Cybersecurity Challenges and Strategies Across Sectors and Government Agencies

snova
New York

Computer Science, Technology and Applications Series

Artificial Intelligence: Policy Perspectives and Global Impacts
Sonja Buckley (Editor)
ISBN: 979-8-89530-859-2
eBook ISBN: 979-8-89530-960-5

Immersive Technologies: The Role of Augmented and Virtual Reality in Civilian and Military Use
Rosalie T. Bryant (Editor)
ISBN: 979-8-89530-796-0
eBook ISBN: 979-8-89530-910-0

Harnessing the Power of IoT-Enabled Machine Learning in Healthcare Applications
Mritunjay Rai, PhD,
Ravindra Kumar Yadav, PhD,
Neha Goel, PhD,
and Mahesh Kumar H. Kolekar, PhD
ISBN: 979-8-89530-626-0
eBook ISBN: 979-8-89530-761-8

The Future of Machine Learning with Automation in Engineering
Sandeep Gupta, PhD
ISBN: 979-8-89530-556-0
eBook ISBN: 979-8-89530-607-9

Big Data, Big Impact: Navigating Competition, Privacy, and Reform
Jessica Andrews (Editor)
ISBN: 979-8-89530-538-6
eBook ISBN: 979-8-89530-565-2

Computational Arts and Creative Products: Languages, Spaces and Practices
Alessandra Micalizzi, PhD
ISBN: 979-8-89530-426-6
eBook ISBN: 979-8-89530-499-0

More information about this series can be found at
https://novapublishers.com/product-category/series/computer-science-technology-and-applications/

Marybeth Wiskoff
Editor

Cybersecurity Challenges and Strategies Across Sectors and Government Agencies

snova
New York

Library of Congress Cataloging-in-Publication Data

ISBN: 979-8-90134-039-4 (Hardcover)
ISBN: 979-8-90134-065-3 (eBook)

Published by Nova Science Publishers, Inc. † New York

Contents

Preface

Cybersecurity refers to the security of our devices, infrastructure, data, and users of computers, computer networks, information and communication technology, virtual systems, or computer-enabled control of physical components. Students, educators, patients, and health care providers across the country rely on countless programs and IT systems to learn with online tools, get a prescription, do a telehealth appointment, and so much more. It is easy to take for granted how critical technology is to fundamental tasks like collecting and protecting the personal data of students and patients.

Federal agencies are responsible for collecting, processing, storing, and disposing of massive amounts of digital information related to individuals, businesses, and sensitive government matters. As a result, even the slightest cyber vulnerability within government agencies can manifest as a large-scale breach, threatening our nation's economic prosperity, national security, and personal privacy.

This book reviews the current challenges in protecting individual privacy and national security.

Chapter 1

Cybersecurity in the Health and Education Sectors*

Committee on Health, Education, Labor, and Pensions

Wednesday, May 18, 2022
U.S. Senate, Committee on Health, Education, Labor, and Pensions,
Washington, DC.

The Committee met, pursuant to notice, at 10:01 a.m., in room 216, Hart Senate Office Building, Hon. Patty Murray, Chair of the Committee, presiding.

Present: Senators Murray [presiding], Casey, Baldwin, Murphy, Hassan, Hickenlooper, Cassidy, Braun, Scott, and Tuberville.

Opening Statement of Senator Murray

The CHAIR. Good morning. The Senate Health, Education, Labor, and Pensions Committee will please come to order. Today we are having a hearing on cybersecurity in the health and education sectors. I will have an opening statement followed by Senator Cassidy, and then we will introduce our witnesses. After they give their testimony, Senators will each have 5 minutes for a round of questions.

---

* This is an edited, reformatted and augmented version of Hearing of the Committee on Health, Education, Labor, and Pensions, United States Senate, One Hundred Seventeenth Congress, Second Session, Publication No. S. HRG. 117–398, dated May 18, 2022.

In: Cybersecurity Challenges and Strategies Across Sectors …
Editor: Marybeth Wiskoff
ISBN: 979-8-90134-039-4

Again, while we were unable to have this hearing fully open to the public or media for in-person attendance, live video is available on our Committee website at help.senate.gov. And again, if you are in need of accommodations including closed captioning, please reach out to the Committee or the Office of Congressional Accessibility Services.

Every day, students, educators, patients, and health care providers across the country rely on countless programs and IT systems to learn with online tools, to get a prescription, do a telehealth appointment, and so much more.

It is easy to take for granted how critical technology is to fundamental tasks like collecting and protecting the personal data of students and patients. Keeping track of course requirements, lesson plans, student financial aid, or providing information about prescriptions, allergies, and surgeries, information with potentially life and death consequences.

During the past few years, COVID–19 has made technology even more central in health care and education, as patients and providers have made greater use of telehealth services to make care accessible and schools are helping close the digital divide by connecting students to the internet and devices.

With that increased reliance on technology, we must also increase the attention given to the challenges that technologypresent. A critical part of that is closing the digital divide and ensuring all of our communities have access to the internet, which is why I fought so hard to invest in universal broadband and digital equity in our bipartisan infrastructure law. But we can't just call it a day after we make technology easy to use or access. We need to make sure it is also safe and secure.

We need to address cybersecurity attacks and ensure they are treated like the National Security threat they are because cyberattacks are on the rise. In 2020, 70 percent of hospitals surveyed said they had faced a significant security incident within the past 12 months. And between 2016 and 2021, there were over 1,300 school cybersecurity incidents in the U.S. and that is just counting the ones that were publicly disclosed.

In my home State of Washington, we know that there were at least 44 data breaches in the health care sector last year and at least 35 in education. And the number of cyber-attacks in our state overall increased significantly from 2020, with the number of large scale attacks affecting over 50,000 people having tripled.

During this pandemic, we also saw hackers infiltrate our state's unemployment insurance system, a breach that exposed the information of over a million people across my state. These attacks can come from a wide variety of sources, individual hackers, organized crime, and even hostile state actors, as we have seen most recently in Russia's invasion of Ukraine.

This is a serious National Security threat and families need to know we are taking action to keep them safe from our enemies here. Because we know our biggest global adversaries, Russia, China, North Korea, Iran have been putting resources into sharpening their cyber-attack capacity.

Cyber-attacks can also take a wide variety of forms. Data breaches that expose sensitive information from health information adversaries might use to threaten National Security to private financial information about patients, students, and staff, distributed denial of service attacks that can be used by hostile countries and others to make computers and networks unresponsive and shut down services, or ransomware attacks where foreign actors or other dangerous organizations hold essential services and data hostage unless a large financial ransom is paid.

Even when a hospital or school is doing everything right, there are always new threats they may not be able to be prepared for. And every organization is still vulnerable to attacks on the tech vendors that they rely on. For example, a 2019 cyber-attack on Pearson affected over 13,000 students and a breach at another education vendor last year, Blackbaud, exposed the financial information of 17,000 students just from my home State of Washington alone.

The fallout from these attacks can be devastating and wide ranging. Hospitals can get locked out of the electronic health care records they need to understand a patient's condition or software needed to schedule surgeries or track prescriptions or get lab results and divert ambulances. I have even heard from health departments back in Washington State about how responding to cyber-attacks has pulled resources and staff from their COVID vaccination efforts. These kinds of challenges don't just cause major headaches or losses and expenses, they put patients in danger, they undermine our National Security, and in some cases, they even cost lives.

Meanwhile, our schools are at risk of getting locked out of online programs that students use to get in turn in assignments or teachers used to post and track grades, and administrators use to layout courses and schedules for the semester. Hacks can disrupt routine and functions like payroll, and can leave patients, students, and staff exposed to identity theft. And that can be especially concerning for K–12 students, as it often isn't clear to students or parents that a child's identity has been stolen until they try to open a bank account or request student aid, which may not happen for several years.

Cyber-attacks also have huge implications for our Country as a whole. They can undermine our competitiveness on the world stage. And the possibility of a cyber-attack coordinated by our enemies to take out health care facilities, especially at a moment of crisis, is a serious threat. So we have to make sure we are ready and vigilant.

That is why I am glad President Biden signed into law legislation we passed to require more reporting of cyber incidents and to study the impact of cyber-attacks on K–12 schools. It is why I am now watching closely as HHS works to strengthen its information security systems and as ED works to help protect K–12 schools from cyber-attacks, and it is why today's hearing is so important.

I want to hear from all of our witnesses about how we can address urgent challenges, like how do we recruit, train, and retain more cybersecurity experts, especially in the health and education sectors where there is a big shortage? What are some best practices that schools and health care providers should be implementing? And how can we better connect organizations to share information like this that will help prevent, mitigate, and respond to cybersecurity incidents? How can we improve disclosure of cybersecurity incidents so people will know when and how they have been affected by a hack, what they might do about it, and how can they protect themselves? And what are we doing to prepare for attacks from hostile foreign actors? How do we make sure we don't just keep up but keep ahead of Russia, China, North Korea, Iran, and others?

It is especially critical to me that we are treating cyber-attacks like the National Security threat we know they are. These are incredibly important questions for families back at home in Washington State and across the entire country whose privacy, finances, futures, and even lives depend on making sure we have good answers and take clear steps to put them in practice.

I look forward to hearing from all of our witnesses today about these issues and really appreciate all of you being here. With that, I will turn it over to Senator Cassidy for his opening remarks.

Opening Statement of Senator Cassidy

Senator CASSIDY. Thank you, Madam Chair. Good morning. Thank you all for attending today's hearing on cybersecurity in the health and education sectors. Looking at you out there, I feel like I am Vladimir Putin meeting with his generals, like on a table 60 yards long. But thank you for being here. In April 2020, the FBI announced that it expected cyber-attacks to increase as a result of a shift to virtual environments during the pandemic. Their prediction was correct.

While cyber threats impact nearly every aspect of our daily lives, we are discussing just two. According to data from the K through 12 Cyber Security Resource Center, K–12 schools have experienced an 18 percent increase in cyber-attacks in 2020 compared to 2019. Specifically, 317 school districts across 40 states suffered 408 publicly disclosed cyber security incidences in 2020.

Microsoft Security Intelligence found that 61 percent of nearly 7.7 million enterprise malware encounters reported in May 2020 came from the education sector, making it the most affected industry. With regard to health care, nearly 50 million people in the U.S. had their sensitive health data breached in 2021, more than triple 2018 numbers.

Just last month, U.S. Federal agencies led by the Cybersecurity and Infrastructure Security Agency issued the strongest warning yet of cyber-attacks on critical infrastructure by Russian government security and intelligence services retaliating against any organization providing support to Ukraine. So what exactly are these cyber threats and incidences in both health and education, the industries being hit by ransomware and phishing attacks? In the health industry, patient care is time sensitive.

As a doctor, I cannot express enough the importance of timeliness in care. Cyber-attacks to delay care cost American lives, and that was particularly during the pandemic. A September 2021 CISA report found that ransomware cyber-attacks on hospitals led to significant and sustained hospital strain and related consequences such as IT network failure, ambulance diversion, strain on ICU bed utilization, and increased mortality.

We must talk today about stopping adversaries from denying our patients the care that is needed. Cyber-attacks are never a victimless crime. In K through 12, phishing attacks stealing data from our youngest children are especially concerning because it can take years to discover that a child's identity has been stolen. In the meantime, the thieves can open credit cards and mount up large debts with a child's identifying information.

Ransomware attacks, on the other hand, show themselves immediately and can result in significant disruptions in the classroom. These attacks come at a high cost, both in the ransom paid and the work it takes to restore systems. One higher education example, University of California San Francisco Medical School paid $1.14 million to hackers who encrypted and threatened to publish sensitive information stolen from the institution.

In another health care example, universal health care services, or UHC, experienced a cyber-attack in October 2020, costing UHC $67 million in lost revenue and recovery efforts. Collaboration with and among the private sector is essential to solving this problem. Existing partnerships with organizations like some of the ones you represent, as well as closer collaboration among Federal agencies, are key ingredients we must pursue as a long term solution to cyber vulnerability.

A strong cyber defense to protect our Country from virtual threats is becoming just as important as a strong military and police force to defend from physical threats. From the bipartisan infrastructure bill to military aid for Ukraine, nearly every comprehensive piece of legislation has to consider and address the importance of cybersecurity.

Continuing that discussion in regards to Americans health and education is also needed. It is important that the Committee is doing this today. With that, I look forward to hearing from our witnesses about how to improve cybersecurity protocols on the Federal level. And I yield.

The CHAIR. Thank you, Senator Cassidy. I will now introduce today's witnesses. Our first witness is Denise Anderson, President and CEO of the Health Information Sharing and Analysis Center, or ISAC a nonprofit organization dedicated to protecting the health sector from physical and cyber-attacks and incidents by serving as a trusted and timely resource for information.

Ms. Anderson is also Chair of the National Council of ISACs, on the Board of Directors for the Global Resilience Federation, on the Cyber Working Group Executive Committee for the Health and Public Health Sector Coordinating Council and engaged in a number of other groups and initiatives focused on cyber issues in the health care sector.

Ms. Anderson, thank you for joining us today. I look forward to your testimony. And with that, I am going to turn over to Senator Hassan, who will introduce our next witness, Joshua Corman.

Senator HASSAN. Well, thank you so much, Chair Murray. It is a real pleasure to introduce our second witness today, Mr. Joshua Corman from Dover, New Hampshire. He is joined today by his fiance, Andra. Thank you for being here as well. Mr. Corman is a founder of a volunteer organization called I Am the Cavalry, which focuses on using the cybersecurity skills of its members to protect public safety.

He also recently served as the Chief Strategist on the Cybersecurity and Infrastructure Security Agency, or CISA's COVID Task Force, where he worked to protect the healthcare sector from cyberattacks and cyber espionage, as the COVID–19 pandemic strained the sector.

He has previously served in several different senior cybersecurity and technology roles, including as Chief Security Officer at PTC, a software company, Director of the Cyber Statecraft Initiative for the Atlantic Council, and Chief Technology Officer for Sonatype, a cybersecurity company. He also serves as an adjunct faculty for the Chief Information Security Officer Certificate Program at Carnegie Mellon University.

As someone who has worked with Members of both parties to strengthen cybersecurity at all levels of Government, especially in small communities, I appreciate Mr. Corman's work very much. Welcome, and thank you for your service, Mr. Corman. I look forward to your testimony today.

The CHAIR. Thank you, Senator Hassan. Today, we will also be hearing from Amy McLaughlin, a knowledgeable technology and information security leader with experience in education, finance, medical, and Government sectors. Ms. McLaughlin is the Cybersecurity Program Director at the Consortium of School Networking.

That is an organization focused on meeting the technology needs of K–12 leaders and supporting the entire IT system, team and school systems. She is also the Executive Director of Technology and Solutions Architecture at Oregon State University. Thank you for joining us today. We look forward to your testimony.

Finally, our last witness today is Helen Norris. She is Vice President and Chief Information Officer at Chapman University. She is responsible for leading the university's information technology strategy and services and overseeing the university library.

She is also a Board Chair of EDUCAUSE, a nonprofit whose mission is to advance higher education through the use of information technology. We look forward to hearing from you today as well. And thank you again to all of you for joining us today. With that, we will begin testimony. Ms. Anderson, we will start with you.

Statement of Denise Anderson, President and CEO, Health Information Sharing and Analysis Center, Oakton, VA

Ms. ANDERSON. Good morning, Chair Murray, and Members of the Committee. My name is Denise Anderson, as you mentioned, and I am

President and CEO of the Health ISAC. I am also representing the Health Sector Coordinating Council Cybersecurity Working Group. I want to thank you for the opportunity to speak today. Health ISAC is a global nonprofit. Our members range from small to large organizations and represent approximately two- thirds of the U.S. health and public health GDP.

Members include providers, academic medical centers, and medical device and pharmaceutical manufacturers, among others. Recently, Health ISAC published its report on the current and emerging health care cyberthreat landscape. And last month, Health ISAC worked with Microsoft to take down a Zloader malware family through coordinated legal and technical actions.

The takedowns struck a major blow against cybercriminals using ransomware to extort hospitals and other victims. The Health Sector Coordinating Council Cybersecurity Working Group is a volunteer coalition of 320 organizations. Membership is open to any organization that meet certain criteria. It is organized into task groups that work to develop best practices for various health care cybersecurity disciplines.

The CWG has produced 15 best practices publications which are freely available via their public website. Both Health ISAC and the CWG worked closely with HHS and the FDA as well as CISA. Our ongoing engagement includes weekly calls with the leadership in each organization to assess and discuss issues facing the sector. With the rise in digital health care, the proliferation of advances in technology, and the efficiencies of connecting devices and data, the cyber threat surface in health care has ballooned and the threat actors have followed.

The focus has traditionally been on data and privacy, but if providers cannot deliver services or data is manipulated or destroyed, patient lives can be at risk. Ransomware has had a big impact on the health sector. According to the FBI's 2021 Internet Crime Report, the sector experienced at least 148 ransomware attacks between June and December 2021, resulting in millions of dollars of losses.

Conti and its Ryuk Ransomware have been especially prolific. Ryuk has been linked to more than 200 ransomware attacks impacting health facilities, with revenue losses amounting to nearly $100 million and remediation costs of $500 million. A high profile attack as a result of Conti was against the national health system in Ireland in May 2021. The attack brought down all of their IT systems and resulted in canceled surgeries and delayed medical care. It took 4 months to recover from that incident.

The other impact of ransomware is the downstream effects when suppliers are attacked. When a human resources firm was attacked in December 2021, hospitals were forced to manage payroll and staff scheduling manually during a surge in COVID–19 infections. In January 2021, a manufacturer essential in providing packaging for COVID–19 treatments was attacked and pharmaceutical manufacturers experienced slowdowns in package production and shipping during a vital period in the pandemic.

The COVID–19 pandemic spurred several incidents. Threat actors accessed sensitive documents for a COVID–19 vaccine at the European Medicines Agency, where the documents were stored. Actors attacked and blocked access to an Italian COVID–19 vaccination booking system, and organizations offering cold storage and delivery processes for keeping vaccines at safe temperatures were targeted.

A concerning threat actor trend has been the intention and ability to target the IT supply chain, such as the SolarWinds attack, to gain access to a larger group of victims. Vulnerabilities also posed a huge problem for the sector. This reported vulnerabilities increased for a fifth straight year. Over 18,000 were reported in 2021, and almost 20 percent of those were considered high risk.

With the tensions between Russia and Ukraine high, many fear a fall out like what occurred during the 2017 Petya attacks that impacted over 300 companies and cost over $10 billion. In February, Russian actors attacked Viasat, 1 hour before Russia invaded Ukraine. Internet users and wind turbines producing electricity in Europe were impacted. Even if health care is not directly targeted, cascading impacts such as access to communications and electricity can be substantial.

The health sector is highly interconnected. Sensitive patient information must move between entities to facilitate proper patient care and history. Hospitals use tens of thousands of medical devices, expensive devices are not easily replaced, and run on software that is no longer patched or supported.

In addition, many of these devices run 24 hours a day, 7 days a week, 365 days a year, so taking them offline or patching them is not—is complicated. As can be seen by the contributions of the CWG and Health ISAC, industry dedicates endless hours to help ensure the sector is strong and secure.

The publications, webinars, workshops, exercises, the many alerts are free and open to the sector. The Zloader takedown will benefit countless organizations inside and outside of healthcare, and we look to do more of the same. Despite the number of great initiatives and efforts underway, we can no longer look at the challenges through just a cyber and or physical lens but must consider all threats to operational resilience.

As evidenced by Hurricane Maria in Puerto Rico and the impact on IV bag supply, ransomware attacks which have crippled the health care delivery, and the COVID–19 shut down in China affecting the supply of contrast fluid used in imaging, health organizations must constantly be focused on all threats to health care delivery and patient safety.

The health sector should be supported and incentivized in this vital effort. This concludes my testimony. Thank you again for the opportunity and look forward to your questions.

[The prepared statement of Ms. Anderson follows:]

Prepared Statement of Denise Anderson

ISAC Background

Chair Murray, Ranking Member Burr, and Members of the Committee, my name is Denise Anderson. I am President and CEO of the Health Information Sharing & Analysis Center (Health-ISAC), Chair of the National Council of ISACs (NCI) and serve on the Executive Committee of the Health Sector Coordinating Council Cybersecurity Working Group (HSCC CWG). I want to thank you for this opportunity to address the Committee on Health, Education, Labor, and Pensions about the industry perspective on cybersecurity threats to the Health sector and the resulting challenges and impacts, as well as the activities the sector is undertaking to combat these threats including collaborating and coordinating within, between and across the public and private critical infrastructure sectors.

ISACs were formed in response to the 1998 Presidential Decision Directive 63 (PDD 63), which called for the public and private sectors to work together to address cyber threats to the Nation's critical infrastructures. After 9/11, in response to Homeland Security Presidential Directive 7 (its 2013 successor, Presidential Policy Directive 21) and the Homeland Security Act, ISACs expanded their role to encompass physical threats to their respective sectors. Many ISACs have been in existence over a decade and in some cases over two decades.

ISACs are industry driven, trusted communities that promote the sharing of timely, actionable, and reliable information for their respective critical infrastructure sectors and provide forums for owner and operator sharing around threats, incidents, vulnerabilities, best practices, and mitigation strategies. ISACs are operational in nature and have strong reach into their sectors to gather and disseminate information quickly and efficiently. ISACs have been thriving and growing in recent years as owners and operators have seen the benefit to participating in these trusted communities, which is a testament to the value ISACs deliver to their members. ISACs coordinate with each other through the National Council of ISACs (NCI), a voluntary organization formed in 2003.

Health-ISAC Background

Health-ISAC, (www.h-isac.org) founded in 2010, is a 501(c)6 nonprofit organization and is funded primarily by its member firms through member dues. Since 2010 the membership has expanded to over 700 organizations including healthcare delivery organizations (HDOs), providers, academic medical centers, medical research and development centers, medical materials manufacturers and distributors, pharmaceutical and medical device manufacturers, retail pharmacies, laboratories and radiological centers, telehealth providers, electronic health record providers and pay ers representing approximately two-thirds of the US Health and Public Health GDP.[1]

Health-ISAC members represent 79 percent of the top 103 hospital chains in the United States, 61 percent of the top 51 global medical device manufacturers, 84 percent of the top 25 global pharmaceutical manufacturers, 93 percent of Fortune 500 healthcare companies in the United States and 86 percent of electronic health record providers in the United States. Our members range from small organizations with less than one million dollars in annual revenue to large Fortune 50 organizations with over 238 billion dollars in annual revenue.

Health-ISAC is a global organization that has members headquartered in over 20 countries and membership is growing rapidly. Health-ISAC saw its largest member growth ever in 2021.

The mission of Health-ISAC is to empower trusted relationships in the global healthcare industry to prevent, detect and respond to cyber-and physical security events so that members can focus on improving health and saving lives.

---

[1] Based on the annual revenue of all Health-ISAC member organizations. ($2.3 Trillion).

Besides offering a trusted forum and community for sharing information around threats, vulnerabilities, best practices and mitigation strategies, Health-ISAC offers a number of other services such as global workshops and webinars, four annual summits—two in the United States, one in Europe and one in Asia, daily cyber and physical reports, alerts, targeted threat alerts, a monthly newsletter, a weekly blog on cybersecurity issues in healthcare, white papers, monthly member-only threat briefings, monthly podcasts, exercises, special interest groups, a number of working groups and committees and various technical tools and partner programs for members to use in their environments. In addition, the Health-ISAC Threat Intelligence Committee (TIC) sets the sector cyber threat level monthly, or as needed, and provides valuable insight and mitigation strategies when threats arise, or incidents occur.

Health-ISAC has numerous sharing and collaboration channels, including platforms where hundreds of thousands of actionable indicators and threat actor tactics, techniques, and procedures (TTPs) are shared. Health-ISAC was one of the first organizations to adopt STIX and TAXII, which are protocols for automated indicator and intelligence sharing and fosters a robust member machine-to-machine sharing environment. Health-ISAC uses the Traffic Light Protocol, (TLP) an information owner dissemination determination protocol for sharing of information. TLP RED is the most restricted sharing protocol, with TLP WHITE, the broadest. Over 100,000 individuals have access to our TLP GREEN and TLP WHITE alerts.

In 2021, for example, Health-ISAC:

- Provided alerts, papers, webinars, thought leadership and facilitated collaboration on myriad incidents during the year including SolarWinds, Accelion, ProxyLogon, PrintNightmare, VPN Vulnerabilities, in Fortinet, Pulse and Citrix, Colonial Pipeline, JBS Meats, Irish National Health Service, Kaseya, Geopolitical Tensions, Hurricane Ida and other physical threats, and Log4j.
- Added 119 new members amounting to a member community of over 5,500 individuals.
- Nearly tripled the number of member organizations using automated indicator sharing.
- Conducted 12 highly attended Monthly Member Threat Briefings, published 242 Finished Intelligence Reports, sent over 419 Targeted Alerts, held ten Threat Operations Center (TOC) Spotlight threat and

vulnerability webinars, and distributed over 65,812 actionable indicators of compromise.

- Worked with security researchers to develop four pre-public alerts and vulnerability notifications impacting millions of medical devices.
- Stood up several new programs including a new webinar program, Continue the Conversation for members to bring subject matter expert panels and discussions around hot topics from the chat channels, the Microsoft Patch Tuesday Podcast and TOC Open House Office Hours.
- Hosted an Analytics Training Workshop, offered 63 webinars, and held three successful global in-person Summits, with our Fall Summit attendance close to pre-pandemic numbers. Health-ISAC also conducted nine customized exercises and in 2022 published an After-Action report from our 2021 Rethinking Resiliency exercise series.
- Planned, and held the Hobby Exercise, a tabletop exercise designed to engage the Health sector and strategic partners, including those in government, on significant security and resilience challenges. The overarching objective is to inform and provide opportunities for continuous organizational improvement while increasing Health sector resiliency. The annual exercise is named for Oveta Culp Hobby, the first U.S. Secretary of Health, Education and Welfare. The 2021 After-Action Report illustrating findings from the exercise was recently published in March 2022.
- Worked with Cisco to conduct a well-received 2-day Leadership Development Course for rising CISOs at the 2021 Fall Summit. This was also held at our Spring Summit in May 2022.
- Produced four white papers, developed Pharmaceutical and Supply Chain Guidance for practitioners and healthcare CISOs, and expanded physical threat information deliverables for Health sector organizations. Also published Full and Lite versions of copyrighted Health-ISAC Questionnaires for Third-Party Risk Management. In 2022 we also published a white paper on Securing the Modern Pharmaceutical Supply Chain.
- Offered valuable tools for members such as third-party risk management, digital risk protection and internet traffic visualization through our Community Services Program.
- Facilitated five Committees, over 15 Working Groups and three Councils devoted to topics such as Cybersecurity Analytics,

Information Security Incident Response, Security Engineering and Architecture, Business Resiliency and Cybersecurity Awareness and Training.

- Continued to build on our work to improve security across the Medical Device Community with over 25 medical device public advisories, two Food and Drug Administration (FDA) Town Halls at Health-ISAC Summits and curated medical device information related to Log4j and other vulnerabilities on the Health-ISAC website. Our Medical Device Cybersecurity Information Sharing Council is comprised of 331 individuals from 135 organizations with half of the group comprised of Healthcare Delivery Organizations (HDOs) and the other half comprised of Medical Device Manufacturers (MDMs).
- Conducted over 30-member interest surveys on topics such as SolarWinds Impact, Security Workforce Size and Strategy, and Security Operations Centers Resourcing.

In 2022, to date, Health-ISAC has engaged in five major activities of note. The first is the publishing of the first annual Health-ISAC report on the Current and Emerging Healthcare Cyber Threat Landscape in both TLP GREEN and TLP WHITE versions. The report features survey results on member threat perspectives, as well as, top issues from 2021 and a look ahead into 2022 (https://h-isac.org/health-isacs-first-annual-current-and-emerging-healthcare-cyber-threat-landscape-executive-summary/). The second is the publishing of the 2021 Health-ISAC Annual Report (https://h-isac.org/2021-annual-report/). Third, the ISAC held several webinars, produced alerts and briefings, and published a joint bulletin with the Health Sector Cybersecurity Coordination Center (HC3), part of the Department of Health and Human Services (HHS), regarding the geopolitical tensions in Russia. The ISAC emphasized several messages to the sector that resulted from Classified briefings conducted by the White House, Cybersecurity and Infrastructure Security Agency (CISA), and its partners and stood up a working group of members directly impacted by the situation so that they could share challenges, issues, and best practices with each other. Fourth, Health-ISAC worked on another pre-public vulnerability disclosure with CISA and CyberMDX/Forescout on Access: 7 vulnerabilities found in PTC Axeda agenda and Axeda Desktop server.

Fifth, in April 2022, Health-ISAC worked with Microsoft and others to take down the Zloader malware family, one of the most notorious cybercrime operations responsible for ransomware attacks against hospitals in the United States and around the world. The takedown was accomplished through coordinated legal and technical actions and disrupted massive botnets using the Zloader malware family, striking a major blow against cybercriminal operators using Ransomware, such as Ryuk, to extort victims.

With the seizing of hundreds of domain names used by the Zloader malware to remotely command and control victim computers, Microsoft will use the intelligence gained from this takedown to partner with Law Enforcement, Internet Service Providers and Computer Emergency Response Teams around the world to help remediate infected computers, making the Internet safer for consumers and businesses worldwide. Together, these aspects of the operation are expected to undermine the criminal infrastructure that relies on these botnets every day to make money and helps to provide new tools for the industry to work together to proactively fight cybercrime.

At Health-ISAC, our mission is much bigger than the ISAC. We believe building a stronger community both inside and outside of the sector leads to better patient care and a healthier world.

Health Sector Coordinating Council Cybersecurity Working Group Background

Healthcare is designated under U.S. national policy as ‘‘critical infrastructure’’ along with 15 other industry sectors, such as financial services, energy, telecommunications, water, transportation and more, represented by industry-organized ‘‘Sector Coordinating Councils (SCCs).’’ These SCC’s and their government counterparts form a national public-private partnership coordinated overall by the U.S. Department of Homeland Security through the National Infrastructure Protection Plan (NIPP). The Health Sector Coordinating Council (HSCC) serves as an official advisory council to its government counterparts—HHS and FDA—with a formally designated critical infrastructure protection function distinct from the advocacy and member services roles of traditional industry associations. The HSCC, HHS and FDA work jointly to identify and mitigate systemic threats to critical healthcare infrastructure, such as pandemics, major weather events, terrorism, active shooters, and cyber-attacks, with a mission to identify cyber and physical risks to the security and resiliency of the sector, develop guidance and policies for mitigating those risks, and facilitate threat preparedness and incident response. The Office of the White House National Cyber Director has identified and engaged the HSCC as a model to accelerate a national healthcare cyber resilience strategy.

The HSCC Cybersecurity Working Group (CWG) is a volunteer coalition of 320 organizations that operate under a charter-based governance structure with an elected Chair, Vice-Chair and Executive Committee. Membership is open to any organization that is; (a) a covered entity or business associate under HIPAA; (b) a Health plan or payer; (c) regulated by FDA as medical device or pharmaceutical company; (d) regulated by HHS Office of the National Coordinator as a Health IT company; (e) a public health organization and (f) a healthcare industry association or professional society. A small allotment of an ‘‘Advisor’’ member category of consulting and security companies is permitted to participate and support CWG initiatives pro-bono.

When working with our government partners, the industry-led Cybersecurity Working Group becomes the Joint Cybersecurity Working Group, which identifies and develops preparedness measures against cybersecurity threats to the security and resiliency of the Health sector. It is organized into outcome-oriented task groups (currently 13) that meet regularly to develop best-practices for various healthcare cybersecurity disciplines such as 405(d) Health Industry Cybersecurity Practices, Supply Chain Cyber Risk Management, Five-Year Plan, Emerging Technology, Workforce Development, Measurement, Policy, Outreach and Awareness and Risk Assessment and Medical Technology Security including sub-groups around the Joint Security Plan Update, MedTech Legacy Devices, and MedTech Vulnerability Communications.

The CWG has produced 15 major best-practices publications since 2019, freely available to sector stakeholders and the public via its website (HealthSectorCouncil.org). These publications include Health Industry Cybersecurity Practices, Health Industry Cybersecurity Tactical Crisis Response Guide, Health Industry Cybersecurity Securing Telehealth and Telemedicine, Model Contract Language for Medtech Cybersecurity Medtech Vulnerability Communications Toolkit and Operational Continuity Cyber Incident.

Many of these HSCC CWG task group initiatives and deliverables directly address the many important recommendations contained in the 2017 HHS report of the Health Care Industry Cybersecurity (HCIC) Task Force, which was established by the Congress in Section 405(c) of the 2015 Cybersecurity Information Sharing Act and was composed of industry and government experts in healthcare and cybersecurity. At the time, the report characterized the healthcare industry’s cybersecurity preparedness as being ‘‘in critical condition.'' As the Health Sector Coordinating Council has been focused on developing cybersecurity best practices and tool kits— by the sector, for the sector—we hope that as more healthcare organizations implement these scalable practices over time, we will raise the sector's preparedness diagnosis to ''stable.'' But in the business of cybersecurity, we are never done, only better.

To support the development of these initiatives, our preparedness, information sharing and incident response, both Health-ISAC and the HSCC CWG work closely with HHS and FDA, both of which serve as our CWG cochairs and Sector Risk Management Agency (SRMA), as well as, CISA. Our ongoing partnership engagement includes holding weekly calls with the leadership in each organization to assess and discuss issues facing the sector.

The Cyber Threat Landscape in Healthcare

Ten years ago, 'cyber' and 'healthcare' were not even placed in the same sentence. Today because of the rise in digital healthcare, the proliferation of advances in technology and the efficiencies of connecting devices and data, the cyber threat surface in healthcare has ballooned and the threat actors have followed. Threat actors have many motivations to attack whether for financial reasons, disruption, intellectual property theft, revenge or to make a political statement.

Unfortunately, the stakes are very high. The focus has traditionally been on data and privacy but if HDOs, providers, or their suppliers cannot deliver services, as was seen in numerous ransomware attacks, or data is manipulated or destroyed, patient lives can be at risk.

There are essentially five malicious actor groups that are responsible for threats to healthcare, which include Nation States such as Russia and China, Cyber Criminals, Hacktivists, Terrorists, and Insiders who can be malicious or non-malicious. Their motivations range from Advantage—intellectual property theft, gain a foothold for further disruption, espionage, blackmail—Ego—notoriety, revenge—Ideology—political, social, cultural and Greed—money, power.

The various actor groups use several Tactics, Techniques and Procedures (TTPs) to conduct their activity. Some TTPs are Phishing and Spearphishing, Ransomware, Wipers, Distributed Denial of Service (DDoS), Business Email Compromise, Remote Access, Supply Chain Attacks, Scanning and Exploiting Vulnerabilities, Social Engineering and Credential Theft.

In November 2021, Health-ISAC conducted a survey of its members asking them to rank order the Top 5 ''greatest cybersecurity concerns'' facing their organizations for both 2021 and 2022. The survey included cyber (e.g., CISO) and non-cyber executives (e.g., CFO), multiple healthcare subsectors (e.g., Providers, Pharmaceutical Manufacturers, Payers, Medical Device Manufacturers, Health Information Technology), as well as, healthcare organizations of varying sizes and budgets. The Top 5 threats, which were the same for both 2021 and 2022 were:

1) Ransomware Deployment
2) Phishing/Spear-Phishing Attacks
3) Third-Party/Partner Breach
4) Data Breach
5) Insider Threat

Ransomware has had a big impact on the Health sector and threat actors have evolved their techniques over the last 2 years from simply just asking for a payment to unlock files to blackmailing organizations with threats to release records to the public. According to the Federal Bureau of Investigation (FBI) Internet Crime Complaint Center's (IC3) 2021 Internet Crime Report, the Health sector experienced at least 148 ransomware attacks between June 2021 and December 2021 resulting in millions of dollars of losses.

Ransomware family groups that have been particularly prolific in the healthcare sector include Conti and its Ryuk Ransomware. Ryuk has been linked to more than 200 ransomware attacks impacting hospitals, public health departments, nursing homes and patient care facilities around the world since 2018. The attacks resulted in the temporary or permanent loss of IT systems that support many of the provider delivery functions in modern hospitals resulting in canceled surgeries and delayed medical care. Some examples of impacts caused by Ryuk at patient care facilities in the United States since 2018 include:

- Ryuk attack forced ambulances to divert, causing a 90-minute delay in emergency patient services.
- Ryuk disrupted delivery of chemotherapy treatments for cancer patients.
- Ryuk forced hospitals to cancel elective procedures.
- Ryuk caused delays in reporting of laboratory results.

- Ryuk caused delays in scheduling appointments for maternity and oncology patients.
- Ryuk caused more than 3 weeks of downtime for the Electronic Health Records management system.
- Ryuk impacted systems at nursing homes, causing patient records to be unavailable and prohibiting pharmaceuticals orders from being placed, and
- Ryuk leaked sensitive patient data including treatments, diagnoses, and other information of hundreds of thousands of people.

Hospitals reported revenue losses due to Ryuk infections of nearly $100 million from data Health-ISAC obtained through interviews with hospital staff, public statements, and media articles. The Ryuk attacks also caused an estimated $500 million in costs to respond to the attacks—costs that include ransomware payments, digital forensic services, security improvements and upgrading impacted systems plus other expenses. A high-profile attack as the result of Conti/Ryuk was against the Health Service Executive (HSE), the national health system in Ireland consisting of 54 hospitals, in May 2021. The attack brought all the IT systems within HSE nationwide down and it took 4 months to completely recover from the incident.

Other Ransomware families are REvil/Sodinokibi, Hive, Lokibot, Pysa and Clop. Health-ISAC assesses that in 2022, Ransomware will continue to proliferate, and cybercriminals will target critical systems to the operations of healthcare organizations to force healthcare organizations to pay a ransom quickly and not allow time for investigation or forensic examination prior to paying the ransom demanded.

The other impact of Ransomware is the downstream effects that result when suppliers are attacked. When Kronos, a Human Resources Management Solutions firm widely used in healthcare, was attacked in December 2021, numerous hospitals were impacted. Hospitals were forced to manage payroll, staff scheduling, and issuing staff IDs manually during a surge in COVID–19 infections. In January 2021, when WestRock, a packaging solutions manufacturer that was essential in providing packaging for COVID–19 vaccines, treatments, and diagnostics, was hit with a Ransomware attack, pharmaceutical manufacturers were impacted by slowdowns in package production and shipping during a vital period in the pandemic.

The COVID–19 Pandemic was a factor in several incidents that took place over 2020 and 2021. Nation State activity has always been present in the sector, but it was especially visible during the COVID–19 pandemic with the desire to gain knowledge about vaccines, diagnostics and therapeutics related to COVID–19. Threat actors accessed documents covering the regulatory submission for Pfizer and BioNTech's COVID–19 vaccine candidate BNT162b2 at the European Medicines Agency (EMA) where the documents had been stored on EMA's servers. There were also several incidents such as when threat actors attacked and blocked access to an Italian COVID–19 vaccination booking system. Other activities targeted organizations offering cold storage and delivery processes for keeping vaccines at safe temperatures with phishing and spear-phishing campaigns.

A concerning threat actor trend has been the intention and ability to target IT providers, Managed Service Providers and Enterprise Management Software Systems to gain access to a larger group of victims. For example, in February 2020, threat actors affiliated with Russia's SVR (foreign intelligence service) injected malicious code into an update for SolarWinds Orion, a network monitoring software used by several organizations including the U.S. Federal Government. The malicious code went undetected until December 2020 and infected over 18,000 machines through the supply chain. Other high profile supply chain compromises included Kaseya and Accenture. Likely heading into 2022 threat actors will evolve this tactic and focus on compromising cloud providers to gain access to the sensitive data and networks of multiple victims.

Vulnerabilities also posed a huge problem for the sector. According to a graph published by the National Institute of Standards and Technology (NIST), vulnerabilities increased for a fifth straight year with 18,378 reported in 2021. Of that number, 3,646 were considered high-risk. Of particular note were the PrintNightmare vulnerability, the Microsoft Exchange Proxy Shell Attack vulnerability, and the Apache Log4j vulnerability which had very broad implications across the sector.

In 2022 there has been increased focus on Nation State activity and related criminal cyber activity surrounding the geopolitical events occurring between Russia and Ukraine. Many fear a fall-out from Russian activities against Ukraine such as what occurred during the 2017 Petya/Not Petya attacks that impacted over 300 companies, many of which were large multi-national corporations, and cost over $10 billion. Recent reporting shows Russian threat actors attacked Viasat, a US provider of high-speed satellite broadband services, 1 hour before Russia invaded Ukraine. Thousands of satellite terminals were affected impacting myriad internet users in Europe as well as over 5,800 wind turbines producing electricity. Even if healthcare is not directly targeted, cascading impacts such as access to communications and electricity can be substantial. Health-ISAC assesses that threat actor cyber activities will continue to rise and evolve, and the sector needs to be ever vigilant, as well as, develop robust enterprise risk management and resiliency strategies.

The Unique Nature of Healthcare

The Health sector is highly inter-connected. Unlike in other sectors, healthcare data must be portable. Sensitive patient information must move between various medical providers, pharmacies, diagnostic facilities, and payers to facilitate proper patient care and history, as well as, payment for those services. Many healthcare facilities such as hospitals operate in environments that are accessible to the public. Hospitals employ tens of thousands of medical devices, many using outdated operating systems, and many of which are connected to a network. These devices are made by a variety of manufacturers with various levels of security and patching protocols built in. Expensive equipment such as Magnetic Resonance Imaging (MRI) machines are not easily replaced and run on software that is no longer patched or supported. In addition, many of these devices run 24 hours a day, 7 days a week, 365 days a year, so taking them offline for patching or other security needs is complicated.

When supply chains are tightened or non-existent for various reasons, or pandemics or natural or man-made regional disasters occur, stretched supplies and staff become an additional factor.

Coupled with a diverse base within the sector, a highly regulated environment, complex siloed departments, a lack of skilled cyber staff, a lack of cyber security situational awareness, a lack of knowledge and training for the medical staff as well as at the CEO and Board level, and lack of cyber security strategy including a risk management approach, the Health and Public Health sector faces enormous challenges.

Meeting the Challenge

Despite the numerous challenges, many organizations in the Health sector have taken great strides to make certain their environments are as protected and resilient as they can be. As can be seen by the contributions of the Health

Sector Coordinating Council Cybersecurity Working Group and Health-ISAC, countless individuals dedicate numerous hours of their time to help ensure the sector is strong and secure. Both the HSCC CWG and Health ISAC have robust communities that thrive on collaboration in their mission. As is the tradition in medicine, members of these two organizations truly care about patient welfare and safety and the protection of the ecosystem that contributes to them. Members share best practices, indicators of compromise, mitigation strategies and other vital information to accomplish this. When the Petya/Not Petya attacks of 2017 took place, some 60 individuals of approximately 34 Health-ISAC member firms came together and within 48 hours, determined what the actual attack was, the attack vector, how it spread and how to stop it and the shared their findings not just within the sector but globally via the Health-ISAC website and alerts. The publications produced, webinars and workshops held, exercises conducted and TLP WHITE alerts are open to the sector and are free. In 2021, Health-ISAC delivered targeted alerts to 49 healthcare companies that were non-members. The Zloader takedown will benefit countless organizations inside and outside of the sector and industry is looking to do more in this space.

Despite the number of great initiatives and efforts underway within the sector, the sector needs to be vigilant. We can no longer look at the challenges through just a cyber-or physical security lens, but must employ enterprise risk management to consider all threats to operational resilience. As evidenced by Hurricane Maria in Puerto Rico and its impact on the availability of IV bags, ransomware attacks on healthcare and healthcare suppliers, which have crippled healthcare delivery, the COVID–19 shutdown in Shanghai that has tightened the supply of contrast fluid used for imaging, which has forced physicians to prioritize which patients can get CT scans, MRIs and more, healthcare organizations must constantly be focused on all threats to healthcare delivery and patient safety. The healthcare sector should be supported and incentivized in this vital effort.

Congress can help meet this challenge by focusing on three key areas:

1. Education, Recognition and Facilitation of the Importance of Information Sharing

One of the greatest challenges for Health-ISAC and all ISACs is the lack of awareness amongst the critical infrastructure owners and operators, particularly the smaller owners and operators, that the ISACs and SCCs exist and have valuable tools available to improve security—many of which are free to use. Numerous incidents have shown that effective information sharing amongst robust trusted networks of members works in combatting cyber threats.

Government, and specifically the SRMAs should regularly and consistently encourage owner/operators and especially at the Board and CEO level to join their respective ISACs and Sector Coordinating Councils. This has been very effective in the financial sector where the United States Department of the Treasury, the regulators and state agencies have been strongly encouraging membership in the FS-ISAC as a best practice.

The SRMAs indeed have a policy reference for this kind of advisory to their sector representatives: the NIST Cybersecurity Framework. This Framework, developed over the course of a year collaboratively by government and private sector stakeholders, lays out a cyber risk management framework linked to five core functions: identify, protect, detect, respond, and recover. Among the functional categories identified as part of a mature cyber risk management strategy is external communications and coordination around cyber security threats, response, and best practices. In other words, membership in an ISAC or ISAO and/or the SCC is an essential element of a successful cyber risk management strategy.

Another way to facilitate sharing and build robust communities is by providing financial incentives through tax breaks or other means to critical infrastructure organizations that join their respective ISACs and/or SCCs.

2. Provide Incentives for Adoption of Cybersecurity Best Practices

Cyber threat actors are agile, in many cases run their operations as businesses, are sophisticated and constantly evolve their TTPs to infiltrate an organization's defenses and achieve their goal. It is much easier to attack versus defend and healthcare organizations are often at a disadvantage, especially smaller organizations that do not have financial and infrastructure resources. Due to the huge growth in cybercrime and large ransomware payouts, sophisticated and organized criminal groups will be able to invest heavily into R&D and develop new ways to conduct automated and effective scams. The criminals will leverage machine learning, artificial intelligence, and deep fakes to perpetrate efficient and effective criminal campaigns. Therefore, it is essential to support healthcare organizations by incentivizing them to adopt at a minimum basic cybersecurity and risk management strategies. Some good best practices include employing multi-factor authentication (MFA) and other access controls, having a layered defense, using endpoint security, developing network segmentation, building prevention and detection strategies, backing up data and training staff on cyber impacts and policies.

3. Establish Cyber Security Professionals as SRMA Liaisons

With the challenging nature of the Health sector and the steady rise in cyber threats and incidents, there should be a cyber security professional within HHS to act as a strong, government liaison and advocate for the public private partnership when it comes to cyber matters. It has become increasingly apparent that industry needs a government representative who understands cyber security issues, threats, vulnerabilities and impacts as well as the blended threats between physical and cyber security. Having an established, clear government 'go-to' lead in this area is imperative to strengthening the partnership and improving the overall cyber security posture of the Health and Public Health sector.

This concludes my testimony. Thank you again for the opportunity to present this testimony and I look forward to your questions.

[Summary Statement of Denise Anderson]

The testimony will provide descriptions of Health-ISAC, ISACs in general, and the Health Sector Coordinating Council Cybersecurity Working Group, including the numerous initiatives that are taking place within industry to help secure the sector and keep it resilient in the face of threats. It will look at the cyber threat landscape in healthcare and will include the major threat actor groups, threat actor motivations, as well as, threat actor Tactics, Techniques and Procedures (TTPs). The testimony will provide a summary view of the top five ''greatest cybersecurity concerns'' Health-ISAC members see facing their organizations for both 2021 and 2022. Also covered are Ransomware, downstream impacts of Ransomware, Supply Chain attacks, vulnerabilities, and Nation State activity—especially related to COVID–19 and the development and distribution of vaccines, diagnostics, and therapeutics, as well as the recent geopolitical tensions between Russia and Ukraine. The unique nature of healthcare and its myriad challenges, such as the necessity of portable data, 24-by–7-by 365 operations, equipment and devices that are no longer supported, but not easily replaced, reliance upon other critical infrastructure and supply chains, all exacerbated when pandemics, natural and man-made events take place, will be described. Finally, three suggestions are made where Congress and Government can help the Health sector in its efforts to improve security and resilience.

The CHAIR. Thank you very much. Mr. Corman.

Statement of Joshua Corman, Founder, I Am the Cavalry, Dover, NH

Mr. CORMAN. Chair Murray, Senator Cassidy, distinguished Members of the Senate Health Committee, thank you for the time to speak to you today about some pretty grave matters that weigh heavy on my heart——

The CHAIR. Is your mic on?

Mr. CORMAN. I will try that again.

The CHAIR. Very good.

Mr. CORMAN. Chair Murray, Senator Cassidy, and distinguished Members of the Senate Health Committee, thank you for the opportunity today to talk about these grave matters that weigh heavy on my heart.

As described, I am Josh Corman. I am the founder of a volunteer grassroots group of hackers trying to save lives through security research. In recognition that the cavalry isn't coming, we asked, what are you willing and able to do? Will you be part of that solution? Will you be a voice of reason and technical literacy and a helping hand to work with policymakers such as yourselves to make things safer?

Our problem statement was simple, our dependence on connected technology was growing faster than our ability to secure it in areas affecting public safety, human life, and National Security. What we were doing 9 years ago was trying to build the trust and the foundation so that we could prevent loss of life.

There is a promise in a parallel to connect to technology. We always adopt things that are immediate and obvious benefits. We have a very hard time determining the delayed consequences of those choices. And I warned the teams, people would have to die first before anyone would listen to us.

To our delight and surprise, bravery from Dr. Suzanne Schwartz at FDA took bold action to try to make sure we raised the bar for minimum cybersecurity hygiene for medical devices and issued the first ever safety communication for a medical device purely for cybersecurity reasons and no one had died. They sent a shot over the bow to the industry of 10,000 medical device makers that the dependence we place on connected technology should be worthy of that trust.

These are devices like this little pacemaker, some of which have found a sync—a hardcoded three digit password is sufficient to affect the hearts and functions of 750,000 patients. We have similarly compromised insulin pumps to give a second lethal dose of insulin without authentication done by a diabetic himself. We have found bedside infusion pumps that should deliver a 3-hour dose of a calcium channel blocker could empty the contents in 30 seconds.

We have done these through clinical E.R. hacking simulations in consultation and collaboration with Federal agencies, with medical practitioners, with physicians to see, can we handle these disruptions to the technologies we take for granted? Through that work, I got to serve on the 2015 405c Congressional Task Force on Health Care Industry Cybersecurity.

Because of the trust built there, when the country and the world faced the pandemic of the COVID–19 virus, Director Krebs, using the Cares Act hiring authority, asked me to serve my country and design and implement what became this as a COVID task force. Senator Cassidy, that report that you referred to, we looked harder and closer at the ability, the Nation's ability to provide medical care than anyone had before. And armed with the extreme pressures and strains of the pandemic, we could use data science to calculate how ICU strain dramatically caused loss of human life.

We found that if the country's ICU beds hit 75 percent, you would see 18,000 lost Americans in 2 weeks with additional amounts four and 6 weeks later. And if you hit 100 percent ICU strain, you would see 80,000 lost Americans. And unlike the losses to COVID, these were 25 to 44 year olds primarily.

The question became, can these cybersecurity failures affect patient care and human life? And we were able to determine the answer was yes. Delays in integrated care affect mortality rates. The seminal New England Journal of Medicine article showed that a 4.4 minute longer ambulance ride during a U.S. marathon had a statistically significant impact on mortality rates 30 days later. Similarly, with strokes, the golden hour or golden hours is one, three, or 4 hours can affect patient care, if you can walk again, if you can talk again.

A 4.4 minutes can affect the mortality for heart. And 4 hours is the difference between life and death for brain. What do 4 weeks of downtime for the State of Vermont or for the protracted impacts to Scripps Health Care in San Diego? These failures further strained already record strained health care delivery, introducing a loss of life, not just of elderly with 65 years or four or more comorbidities, but critical infrastructure aged workforce that we depend upon, and in parallel with these record high strains, as these losses of life succumb to COVID, non-covid conditions, injury, burn- out, retirement, and alterations to their family support structure.

If we zoom out to Maslow's hierarchy of needs, in the last 2 years, we have seen successful compromises of the water we drink, the food we put on our table, the oil and gas that fuels our cars in our homes, the schools our children attend, the municipalities who run our towns or our cities, the timely access to patient care during a pandemic. I myself suffered degraded and delayed care, which imperiled my ability to serve the country during these 2 years.

We are overdependent on the panel things and while we are doing many correct things and this body themselves have taken bold action, these voluntary practices where we take our time have not proven sufficient to transcend the market failures. The adversaries are setting the pace.

We are messing with Maslow. It is not tenable for an individual nor a nation. And with the threats or further attacks from Putin and other nations or adversaries, we need bold action, and we need it now. Any crisis of confidence in the public to trust these baseline functions is unacceptable. We need to be better. We have a head start.

I have in my testimony areas where we can stem the bleeding in the foreseeable future, but it will take much more substantive action. I look forward to answering your questions.

[The prepared statement of Mr. Corman follows:]

Prepared Statement of Joshua Corman
For Senate Health, Education, Labor & Pensions Committee (HELP)
Full Committee Hearing "Cybersecurity in the Health and Education Sectors," May 18, 2022

Opening

Chair Murray, Ranking Member Burr, and distinguished Members of the Senate Committee on Health, Education, Labor, and Pensions, thank you for the opportunity to testify today.

My name is Joshua Corman. I am a Philosopher, Hacker, Protector, and Puzzler… driven to make the world a safer place. Nearly 9 years ago, I founded "I am The Cavalry" (dot org) - a volunteer, cyber safety initiative focused on public safety and human life in the internet of things – or as we like to say: *"where Bits & Bytes meet Flesh & Blood"*. Most recently, I designed and drove what became the *CISA COVID Task Force* (under the CARES Act emergency hiring authority). I am an adjunct faculty for the CISO Certificate Program at Carnegie Mellon University's Heinz College. Lastly, I testified to the *2016 Presidential Commission on Enhancing National Cybersecurity*[2] and served on the (405c) *Health Care Industry Cybersecurity Task Force*[3] – initiated by Congress in the Cybersecurity Act of 2015.

Bottom Line up Front

Attacks on healthcare are increasing in volume, variety, and impact - with consequences now include the loss of life. While directionally-correct steps have been taken, we're getting worse faster than we're getting better. Bold actions and assistance will be required to change this trajectory, address these market failures, lack of incentives, and historical under-investments.

I'd like to bring you good news. However, the more consequential the subject matter, the more important it is to be forthright and avoid exaggeration

---

[2] 2016 Presidential Commission on Enhancing National Cybersecurity https://www.nist.gov/system/files/documents/2016/12/02/cybersecurity-commission-report-final-post.pdf.

[3] Health Care Industry Cybersecurity Task Force Report https://www.phe.gov/Preparedness/planning/CyberTF/Documents/report2017.pdf.

in either direction. The candid truth is, I am more concerned about the cybersecurity of US healthcare than I ever have been.

Note: For events which occurred during my emergency Federal service (which ended January 14, 2022), I will err on discussing public and/or published materials.

Attackers have gotten stronger, but defenders have not - and many got weaker. The number of healthcare attacks have grown. The costs of the ransom payments have grown.[4] The impact of attacks are no longer merely measured by record count, fines, ransom payments, or recovery costs… but including double-digit millions of lost revenue and worse… degraded patient care and human life.[5] Crisis adjustments, made in a hurry, added more technologies and attack surfaces. Financial constraints have forced reduced investments in cybersecurity staff and operating budgets.

The majority of healthcare regulations have focussed on the confidentiality of records. However, "*Cyber Safety is Patient Safety*". I love my privacy; I'd like to be alive to enjoy it. Yes, defensible connected technologies will require investment - as will the talent to defend them. Scrubbing-in before surgery takes time/money – *and* this vital hygiene practice dramatically reduces post-op infection, complications, and mortality rates. As technology increasingly plays a role in the delivery of modern healthcare, cyber-hygiene is no longer negotiable. While many have exclaimed they can't afford to do more, I tried to channel my inner Stan Lee: With Great Connectivity, Comes Great Responsibility…

With seams and cracks in healthcare noted in our 2017 405c report,[6] the pandemic widened and shattered those issues for many.

The pandemic brought an untenable, perfect storm of a record high need for patient care in the face of record high adversary activity, and severely diminished resources with which to defend the healthcare delivery environments.[7]

---

[4] RTF Report: Combating Ransomware - A Comprehensive Framework for Action: Key Recommendations from the Ransomware Task Force https://securityandtechnology.org/ransomwaretaskforce/report/.

[5] CISA Insights Provide Medical Care is in Critical Condition: Analysis and Stakeholder Decision Support to Minimize Further Harm https://www.cisa.gov/sites/default/files/publications/CISA_Insight_Provide_Medical_Care_Sep2021.pdf.

[6] Health Care Industry Cybersecurity Task Force Report https://www.phe.gov/Preparedness/planning/CyberTF/Documents/report2017.pdf.

[7] Ransomware Hits Dozens of Hospitals in an Unprecedented Wave https://www.wired.com/story/ransomware-hospitals-ryuk-trickbot/.

Degraded and delayed care affects patient outcomes.[8] Cybersecurity disruptions can cause and exacerbate delays and degrade care for a hospital, town, region, or even at the state level.[9]

Zooming out, while the country has 16 designated critical infrastructure sectors - with 55 National Critical Functions spanning them - Healthcare and "provide Medical Care" during the pandemic may be respective first among equals. Overall pandemic strains have not merely affected the general population, but have had material impact to the skill-workers and the critical infrastructure workforce that support foundational, life-line critical functions that underpin society (food, water, power, transportation, and brittle supply chains, etc.). As the CISA COVID Task Force came to an end in January, I was alerting CISA, the White House, Federal and Private Sector leadership of material erosions (10, 20, and 30%) to critical infrastructure workforce and difficult-to-replace skill workers - as they succumb to: death from COVID, death from non-COVID, injury, burnout, retirement, and alterations to their family support structure.

Adversaries are disrupting the bottom of Maslow's Hierarchy of Needs.[10] Insecurity at the base of his famous pyramid is not tenable for an individual - and certainly not sustainable for a country. Do not mess with Maslow…

Context

My sentiment below becomes more true with each passing year:

> Through our over dependence on undependable IT, we have created the conditions such that the actions of any single outlier can have a profound and asymmetric impact on human life, economic, and national security.

When I first wrote this, my hope was to prevent high consequence failure in cyber-physical-systems and critical infrastructure. Yet over the last 2 years, we have seen successful attacks and disruptions to:

---

[8] Delays in Emergency Care and Mortality during Major U.S. Marathons https://www.nejm.org/doi/full/10.1056/nejmsa1614073.

[9] Hospitals say cyberattacks increase death rates and delay patient care https://www.theverge.com/2021/9/27/22696097/hospital-ransomware-cyberattack-death-rates-patients.

[10] Maslow's hierarchy of needs https://en.wikipedia.org/wiki/Maslow%27s_hierarchy_of_needs

- The *water* we drink[11,12]
- The *food* we put on our tables[13,14,15,16]
- The *oil & gas* that fuels our cars and our homes[17]
- The *schools* our children attend[18,19,20]
- The timely *access to patient care* - with mortal consequences - during the strains of a pandemic[21,22]
- The *municipalities* who run our towns and our cities[23,24,25]

---

[11] A Hacker Tried to Poison a Florida City's Water Supply, Officials Say https://www.wired.com/story/oldsmar-florida-water-utility-hack/.

[12] Hackers Tried to Poison California Water Supply in Major Cyber Attack https://www.newsweek.com/san-francisco-water-plant-hack-cyber-attack-poison-supply-1601798.

[13] Ransomware Hits a Food Supply Giant—and Underscores a Dire Threat https://www.wired.com/story/jbs-ransomware-attack-underscores-dire-threat/.

[14] Ransomware gang strikes Iowa agriculture business New Cooperative, the latest hack on food supply chain https://www.cyberscoop.com/blackmatter-new-cooperative-ransomware-iowa/.

[15] 'Cyber event' knocks dairy giant Schreiber Foods offline amid industry ransomware outbreak https://www.cyberscoop.com/schreiber-foods-cyber-event-ransomware-agriculture-food/.

[16] AGCO's business operations disrupted by ransomware attack https://www.security magazine.com/articles/97576-agcos-business-operations-disrupted-by-ransomware-a ttack.

[17] Hackers Breached Colonial Pipeline Using Compromised Password https://www.bloomberg.com/news/articles/2021-06-04/hackers-breached-colonial-pipeline-using-compromised-password.

[18] Ransomware Has Disrupted Almost 1,000 Schools in the US This Year https://www.vice.com/en/article/4awyvp/ransomware-has-disrupted-almost-1000-schools-in-the-us-this-ye ar.

[19] Texas, California, New York, Louisiana, Missouri lead list of states with most ransomware attacks on schools: report https://www.zdnet.com/article/texas-california-new-york-and-louisiana-missouri-lead-list-of-states-with-mo st-ransomware-attacks-on-schools-report/.

[20] Hackers prey on public schools, adding stress amid COVID pandemic - Albuquerque, NM https://www.pbs.org/newshour/education/hackers-prey-on-public-schools-adding-stress-amid-covid-pande mic.

[21] Patients of a Vermont Hospital Are Left 'in the Dark' After a Cyberattack https://www.nytimes.com/2020/11/26/us/hospital-cyber-attack.html.

[22] Ransomware Attack Hits Universal Health Services https://www.wsj.com/articles/ransomware-attack-hits-universal-health-services-11601341873.

[23] Amid a surge in ransomware attacks, cities are taking some of the biggest hits https://www.washingtonpost.com/politics/amid-a-surge-in-ransomware-attacks-cities-are-takingsome-ofthe-biggest-hits/2021/09/02/9bd5d654-0a84-11ec-aea1-42a8138f 132a_story.html.

[24] Hackers have been holding the city of Baltimore's computers hostage for 2 weeks https://www.vox.com/recode/2019/5/21/18634505/baltimore-ransom-robbinhood-mayor-jack-young-hacke rs.

[25] Four months on from a sophisticated cyberattack, Alaska's health department is still recovering https://www.zdnet.com/article/four-months-on-from-sophisticated-cyber-attack-alaskas-health-services-is- still-recovering/.

- ....even *Federal agencies* charged with public safety and national security...[26,27]

...stuff... is on fire...

We were prone. We were prey. Our predators finally noticed. Their largely-unchecked aggression has emboldened them. With blood in the water from the strains of the pandemic, healthcare found itself in a feeding frenzy.

Escalation over the Last Few Years in Healthcare

In early 2016, because of hard-earned trust built between I am The Cavalry and the FDA,[28] I had the privilege to serve on the CISA 2015 405c Congressional Task Force on these matters.[29] Our task force started shortly after an untargeted SamSam ransomware hit Hollywood Presbyterian Hospital in LA - diverting ambulances to other facilities, canceling surgeries, and even moving critical care patients.[30] It ended near Mother's Day weekend 2017 with WannaCry wreaking havoc on UK healthcare - manifesting many of our worst fears.[31] Prior to knowing this would happen, the banner graphic in our report to congress earlier that week stated bluntly:

---

[26] DHS, DOJ And DOD Are All Customers Of SolarWinds Orion, The Source Of The Huge US Government Hack https://www.forbes.com/sites/thomasbrewster/2020/12/14/dhs-doj-and-dod-are-all-customers-of-solarwinds-orion-the-source-of-the-huge-us-government-hack/?sh=a170ec825e68.

[27] Suspected Russian hackers spied on U.S. Treasury emails - sources https://www.reuters.com/article/us-usa-cyber-amazon-com-exclsuive/exclusive-u-s-treasury-breached-by-hackers-backed-by-foreign-government-sources-idUSKBN28N0PG.

[28] Hippocratic Oath for Connected Medical Devices https://iamthecavalry.org/ issues/medical/oath/.

[29] Health Care Industry Cybersecurity Task Force Report https://www.phe.gov/Preparedness/planning/CyberTF/Documents/report2017.pdf.

[30] Ransomware takes Hollywood hospital offline, $3.6M demanded by attackers https://www.csoonline.com/article/3033160/ransomware-takes-hollywood-hospital-offline-36m-demanded- by-attackers.html.

[31] NHS could have avoided WannaCry hack with 'basic IT security', says report https://www.theguardian.com/technology/2017/oct/27/nhs-could-have-avoided-wannacry-hack-basic-it-se curity-national-audit-office.

"Healthcare Cybersecurity Is in Critical Condition"

Almost exactly five years later, the situation has grown much more severe.[32] Without bold leadership and swift action, I fear we're not yet to the worst of it.

In June of 2017, while in Tel Aviv CyberWeek explaining to our UN counterparts how lucky we all got with WannaCry, Russia's NotPetya escaped its intended blast radius of Ukraine causing more than $10B of damage worldwide - with $1B alone to Merck Pharmaceuticals.[33] It was at that time that I challenged that international policy cohort to consider a "Cyber-No-Fly-Zone" on at least hospitals (chronicled in the *Sandworm* book).[34] I argued that harms from cyber-munitions against hospitals - intentional or otherwise - should be severely punished and sanctioned. While most allies are loath to enact norms or treaties about cyber-conflict, it is routinely discussed that attacks from a Nationstate, harming country-designated "critical infrastructure" could constitute an act of war.[35] NOTE: Healthcare is designated Critical Infrastructure.

Over the next few years, the ransomware revolution grew bolder and more sophisticated, expanding their appetite to more types of prey.[36] The unavailability of what's important to *you*, can be made valuable to *them*.

As the pandemic reached US soil in early 2020, in the Sandbox at the RSA Conference, I warned then-Director Krebs that I expected a larger volume and variety of ransom attacks on hospitals. I offered a "director's cut" of our 2017 report to congress for him and his team - when the time was right. A few weeks later he called. He did not ask for the briefing. Instead, he asked if I would serve my country for a year. I'll next outline what happened over the next two years.

---

[32] 5 Years That Altered the Ransomware Landscape https://www.darkreading.com/endpoint/five-years-that-changed-the-ransomware-landscape.

[33] The Untold Story of NotPetya, the Most Devastating Cyberattack in History https://www.wired.com/story/notpetya-cyberattack-ukraine-russia-code-crashed-the-world/.

[34] Sandworm by Andy Greenberg https://www.penguinrandomhouse.com/books/597684/sandworm-by-andy-greenberg/.

[35] Tallinn Manual 2.0 on the International Law Applicable to Cyber Operations https://www.cambridge.org/core/books/tallinn-manual-20-on-the-international-law-applicable-to-cyber-oper ations/E4FFD83EA790D7C4C3C28FC9CA2FB6C9.

[36] WSJ Mounting Ransomware Attacks Morph Into a Deadly Concern https://www.wsj.com/articles/mounting-ransomware-attacks-morph-into-a-deadly-concern-11601483945.

Cyber-Attacks during COVID-19

As feared, unscrupulous threat actors started attacking hospitals and medical supply chains for vital and scarce supplies like Personal Protective Equipment (PPE).[3736] Scores of volunteer cybersecurity do-gooders formed groups like the CTI League (Cyber Threat Intelligence League) to assist governments in identifying bad actor infrastructure.[3837] CISA had already launched what they

---

[37] PPE, COVID-19 Medical Supplies Targeted by BEC Scams https://threatpost.com/ppe-covid-19-medical-supplies-bec-scams/154806/.

[38] CTI League https://cti-league.com/.

called PROJECT TAKEN to help hospitals (approximately 85% of whom lacked a single, experienced cybersecurity person on staff).[39,40] As I was being on-boarded through the CARES Act, the country was additionally organizing around what became Operation Warp Speed (OWS). Our eventual CISA COVID Task Force took responsibilities with both - across the interagency.[41]

In addition to engaging and attempting to protect OWS entities, my initial focus was prioritizing a long list of smaller, but potentially vital suppliers to the official OWS funded entities. Using a strategy I dubbed our "Ball Bearings" analysis… We spotted smaller, weak links in the vaccine supply chains who if disrupted could have a profound impact on American lives and interests.[42,43] A recurring uncomfortable reality was that most of these entities lacked even the most basic of cybersecurity. As was the case with healthcare delivery organizations (HDOs), these ball bearings were "*Target Rich, but Cyber Poor*". We were going to have to meet them where they are, and bring fit-for-purpose methods to identify and buy down the risks that we could. This later became the foundation for what I've been calling the "*Pragmatic Security Suite.*"

September saw an uptick in attacks on hospitals. The large, publicly traded hospital network known as UHS suffered a fairly serious ransomware attack.[44] This was my first big opportunity to work across the interagency. It was far more challenging than I was expecting. The good news: this was part of why the CARES Act was enacted – to help combine experience and skills to better serve the public throughout the pandemic.

---

[39] US cyber officials try to channel Liam Neeson in responding to coronavirus threats https://www.cyberscoop.com/project-taken-liam-neeson-dhs-cybersecurity-coronavirus/.

[40] Health Care Industry Cybersecurity Task Force Report https://www.phe.gov/Preparedness/planning/CyberTF/Documents/report2017.pdf.

[41] THE COVID-19 VACCINES WEREN'T HACKED — THIS TASK FORCE IS ONE REASON WHY https://www.theverge.com/2021/7/8/22568397/covid-vaccine-cybersecurity-cisa-task-force.

[42] CyberCast Season 3 Episode 18 - How CISA's COVID-19 Task Force Protected Hospitals and the Vaccine Supply Chain https://www.youtube.com/watch?v=gI40RaxCflk.

[43] Business Insider - Meet the government worker who cut through months' worth of federal bureaucracy in 10 days to help millions of Americans get vaccinated https://www.businessinsider.com/cisa-kenrda-martin-covid-vaccine-bureaucracy-2021-6.

[44] UHS Hospitals hit by Ryuk ransomware, forced to shut down systems https://www.securitymagazine.com/articles/93482-uhs-hospitals-hit-by-ryuk-ransomware-forced-to-shut-d own-systems.

Given that UHS is publicly traded, several of the impacts were eventually disclosed - including a declared $67MM in lost revenue from the ordeal.[45,46]

While many across the healthcare sector discussed the growing impacts of records lost, fines levied, dollars paid to ransoms and restoration services, and now significant lost business… I began to fear that these service disruptions would be measured in degraded and delayed care, patient outcomes, and even lost lives.

Not long after the UHS experience, I helped to rally HHS, FBI, and CISA to issue a joint three-agency (Tri-Seal) Alert to warn the sector of a credible threat to disrupt plural US Healthcare entities concurrently - in close proximity to the US Presidential Election.[47] While we did our best to warn, far too many already strained hospitals fell victim to these more aggressive attacks. At the time, there were some who doubted the intelligence,[48] but in subsequent coverage and reporting from WIRED, the Wall Street Journal, and others… proved the intent to disrupt and intercepted communications reveal just how serious and perilous this was for the country.[49] These attacks felt at least state-tolerated… but more recent reporting suggests they were even state directed.[50] Not only are hospitals designated critical infrastructure, but they are also more taxed and strained than sustainable - without cyber-disruption.

Some victims of this campaign suffered severe and protracted effects on patient care. One such public example was in Vermont - covered in a harrowing story in the NYT.[51] In an attempt to assist future victims, the University of Vermont Medical Center eventually published a detailed report of how this attack affected their oncology capabilities.[52]

---

[45] Cyberattacks Cost Hospitals Millions During Covid-19 https://www.wsj.com/articles/cyberattacks-cost-hospitals-millions-during-covid-19-11614346713.

[46] United States Securities and Exchange Commission - United Health Services, Inc. https://www.sec.gov/Archives/edgar/data/0000352915/000156459022006717/uhs-10k_20211231.htm.

[47] Alert (AA20-302A) - Ransomware Activity Targeting the Healthcare and Public Health Sector https://www.cisa.gov/uscert/ncas/alerts/aa20-302a.

[48] Healthcare Providers Were Warned of a Ransomware Surge Last Fall. Some Still Aren't Sure How Serious the Threat Was https://therecord.media/healthcare-providers-were-warned-of-a-ransomware-surge-last-fall-some-still-are nt-sure-how-serious-the-threat-was/.

[49] Ransomware Hits Dozens of Hospitals in an Unprecedented Wave https://www.wired.com/story/ransomware-hospitals-ryuk-trickbot/.

[50] Leaked Ransomware Docs Show Conti Helping Putin From the Shadows https://www.wired.com/story/conti-ransomware-russia/.

[51] Patients of a Vermont Hospital Are Left 'in the Dark' After a Cyberattack https://www.nytimes.com/2020/11/26/us/hospital-cyber-attack.html.

[52] JCO Oncology Practice: Cancer Care in the Wake of a Cyberattack: How to Prepare and What to Expect https://ascopubs.org/doi/full/10.1200/OP.21.00116.

Major attacks would later degrade and delay care in other regions and states. After the Scripps attacks in San Diego, Dr. Christian Dameff began writing about how an attack on one hospital can drive significant surplus case loads onto proximal, alternative care facilities - with cascading effects.[53,54,55,56]

Excess Deaths and Loss of Life

Delays affect mortality rates.[57] Cyberattacks can cause delays - big ones.[58]

In early 2021, I asked the team an uncomfortable question: Can these cyberattacks contribute to loss of life?

With some analysis and data science, we were able to measure how they can. The simplified abstraction is this:

Ransoms can strain hospitals to levels associated with Excess Deaths.[59]

We studied a state hit hard by ransomware - for a statistically significant observation period. In the same state, with the same population, during the same pandemic, controlling for hospital type and size, locations hit by ransom both achieved these excess death danger zones sooner and stayed there longer than their peers.

Sanitized versions of these models and methods were published in late 2021.

On October 1st, CISA Published a collection of this analysis in a report called: *"Provide Medical Care Is In Critical Condition."*[60] The Excess Death

---

[53] San Diego EDs Deluged With Patients After Cyberattack https://www.medpagetoday.com/meetingcoverage/acep/95357.

[54] Annals of Emergency Medicine - Research Forum Abstract: 108 Emergency Department Crowding Resulting from a Local Health System Cyberattack https://www.annemergmed.com/article/S0196-0644(21)00959-8/fulltext.

[55] Annals of Emergency Medicine - Research Forum Abstract: 7 Impact of a Hospital Cyberattack on EMS Arrivals at Neighboring Emergency Departments https://www.annemergmed.com/article/S0196-0644(21)00856-8/fulltext.

[56] Annals of Emergency Medicine - Research Forum Abstract: 162 Regional Emergency Department Census Impacts During a Cyber Attack https://www.annemergmed.com/article/S0196-0644(21)01014-3/fulltext.

[57] Delays in Emergency Care and Mortality during Major U.S. Marathons https://www.nejm.org/doi/full/10.1056/nejmsa1614073.

[58] Hospitals say cyberattacks increase death rates and delay patient care https://www.theverge.com/2021/9/27/22696097/hospital-ransomware-cyberattack-death-rates-patients.

[59] The Pandemic Revealed the Health Risks of Hospital Ransomware Attacks https://www.theverge.com/2021/8/19/22632378/pandemic-ransomware-health-risks.

[60] CISA Insights Provide Medical Care is in Critical Condition: Analysis and Stakeholder Decision Support to Minimize Further Harm https://www.cisa.gov/sites/default/files/publications/CISA_Insight_Provide_Medical_Care_Sep2021.pdf.

/ Hospital Strain data science instrument was subsequently published on November 18th, 2021 in the CDC MMWR (Morbidity and Mortality Weekly Report) called “Impact of Hospital Strain on Excess Deaths During the COVID-19 Pandemic.”[61] To make these dense reports more accessible, we recorded a short CISA Webinar as well.[62]

As CISA was about to publish our statistical evidence regarding loss of life, the Wall Street Journal published a front page story about a baby who died after a complicated birth at an Alabama hospital that had recently suffered disruptions from a cyberattack.[63]

A Bit More on the Excess Deaths

The CISA COVID Task Force had been analyzing risks and system dynamics related to the National Critical Function (NCF) known as “Provide Medical Care”. In February 2021, when the country hit the sobering milestone of 500,000 Americans lost to COVID,[64] we had also achieved an additional 150,000 Americans lost to what the CDC tracks as Excess Deaths. Excess Deaths are defined as the difference between expected deaths and actual deaths - by month, condition, and state. As we dug into the year of Excess Deaths, several things concerned us. Unlike COVID deaths affecting primarily 65+ year olds, 25-44 year olds were the fastest growing portion of these Excess Deaths. A review of the top causes revealed several time-sensitive conditions for which delayed access to care is known to affect mortality rates (heart, brain, pulmonary, etc). I know from my Cavalry and 405c Task Force work that, for example:

Even 4.4 minutes can affect mortality rates for heart attacks (NEJM)[65] 1-4 hours is critical to save brain/life with strokes; the Golden hour(s).

---

[61] CDC MMWR Impact of Hospital Strain on Excess Deaths During the COVID-19 Pandemic — United States, July 2020–July 2021 https://www.cdc.gov/mmwr/volumes/70/wr/mm7046a5.htm.

[62] CISA COVID Task Force: “Provide Medical Care is in Critical Condition” December 2021 https://www.youtube.com/watch?v=F-uh-lx_KKU&t=6s.

[63] WSJ Hospital Hit by Hackers, a Baby in Distress: The Case of the First Alleged Ransomware Death https://www.wsj.com/articles/ransomware-hackers-hospital-first-alleged-death-11633008116.

[64] Entering uncharted territory, the U.S. counts 500,000 Covid-related deaths. https://www.nytimes.com/2021/02/22/us/us-covid-deaths-half-a-million.html.

[65] Delays in Emergency Care and Mortality during Major U.S. Marathons https://www.nejm.org/doi/full/10.1056/nejmsa1614073.

We chose to study these Excess Deaths more closely - and to hopefully find ways to mitigate these losses of life.

One of our findings was stunning. We found a strong positive correlation between Adult Intensive Care Unit (ICU) Bed utilization and Excess Deaths two, four, and six weeks later. In the model, if the country hit 75% ICU Bed utilization, you'd expect 18,000 lost Americans in two weeks. If the model hit 100%, it would indicate 80,000 lost Americans in two weeks. Delayed and degraded care affects outcomes for time sensitive conditions. ICU strain significantly added delays. Cyberattacks made them worse.

Morbidity and Mortality Weekly Report

FIGURE. Estimated number of excess deaths* 2 weeks after corresponding percentage of adult intensive care unit bed occupancy — United States, July 2020–July 2021

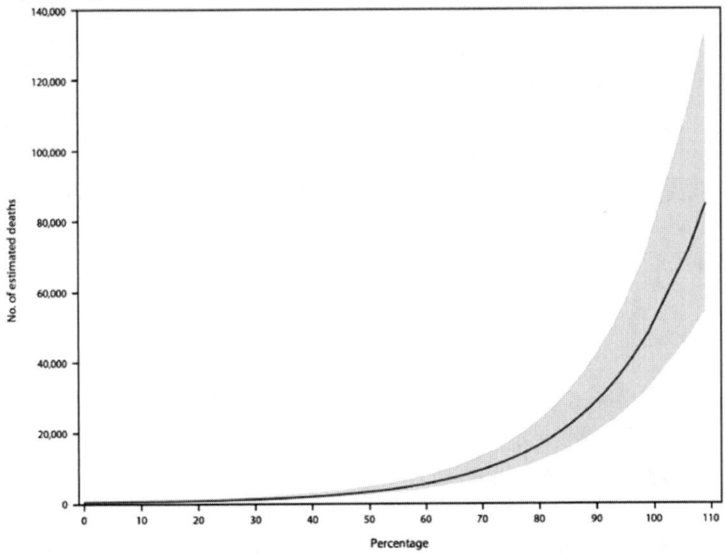

* Upper and lower boundaries of shaded area indicate 95% CIs.

Cybersecurity & Infrastructure Security Agency, unpublished data, 2021). As hospitals exceed 100% ICU bed capacity, 80,000 (95% CI = 53,576–132,765) excess deaths would be health care and public health sectors, with excess deaths emerging in the weeks after a surge in COVID-19 hospitalizations. The results of this study support a larger body of evidence

While this Excess Death math is a feature of the pandemic strains, the systems analysis revealed the elevated risk of loss of life when (for example) ambulance diversions are too far away for the time-sensitive conditions. Also, with the financial strains from covid and the substantive losses of skill workers in healthcare, we will not return to safer capacity levels for some time.

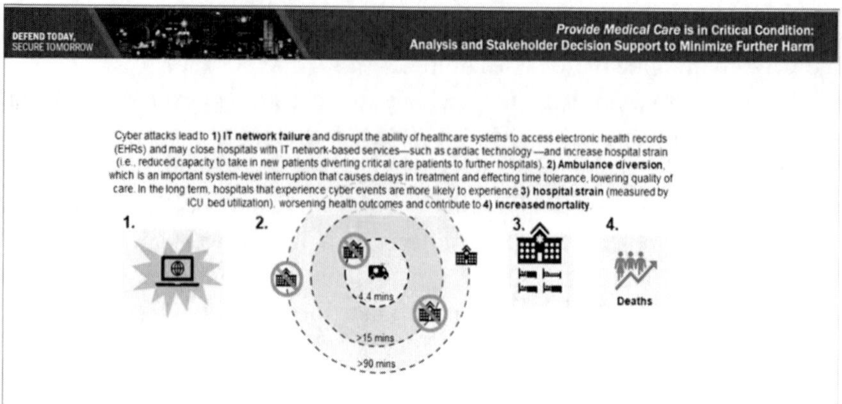

Figure 8 - Conceptual Model of Impact of Cyber Attack on Patient Outcomes

Pragmatism for the Target Rich; Cyber Poor

Years ago, my colleague from industry, Wendy Nather coined: "Living Below the Security Poverty Line."[66] Throughout my emergency Federal Service, and with a focus on Critical Infrastructure, I channeled this into what I've been calling *Target Rich;*

Cyber Poor. An entity can be *Cyber Poor* if there is a deficiency in one or more of the following three areas:

- Insufficient Information/Awareness
- Insufficient Incentives (Carrots/Sticks)
- Insufficient Resources

Going back to the 405c Task Force Report, our estimate was that 85% of the healthcare delivery organizations in the country lack a single, experienced cybersecurity person on staff. We saw similarly prone targets in the vaccine supply chain ball bearings. We saw similar conditions in Water & Waste Water, in Food Production, etc.

There is a massive split between the Haves and the HaveNots of critical infrastructure. The Haves might attempt "Best Practices" and are likely in or around Sector Coordinating Councils and ISACS and running the race. The

66 Security Ledger Episode 223: CISA Looks To Erase The Security Poverty Line https://securityledger.com/2021/08/episode-223-cisa-looks-to-erase-the-security-poverty-line/.

HaveNots of the Cyber Poor may not even be at the starting line. It became clear to me that we would need to reckon with these HaveNots - meet them where they are, and identify and buy down risk… Crawl, then Walk, then Run.

During the Microsoft Exchange attacks,[67] I watched the Cyber Poor / Resource Poor being encouraged to "Implement Zero Trust" or "Just Do Best Practices". Many were asking if software updates would be provided for their Unsupported versions of Exchange. The Chief Data Scientist of Rapid7, Bob Rudis, then surveyed the Internet to find that the dominant versions of Exchange were unsupported. This was especially bad in healthcare. I decided that day that we needed to invert the script. I started working on CISA's "Bad Practices" - the most dangerous practices for owners and operators of critical infrastructure.[68] This list currently has three entries including: the first of which, the use of Unsupported and End of Life Software in service of Critical Infrastructure.

Next I shifted to something I teach my CMU students: S.O.S. Get your "stuff" off search.[69] See what your adversaries see about your internet facing infrastructure. We wrote CISA's Stuff Off Search program. A free way to see if your assets are showing - and how to reduce that attack surface.

We use S.O.S. as a gateway to the free, taxpayer funded CISA Cyber Hygiene (CyHy) Scanning Service – which will send daily scan results of known vulnerabilities to you.[70] And since you likely cannot fix all of them, the CISA KEV list can tell you the Known Exploited Vulnerabilities to prioritize first.[71]

Since attacks are likely to be successful, perhaps the best way to know how you might fare is to practice failure with lightweight table top crisis simulations (also offered by CISA).[72]

We rolled these together into a collection we informally called the Pragmatic Security Suite… a short set of self service webinar videos.[73]

Be under no illusions… these will not make the Cyber Poor immune to attackers. But they may be the difference in opportunistic attacks. This starts

---

67 The Microsoft Exchange Server hack: A timeline https://www.csoonline.com/article/ 3616 699/the-microsoft-exchange-server-hack-a-timeline.html.

68 CISA Bad Practices https://www.cisa.gov/BadPractices.

69 CISA Stuff Off Search https://www.cisa.gov/publication/stuff-off-search.

70 CISA Cyber Hygiene Services https://www.cisa.gov/cyber-hygiene-services

71 CISA Known Exploited Vulnerabilities Catalog https://www.cisa.gov/known-exploited-vulnerabilities-catalog.

72 CISA Tabletop Exercises Packages https://www.cisa.gov/cisa-tabletop-exercises-packages.

73 The Pragmatic Cyber Security Series https://www.cisa.gov/pragmatic-cyber-security-webinar.

their journey… but there will need to be strong incentives and assistance to advance this journey.

Good Steps - In Need of Acceleration

There are some bright spots, but these efforts need to move more quickly.

- The FDA CyberSecurity Pre-Market[74] and Post-Market[75] Guidance: Suzanne Schwartz has leaned-in and shown bold leadership. She needs more support and authority to drive these advances more quickly.[76,77] Hospitals are desperate for these fortifications. This is helpful for FDA approved technologies, but EHRs and other non-FDA regulated. healthcare tech require similar levels of care
- SBOM[78] (Software Bill of Materials): This Software Supply Chain foundational enabling artifact/practice is in the FDA Pre-Market Draft,[79] enjoyed an 3.5 voluntary cultivation via NTIA,[80,81] made it into President Biden's CyberSecurity Executive Order,[82,83] and is *increasingly* proving its necessity on large scale issues like the most recent Log4j exposures.[84],[85] Parts of industry still fear this

[74] Cybersecurity in Medical Devices: Quality System Considerations and Content of Premarket Submissions Draft Guidance for Industry and Food and Drug Administration Staff https://www.fda.gov/media/119933/download.

[75] Postmarket Management of Cybersecurity in Medical Devices https://www.fda.gov/regulatory-information/search-fda-guidance-documents/postmarket-management-cybersecurity-medical-devices.

[76] H.R.7084 - PATCH Act of 2022 https://www.congress.gov/bill/117th-congress/house-bill/7084/text.

[77] S.3983 - PATCH Act https://www.congress.gov/bill/117th-congress/senate-bill/3983/text.

[78] NTIA Software Bill of Materials https://www.ntia.gov/sbom.

[79] 115th Congress of the United States Committee on Energy and Commerce Letter from Chairman Walden to Acting Secretary Hargan https://republicans-energycommerce.house.gov/wp-content/uploads/2017/11/20171116HHS.pdf.

[80] NTIA Launches Initiative to Improve Software Component Transparency https://www.ntia.doc.gov/blog/2018/ntia-launches-initiative-improve-software-component-transparency.

[81] NTIA Software Component Transparency https://www.ntia.gov/SoftwareTransparency.

[82] EO 14028: Improving the Nation's Cybersecurity https://www.federalregister.gov/documents/2021/05/17/2021-10460/improving-the-nations-cybersecurity.

[83] EO 14028: The Minimum Elements For a Software Bill of Materials (SBOM) https://www.ntia.doc.gov/report/2021/minimum-elements-software-bill-materials-sbom.

[84] Log4j is why you need an SBoM https://blog.reversinglabs.com/blog/log4j-is-why-you-need-an-sbom.

[85] Nature: Building resilient medical technology supply chains with a software bill of materials https://www.nature.com/articles/s41746-021-00403-w.

transparency and want to go more slowly than we can afford. The Healthcare Proof of Concept team developed an open source tool "Daggerboard" to ingest/manage SBOMs to protect hospitals… its full value will grow as SBOMs become more readily available

- Medical/Clinical Hacking Simulations: I am The Cavalry teamed with doctors to start the Cyber Med Summits[86,87,88] - now a formal 501(c)(3) non-profit. ER & OR hacking simulations and table-top exercises show healthcare stakeholders how real medical technology hacks affect patient care. We have hacked insulin pumps, pacemaker defibrillators,[89,90] bedside infusion pumps, imaging systems, blood bank databases, building automation systems, EHRs, and more. Experiential learning forums like these could inform and inspire more awareness-sooner.
- Mandatory Breach Reporting[91] to CISA: I was pleased to see this passed into law, but disappointed to see a multi-year rule making process. With so many attacks and such poor reporting, we need to move as quickly as possible. We cannot shift to studying and preventing attacks without adequate and timely visibility into them
- Bad Practices[92] are declared: Who will help to drive them toward extinction? Sector Specific Regulators? FTC? SEC? The Insurance Industry is talking about their role… I could see arguments around due care and negligence getting traction if encouraged
- SRMAs (Sector Risk Management Agencies) are now in statute: but/and the interagency, shared responsibility model with CISA (and FBI, etc) is far from where it needs to be. Our CISA Covid Task Force got a lot of great things accomplished outside of interagency comfort zones… and I fear those positive models have diminished since our

---

[86] CyberMed Summit https://www.cybermedsummit.org/.

[87] ABC Nightline: Fears of hackers targeting US hospitals, medical devices for cyber attacks https://abcnews.go.com/Health/fears-hackers-targeting-us-hospitals-medical-devices-cyber/story?id=4834 8384.

[88] Mark Albert: Efforts to protect patients from cyberattacks grow https://www.wisn.com/article/efforts-to-protect-patients-from-cyberattacks-grow/27493371#.

[89] Digital Defenses for Hacked Hearts: Why Software Patching Can Save Lives https://www.jacc.org/doi/10.1016/j.jacc.2018.03.540.

[90] FDA Warning Letter - Abbott (St Jude Medical Inc.) https://www.fda.gov/inspections-compliance-enforcement-and-criminal-investigations/warning-letters/abbott-st-jude-medical-inc-519686-04122017.

[91] H.R.2471 - Consolidated Appropriations Act, 2022 https://www.congress.gov/bill/117th-congress/house-bill/2471/text.

[92] CISA Bad Practices https://www.cisa.gov/BadPractices.

task force was ended. Cybersecurity is a team sport… the sooner we find the optimal shared responsibility model… the sooner we can do what the country needs us to… Perhaps the newly formed ONCD in the White House can assist here

Failed Markets & Getting Beyond Voluntary

Congress has acted in directionally-correct ways - plural times.[93,94] Industry prefers voluntary… and yet, we're now seeing more and more devastating attacks to healthcare.[95,96,97] Critical Infrastructure needs to work.

The NIST CYbersecurity Framework is voluntary - and nearly a decade later, OIG reports show we still have poor visibility into if it is being used or not.[98] The Cybersecurity Act of 2015 reduced the risk of information sharing and provided some safe harbor for reporting to CISA, yet it isn't being used for more than a tiny fraction of publicly observable attacks. FDA has done a great job raising the bar for the Cybersecurity of new devices and have even issued safety communications and affected recalls.[99,100] Yet hospitals continue to use these recalled devices and unsupported devices - as the norm. Without HHS CMS and/or Joint Commission requirements, we will remain prone. And… With mandatory minimums, there may need to be assistance. Our 405c Task Force had suggestions for Cash-For-Clunkers-like models for technology refresh programs to remove the most dangerous equipment from

---

[93] 115th Congress of the United States Committee on Energy and Commerce Letter from Chairman Walden to Acting Secretary Hargan https://republicans-energycommerce.house.gov/wp-content/uploads/2017/11/20171116HHS.pdf.

[94] H.R.4611 - DHS Software Supply Chain Risk Management Act of 2021 https://www.congress.gov/bill/117th-congress/house-bill/4611/text.

[95] RTF Report: Combating Ransomware - A Comprehensive Framework for Action: Key Recommendations from the Ransomware Task Force https://securityandtechnolo gy.org/ransomwaretaskforce/report/.

[96] Nine security lessons from the 'Conti cyber attack on the HSE' report https://bhconsulting.ie/nine-security-lessons-from-the-conti-cyber-attack-on-the-hse-report/.

[97] Mark Albert: Efforts to protect patients from cyberattacks grow https://www.wisn.com/article/efforts-to-protect-patients-from-cyberattacks-grow/27493371#.

[98] Medicare Lacks Consistent Oversight of Cybersecurity for Networked Medical Devices in Hospitals https://oig.hhs.gov/oei/reports/OEI-01-20-00220.asp.

[99] LifeCare PCA3 and PCA5 Infusion Pump Systems by Hospira: FDA Safety Communication - Security Vulnerabilities. https://wayback.archive-it.org/7993/20170112164109/http:/www.fda.gov/Safety/MedWatch/SafetyInformation/SafetyAlertsforHumanMedicalProducts/ucm446828.htm.

[100] FDA warns of security flaw in Hospira infusion pumps https://www.reuters.com/article/hospira-fda-cybersecurity-idCNL1N10B2GY20150731.

rotation. HIMSS surveys show legacy & unsupported software remains unaddressed.[101]

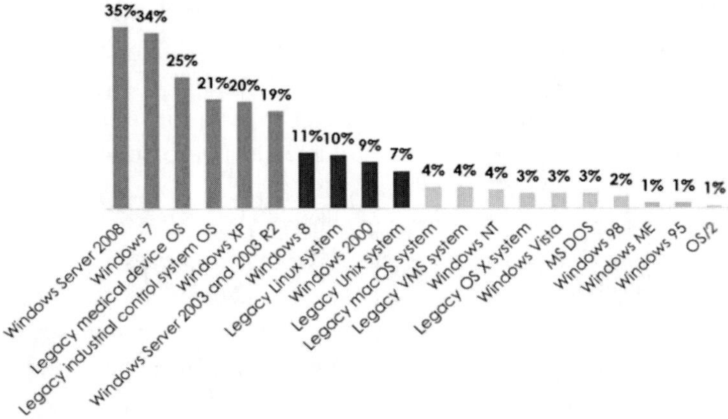

Seatbelts weren't voluntary. I don't believe fire escapes were voluntary - nor kitchen sanitation codes for commercial restaurants. Public Safety isn't free. The lack of sufficient public safety and public good is also dis-economic. Further crisis of confidence in the public in modern healthcare will drive devastating harms to the public safety, economic, and national security.

The Therac-25 radiation delivery machine's software design flaws killed people.[102,103] At the time, they wanted to give it a few more years before we introduced liability to software.[104,105] That was 37 years ago. We're now seeing more brazen adversaries, more nation state use of cyberwarfare, and more frequent and consequential attacks on designated critical infrastructure.

As the world is increasingly depending upon digital infrastructure,[106] that infrastructure needs to be more dependable.

The cybersecurity of healthcare is not trending in the right direction. We can do something about that. We must.

---

[101] 2021 HIMSS Healthcare Cybersecurity Survey Report https://www.himss.org/resources/himss-healthcare-cybersecurity-survey.

[102] An investigation of the Therac-25 accidents https://ieeexplore.ieee.org/document/274940.

[103] The Therac-25: 30 Years Later https://www.computer.org/csdl/magazine/co/2017/11/mco2017110008/13rRUxAStVR.

[104] 2014 RSAC Webinar - Software Liability?: The Worst Possible Idea (Except for all Others) https://www.rsaconference.com/library/webcast/webcast-software-liability-the-worst-possible-idea-except-for-all-others.

[105] 2017 RSAC Talk: SW Liability? Uncomfortable Truths Require Uncomfortable Response https://youtu.be/yGIAC6zxVnc.

[106] Andrea Matwyshyn - Internet of Bodies https://scholarship.law.wm.edu/wmlr/vol61/iss1/3/.

[Summary Statement of Joshua Corman]

Attacks on healthcare are increasing in volume, variety, and impact—with consequences now including the loss of life. While directionally correct steps have been taken, we're getting worse faster than we're getting better. Bold actions and assistance will be required to change this trajectory, address these market failures, lack of incentives, and historical under-investments.

Attackers have gotten stronger, but defenders have not—and many got weaker. The number of healthcare attacks have grown. The costs of the ransom payments have grown.[107] The impact of attacks are no longer merely measured by record count, fines, ransom payments, or recovery costs . . . but include double-digit millions of lost revenue and worse . . . degraded patient care and human life.[108] Hurried crisis adjustments added more technologies and attack surfaces. Financial constraints forced reduced investments in cybersecurity staff & operating budgets.

''Cyber Safety is Patient Safety''. I love my privacy; I'd like to be alive to enjoy it. Defensible connected technologies will require investment—as will the talent to defend them. Scrubbing-in before surgery takes time/money—and this vital hygiene practice dramatically reduces post-op infection, complications, and mortality rates. As technology increasingly plays a role in the delivery of modern healthcare, cyberhygiene is no longer negotiable. Many exclaim they can't afford to do more. I hear Stan Lee: With Great Connectivity, Comes Great Responsibility ...

The pandemic brought an untenable, perfect storm of a record high need for patient care in the face of record high adversary activity, and severely diminished resources with which to defend the healthcare delivery environments.[109]

Degraded and delayed care affects patient outcomes. Cybersecurity disruptions can cause and exacerbate delays and degrade care for a hospital, town, region, or even at the state level. Adversaries are disrupting the bottom of Maslow's Hierarchy of Needs. Insecurity at the base of his famous pyramid is not tenable for an individual—and certainly not sustainable for a country. Do not mess with Maslow . . . Last, purely voluntary efforts have not proven

---

[107] RTF Report: Combating Ransomware https://securityandtechnology.org/ ransomwaretask force/report/.

[108] CISAInsights Provide MedicalCare is in CriticalCondition https://www.cisa. gov/sites/ default/files/publications/CISA-Insight-Provide-Medical-Care-Sep2021.pdf.

[109] Ransomware Hits Dozens of Hospitals in an Unprecedented Wave https://www.wired.com/ story/ransomware-hospitals-ryuk-trickbot/.

able to transcend these market failures-and we're on a troubling trajectory with increasingly aggressive nationstates attacks. We have useful building blocks, but they require more speed & support. As the world is increasingly depending upon digital infrastructure, that infrastructure needs to be more dependable.

The CHAIR. Thank you.
Ms. McLaughlin.

Statement of Amy Mclaughlin, Cybersecurity Prorram Director, Consortium of School Networking, Corvallis, OR

Ms. MCLAUGHLIN. Chair Murray, Senator Cassidy, and Members of the Committee, it is an honor to be here with you today to talk about the cybersecurity threats and challenges facing K–12 education. As mentioned earlier, I am Amy McLaughlin. I maintain multiple cybersecurity certifications and have over 20 years' experience as a cybersecurity professional that spans state and local Government, K–12 and higher education, and health care.

I serve as the Cybersecurity Program Director for the Consortium of School Networking, CoSN, the national organization dedicated to meeting the needs of K–12 education technology leaders. K–12 school districts face increasing attacks and threats. Today's cyber threats largely come from organized crime, nation state actors, and terrorist organizations.

The most prevalent threats facing K–12 schools are ransomware attacks designed to encrypt and block data access to computer systems until a ransom is paid, phishing attacks that inundate education employees with fraudulent emails, attempting to trick them into responding with sensitive data, distributed denial of service attacks that flood the target networks making them inaccessible, and cybersecurity—or cyber-attacks against vendors providing services to multiple districts that result in wide scale impacts.

The impacts of cyber-attacks on K–12 school districts, teachers, and students include lost instructional time, damage to schools' reputations, high financial costs of cyber incidents, rising cybersecurity insurance costs, financial and credit hardships for students and employees from the loss of their personal data, and rising mental health impacts, including increases in anxiety and depression.

These impacts are being realized around the country. In Toledo, Ohio, and Fairfax County, Virginia, attackers threatened to make personal information of students and educators public. School districts in Baltimore, Maryland and Hartford, Connecticut were forced to shut down and cancel several days of school due to ransomware. And on the first day of classes, the Miami-Dade County Public Schools in Florida, the fourth largest U.S. district, saw their networks overwhelmed by denial of service attack.

K–12 schools and districts experience significant challenges in protecting themselves from cyber-attacks. Most districts see cybersecurity as a technical issue, and it isn't. It is an issue that requires everybody in an organization to understand and be part of the solution and understand their role in protecting the organization. Safeguarding technologies are expensive, and the leading K–12 funder, the E-Rate program, does not fund cybersecurity or network defenses.

School districts struggle to hire cybersecurity professionals. With almost 500,000 unfilled positions in cybersecurity in the United States, districts cannot compete with private sector salaries and opportunities. Digital equity is a significant challenge as cyber issues, security issues disproportionately impact our school districts who have less funding available to support and secure their technologies.

The addition of Internet of Things devices to networks demand additional protections the districts are unable to fund and unprepared to deliver. Our K–12 school systems are taking many steps already to improve and expand protections for data and IT systems, including training their IT staff in cybersecurity, training their end users to protect themselves from cyber-attack, backing up data to offsite facilities to recover faster from ransomware attacks, and upgrading their password requirements from basic eight character passwords to stronger pass phrases and implementing multiple factor authentication.

But there are additional Federal actions that should be taken to help our schools and districts improve their cybersecurity defenses. E-Rate needs to be updated to include cybersecurity and expand the E-Rate definition of firewalls to encompass next generation firewalls and services.

We need to encourage the U.S. Department of Education through the Privacy Technical Assistance Center to expand guidance materials and coordinate services across Federal agencies. We need support for implementation of Representative Matsui's 2021 Enhancing K–12 Cybersecurity Act, which CoSN has endorsed.

We need funding, additional funding for MS-ISAC to provide their fee based services to K–12 free of charge. Additionally, funding university and college run security operations centers, or SOCs, which offer cost effective services for K–12 schools and train new cybersecurity professionals, is an excellent opportunity, and we need to help schools hire expert staffing.

Our K–12 districts are on the front lines of protecting their data and systems against much larger, better funded organizations and a rapidly evolving cyberthreat environment. They need access to staffing and technical resources and continue to securely deliver education. I thank you for your time and look forward to your questions.

[The prepared statement of Ms. McLaughlin follows:]

Prepared Statement of Amy Mclaughlin

Chair Murray, Ranking Member Burr and Members of the Committee:

It is an honor to be with you today to talk about the cybersecurity threats and challenges facing K-12 education. I'm Amy McLaughlin, I maintain multiple cybersecurity certifications including the Certified Information Systems Security Professional (CISSP), and Certified Information Systems Manager (CISM). I have over 20 years of experience as a cybersecurity professional that spans state and local government, K-12 and higher education, and health care. I serve as the Cybersecurity Program Director for the Consortium of School Networking (CoSN) the national organization dedicated to meeting the needs of K-12 education technology leaders.

These challenges were daunting before the COVID–19 pandemic, and the rapid deployment of millions of one-to-one mobile devices to shift schools to remote and hybrid learning expanded the technology footprint and increased opportunities for malicious attacks.

The threats faced by K 12 schools and the education sector are very serious and constantly changing. Gone are the days where cyber threats came from individual ''script kiddies'' who sought to access systems, write viruses and worms just to see if they could. Today's cyber threats come from organized crime, nation state actors, and terrorist organizations[110] who have three objectives—use cybercrime to make money through ransoming data or stealing and selling data, collecting data for future use, and disrupting U.S.

[110] *https://www.cisa.gov/uscert/ics/content/cyber-threat-source-descriptions.*

infrastructure and daily life with attacks on our ability to offer a free public education. In addition to external threats, education faces internal threats from students who can quickly and easily learn how to buy or conduct disruptive attacks online.

Attacks against the K-12 system are increasing. In December 2020, the Federal Bureau of Investigation (FBI), the Cybersecurity and Infrastructure Security Agency (CISA), and the Multi-State Information Sharing and Analysis Center (MS-ISAC) issued a TLP: WHITE level Joint Advisory[111] identifying K-12 as targets of opportunity for cyber actors and identified increased attacks against education organizations.

The increase in attacks is reflected in the data around ransomware attacks. The 2020 Joint Advisory cited the MS-ISAC data indicating that ''the percentage of reported ransomware incidents against K–12 schools increased at the beginning of the 2020 school year. In August and September, 57 percent of ransomware incidents reported to the MS-ISAC involved K–12 schools, compared to 28 percent of all reported ransomware incidents from January through July.'' This trend continued into 2021 and continues to be a significant issue going into 2022. Bad actors do not discriminate by location. Cyberattacks hit the biggest urban and suburban school districts as well as the smallest rural schools.

Our K-12 schools and districts recognize the serious privacy, monetary, and operational significance of the cyber threats. CoSN's 2022 Ed Tech Trends report identified cybersecurity as the top unmet technology need stating that even before the pandemic required schools to move more services online cybersecurity has been a top concern for districts. In a situation where even well-funded corporations in the private sector struggle to address cybersecurity issues, poorly funded districts are at a disadvantage. One respondent called the need for more cybersecurity funding as ''desperate.''

Cybersecurity is not only an unmet technology need; it is an organizational culture challenge. K-12 organizations are vulnerable to cyber actors who leverage phishing attacks and social engineering skills to attack school systems with ransomware and other malware or obtain login credentials to access and hack systems. These attacks exploit the helpful and service-oriented focus of school staff and teachers to perpetrate malicious attacks. School district technology leaders work to help staff and teachers recognize these tricks but cybersecurity education must become a more systemic part of educator preparation and professional development and other staff training.

---

111 *https://www.cisa.gov/uscert/ncas/alerts/aa20-345a.*

There are many cybersecurity threats facing K–12 schools. In lieu of providing an exhaustive list, I'll share with you the most prevalent threats:

Ransomware and other malware attacks are often the most destructive and disruptive threat facing education. Ransomware is malicious software designed to encrypt files and block access to computer systems until a sum of money is paid. The more advanced forms of ransomware not only encrypt files, they also exfiltrate the files to the attacker who can then hold the data hostage, resell the data on the dark web, or collect the data for later uses that are, as yet, unknown and, in the case of data stolen by nation state actors, may become a national security threat. Just to be clear, these bad actors are stealing the most damaging and sensitive student, family, employee, and district financial data held by school districts and disseminating it to the highest bidder.

The State of Louisiana experienced the devastating impact of ransomware in 2019 when Louisiana's Governor had to declare a state of emergency after a series of cyber-attacks shut down phones and locked and encrypted data at three of the state's school districts.[112] The attack disrupted teaching and learning and ransomware response ultimately cost the state over $2.3 million.[113] 75,000 students in Albuquerque, NM missed 2 days of school in a 2022 ransomware attack.[114]

Second, education is inundated with ongoing phishing attacks through school district and other email systems. Phishing is an attack that leverages sending fraudulent emails purporting to be from reputable companies and organizations in order to trick individuals to reveal personal information, such as passwords and credit card numbers or send data directly to the cyber actor for example, W2 forms and gift card numbers. ''Phishing attacks are responsible for more than 80 percent of reported security incidents. According to CISCO's 2021 Cybersecurity Threat Trends report, about 90 percent of data breaches occur due to phishing. Spear phishing is the most common type of phishing attack, comprising 65 percent of all phishing attacks. The 2021 Tessian research revealed that employees receive an average of 14 malicious emails every year.''[115]

---

112 https://www.cnbc.com/2019/07/26/louisiana-declares-state-of-emergency-after-cybercriminals-attack-school-districts.html.

113 https://www.theadvocate.com/baton—rouge/news/politics/legislature/article-caf129ae-5e62-11ea-912b-77e0d8405441.html.

114 https://www.usnews.com/news/best-states/new-mexico/articles/2022-01-18/albuquerque-schools-confirm-ransomware-attack-resume-class.

115 https://spanning.com/blog/cyberattacks-2021-phishing-ransomware-data-breach-statistics/.

Third, schools are frequently victims of (DDOS) distributed denial of service attacks. DDOS attacks occur when multiple machines are operating together to attack one target, they flood the target network, server or system, with traffic and illegitimate activity disabling the systems and making them inaccessible. As the FBI, CISA, MS-ISAC Joint Advisory noted, the availability of DDoS-for-hire services provides opportunities for any motivated malicious cyber actor to conduct disruptive attacks regardless of experience level, including students. Miami-Dade School District experienced a particularly disruptive DDoS attack in September 2020 that impacted the districts ability to offer 200,000 students remote learning for the first 2 days of the school year.[116] This attack was perpetrated by a 16-year old high school junior.[117]

A less obvious, but large threat to K-12 schools, are cyber-attacks against third party companies that provide essential operational and instructional technologies. Many K-12 school systems leverage software as a service providers and cloud hosted systems to deliver important technologies for supporting teaching, learning and the delivery of school services including student information systems, learning management systems, ERP systems for finance and human resources, and more. Attacks against third party services providers can result in wide scale outages for schools and widescale data theft or data destruction. Examples of vulnerable and exploited third-party tools that have impacted K-12 education include the 2020 SolarWinds hack,[118] the 2021 Log4J vulnerability that had organizations scrambling to identify vulnerable systems and remediate them,[119] and the 2022 data breach at Illuminate Education which impacted at least 24 districts.[120]

Additional threats include social engineering, end of life and unsupported software and operating systems, open and exposed Internet of Things (IoT) systems, video conference disruptions, website defacement and hacktivism, and more.

The impacts of cyberattacks on K-12 school systems are extensive. Students are directly impacted by lost instructional time when schools are closed as a result of ransomware or other debilitating attacks. Successful

---

116 https://thehill.com/policy/cybersecurity/514802-miami-dade-school-district-virtual-classes-disrupted-by-cyberattack/.

117 https://www.nytimes.com/2020/09/03/us/miami-dade-school-cyberattack.html.

118 https://www.zdnet.com/article/sec-filings-solarwinds-says18000-customers-are-impacted-by-recent-hack/.

119 https://www.cisa.gov/uscert/apache-log4j-vulnerability-guidance.

120 https://thejournal.com/articles/2022/05/03/illuminate-education-data-breach-impacted- at-least-24-districts-18-charter-schools-in-ny.aspx.

cyberattacks damage the reputation of schools and undermine trust of students and parents in the ability of school districts to protect student data and maintain consistent services. Cyberattacks are a crime, yet school districts who are victimized by these sophisticated criminal operations face blame for the crime.

The cost of responding to a cybersecurity incident, restoring systems, and providing services to impacted students and staff is high. In 2021, the average data breach by in the education sector costs $3.79 million.[121] The cost per individual record lost to a data breach can exceed $165 per record. These costs roll over to other schools and districts as insurance companies raise cybersecurity premiums and deductibles. Cybersecurity insurance costs for K-12 are rising by 25–300 percent with more limited coverage and high deductible.[122]

School districts across the country are facing rising insurance costs regardless of whether they have had a cybersecurity incident or not. Not only are insurance premiums increasing, the ability to even become insured has now become predicated on successful completion of a risk assessment and implementation of specific cybersecurity safeguards. The costs of new cybersecurity safeguards and rising insurance premiums prices many school districts out of the insurance market.

There are individual financial and psychological impacts to staff and student victims of cybersecurity attacks. Individuals whose identities are stolen face financial hardship from the loss of their personal data, and students whose identities are stolen may not realize the full financial impact until much later. Since 2017 there has been a growing trend of sales of student data on the dark web. Identities of students who are too young to have existing credit accounts are valuable commodities.

Students under 18, without existing credit accounts, have found themselves victims of identity theft and credit card fraud when stolen data is used to open accounts using their information. Often the fraudulent accounts go undetected until students apply for financial aid for college, or attempt to

---

[121] Cost of a Data Breach Report 2021, IBM Security https://doc-0k-5g-apps-viewer.googleusercontent.com/viewer/secure/pdf/pp9sepf14apgmvrtn4gr78ef7erikjgp/ke3i7gc3usr03dhfesplfnjgpfsrg4d1/1652374200000/drive/14468447276760910654/ACFrOgDH7U4d-azWxsI9zUMG-du0g1d1xPAzRyNRZOZ80u9mK7921h7ZxHLm0C2HHrjSTa-LsSLDcpD-iREpwtCR4j-9Y6RT8Kdpooo7pTum8mhiQ9IZ0kRnnJtex2inBASkqwbNCRUozGq4Vg1B?print=true.

[122] https://www.businessinsurance.com/article/20220216/NEWS06/912347780/ Perspec tives-New-lessons-for-K-12-schools-on-cyber-security,-insurance-cover-#:-:text=K—2D12—20schools—20face—20a,deductibles—20and—20narrower—20coverage—20terms.

obtain credit for the first time only to discover their credit is destroyed and their finances are crippled by data theft from a previous cyber-attack.

Data breaches and identity theft also result in mental health impacts. According to a recent survey by the nonprofit Identity Theft Resource Center, ''86 percent of identity theft, victims reported feeling worried, angry and frustrated, nearly 70 percent felt they could not trust others and felt unsafe, and nearly 85 percent reported disturbances in their sleep habits and 77 percent reported increased stress levels, and nearly 64 percent, they had trouble had trouble concentrating.''

K–12 schools and districts experience significant challenges in protecting themselves from cyberattack. First, school districts are not funded to purchase in depth cybersecurity technologies to safeguard their systems and data. These technologies are expensive and existing mechanisms funding high speed internet access, such as the E-rate program, do not fund network defenses.

Staffing and the ability to hire cybersecurity professionals is another challenge school districts face. There are not enough cybersecurity professionals available and school districts can't afford them. According to, ''Only a fifth (21 percent) of districts have a full-time equivalent (FTE) employee dedicated to network security, the same percentage as the prior year. This means that cybersecurity protection is a part-time responsibility in a large majority of school districts . . . In lieu of a full-time cybersecurity position, districts address cybersecurity in a variety of ways. A third (33 percent) of districts include the responsibility as part of another job.''

Today there are almost 500,000 unfilled cybersecurity positions in the United States that number is projected to increase. School districts struggle to find qualified cybersecurity staff who will work for a K–12 salary. The competition for skilled cybersecurity professionals also results in districts making tough choices between hiring one or two teachers or hiring a cybersecurity professional.

Ensuring cybersecurity equity in education is a significant challenge. Every school district faces cybersecurity threats, but they disproportionately impact school districts with less funding available to staff, support, and secure their technologies. Often, rural, and low-income schools and districts have less funding available to hire dedicated expert staff and maintain their technology up-to-date resulting in higher risk of unsupported and aging systems vulnerable to attack.

Recognizing the many attack vectors and challenges they face, K–12 school systems are taking many steps to improve and expand protections for data and IT systems. The 2022 CoSN Ed Tech Leadership Survey identified the following steps being taken to protect data and systems:

- 65 percent of schools and districts responding to the survey focusing on IT staff training to help grow the skills of their staff in the cybersecurity space. In lieu of hiring trained cybersecurity professionals, districts are seeking to grow these skills internally.
- 63 percent are investing in end-user training which can address the 55 percent are leveraging offsite backups which is the No. 1 step districts can take to be able to recover quickly from a ransomware attack.
- 54 percent were working with staff to upgrade their passwords to expand from a basic eight-character password to a stronger passphrase of at least 12 characters. Increasing the number of characters in a password from eight to 12 characters increases the time a supercomputer needs to brute- force crack a password from minutes to centuries.[123]

There are additional steps that can be taken at a national level to help schools and districts improve cybersecurity defenses and services across the country.

1) Update E-rate's definition of firewall to encompass next-generation firewalls and services. CoSN[124] filed a petition with the Federal Communications Commission in 2021 requesting this change. This does not require legislation and the FCC can and should immediately take this action.
2) Encourage the U.S. Department of Education through the Privacy Technical Assistance Center to expand guidance materials and coordinate services across Federal agencies to provide a comprehensive menu of products.
3) Support the implementation of Rep. Matsui's 2021 Enhancing K–12 Cy- bersecurity Act,[125] which CoSN has endorsed.
4) Fund MS-ISAC to provide their fee-based services to K-12 free of charge and expand staffing of their Security Operations Center.

[123] Firewalls Don't Stop Dragons, Fourth Edition, Cary Parker, Apress, p.109.

[124] *http://d31hzlhk6di2h5.cloudfront.net/20190903/cc/f3/72/41/228e09116606c764f2d2f2c4/CoSN-Cat-Two-Filing-Final-2019.pdf.*

[125] *https://www.Congress.gov/bill/117th-congress/house-bill/4005-q=—7B—22search—22— 3A —5B—22hr-3—22—5D—7D&s=1&r=64.*

5) Fund university and college run Security Operations Centers (SOCs). Colleges and universities are developing non-profit SOCs offer cost-effective services for K-12 schools and train new cybersecurity professionals increasing the number of people capable of filling open positions.
6) Help schools hire expert staffing.

Our K-12 school districts are on the front lines of protecting their data and systems against much larger, better funded organizations, and a rapidly evolving cyber threat environment. To borrow a quote from ''Hamilton'' they are ''outgunned, outmanned, outnumbered, out planned.'' They need access to staffing and technical resources to continue to securely deliver on the mission of delivering education.

[Summary Statement of Amy Mclaughlin]

K-12 school districts face increasing attack and threats. Today's cyber threats largely come from organized crime, nation state actors, and terrorist organizations.

The most prevalent threats facing K-12 schools are:

- Ransomware attacks designed to encrypt files and block access to computer systems until a sum of money is paid are increasing.
- Phishing attacks that inundate education employees with fraudulent emails attempting to trick them into responding with sensitive data.
- Distributed denial of service attacks (DDOS) that flood the target networks making them inaccessible.
- Cyber-attacks against vendors providing services to multiple districts with widescale impacts

The impacts of cyberattacks on K-12 school districts, teachers and students include:

- Lost instructional time
- Damage to schools reputations
- Financial costs of cyber incidents
- Rising cybersecurity insurance costs

- Financial and credit hardships for students and employees from the loss of their personal data
- Mental health impacts including anxiety and depression

K–12 schools and districts experience significant challenges in protecting themselves from cyberattack

- Safeguarding technologies are expensive and the leading K-12 technology funder—the E-rate program—does not fund network defenses
- School districts struggle to hire cybersecurity professionals. With almost 500,000 unfilled cybersecurity positions in the United States, districts can't compete with private sector salaries
- Digital equity is a significant challenge as cybersecurity issues disproportionately impact school districts with less funding available to support and secure their technologies
- The addition of Internet of Things (IoT) devices to networks demand ad- ditional protections

Our K–12 school systems are taking many steps to improve and expand protections for data and IT systems including:

- Training IT staff training in cybersecurity
- Training end-users to protect themselves from cyber attacks
- Backing up data to offsite locations to facilitate faster recovery from a ransomware attack
- Upgrading password requirements from a basic eight-character password to a stronger passphrase of at least 12 characters and implementing multi-factor authentication

There are additional Federal actions that should be taken to help schools and districts improve cybersecurity defenses:

1) Update E-rate's definition of firewall to encompass next-generation fire- walls and services.
2) Encourage the U.S. Department of Education through the Privacy Technical Assistance Center to expand guidance materials and coordinate services across Federal agencies.

3) Support implementation of Rep. Matsui's 2021 Enhancing K–12 Cyber- security Act, which CoSN has endorsed.
4) Fund MS-ISAC to provide their fee-based services to K–12 free of charge and expand staffing of their Security Operations Center.
5) Fund university and college run Security Operations Centers (SOCs) which offer cost-effective services for K-12 schools and train new cybersecurity professionals.
6) Help schools hire expert staffing.

The CHAIR. Thank you very much. Ms. Norris.

Statement of Helen Norris, Vice President and Chief Information Officer, Chapman University, Orange, CA

Ms. NORRIS. Let me begin by thanking, Chair Murray, Senator Cassidy, and the Members of the Committee for the opportunity to address you on this important topic. I am Helen Norris, the Chief Information Officer at Chapman University.

As the CIO, I oversee all technology for the institution, including our cybersecurity practice. Chapman is a mid-sized private university in Southern California with about 10,000 students. However, I have worked across a variety of institutions since 1997, including the University of California at Berkeley and the California State University.

Through my experience at these three universities, I have observed the cybersecurity threat landscape change over the years. When I arrived at Berkeley in 1997, we did not even have one IT professional that worked in information security.

Now, many colleges and universities have cyber—have large departments, have entire departments to deal with the threats that we face. We must defend against a variety of threats, including ransomware, phishing, hacking, and social engineering. We manage sensitive student financial and employee data.

Universities that include medical centers and teaching hospitals have even greater challenges in managing personal health information for individuals. Our systems have grown into complex environments that include large data center and growing—large data centers and a growing set of third party partners.cj.

The scope and intensity of our operations presents challenges to keeping them secure, and we know that bad actors are always looking to turn our difficulties into their opportunities. As I describe cybersecurity challenges, however, I do want to note that higher education is not monolithic. There are approximately 6,000 institutions across the country and there is incredible variety among them.

The challenges related to cyber security differ across types of institutions, but there are some common themes. First, addressing cybersecurity threats is expensive. Investment in this area varies depending on the type of institution.

A large research university or one with a medical center might employ a good sized cybersecurity department. But a smaller university or a community college with more financial limitations will be challenged to do so, even though they must protect sensitive student data in a similar way.

Second, the complexity of this work is enormous. New threats emerge with alarming speed, and we must pivot to address them as they arise. The challenge is not just for our information security professionals. Cybersecurity threats impact our entire community. In higher education, we often say that cybersecurity is everyone's job, as we all face threats of ransomware, phishing, and hacking.

Institutions are also challenged by the increasing number and complexity of cybersecurity regulations, which generate costs that draw resources away from managing risks. My peers and I would welcome the chance to work with agencies to standardize and streamline requirements so we can focus our limited resources on maximizing cybersecurity. While the challenges we face are real and complex, higher education is sophisticated in cybersecurity threat mitigation and protection.

As noted, most institutions have added resources in this area to directly address risks. Our teams protect our networks and our systems in a variety of ways. Some of these involve technical measures like firewalls, encryption, and network segmentation. But much of the work these groups do is outreach to our community. Many security incidents occur when an individual falls into a trap set by a hacker.

A large part of our work is an education—is educational, ensuring that our students and others have the tools that they need to protect themselves. Colleges and universities also address cybersecurity by combining our strength through collaboration to protect the entire ecosystem. We share information on new threats, best practices, and community sourced tools.

We also work closely with partners in Federal and state agencies, particularly the FBI and CISA. Institutions want to continue to buildupon our response to the threats that are out there, and we see partnering at the Federal level as critical to that. We encourage continued and growing collaboration between our community and Federal agencies.

We also welcome ongoing dialog with this Committee as it considers further the cybersecurity challenges and opportunities we face. We believe that engagement and partnership with colleges and universities will help ensure effective approaches to bolstering cybersecurity.

With that in mind, I encourage you to reach out to colleges and universities in your states so that you can hear directly from them about their experiences and what would most help them to succeed in this critical area.

In closing, I want to thank you again for giving me the opportunity to address you, and I look forward to your questions.

[The prepared statement of Ms. Norris follows:]

Prepared Statement of Helen Norris
Senate Help Committee Cybersecurity in the Health and Education Sectors
Testimony of Helen Norris

Chair Murray, Ranking Member Burr, and Members of the Committee,

Thank you for holding today's hearing on cybersecurity in the education and health sectors and for providing me with the opportunity to testify about the cybersecurity landscape in the higher education sector. My name is Helen Norris and I am the Chief Information Officer at Chapman University. As the CIO, I am responsible for all technology at the institution and oversee our cybersecurity practice. Chapman is a midsize private university, with about 10,000 students, in Southern California. However, I have worked in higher education across a variety of institutions since 1997, including UC Berkeley, a large research university, and the California State University.

I will focus my testimony today on cybersecurity threats and challenges in the higher education sector, the impact those threats have on a campus community, and the steps that cybersecurity professionals and their colleagues are taking to prevent, mitigate, and respond to these challenges.

Cybersecurity Threats and Challenges in Higher Education

The cybersecurity threat landscape has grown and transformed over the years. Colleges and universities are a target for hackers and need to defend against threats in the form of ransomware, hacking, phishing and social engineering as they manage sensitive data, including student data. We manage personal data pertaining to our employees, and financial data including payment and banking information. Universities that include medical centers and teaching hospitals face an additional layer of cybersecurity considerations as they also manage personal health information.

It is important to understand that university data systems are highly complex environments to manage and that those systems have both grown in number and data content over recent years. This complexity accelerated even further during the pandemic, as we found ourselves supporting at-home work and a vastly increased online presence in teaching and research. These developments necessitated that we expand our "protection zone" beyond the institution's network to encompass a national or global workforce and student body. This is all within a diverse technical infrastructure that includes our data centers and third-party partners. Colleges and universities must keep these realities in mind as they evaluate and assess the cybersecurity threats that exist today and the challenges those threats pose to the campus community. The scope and intensity of our data operations presents challenges to keeping them secure, and we know that bad actors are looking every day for ways to turn our difficulties into their opportunities.

I would note that higher education is not monolithic. There are approximately 6,000 Title IV institutions across the country, and there is incredible variety amongst them, including community colleges, research institutions, HBCUs, small private institutions and so on. The challenges related to cybersecurity are different across these institutions, although there are some common themes.

First, the need to address cybersecurity threats is an expensive endeavor, particularly in a sector that faces other budget pressures, such as an across-the-board rise in costs, delays in the post- pandemic recovery of enrollments, and the need to maximize college affordability. It has become necessary for universities to invest in this area, especially in terms of hiring information security professionals, as well as acquiring security tools and services. This investment varies depending on the type of institution. A large research university or one with a medical center might employ a good-sized information security department. But a smaller university or a community college with more financial limitations simply can't afford to do this, even though they must protect similar information on behalf of their students and their community. In addition to the cost of this operation, cybersecurity is a highly competitive field, and the nation as a whole simply does not have enough human resources currently to meet the demand.

Universities are at a disadvantage in competing with employers in the tech sector when hiring information security professionals, where the jobs are better-paying and seem more attractive. It is difficult for higher education institutions to develop and retain a skilled cybersecurity workforce. One approach we have taken to addressing this challenge is to integrate our students into our workforce, an action that brings benefits for all.

In addition to the human resources needed to manage the risk, the complexity of the work is enormous. We are constantly dealing with new threats but also new and sometimes conflicting regulations and requirements. We have ever-growing lakes of data with privacy implications that must be protected. New threats are introduced with alarming speed, and we must pivot to address them as they arise. To manage these ever-growing threats, a variety of tools are developing in the marketplace. Universities need highly skilled-integration engineers and security experts to blend these tools together and implement the full monitoring, notification, and automated steps taken at each layer of our environment. Over time, we do expect artificial intelligence to improve the ability of these tools to deliver these protective actions more efficiently and independently.

Even more expensive than managing the risk is the cost of addressing an incident when one occurs. Ransomware is now among the most well-known types of security incident. In this situation, a hacker essentially "kidnaps" the victim's data by encrypting it and will only share the key to decrypt the data when a ransom is paid. While we don't have exact figures on how often this occurs in any sector, we know that a number of successful ransomware attacks, some very high profile, have occurred at colleges and universities. Ransomware attacks are usually carried out by offshore hackers, which makes addressing them even more challenging. It can be highly lucrative for these individuals, and usually there is very little risk to them with this activity.

Ransomware tactics and techniques have continued to evolve in recent years, demonstrating threat actors' growing technological sophistication and an increased ransomware threat to organizations globally. For example, ransomware threat actors are now using double and triple extortion by threatening to:

1) Publicly release stolen sensitive information,
2) Disrupt the victim's internet access, and/or
3) Inform the victim's partners, shareholders, or suppliers about the incident.

Ransomware attacks on universities have been highly disruptive, shutting down the daily operations of the university until the ransom is paid, or the data can be recovered in other ways, a process that usually takes days or weeks. All of this is costly for colleges and universities in financial terms and is also highly disruptive for the institutional community that lacks access to those systems or data during this downtime. An article from the EDUCAUSE review included here as Appendix 1 illustrates some of the impact of a ransomware incident. Quoting from the article: "The impact of a ransomware attack can be devastating. For example, a West Coast university was the victim of a ransomware attack involving data within their school of medicine's research department. After the university realized hackers had encrypted valuable research data, the school chose to pay the hackers $1.14 million in cryptocurrency in hopes that the hackers would provide a decryption key. Fortunately, the school reported that it received a key to restore access to the files and copies of the stolen documents. The FBI recommends against ever paying a ransom to ransomware attackers, as there is no guarantee that the data will be recovered, and paying the ransom encourages the hackers to repeat the attack. The FBI encourages victims of ransomware attacks to contact their local FBI field office to request assistance.

Most types of cyberattacks are happening globally. In England, a top university recently suffered a ransomware attack that forced the school to shut down nearly all of its IT systems. The school was forced to delay the start of the next term while IT teams scrambled to investigate the attack and determine the effect on their systems. The impact of ransomware is not always just a monetary loss, as the disruption to a school's term start will affect many other programs and schedules down the road."

Even when the security teams are successful in avoiding an interruption in services or paying a ransom, hacking incidents are still disruptive and time-consuming. In 2020 a university in California discovered that hackers had infiltrated its systems. While the team successfully shut down the initial attack immediately, they later learned that the cybercriminals had stolen passwords that gave them access to the campus systems for a much longer period.

As in other sectors, higher education is at risk of data breaches, often, as described above, as part of a ransomware attack. In most states, there is a requirement to notify individuals when certain aspects of their personal data have been exposed. This is indeed appropriate. However, it can be an expensive and disruptive process for the institution. In 2017, IBM and the Ponemon Institute published research that showed that the average cost of a breach that involves data exposure can result in costs to the university of $245 per record. The financial impact of a significant breach, which may involve hundreds or thousands of records, can be devastating to a university.

Higher education institutions also face a complex regulatory environment in relation to cybersecurity. Recent revisions by the Federal Trade Commission (FTC) to its Safeguards Rule established under the Gramm-Leach-Bliley Act (GLBA) have greatly expanded the number and scope of requirements with which college and university cybersecurity programs must comply starting late this year. These new mandates are all the more pressing since Safeguards Rule compliance is also a condition of the agreement that institutions must sign to participate in Title IV Federal Student Aid programs authorized under the Higher Education Act. The revised Safeguards Rule directives delve deeper than ever before into institutional cybersecurity, applying to systems that are connected to systems that contain covered information and specifying particular human resources practices that institutions must adopt in relation to their information security staff, among many other things. While colleges and universities are working hard to meet the FTC's December deadline for compliance, many will certainly be challenged to address the significant expansion of Safeguards Rule requirements by the end of the year.

When releasing the new version of its regulations, the FTC also asked for public comment on a proposal to add an incident reporting requirement to the Safeguards Rule. The FTC has not yet indicated whether a final rule on this issue will be released or what its final form will be if so, but the higher education community was generally satisfied with the proposed regulation as initially presented. However, an additional incident reporting requirement from the FTC would exist alongside state data breach reporting requirements that vary across the 50 states. Higher education institutions try to account for the current diverse array of reporting laws and regulations by designing institutional incident response and breach notification processes around their common elements. Differences still exist, though, and simply being prepared to track and address those differences in relation to any given incident carries with it significant administrative overhead. Therefore, additional reporting requirements, such as the FTC's proposed incident reporting requirement, that may themselves seem manageable in isolation should be understood as introducing more layers to an already tall stack of compliance measures that institutions have to follow, and those efforts present additional costs with which institutions, as well as students and other stakeholders, have to contend.

Colleges and universities also know that, in addition to complying with the Safeguards Rule, they will eventually be required by the U.S. Department of Education to follow the cybersecurity guidelines for "controlled unclassified information (CUI)" developed by the National Institute of Standards and Technology (NIST). This stems from the fact that "education records" as defined by the Family Educational Rights and Privacy Act (FERPA) are considered CUI under the National Archives and Records Administration (NARA) CUI Program established as a result of Executive Order 13556, "Controlled Unclassified Information." The Office of Federal Student Aid has previously stated that it considers Federal Student Aid data shared with institutions to facilitate the awarding and distribution of federal student financial aid to fall under the "education records" CUI category, and thus it intends to work toward ensuring institutional compliance with the NIST CUI guidelines in the years ahead. Institutions that conduct relevant research for the U.S. Department of Defense (DoD) must already follow these guidelines in relation to the DoD CUI (or covered defense information (CDI)) related to those projects, with the guidelines also forming an integral part of DoD's Cybersecurity Maturity Model Certification (CMMC) Program. The application of the guidelines to student financial aid information, however, will greatly expand their scope of impact across colleges and universities as well as within institutions, given that the CUI requirements are associated with student financial aid data that will generally find its way into multiple institutional administrative systems. While many institutions have a working knowledge of the NIST CUI guidelines and may in fact be complying with them now, many others know that meeting the standards will be one more resource-intensive exercise on top of compliance efforts, such as fulfilling the new Safeguards Rule provisions, that are already underway. (Please see Appendix 2 for the supporting documents regarding the regulatory issues discussed in this and the immediately preceding paragraphs.)

Colleges and universities take compliance with federal and state cybersecurity requirements very seriously. Beyond regulatory compliance, we take even more seriously our obligation to our students, their families, and our stakeholder communities to secure the data with which we are entrusted and to provide secure environments in which learning, research, and service can take place. The ever-growing number and complexity of the compliance requirements that we face, however, presents an ever-expanding set of administrative burdens and associated costs that may detract from our capacity to manage the actual cybersecurity risks confronting our institutions, both now and in the future. Higher education technology and cybersecurity leaders would welcome the opportunity to explore with policymakers and regulators how these requirements might be streamlined to ensure that we can maximize the value of our cybersecurity resources to maximizing our cybersecurity effectiveness.

Impacts on Students, Staff, Patients and Families

Students are also directly and personally impacted by the disruption of an actual breach. Ransomware attacks can cripple the university's ability to operate by taking down critical systems for an extended period of time, as noted in the earlier example from the United Kingdom. During that time, students lose access to critical services that they need from the institution. This may include the ability to communicate with their faculty as well as the ability to manage their assignments and tests, directly impacting their educational experience. In some instances, colleges and universities have chosen to shut down all services, including canceling classes, until they are confident that they have eliminated the threat from the system or systems in question. Students are also impacted during a data breach if their own data is exposed, creating the risk of negative personal and financial impacts.

Incidents that impact individuals, however, are most often at a smaller scale than a major data breach or ransomware incident. Students in particular must be ever-vigilant to the ongoing attempts by hackers to trap them via email scams based on social engineering. There are many incidents in which a student "falls for" an email scam fraudulently offering a part-time job or threatening to share embarrassing personal information, and the student actually loses money in the process. These phishing attacks involve a hacker impersonating a trusted authority and convincing the victim to share his or her personal information, or even send money to the individual. Students are often victims of a particularly common form of this scam comprised of a fake job offer. In the past we have seen increases in this activity at specific times of the year, such as holidays or tax time, and higher education institutions are often and explicitly targeted.

How Colleges and Universities Prevent, Mitigate and Respond to These Challenges

While the challenges we face are real and complex, the higher education sector is sophisticated in cybersecurity threat mitigation and protection. As noted, most of us have invested resources to build effective cybersecurity capacity. Our information security teams deploy a variety of technologies and processes to protect institutional networks and systems. During the pandemic, as our staff, faculty and students all needed to work, teach, and learn remotely, colleges and universities had the need to implement and extend our technical protections to off-site locations. Some of the technical tools we use to respond to cybersecurity challenges are outlined below:

- Implementing multi-factor authentication to govern system access;
- End Point Detection and Response Systems (EDR), which protects systems both on and off the campus network;
- The use of technology such as firewalls to protect the physical network;
- Encrypting our most sensitive data;
- Network segmentation, which puts our more valuable and sensitive data in a more secure section of the network;
- Addressing software vulnerabilities by applying patches provided by our partners;
- Utilizing virtual private network (VPN) technology to encrypt data when it is accessed from a remote location;
- Using modern monitoring technology to root out suspicious activity on our networks and investigate those activities.

While we often tend to think of cybersecurity as focusing on technical solutions, it is in fact a very human issue and many of the efforts in colleges and universities to combat cybersecurity threats involve outreach to our stakeholders. For example, as previously noted, many security incidents result from an individual falling into a trap set by a hacker through phishing. Higher education information security professionals strive to ensure that the members of our institutional communities have the tools to protect themselves from such incidents—tools that will help them recognize these traps and avoid them altogether, creating a strong human firewall for our institutions. Examples include:

- As noted above, implementing multifactor authentication to govern systems access and educating our community on its importance;
- Phishing campaigns designed to educate our students, faculty and staff on this risk; and
- General outreach and education, which includes sharing information about current threats.

Colleges and universities also address cybersecurity challenges by amplifying our strength through collaboration. As noted previously, there is a great variety in the type of institutions and how they are resourced. Less well-resourced colleges and universities may not individually have the level of human resources needed to manage the range of threats they face on their own. But the overall community comes together to protect the entire ecosystem. Through organizations like EDUCAUSE, Internet2 and REN-ISAC, we share information on new threats, best practices and community-sourced tools. In addition, we work closely with partners in many federal and state agencies, particularly the FBI and CISA. Many institutions develop relationships with their local FBI cybersecurity teams in advance of an incident. This collaboration helps us to avoid problems, and it also enables us to respond more quickly when an incident does occur. CISA offers a variety of free cybersecurity services and tools to colleges and universities, including an online database of known exploited vulnerabilities that is a critical tool, and even free vulnerability scanning. (https://www.cisa.gov/free-cybersecurity-services-and-tools) That means that CISA will test an institution's internet-facing systems to find weaknesses. Literally hundreds of colleges and universities take advantage of these great services, and they are a critical part of our defense.

Finally, while we plan and protect, universities also prepare for the worst using several different techniques. Most universities have created incident response plans (IRPs) that outline what we should do in the event of a cybersecurity incident such as a ransomware attack. Universities generally test these plans on a regular basis via tabletop exercises that allow them to evaluate their preparedness for an event and adjust their plans as necessary. Some institutions also carry cyber insurance that aids them in the event of an incident, with their insurance carriers also providing guidance in the preparation and testing of an IRP. Unfortunately, cyber insurance has become prohibitively expensive for some institutions, and looking to the future, the growing cost of cyber insurance remains a concern for higher education as a whole.

In summary, colleges and universities usually take a multi-layered approach to security by:

- Utilizing technical tools to protect our networks and technical environments from unauthorized access by hackers;
- Using outreach, communication and education to protect our institutional communities from phishing for data and credentials, email scams and ransomware;
- Actively engaging with federal agencies and the higher education community in general to increase our own awareness of current threats and risks, allowing us to avoid becoming a victim of those new threats; and
- Preparing and planning for an incident should one occur.

In conclusion, I would again like to thank the Committee for your attention to this important issue. I look forward to continued collaboration and conversation on this topic.

Appendix 1

Why IT Matters to Higher Education
EDUCAUSE
REVIEW

The Increasing Threat of Ransomware in Higher Education

Steve Scholz, William Hagen and Corey Lee
Tuesday, June 22, 2021
Cybersecurity and Privacy
7 min read

Cyberattacks are increasing in frequency and impact. Defending against ransomware attacks requires a tiered approach to security with a Zero Trust model at the heart of the methodology.

Credit: posteriori / Shutterstock.com © 2021.

During the pandemic, several major cyberattacks have unfolded, resulting in severe impacts to organizations and individuals. One of the most talked-about cyberattacks in 2020 was the SolarWinds breach, in which hackers gained access to nearly 18,000 clients of SolarWinds. The victims of the attack include Fortune 500 companies and multiple US government agencies.

In May 2021, Colonial Pipeline Company, a major refined-oil products supplier responsible for 45 percent of the East Coast's fuel supply, was hit in the largest-known hack to date on US energy infrastructure. The attack caused Colonial Pipeline to shut down its entire system, leading to panic and a disruption in gasoline supply across the East Coast of the United States.[126] In order to unlock encrypted files and get the pipeline back up and running, Colonial Pipeline paid hackers $4.4 million in Bitcoin for a decryption key.

Recently, the number of ransomware attacks similar to the attack on Colonial Pipeline has increased dramatically. The number of ransomware attacks more than doubled as cybercrime operations increased throughout the coronavirus pandemic. These attacks grew not only in frequency but also in sophistication and ransom demand. In 2018, the average ransom demanded

[126] Will Englund and Ellen Nakashima, "Panic Buying Strikes Southeastern United States as Shuttered Pipeline Resumes Operations," Washington Post, May 12, 2021.

from a victim was $8,000. In 2020, the average demand grew to $170,000, with high-end demands exceeding $1 million.[127]

Ransomware attacks are not only affecting businesses; colleges and universities are also prime targets for attacks. Surprisingly, education is the most affected sector for malware attacks when compared to other industries like business and professional services, retail and consumer goods, and high tech. Within the last thirty days, educational organizations have been the target of more than 6.1 million malware attacks, while the second-most affected industry (business and professional services) has only seen 900,000 attacks.[128] An analysis of ransomware campaigns within higher education found that ransomware attacks against colleges and universities have more than doubled since the onset of the coronavirus pandemic.[129]

The FBI's Cyber Division recently warned that ransomware poses a huge risk for higher education, as cybercriminals using this type of attack are now focusing heavily on colleges and universities.[130] The FBI became aware of a new type of ransomware attack—using a new type of malware known as PYSA—where unidentified cyber actors are specifically targeting higher education, K–12 schools, and seminaries.

These actors use PYSA to exfiltrate data from victims prior to encrypting the victims' systems to use as leverage in eliciting ransom payments.

What Is Ransomware?

Ransomware is a malicious form of malware, where hackers deploy a malicious computer code to block an organization's access to its own computer network to extort a ransom. The types and complexity of ransomware attacks have increased rapidly over time, and today many ransomware attacks see cybercriminals gaining access to an organization's data and then holding it hostage with military-grade encryption.

---

[127] John Leyden, "Ransomware Attacks More Than Doubled Last Year as Cybercrime Operations Scale Up during Coronavirus Pandemic," The Daily Swig (website), March 8, 2021.

[128] Microsoft Security Intelligence, Global Threat Activity Map by Industry, Microsoft (website), accessed June 4, 2021.

[129] Cybersecurity in Higher Education, research report, (New York, NY: BlueVoyant, February 2021).

[130] Federal Bureau of Investigation Cyber Division, Increase in PYSA Ransomware Targeting Education Institutions, FBI FLASH, Alert Number CP-000142-MW, March 16, 2021.

There are three main types of ransomware (listed below in order of increasing severity and complexity):

- Scareware: This type of ransomware typically includes rogue security software and tech-support scams. In this type of ransomware, the victim may receive a pop-up message claiming that malware was discovered on their system, and the only way to eradicate the malware is to pay for the security software to remove it. In most cases, this type of attack poses little actual risk to files and data.
- Screen lockers: When a screen locker attack is deployed, the victim is locked out of their computer entirely. Upon startup, a full-size window will appear demanding ransom payment and prohibiting the victim from using their computer.
- Encrypting ransomware: This is the most complex and devastating type of ransomware. Cybercriminals will gain access to the victim's system, seize their files, encrypt them, and then demand payment for decrypting and returning the files.

When faced with an encryption ransomware attack, the victim is left with only a few choices: they can either pay a ransom to the criminals (which does not guarantee the criminals will return the data), attempt to break the encryption on their data, or restore their data and systems from backups.

In a ransomware attack, hackers typically search out an organization's most valuable data. High-profile ransomware attacks sometimes target organizations that are conducting research where the data is highly confidential. In other cases, the data the attackers might be after could be confidential data about a university's students, including social security numbers, addresses, and birthdates. Another common target for ransomware attacks is any type of data or system that could make it impossible for an organization to function.

Because of the data they possess, higher education institutions are key targets for ransomware attacks.

However, even smaller universities and colleges, as well as those without an emphasis on research, are prime targets for this type of cyberattack. Regardless of whether an institution considers its data to be valuable, chances are that cybercriminals do. Higher education institutions inherently gather and store large amounts of confidential student data and therefore must protect themselves against ransomware attacks.

Even more concerning than traditional malware-based ransomware attacks are human-operated ransomware attacks, which pose a huge threat to organizations of all types. An advanced type of ransomware, human-operated ransomware attacks are becoming more frequent and costly. In a human-operated attack, a cybercriminal is actually controlling the attack in real-time, and after gaining access to a victim's system, the criminal quickly scans through files and locations— while also preventing any antivirus alerts—to pinpoint and steal the most valuable data.

In these types of attacks, the attacker will often exhibit extensive knowledge of systems administration and common network security misconfigurations, perform thorough reconnaissance, and adapt to what they discover in a compromised network. Existing antivirus solutions are often not a strong enough defense when an organization is faced with this type of hands-on-keyboard ransomware attack.

The Impact of Ransomware Attacks

The impact of a ransomware attack can be devastating. For example, a West Coast university was the victim of a ransomware attack involving data within their school of medicine's research department. After the university realized hackers had encrypted valuable research data, the school chose to pay the hackers $1.14 million in cryptocurrency in hopes that the hackers would provide a decryption key.

Fortunately, the school reported that it received a key to restore access to the files and copies of the stolen documents. The FBI recommends against ever paying a ransom to ransomware attackers, as there is no guarantee that the data will be recovered, and paying the ransom encourages the hackers to repeat the attack. The FBI encourages victims of ransomware attacks to contact their local FBI field office to request assistance.

Most types of cyberattacks are happening globally. In England, a top university recently suffered a ransomware attack that forced the school to shut down nearly all of its IT systems. The school was forced to delay the start of the next term while IT teams scrambled to investigate the attack and determine the effect on their systems. The impact of ransomware is not always just a monetary loss, as the disruption to a school's term start will affect many other programs and schedules down the road.

Developing a Strategy to Help Prepare for Ransomware Attacks

Defending against ransomware attacks requires a tiered approach to security with a Zero Trust model at the heart of the methodology. So, how does Zero Trust work? Zero Trust follows three guiding principles: verify explicitly, use least privileged access (LPA), and assume breach.

- Verify explicitly: Zero Trust closes gaps in multi-factor authentication (MFA) coverage by requiring explicit verification across the network. Instead of assuming trust based on weak assurances like network locations, Zero Trust uses all available data—identity, endpoint, and network data—to authenticate all access requests, no matter where they came from or what they're accessing.
- Use least privileged access (LPA): Zero Trust makes it harder for attackers to negatively impact key systems and data by limiting users' access to the resources, devices, and environments they need. Without widespread privileges and access, attackers have fewer opportunities to move laterally within the network beyond an initial breach.
- Assume breach: As a final fail-safe, Zero Trust operates under the assumption that a breach has already happened or soon will. This means deploying redundant security mechanisms, collecting system telemetry, using that telemetry to detect anomalies, and—wherever possible—automating insight generation to enable near-real-time prevention, response, and remediation.

IT professionals play an important role in security and are the foundation of an approach to preventing ransomware. Many observed ransomware attacks leverage malware and tools that are easily detected by antivirus security software. Observed affected servers also often lack firewall protection and MFA, have weak domain credentials, and use non-randomized local admin passwords.

Oftentimes, these protections are not deployed because there is a fear that security controls will disrupt operations or impact performance. IT professionals can help determine the true impact of these settings and collaborate with security teams on mitigations. Attackers often prey on settings and configurations that many IT admins manage and control. Given the key role they play, IT professionals should be part of security teams to defend against ransomware attacks.

When considering complex, human-operated ransomware attacks, traditional solutions like MFA and antivirus are a good start but will not completely defend an organization against a knowledgeable cyberattacker. The only way to defend against these types of events is a twofold approach involving top-of- the-line endpoint detection and response paired with a user entity behavior analytics (EUBA) solution. This is the only way to pinpoint if there is an attacker on the inside of a system who has managed to evade or silence antivirus alerts.

Microsoft has the tools and expertise needed to ensure your security system is able to prevent ransomware attacks.

Contact your Microsoft account representative to discuss your security needs and learn how higher education institutions are defending against ransomware attacks.

Additionally, you can learn more about Microsoft's approach to defending against these types of cyber-attacks and *human-operated ransomware on Microsoft Docs.*

Steve Scholz is Principal Technical Specialist for Security, Compliance and Identity, US Education, at Microsoft.

Bill Hagen is a Senior Director of Security addressing industry, partner, and customer requirements at Microsoft.

Corey Lee is Senior Consultant and Zero Trust Architect at Microsoft.

Microsoft is a supporting partner of EDUCAUSE.

Cyber Threat Intelligence , Cybersecurity , Encryption , Endpoint Detection and Response (EDR), Incident Management and Response , Intrusion Detection and Prevention , Security Risk Management, Vulnerability Management, Zero Trust

Appendix 2

Why IT Matters to Higher Education
EDUCAUSE
REVIEW

Policy Analysis: Revised, Highly Prescriptive FTC Safeguards Rule

Jarret Cummings
Thursday, December 2, 2021
Policy
20 min read

The Federal Trade Commission (FTC) has released a revised version of the Safeguards Rule. The revised Rule will impose many new requirements on institutional cybersecurity operations in relation to student financial aid and other "customer" information.

Credit: Jarretera / Shutterstock.com © 2021.

Note: The Federal Trade Commission officially published its revised Safeguards Rule in the Federal Register on December 9, 2021, making December 9, 2022, the deadline for institutions to achieve compliance with the new requirements of the revised Rule. The text below has been updated as of March 9, 2022, to reflect this change. Some of the document links have been revised as well to reflect new, post-publication locations of the respective resources.

When the Federal Trade Commission (FTC) proposed to revise the Safeguards Rule (the Rule) in 2019, EDUCAUSE joined with the American Council on Education (ACE) and several other associations to submit comments asking for a number of changes and clarifications.[131] Those comments derive largely from an analysis (written by EDUCAUSE members and staff) of the FTC's proposed revisions to the Rule.[132] In light of the initial comments that the FTC received, including ours, the agency held an online listening session during the summer of 2020. Among the select stakeholder panelists the FTC invited to participate were a few EDUCAUSE member CIOs and CISOs. However, the FTC did not provide any insights into how the feedback it received on its proposed rulemaking might influence the form that its revised cybersecurity regulations would take. The agency *released* the latest version of the Safeguards Rule on October 27.[133] This version is largely unchanged from the FTC's original draft. *(Note: The pre- publication draft originally made available by the FTC on October 27, 2021, was replaced by a pre-publication version posted to the online version of the Federal Register on December 8, 2021. The references and links to the pre- publication draft of the revised Rule have been updated to reflect the December 8 version in the online Federal Register since that is the pre-publication form of the document still available. The same is true for the supplemental notice of proposed rulemaking regarding a possible Safeguards Rule reporting requirement. The December 8 version of that document is the pre-publication version still available, so relevant references and footnotes have been updated accordingly.)*

Given the extensive edits, clarifications, and changes that we requested,[134] the FTC's decision not to substantially revisit its regulatory proposal is disappointing. That said, the analysis of public comments provided with the FTC's pre-publication copy of the new Rule contains an important acknowledgment from the agency that sets the context for interpreting and applying the numerous provisions with which colleges and universities will now have to comply:

> Although the Final Rule has more specific requirements than the current Rule, it still provides financial institutions the flexibility to

---

[131] Federal Trade Commission, "Standards for Safeguarding Customer Information (Notice of Proposed Rulemaking; Request for Public Comment)," Federal Register, Vol. 84, No. 65, April 4, 2019, pp. 13158-13177; Jarret Cummings, "Higher Ed Community Responds to Proposed Safeguards Rule Change," EDUCAUSE Review, August 14, 2019.

[132] Please see Jarret Cummings, "Safeguards Rule Comments Deadline Extended to August 2," EDUCAUSE Review, June 7, 2019, for more details.

[133] Federal Trade Commission, "FTC Strengthens Security Safeguards for Consumer Financial Information Following Widespread Data Breaches," October 27, 2021.

[134] For details, see Jarret Cummings, "Safeguards Rule Comments Deadline Extended to August 2," EDUCAUSE Review, June 7, 2019, and Jarret Cummings, "Higher Ed Community Responds to Proposed Safeguards Rule Change," EDUCAUSE Review, August 14, 2019.

> design an information security program that is appropriate to the size and complexity of the financial institution, the nature and scope of its activities, and the sensitivity of any customer information at issue.[135]

This statement is significant because it is relevant to a point that EDUCAUSE and our higher education association partners pressed throughout our comments on the proposed Rule. We consistently noted that many provisions lacked sufficiently specific guidance to assure a college or university that it had achieved compliance, an issue that we summarized as follows:

> The proposed revised Rule, however, specifies many of the details of those elements while adding more provisions and requirements, but without providing effective guideposts for compliance. That leaves colleges and universities with many questions about whether the proposed Rule's provisions are appropriately limited to the data and functions it covers and how institutions will effectively be able to determine if they are in compliance regardless.[136]6

The statement from the FTC quoted above directly addresses this concern.[137]7 In my view, it reaffirms that an effective approach to the requirements of the Safeguards Rule, including all of its new provisions, remains a matter of discretion for the covered entity in question based on its size and complexity, the nature and scope of its activities, and the sensitivity of the customer information it handles. The Rule identifies the elements that an institution's information security program must include; however, it leaves the determination of how the institution should address those elements (for the most part) to the covered entity, with the understanding that the institution will make those decisions based on, and reasonably justified by, its particular context.

From a compliance standpoint, institutions may view this level of discretion as a double-edged sword based on understandable concerns about their decisions being second- guessed by regulators at some point in the future.

---

[135] Federal Trade Commission, "16 CFR Part 314: Standards for Safeguarding Customer Information (Final Rule)," pre-publication copy, (December 8, 2021): 5.

[136] American Council on Education et al., letter to the Federal Trade Commission, "Request for Public Comment on Notice of Proposed Rule-Making, 'Standards for Safeguarding Customer Information' (Safeguards Rule, 16 CFR 314, Project No. P145407)," August 2, 2019, 3.

[137] FTC, "16 CFR Part 314: Standards for Safeguarding Customer Information (Final Rule),"5.

Given the FTC's position as reflected in the acknowledgment from the agency quoted above and its analysis of public comments on the proposed revisions to the Rule, institutions may best respond by adopting an approach that EDUCAUSE asked the FTC to affirm explicitly in the Rule or its related guidance (which it apparently declined to do in favor of reaffirming the extent of institutional discretion):

> [W]e would urge the FTC to explicitly state in the Rule and subsequent guidance what we believe the proposed revised Rule implies—that institutions may achieve compliance through providing reasonable explanations in their information security program documentation for the choices they make in fulfilling the given provisions.[138]8
>
> In other words, the discretion to determine what constitutes an appropriate way to fulfill a given requirement based on an institution's size and complexity, the nature and scope of its activities, and so forth carries with it the responsibility of ensuring that the measures adopted by the institution are appropriate given what it is, what it does, and what options it may reasonably have available to it as a result.
>
> I used the word "regulators" above, not "the FTC," because the Office of Federal Student Aid (FSA) at the US Department of Education (ED) has made compliance with the FTC Safeguards Rule a requirement of the Title IV Program Participation Agreement (PPA) that institutions must sign to participate in federal student financial aid programs.[139]9 As a result, institutions are ultimately responsible to the FTC directly for complying with the Safeguards Rule, but a determination by FSA that an institution is not complying with the Safeguards Rule may affect its Title IV eligibility and therefore the ability of the students enrolled at the institution to get federal student loans and other forms of federal financial aid.

It remains unclear how FSA will address the changes in the FTC's cybersecurity regulations. Conversations between EDUCAUSE and FSA representatives about the issues that have occurred since the FTC unveiled its rulemaking notice in 2019 did not produce any indication of how FSA would

[138] American Council on Education et al., letter to the FTC, "Request for Public Comment on Notice of Proposed Rule-Making, 3.

[139] "Record Keeping, Privacy, and Electronic Processes," in 2021-2022 Federal Student Aid Handbook in PDF Format, (Washington DC: Office of Federal Student Aid, US Department of Education, 2021), 2- 218, 2-220.

incorporate Safeguards Rule revisions into its compliance expectations. For now, the Safeguards Rule audit objective that FSA had incorporated into the federal single audit process still focuses on confirming a few high-level objectives from the previous version of the Rule:

- That an institution has appointed a person or team to coordinate its information security program
- That it has conducted a relevant risk assessment
- That it has developed information security controls based on its identified risks[140]

FSA will have to work with the Office of Management and Budget to alter the audit objective in light of the FTC's revisions to the Rule, if and when it chooses to do so, and that process will take time.

Meanwhile, EDUCAUSE intends to work with its members and association partners to engage with FSA to understand its Safeguards Rule compliance and audit objective plans as they take shape. We hope such discussions will also provide the opportunity for member representatives to share information about the practical issues and difficulties that different approaches to FSA compliance in this area might present. In this regard, FSA is better positioned to understand the problems that the revised Rule creates for colleges and universities and to tailor its compliance interests to the higher education context.

Turning to the revised Rule itself, even with the understanding that how an institution fulfills a given requirement remains discretionary, the long list of new requirements is still eyeopening. Also, the FTC is now requiring the adoption of several measures that EDUCAUSE argued in 2019 should continue to fall under institutional discretion. In the review that follows, I highlight what I consider to be key points in the revised Rule. I encourage EDUCAUSE members involved in their institution's compliance with the Safeguards Rule to review the revised regulations in their entirety (see pp. 109–128 for the text of the new Rule itself), as some parts of the Rule may be more central to your institution's needs and interests than the ones I identify below.

In addition to releasing the revised Safeguards Rule, the FTC also announced that it would conduct a supplementalrulemaking on the issue of

[140] Jarret Cummings, "The Safeguards Rule Audit Objective Is Here!" EDUCAUSE Review, July 11, 2019.

whether to require entities covered by the Rule to report relevant cyber incidents to the FTC.[141] The higher education comments on the proposed Rule that EDUCAUSE helped to develop in 2019 raised questions about the value of such a reporting requirement, especially as it relates to the burden that the requirement would create for covered entities such as colleges and universities. The new FTC rulemaking notice indicates the agency's desire to minimize the potential burden of Safeguards Rule incident reporting, which may, in turn, lessen higher education's concerns about a proposed requirement. I will be writing a supplemental article in which I review the need to consider whether EDUCAUSE and the higher education community should submit comments on the FTC's proposed incident reporting requirement and, if so, the direction those comments should take. *(Note: The review of the rulemaking notice regarding a possible Safeguards Rule reporting requirement was posted on December 8, 2021. EDUCAUSE joined several associations in submitting comments about the proposed reporting requirement to the FTC on February 7, 2022. An article reviewing the higher education submission, with a link to the comments themselves, was posted on March 3, 2022.)*

The Revised FTC Safeguards Rule: Key Provisions by Section

Please note that the *Code of Federal Regulations (CFR)* reference for the Safeguards Rule is *16 CFR 314.* To find the Safeguards Rule regulations, enter "16 CFR 314" in the search bar on the *Electronic Code of Federal Regulations* web page.

Section 314.5—Effective Date

Keep in mind that most of the new requirements added to the Rule will not take effect until one year after the date of their publication in the *Federal Register. (Note: The revised Safeguards Rule was officially published in the Federal Register on December 9, 2021, and it identifies December 9, 2022, as the compliance deadline for the new requirements incorporated into the revised Rule.)* With that in mind, I will take the second-to-last section, Section

[141] Federal Trade Commission, "16 CFR Part 314: Standards for Safeguarding Customer Information (Supplemental Notice of Proposed Rulemaking)," pre-publication copy, (December 8, 2021).

314.5—Effective Date, out of order since it identifies the following sections as falling under the one-year compliance deadline:

- 314.4(a)—Designate a "qualified individual" to oversee, implement, and enforce the institution's information security program.
- 314.4(b)(1)—Produce a written risk assessment about the institution's customer information that includes a now-mandated set of criteria and requirements.
- 314.4(c)(1)-(8)—"Design and implement safeguards to control the risks you identity through risk assessment," including the following:
  - Technical and physical access controls to ensure only authorized access
  - An inventory of all relevant parts of the IT environment and management of the same consistent with their business priority and the institution's risk strategy
  - Encryption of all customer information in transit over external networks and at rest
  - Procedures for securely developing internal applications and assessing the security of externally developed applications used in relation to customer information
  - Multi-factor authentication for any individual accessing any information system
  - Procedures for the secure disposal of customer information that is no longer needed for business operations or another legitimate business purpose
  - Change management procedures
  - Measures to monitor and log the activities of authorized users and to detect their unauthorized access or use of or tampering with customer information
- 314.4(d)(2)—Implement continuous monitoring of "information systems" (as defined in 314.2) or annual penetration testing with vulnerability assessments at least every six months.
- 314.4(e)—Establish policies and procedures to ensure that your staff receives security awareness training, that you hire qualified information security personnel and provide ongoing professional development for them, and that key members of your information security staff maintain their knowledge of current threats and responses.

- 314.4(f)(3)—Periodically assess the information security risks that your institution's service providers present and the adequacy of the safeguards they deploy to ensure that they are following the provisions of the Rule.
- 314.4(h)—Establish a written incident response plan, including a set of specific elements, for the customer information that the institution controls.
- 314.4(i)—Require your institution's "qualified individual" to submit a written report on key aspects of the information security program to the institution's governing board at least once per year.

All other aspects of the revised Rule take effect thirty days from its publication in the Federal Register, but those aspects essentially concern the current requirements of the Safeguards Rule with modest text edits to accommodate the range of new requirements that will go into effect next year. In other words, the thirty-day deadline for the rest of the revised Rule ensures that covered entities continue to comply with pre-existing requirements while preparing to comply with the new ones. (Note: The revised Rule officially took effect on January 10, 2022; as mentioned, though, the FTC has deferred compliance with the new requirements added to the Safeguards Rule until December 9, 2022.)

Section 314.2—Definitions

- The FTC greatly expands the definitions section— largely to incorporate key terms from its Privacy Rule directly into the revised Safeguards Rule. These terms are important for understanding what the Safeguards Rule covers.
- For example, where the current regulation includes only the definition of "customer information," the revised Rule includes definitions of terms ("consumer," "customer," "nonpublic personal information," "personally identifiable financial information," and so forth) that are central to understanding what "customer information" actually means.
- EDUCAUSE and its partners specifically requested that the FTC add all relevant definitions from the Privacy Rule to the new Safeguards Rule to make it easier for institutions to understand what "customer

information" they need to protect under the Rule, so this change, even at the expense of the Rule's brevity, is greatly appreciated.

- hat said, IT leaders and professionals will likely be well served by working with institutional legal counsel as well as their business offices, registrars, and financial aid colleagues to walk through the interlocking chain of definitions that have to be explored to reach a full understanding of exactly what institutional data constitutes "customer information."
- Since institutions currently must comply with the existing version of the Safeguards Rule, most, if not all, probably already have a good handle on the scope of "customer information." However, with all of the relevant definitions now being included in the Rule itself, evaluating the new compliance requirements presents a good opportunity to review the previous determinations to ensure nothing has been missed.

"Authorized User"

In the revised Rule, the FTC added "customer" to the definition's list of people who might be considered "authorized users" to make clear that the Rule's requirements for multi-factor authentication and user activity monitoring and logging, for example, extend to "customers" that can access their information via the institution's systems.

Depending on how an institution already allows students to access their financial aid and institutional account information, the Rule's new security requirements may or may not pose problems. However, institutions will have to review those requirements in light of students' (or parents') access to account information and make sure all of the required measures are in place in ways that are appropriate to the institution's size, complexity, and so forth.

"Encryption"

In commenting on the proposed Rule, EDUCAUSE and its partners suggested that the FTC add to the definition of "encryption" to link the potential new encryption requirement under the Rule to "industry standards," which would give institutions a frame of reference for complying with the requirement.

Instead, the final version of the revised Rule includes a reference to "current cryptographic standards" as an appropriate measure to secure an associated encryption key.

From a compliance standpoint, I think the end result is the same. In deciding what form of encryption to deploy to meet the Rule's requirement, institutions should document how the method(s)/tool(s) that are chosen reflect current encryption standards and approaches.

"Information System"

As previously mentioned, one of the key definitional changes from the proposed Rule to the Final Rule is the addition of references to "containing customer information or connected to a system containing customer information" in the definition of "information system." As a result, the definition now clearly links systems and related technology covered by the revised Rule's requirements to the customer information for which institutions are responsible under the Safeguards Rule. However, as also noted previously, the addition of "connected to a system containing customer information" likely pulls a much greater degree of an institution's IT environment into the scope of the Rule's requirements than a college or university would find helpful or, in many cases, justified.

This definitional change may point the way, though, to how an institution can modify its IT environment to segregate its "customer information" (with student financial aid and account information likely drawing the lion's share of concern) to limit the extent of the environment that will fall under the Rule's new requirements, such as continuous monitoring or annual penetration testing or biannual vulnerability assessments. There is little doubt, however, that the FTC did not take into account our points about the extent to which student financial aid information might reasonably be distributed across institutional systems and, therefore, the difficulty that the scope of compliance in the revised Rule might pose for a college or university.

Section 314.4—Elements [of a Safeguards Rule-Compliant Information Security Program]

- "Qualified individual" to oversee/enforce the information security program [314.4(a)]

The revised Rule follows the proposed Rule in moving from requiring that an employee or employees be designated to coordinate the institution's information security program to mandating that a single "qualified individual" be appointed to oversee, implement, and *enforce* the program. In our comments on the proposed Rule, we argued that the decision of whether to have individual or team leadership of an institution's information security program should remain a matter of institutional discretion given the great variety of institutional contexts. The FTC determined, however, that streamlining and ensuring accountability by having a single head of the information security program trumped other considerations.

That said, we also noted in our comments on the proposed Rule that the FTC's repeated reference to a chief information security officer in this context, which the agency intended to be just an example, would likely be interpreted as a mandate that all institutions might not be able to address within the anticipated timeframe for achieving compliance. With our feedback and similar comments from other stakeholders in mind, the FTC adjusted its text in the final rule so that it only refers to the need for an institution to appoint a "qualified individual" to lead the information security program. What constitutes being "qualified" will remain subject to institutional discretion based on the institution's size and complexity, the nature and scope of its operations, and so forth.

- Risk assessment [314.4(b)]
    - Under the revised Safeguards Rule, institutions will now have to develop a written risk assessment regarding the security of their customer information. The written assessment will have to cover the following elements:
        - The criteria used to evaluate and classify the relevant security risks that the institution has identified
        - The criteria used to assess "the confidentiality, integrity, and availability of your information systems and customer

information, including the adequacy of the existing controls in the context of the identified risks or threats you face"
        - The ways in which "identified risks will be mitigated or accepted based on the risk assessment and how the information security program will address the risks"
    - The expanded risk assessment requirement in the revised Rule also mandates that institutions periodically update their risk assessments, with when and how to do so left to institutional discretion based on institutional size, complexity, nature, scope, etc.
- Safeguards [314.4(c)]
    - The revised Rule goes into much greater detail about the types of security measures that institutions will need to implement to address the risks they identify in their risk assessments. In fact, one could interpret the specific requirements introduced as the FTC setting minimum baselines under the assumption that any valid risk assessment would identify the risks requiring the measures that the FTC is now imposing by regulation.
    - Under the revised Rule, institutions must take the following actions:
        - Implement and maintain technical and physical access controls on customer information to limit access to authorizedusers and limit those users' access to the scope of their authorizations.
        - Inventory and manage "the data, personnel, devices, systems, and facilities" central to their operations in light of their priority and the institution's "risk strategy."
        - Encrypt all customer information "held or transmitted" by the institution when "in transit over external networks or at rest."
        - The FTC had previously raised the possibility of requiring encryption of customer information while in transit over internal networks as well, so this encryption provision could have been even more cumbersome to manage.
        - The provision also allows for institutions to use "effective alternative compensating controls" when necessary if approved by their "qualified individual."
        - Adopt secure development practices for any internally developed applications and security assessment procedures

for any externally sourced applications thatthe institution uses to "transmit, access, or store customer information."

- "Implement multi-factor authentication for any individual accessing any information system [emphasis added], unless your Qualified Individual has approved in writing the use of reasonably equivalent or more secure access controls."
- Establish policies and procedures for the secure disposal of customer information "no later than two years after the last date" on which the information was used to serve the customer in question unless it is needed for business operations or "for other legitimate business purposes."
- The institution may also maintain the data if required by law or regulation, or if it is held in a fashion that makes "targeted disposal . . . not reasonably feasible."
- In responding to the proposed Rule, EDUCAUSE and its partners argued that "business purposes" might not be understood as the FTC intended in institutions focused on academic purposes, and thus it should use the phrase "legitimate purposes."
- Since the FTC did not take our suggestion, institutions will have to rely on their discretion based on their size, complexity, nature, scope, etc., to determine what constitutes a "legitimate business purpose" given their operations.
- Also, this provision assumes that secure disposal of customer information as required will be based on a periodically reviewed and updated institutional data retention policy designed "to minimize the unnecessary retention of data."
- Adopt change management procedures (presumably for systems, policies, processes, etc., that connect in some meaningful way with customer information).
- Implement measures to "monitor and log the activity of authorized users" and to detect when they have accessed, used, or tampered with customer information outside the scope of their authorization.
- The logging aspect of this provision replaces a separate provision in the proposed Rule that would have required the creation of "audit trails . . . to detect and respond to security events."

    - EDUCAUSE member feedback indicated that simply focusing on user logs would be a more accurate and useful way to address the FTC's concern, and it seems that our comment about the issue in relation to the proposed Rule led to an appropriate change.

- Monitoring and testing safeguards [314.4(d)(1) and (2)]
  - Part 1 of this provision requires institutions to test regularly or otherwise monitor the effectiveness of the safeguards established under their information security program "including those to detect actual and attempted attacks on, or intrusions into, information systems" as defined by the Rule.
  - Part 2, however, specifically mandates either continuous monitoring of information systems (again, as defined by the Rule) or annual penetration testing with vulnerability assessments at least every six months and whenever the institution experiences significant operational changes or an incident that "may have a material impact on [the institution's] information security program."
  - In commenting on the proposed Rule, EDUCAUSE and its partners argued that if, when, where, and how these measures might be deployed should be a matter of institutional discretion based on the findings of the institution's risk assessment in light of its size, complexity, nature, scope, etc., especially given the diversity of institutional types and contexts across higher education.
  - In light of how the Rule defines "information system," limiting the reach of this provision across the institutional IT environment will require careful consideration of where and how customer information is stored and used, as well as which systems and data stores have to be connected to systems and databases containing customer information.
- Human resources policies and procedures related to information security [314.4(e)]
  - This aspect of the revised Rule requires institutions to provide security awareness training for their personnel consistent with the results of their risk assessments.
  - Institutions must also do the following:
    - Use qualified information security personnel to manage security risks and "perform or oversee" their information

security program, whether such personnel are institutional employees or are supplied by a service provider.

        - Ensure their information security personnel have access to security updates and training that will allow them to address security risks at their institution.
        - Verify that "key information security personnel" are maintaining their professional knowledge of the field (i.e., of "changing information security threats and countermeasures").

- Service provider oversight [314.4(f)]
    - The revised Rule adds a requirement that institutions periodically review the information security risks that their relevant service providers pose, including the adequacy of those providers' safeguards.
- Evaluation and revision of the information security program [314.4(g)]
    - The FTC changed this section from the proposed rule to the final rule to cross-reference the requirement about reviewing and revising the institutional information security program with the sections on modifying relevant safeguards based on the results of the institution's written risk assessment [314.4(b)(2)] and its continuous monitoring/annual penetration testing (with at least biannual vulnerability assessments) of relevant information systems [314.4(d)].
- Written incident response plan [314.4(h)]
    - The FTC revised this provision slightly in the revised Rule from how it was presented in the proposed Rule.
        - Rather than saying that covered entities have to develop written incident response plans to cover customer information in their "possession," the text now reads that they must have incident response plans for such information under their "control."
        - This edit responds to our comment on the proposed Rule regarding the need to revise this provision to reflect institutional use of cloud services, where the relevant information may actually be possessed by a cloud services provider and not by the institution directly.

  - Whether "control" works better than "possession" in this context remains debatable. We suggested that the text tie the incident response plan to the customer information for which the institution is "responsible," since there is little doubt that the covered entity remains responsible for the security of its data no matter where it is housed, especially in light of the Rule's service provider oversight provision.
  - To that end, regardless of how the text reads, the FTC's intent is clear: The institution's incident response plan regarding covered customer information must account for relevant service providers as well.
  - The provision identifies several specific items that a compliant incident response plan must include, all of which are consistent with standard incident response principles and practices.
  - Institutions with incident response plans that cover customer information should review the list to establish a crosswalk between their plans and the required elements. Those needing to develop such plans should review the list to ensure that their plans cover all the bases.
- Board reporting [314.4(i)]
  - The revised Rule incorporates the proposed Rule requirement that the head of the institution's information security program submit a written report about the program to the institution's governing board at least once a year.
  - The modest edits to the provision in the revised Rule identify the head of the information security program as its "qualified individual" and specify that written reports should be provided to the board "regularly and at least annually."
  - A Rule-compliant board report must include the following elements:
    - A review of the program's overall status and compliance with the Rule
    - "Material matters" about the program, such as:
    - risk assessment and risk management/control decisions;
    - service provider arrangements;
    - results of testing and security events or violations, and management's responses to them; and
    - recommendations for program changes.

- Section 314.6—Exceptions
  - o Institutions that maintain customer information on fewer than 5,000 consumers (note the difference between "consumer" and "customer" in the definitions) are exempt from having to:
    - develop a written risk assessment [314.4(b)(1)];
    - implement continuous monitoring or penetration testing/vulnerability assessments of their information systems [314.4(d)(2)];
    - develop a written incident response plan [314.4(h)]; or
    - submit a report about their information security program to their governing board or senior executive [314.4(i)].
- In commenting on the proposed Rule, EDUCAUSE and its partners argued that the threshold for exceptions to the requirements of the Rule for higher education institutions should be set by Carnegie classification, not the number of consumer records managed, as Carnegie classification would provide a more appropriate indicator of institutional size (and therefore institutional capacity to manage the requirements in question). With the FTC declining to accept that recommendation, even the smallest accredited colleges and universities are unlikely to qualify for the exceptions to certain Rule requirements given the length of time for which financial aid and student account information is generally maintained.

Jarret Cummings is Senior Policy Advisor at EDUCAUSE.

Compliance , Cybersecurity Policy , Data Security , Encryption , Federal Student Aid , Higher Education Policy , Policy and Law

Why IT Matters to Higher Education
EDUCAUSE
REVIEW

Higher Ed Responds to Proposed Safeguards Rule Reporting Requirement

Jarret Cummings
Thursday, March 3, 2022
Policy
5 min read

The Federal Trade Commission (FTC) has proposed adding a reporting requirement to its Safeguards Rule. EDUCAUSE and its partners recommend that the FTC adopt a few revisions (e.g., delaying the public release of any Safeguards Rule security event report for one year from the submission date).

The Federal Trade Commission (FTC) published its long- awaited revisions to the Safeguards Rule in early December 2021 while giving covered entities, such as colleges and universities, until December 2022 to achieve compliance with the many new provisions of the Rule.[142] At the same time, the FTC also proposed a new Safeguards Rule reporting requirement. Comments on the proposal were due by February 7.[143]

EDUCAUSE worked with member representatives to analyze the FTC's proposed provision. Our findings formed the basis of public comments jointly submitted to the FTC by the American Council on Education (ACE), EDUCAUSE, and several other groups.[144] We determined that, in general, the proposal from the FTC strikes a reasonable balance between meeting its needs as a regulator and minimizing the reporting burden on institutions. A covered entity would only be required to report security events for which it has determined a misuse of customer information (primarily student financial aid information in the case of higher education) involving one thousand or more consumers has occurred or is reasonably likely to occur. Also, the entity would only have to report a few general elements:

---

[142] Jarret Cummings, "Policy Analysis: Revised, Highly Prescriptive FTC Safeguards Rule," EDUCAUSE Review, December 2, 2021.

[143] Jarret Cummings, "Cyber Incident Reporting Under the Safeguards Rule?" EDUCAUSE Review, December 8, 2021.

[144] American Council on Education, et al., letter to the Federal Trade Commission, "Request for Public Comment on Supplemental Notice of ProposedRulemaking, 'Standards for Safeguarding Customer Information' (Safeguards Rule, 16 CFR 314, Project No. P145407), December 9, 2021—Proposed Security Event Reporting Requirement," February 7, 2021.

- The name of and contact information for the organization
- A description of the types of information involved
- The date or date range of the event (if identified)
- A general description of the event itself

While the proposed reporting standard and structure would be workable overall, the FTC raised several questions indicating that it could conceivably take the final version of the regulation in some problematic directions from the higher education perspective. With that in mind, EDUCAUSE and its partner associations provided a few specific points for the FTC to consider, with the goal of keeping the final provision largely within the initial parameters identified in its rulemaking notice.

The FTC clearly indicates in its rulemaking proposal that it wants to make the reports it would receive as a result of the new reporting provision publicly available, and it specifically asks if it should do so. The response from higher education associations argues that the information submitted under the proposed requirement would suit the needs of the FTC as a regulator that is trying to identify where it may need to work with a covered entity on possible compliance issues. It would be too high level, though, to provide meaningful information to students, parents, and other stakeholders and could conceivably raise anxiety among individual members of the campus community about whether their personal information might be involved. Given the likelihood that the public availability of the reports could generate undue concern among institutional stakeholders, EDUCAUSE and its partners suggested that posting all submitted reports to a national, publicly available web page might be counterproductive. If the FTC decides to proceed with such a plan, however, we asked it to consider delaying the public release of any Safeguards Rule security event report for one year from the date of submission. This would ensure that institutions have time to remediate the underlying event fully and communicate with all affected stakeholders before the general public release of the report in question.

The FTC also asked if the proposed requirement should explicitly exclude events involving encrypted information from reporting, which would be consistent with the New York state regulations from which the overall revisions to the Safeguards Rule were drawn. The higher education groups noted that the reporting standard for the new requirement would generally lead to that result regardless, given that institutions would not consider encrypted data subject to misuse or likely misuse in the absence of some reasonable indication of the encryption having been compromised. Thus, we recommended that the FTC clearly state in the final regulation that entities are not required to report events involving encrypted information so long as no reasonable basis exists for thinking that the encryption involved is or is likely to be compromised.

Another key point that we raised concerns whether a covered entity should be allowed to delay reporting to the FTC if a law enforcement agency requests that it not share information about an event unless or until law enforcement gives its approval to do so. EDUCAUSE and its partner associations argued that if enacted, a Safeguards Rule reporting requirement should allow a covered entity to respect the wishes of law enforcement agencies and delay reporting at their request, given the general importance to cybersecurity of identifying and prosecuting bad actors to the extent possible. We noted, however, that the FTC could provide a way via its reporting process for a covered entity to inform the FTC that the entity is subject to such a request and provide contact information for the law enforcement agency or agencies in question. This would allow the FTC to negotiate with law enforcement as necessary about the conditions under which an entity could fulfill its normal reporting responsibilities sooner rather than later if the FTC thought a particular case warranted it.

Given the track record of the FTC concerning its rulemaking leading to the recently revised Safeguards Rule, EDUCAUSE members should assume that the FTC will adopt a Safeguards Rule reporting requirement that is similar to its proposed regulation. It is also highly likely that reports submitted under the new provision will become publicly available, although EDUCAUSE and its partners remain hopeful that the FTC will adopt a delay in providing public access to security event reports as we requested. The proposed Rule indicates that the FTC's final regulation will likely defer compliance for six months from the date of its official publication. With the early December compliance deadline for the new requirements, the FTC could issue the final version of its reporting provision in time for it to take effect at roughly the same time as the overall set of new Safeguards Rule mandates. Whether the FTC can achieve such a goal remains to be seen, but EDUCAUSE will continue to update members on any new developments with the proposed Safeguards Rule reporting requirement as they become available.

Jarret Cummings is Senior Policy Advisor at EDUCAUSE.

Compliance , Data Privacy , Federal Student Aid

Protecting Controlled Unclassified Information in Nonfederal Systems and Organizations

Date Published: February 2020 (includes updates as of January 28, 2021)
Supersedes: SP 800-171 Rev. 2 (02/21/2020)
Planning Note (4/13/2022)

The security requirements in SP 800-171 Revision 2 are available in multiple data formats. The PDF of SP 800-171 Revision 2 is the authoritative source of the CUI security requirements. If there are any discrepancies noted in the content between the CSV, XLSX, and the SP 800-171 PDF, please contact sec-cert@nist.gov and refer to the PDF as the normative source.

CUI SSP template

** There is no prescribed format or specified level of detail for system security plans. However, organizations ensure that the required information in [SP 800-171 Requirement] 3.12.4 is conveyed in those plans.

Author(s)

Ron Ross (NIST), Victoria Pillitteri (NIST), Kelley Dempsey (NIST), Mark Riddle (NARA), Gary Guissanie (IDA)

Abstract

The protection of Controlled Unclassified Information (CUI) resident in nonfederal systems and organizations is of paramount importance to federal agencies and can directly impact the ability of the federal government to successfully conduct its essential missions and functions. This publication...
See full abstract

Keywords

basic security requirement; contractor systems; Controlled Unclassified Information; CUI Registry; derived security requirement; Executive Order 13556; FIPS Publication 199; FIPS Publication 200; FISMA; NIST Special Publication 800-53; nonfederal systems; security assessment; security control; security requirement; nonfederal organizations

Control Families

Access Control; Audit and Accountability; Awareness and Training; Configuration Management; Identification and Authentication; Maintenance; Media Protection; Personnel Security; Physical and Environmental Protection; System and Communications Protection; System and Information Integrity.

Documentation

Publication:
SP 800-171 Rev. 2 (DOI)
Local Download
Supplemental Material:
Security Requirements Spreadsheet (xls)
Security Requirements CSV (other)
README for CSV (txt)
CUI Plan of Action template (word)
CUI SSP template **[see Planning Note] (word)
Mapping: Cybersecurity Framework v.1.0 to SP 800-171 Rev. 2 (xls)
Other Parts of this Publication:
SP 800-171A
Related NIST Publications:
SP 800-172
Document History:
01/28/21: SP 800-171 Rev. 2 (Final)

Topics

Security and Privacy

audit & accountability; awareness training & education; maintenance; security controls; threats

Laws and Regulations

Federal Acquisition Regulation; Federal Information Security Modernization Act.

State Data Breach Notification Chart

(hps://iapp.org/media/resource_center/iappus_state_data_breach_notification_chart.xls

Last Updated: March 2021

U.S. data breach notification laws vary across all 50 states and U.S. territories. Each law must be applied to every factual scenario to determine if a notification requirement is triggered.

territory's data breach notification law concerning entities that own, control or process personal data. The main sheet of this chart, titled "All Data – Alphabetical," lists all states followed by U.S. territories and contains:

- A hyperlink to the state's notification statute.
- The timeframe in which notification to impacted individuals is required.
- Any exceptions to notification requirements.
- If and when notification must be made to a state agency, consumer protection agency or consumer reporting agency.
- Special forms or language that must be included in the notice.
- Whether the statute provides for a private right of action.

Each column can be filtered to allow notification laws with certain features to be hidden or prioritized. As a starting point, a practitioner could filter the "Timeframe for Breach Notification" column to identify which states have the shortest notification window to further investigate the state-specific requirements. For convenience, the IAPP has also included subsequent sheets with three categories of pre-sorted data:

- Shortest notification timeframe.
- Requires a orney general notification (ranked from the lowest number of impacted individuals to highest).
- Requires consumer reporting agency notification (ranked from the lowest number of impacted individuals to highest).

This chart does not include exceptions to or additional compliance requirements with federal laws, such as the Gramm-Leach-Bliley Act or the Health Insurance Portability and Accountability Act. Additionally, an entity must determine if it owns, controls or licenses "personally identifiable information" before it can determine if the "personally identifiable information" was compromised in a "breach" (compared to a security "event" or "incident"), which will be uniquely defined by each law.

NOTE: This tool is for informational purposes only and is not legal advice. State requirements, including any recent changes, should always be verified via official sources. Requirements, if there is a security event, incident or breach, will vary depending on the

Tags: Data Loss (/tag/data-loss), Infosecurity (/tag/infosecurity), Privacy Law (/tag/privacy-law), Privacy Operations Management (/tag/privacy-operations-management), Privacy Research (/tag/privacy-research)

Pease International Tradeport, 75 Rochester Ave.
Portsmouth, NH 03801 USA • +1 603.427.9200

NATIONAL ARCHIVES

visitors, customers, and employees during the COVID-19 (coronavirus) pandemic. NARA's facilities are closed until further notice and in-person services for the public and other Federal agencies have been suspended almost entirely. All ISOO staff are teleworking remotely and we are making every effort to continue providing services whenever possible, using online and remote capabilities. ISOO's ability to serve our customers in a timely manner may be hampered by the current crisis.To ensure a more timely response to your inquiry, please contact us via email at [isoo@nara.gov / cui@nara.gov / iscap@nara.gov] We ask for your understanding and appreciate your patience. ISOO will use its blog, ISOO Overview to communicate with stakeholders on all ISOO matters. Please join for weekly posts.

Please visit the CUI blog: Controlled Unclassified Information for more information.

Established by Executive Order 13556, the Controlled Unclassified Information (CUI) program standardizes the way the Executive branch handles unclassified information that requires safeguarding or dissemination controls pursuant to and consistent with law, regulations, and Government-wide policies. Learn About CUI

CUI Registry

The CUI Registry is the Government-wide online repository for Federal-level guidance regarding CUI policy and practice. However, agency personnel and contractors should first consult their agency's CUI implementing policies and program management for guidance.

Search the Registry: [ ] Go

Categories, Markings and Controls:

- Category List
- CUI Markings
- Limited Dissemination Controls
- Decontrol
- Registry Change Log

Policy and Guidance

- Executive Order 13556
- 32 CFR Part 2002 (Implementing Directive)
- CUI Marking Handbook
- CUI Notices

CUI Glossary

CUI Training

Learn about training tools developed by the Executive Agent for CUI users.

Oversight

Learn about CUI oversight requirements and tools.

CUI Resources

Learn about additional tools for handling CUI, including:

- CUI Coversheet
- CUI Marking Trifold Brochure
- CUI Audio/Photo/Video Markings Brochure
- CUI Destruction Label
- CUI Email Marking Tip
- CUI Media Labels

The U.S. National Archives and Records Administration
1-86-NARA-NARA or 1-866-272-6272

NATIONAL ARCHIVES

CUI Category: Student Records

Banner Marking for Specified Authorities: CUI//SP-STUD

Banner Marking for Basic Authorities: CUI

Category Description:	As per 20 USC 1232g, the Family Educational Rights and Privacy Act of 1974, an education record which is comprised of those records which are directly related to a student.
Category Marking:	STUD
Alternative Banner Marking for Basic Authorities:	CUI//STUD

Banner Format and Marking Notes:	Banner Format: CUI//Category Marking//Limited Dissemination Control Marking Notes: • The CUI Control Marking may consist of either the word "CONTROLLED" or the acronym "CUI", depending on agency policy. • Category marking is optional when marking Basic CUI unless required by agency policy. Example: CUI//Limited Dissemination Control. • Category Marking preceded by "SP-" is required when marking Specified CUI. Example: CUI//SP-Category Marking//Limited Dissemination Control • Whether CUI is Basic or Specified is determined by the applicable Safeguarding and/or Dissemination Authority for a given instance of CUI. • Separate multiple Category Markings by a single forward slash (/) and list Category Markings alphabetically. Example: CUI//Category Marking A/Category Marking B//Limited Dissemination Control • Category Markings for Specified CUI precede Category Markings for Basic CUI. Example: CUI//SP-Category Marking/Category Marking//Limited Dissemination Control • Separate multiple Limited Dissemination Controls by a single forward slash (/). Example: CUI//Category Marking//Limited Dissemination Control/Limited Dissemination Control • Reference 32 CFR 2002.20 , CUI Marking Handbook , Limited Dissemination Controls and individual agency policy for additional and specific marking guidelines

Notes for Safeguarding, Dissemination and Sanction Authorities:

- Whether CUI is Basic or Specified is determined by the applicable Safeguarding and/or Dissemination Authority for that CUI.
- Each "Safeguarding and/or Dissemination Authority" citation links to the statute, regulation or government-wide policy authorizing the control of that information as CUI.
- Each "Sanctions" authority links to the statute, regulation or government-wide policy that includes penalties for CUI misuse of CUI for the associated "Safeguarding and/or

Dissemination Authority" on the same line.

Safeguarding and/or Dissemination Authority	**Basic or Specified**	**Banner Marking**	**Sanctions**
20 USC 1232g(a)(1)(C)	Basic	CUI	
25 CFR 43.14	Basic	CUI	
25 CFR 43.22	Specified	CUI//SP-STUD	
34 CFR 99.30(a)	Basic	CUI	
34 CFR 99.31(a)(6)(ii)	Basic	CUI	
34 CFR 99.33(a)(1)	Basic	CUI	

Authority links are updated based on regular re-publication of the United States Code and Code of Federal Regulations, and the CUI Registry maintenance schedule.

Federal Student Aid

An OFFICE of the U.S. DEPARTMENT of EDUCATION

Published on https://fsapartners.ed.gov/knowledge-center/library /electronic- announcements/2020-12-18/protecting-student-information-compliance-cui-and-glba

POSTED DATE: December 18, 2020
AUTHOR: Federal Student Aid
SUBJECT: Protecting Student Information – Compliance with CUI and GLBA

As instances of data and information breaches rise, it is vital that institutions of higher education (IHEs) protect Controlled Unclassi ed Information (CUI) used in the administration of federal student aid programs authorized under Title IV, of the Higher Education Act, as amended.[145] FSA is nalizing the Campus Cybersecurity Program framework. A multi-year phased implementation will begin with a self-assessment of the National Institute of Standards and Technology Special Publication 800–171 Rev. 2, Controlled Unclassi ed Information in Nonfederal Systems (NIST 800–171 Rev. 2) readiness and outreach activities. We are committed to fully advancing and encouraging all postsecondary institutions implementation of NIST 800-171 controls.

This Electronic Announcement is meant to inform IHEs and their third-party servicers about upcoming activities to ensure compliance with NIST 800–171 Rev. 2. Institutions' compliance is in accordance with 32 C.F.R. Part 2002 and the federal government-wide requirement that institutions receiving CUI from the U.S. Department of Education (Department) comply with NIST 800–171 Rev. 2.[146] FSA has previously encouraged IHEs to review and adopt NIST 800–171 Rev. 2 as a security standard and to support continuing obligations under the Gramm-Leach-Bliley Act (GLBA). Since 2018, many institutions have adopted some or all of the NIST 800–171 recommended requirements. We further encourage use of NIST 800–171 Rev. 2 to help mitigate risks related to CUI.

---

[145] 20 U.S.C. § 1070, et seq.

[146] 32 CFR § 2002.16 (5) ("Agencies should enter into agreements with any non-executive branch or foreign entity with which the agency shares or intends to share CUI.").

In 2021, FSA plans to initiate a self-assessment effort to understand the IHE community's readiness to comply with NIST 800– 171 Rev 2. The self-assessment effort will help the Department determine the cybersecurity posture, maturity, and future compliance of each IHE with NIST 800–171 and other cybersecurity requirements. Our intention is to partner and collaborate with IHEs, and other organizations, to enhance the resilience and maturity across IHEs by establishing a cybersecurity baseline, sharing information, and overseeing compliance with NIST 800–171 Rev. 2 and other cybersecurity requirements.

Instances of data breaches at organizations entrusted with personally identi able information (PII) continue to proliferate and reinforce the need for the Department and IHEs to work together to combat cybersecurity threats and strengthen cybersecurity infrastructure at IHEs. Ensuring the con dentiality, security, and integrity of Title IV information depends on cooperation between the Department, IHEs, and other entities, including state grant agencies, lenders, contractors, and third- party servicers.

We expect federal student aid partners to develop, implement, and enhance information security programs with requisite controls and monitoring that supports all aspects of the administration of Title IV federal student aid programs. These security programs must encompass all systems, databases, and processes that collect, process, and distribute information—including PII—in support of applications for and receipt of Title IV student assistance.

Protecting Student Information – Next Steps

The Department looks forward to continued collaboration with IHEs to protect student data. We are committed to supporting IHEs and are working to provide additional guidelines and best practices to implement the government-wide CUI requirements, leveraging NIST security guidance. In 2021, we will post additional information to provide further information and guidance, including the cybersecurity self-assessment. In the meantime, institutions are strongly encouraged to learn more about NIST 800–171 Rev. 2 and sharing with your IT team to reduce risk surrounding CUI.

Background

The Student Aid Internet Gateway (SAIG) Enrollment Agreement entered into by each Title IV-participating institution includes a provision that the institution "[m]ust ensure that all Federal Student Aid applicant information is protected from access by or disclosure to unauthorized personnel." Institutions are reminded that under various federal and state laws and other authorities—including the HEA;[147] the Family Educational Rights and Privacy Act (FERPA); the Privacy Act of 1974, as amended; the GLBA; and state data breach and privacy laws—institutions may be responsible for losses, nes, and penalties (including criminal penalties) as a result of data breaches.

CUI is government-created or -owned information that requires safeguarding or dissemination controls consistent with applicable laws, regulations, and government-wide policies. National Archives and Records Administration's CUI rule, effective Nov. 14, 2016, 32 C.F.R. Part 2002.16, establishes that agencies must enter into an agreement with a non-executive branch entity to share CUI and require compliance with the standards set forth in the NIST 800–171 Rev. 2. The CUI program standardizes the way the Executive branch agencies handles unclassi ed information that requires safeguarding or dissemination controls pursuant to and consistent with law, regulations, and federal government-wide policies. Most data sourced from the Department and information used in the administration of Title IV programs are considered CUI.

Contact Information

If you have questions about compliance with CUI and GLBA, please contact the Cybersecurity Team at FSA_IHECyberCompliance@ed.gov or by phone at 202-245-6550.

147 See 20 U.S. Code § 1018b ("Any entity that maintains or transmits information under a transaction covered by this section shall maintain reasonable and appropriate administrative, technical, and physical safeguards.").

References

National Institute of Standards and Technology Special Publication 800-171 Rev 2 Protecting Controlled Unclassi ed Information in Nonfederal Systems and Organizations

National Institute of Standards and Technology Special Publication 800-172 Enhanced Security Requirements for Protecting Controlled Unclassi ed Information: A Supplement to NIST Special Publication 800-171 (Final Public Draft)

Federal Trade Commission Safeguards Rule

NIST National Institute of Standards and Technology U.S. Department of Commerce

Manufacturing Innovation Blog

(https://www.nist.gov/blogs/manufacturing-innovation-blog)

Powered by the Manufacturing Extension Partnership https://www. nist.gov/mep)

What Is the NIST SP 800-171 and Who Needs to Follow It?

October 8, 2019

By: Traci Spencer (https://www.nist.gov/blogs/manufacturing-innovation-blog/authors/traci- spencer)

This article originally appeared on IndustryWeek (https://www.industry week.com/sponsored/what-nist-sp-800-171-cybersecurity-f ramework).

Guest blog post by Traci Spencer, Grant Program Manager for TechSolve, Inc., the southwest regional partner of the Ohio MEP, part of the MEP National NetworkTM.

Manufacturers involved in supply chains tied to government contracts can anticipate those awards bringing in additional revenue at levels that might not be possible otherwise. However, being successful in getting and keeping such work means complying with the Federal Acquisition Regulation (FAR) and Defense Federal Acquisition Regulation Supplement (DFARS).

FAR is a set of regulations that governs all acquisitions and contracting procedures associated with the U.S. government. DFARS accompanies FAR as an addition. The Department of Defense (DoD) is the administrative body behind DFARS, but the reach of DFARS requirements extends to more than that organization.

NIST SP 800-171 is a NIST Special Publication that provides recommended requirements for protecting the confidentiality of controlled unclassified information (CUI). Defense contractors must implement the recommended requirements contained in NIST SP 800-171 to demonstrate their provision of adequate security to protect the covered defense information included in their defense contracts, as required by DFARS clause 252.204-7012. If a manufacturer is part of a DoD, General Services Administration (GSA), NASA or other federal or state agencies' supply chain, the implementation of the security requirements included in NIST SP 800-171 is a must.

How Do You Implement NIST SP 800-171?

It's understandable for manufacturers to wonder what they should do to implement NIST SP 800-171 and ultimately get in compliance with DFARS, and whether there are specialized resources available to help them achieve that milestone without preventable pitfalls. The first thing they should keep in mind is that being DFARS compliant likely involves working with a cybersecurity consultant that knows the NIST SP 800-171 requirements inside and out.

It's advisable for small manufacturers to look to their state's Manufacturing Extension Partnership (MEP) Center. Part of the MEP National Network™, a larger organization that connects them to NIST, the representatives at your local MEP Center will have a working knowledge of NIST SP 800-171 and can help companies prepare for DFARS compliance. It can be a short or long process, depending upon the complexities of a company's operating environment and information systems, but implementing NIST SP 800-171 is a necessary process for a company to protect its information.

What Does a Successful Plan Entail?

Manufacturers that want to retain their DoD, GSA, NASA and other federal and state agency contracts need to have a plan that meets the requirements of NIST SP 800-171. DFARS cybersecurity clause 252,204-7012 went into effect on Dec. 31, 2017, and deals with processing, storing or transmitting CUI that exists on non-federal systems — such as those used by a government contractor.

One of the first steps manufacturers should take is to identify where gaps exist that prevent them from being compliant with DFARS. From that point, they can determine how to proceed.

How Should Manufacturers Start Working Toward Compliance?

The MEP National Network offers dedicated resources for manufacturers (https://www.nist.gov/mep/cybersecurity -resources-manufacturers) that need information about a company's cybersecurity posture that can help companies understand what getting compliant with DFARS actually means to them. Companies can see whether DFARS compliance applies to them and view infographics that recommend steps to take to make their factory floors more secure.

The MEP National Network also provides a particular resource that manufacturers will undoubtedly refer to again and again: the NIST Self-Assessment Handbook (https://nvlpubs.nist.gov/nistpubs/hb/2017/NIST.HB.162.pdf) (NIST Handbook 162) (https://nvlpubs.nist.gov/nistpubs/hb/2017/NIST.HB.162.pdf). It spans more than 150 pages and helps readers assess their facilities to conclude how close they are to implementing NIST SP 800-171 to help them understand how close they are to being DFARS compliant. It also helps determine where to focus efforts when making improvements to maximize the impact of each dollar spent on cybersecurity.

For example, the document features content that advises how to go about carrying out an assessment and which applicable employees to talk to regarding security requirements. Manufacturers that read through the handbook will note that each assessment question has an "alternative approach" option. It refers to the fact that manufacturers may find some requirements in NIST SP 800-171 that don't apply to them.

In that case, it's acceptable to use a different but equally effective method of maintaining security — as long as the respective manufacturers notify the correct government authorities about the changes and get approval for them.

Manufacturing plant representatives can also increase their understanding of compliance requirements by watching a webinar (https://bluejeans.com/playback/s/VZevy5gUYLnIO2QOEXrt3GVCoAJp1cWKmK21oR6S1DVG eCtYm fTQo5DG7zNVVm46) that goes through some of the crucial elements of the handbook.

Complexity Shouldn't Be a Barrier

Manufacturers may initially view the cybersecurity requirements for government contracts as too complicated, especially if they have small operations.

However, using the available resources — including local MEP Centers — allows manufacturers to realize it's possible to get in compliance with DFARS, as well as stay in compliance, by implementing the NIST SP 800-171 requirements and to open possibilities for receiving financially rewarding and reputation-boosting government contracts.

A local MEP Center is an ideal resource for manufacturers to use as they start to complete a plan that details how to implement the NIST SP 800-171 cybersecurity requirements.

Each MEP Center has access to public and private sector resources that can help companies get into compliance with more confidence. Locations exist in all 50 states and Puerto Rico (https://www.nist.gov/mep/mep-national-network/connect-your-local-mep- center).

Cybersecurity (https://www.nist.gov/manufacturing-innovation-blog-categories/cybersecurity)

About the Author

Traci Spencer (https://www.nist.gov/blogs/manufacturing-innovation-blog/authors/traci-spencer)

Traci Spencer is the Grant Program Manager for TechSolve, Inc., the southwest regional partner of the Ohio MEP. A member of the MEP National Network Cybersecurity Working Group, she recently completed...

Related Posts

Cybersecurity for the Manufacturing Sector: Reduce Data Integrity Breaches with NIST SP 1800-10 (https://www.nist.gov/blogs/manufacturing-innovation- blog/cybersecurity -manufacturing-sector-reduce-data-integrity), April 21, 2022.

Industrial control systems (ICS) help manufacturers boost productivity, optimize efficiency and advance production lines. Historically, ICS networks were

Supporting Digital Transformation with Legacy Components

(https://www.nist.gov/blogs/manufacturing-innovation-blog/supporting-digital-transformation-legacy -components)
July 20, 2021

"Information is the oil of the 21st century, and analytics is the combustion engine." – Peter Sondergaard, Senior Vice President, Gartner Research Digital

Commonly Misused Terms in Cybersecurity

(https://www.nist.gov/blogs/manufacturing-innovation-blog/commonly - misused- terms-cybersecurity)

June 25, 2021

Words are hard. English is hard. How we manage to communicate anything is nigh a miracle. Sometimes I wish I was Oscar Wilde or Mark Twain or any of the other

About This Blog

Manufacturing Innovation, the blog of the Manufacturing Extension Partnership (MEP) (https://www.nist.gov/mep), is a resource for manufacturers, industry experts and the public on key U.S. manufacturing topics. There are articles for those looking to dive into new strategies emerging in manufacturing as well as useful information on tools and opportunities for manufacturers.

The views presented here are those of the author and do not necessarily represent the views or policies of NIST.

If you have any questions about our blog, please contact us at mfg@nist.gov
(https://www.nist.govmailto:mfg@nist.gov).

About CMMC

Frequently Asked Questions

- NOW THAT CMMC 2.0 IS PUBLISHED, WILL COMPANIES BE REQUIRED TO COMPLY WITH CMMC 1.0?
- WHEN WILL CMMC 2.0 BE REQUIRED FOR DOD CONTRACTS?
- WHY DID THE DEPARTMENT MAKE THESE CHANGES?
- HOW MUCH WILL IT COST TO IMPLEMENT CMMC 2.0?

Cybersecurity is a top priority for the Department of Defense.

The Defense Industrial Base (DIB) is the target of increasingly frequent and complex cyberattacks. To protect American ingenuity and national security information, the DoD developed CMMC 2.0 to dynamically enhance DIB cybersecurity to meet evolving threats and safeguard the information that supports and enables our warfighters.

Overview of the CMMC Program

The Cybersecurity Maturity Model Certification (CMMC) program enhances cyber protection standards for companies in the DIB. It is designed to protect sensitive unclassified information that is shared by the Department with its contractors and subcontractors. The program incorporates a set of cybersecurity requirements into acquisition programs and provides the Department increased assurance that contractors and subcontractors are meeting these requirements.

The framework has three key features:

- Tiered Model: CMMC requires that companies entrusted with national security information implement cybersecurity standards at progressively advanced levels, depending on the type and sensitivity of the information. The program also sets forward the process for information flow down to subcontractors.
- Assessment Requirement: CMMC assessments allow the Department to verify the implementation of clear cybersecurity standards.
- Implementation through Contracts: Once CMMC is fully implemented, certain DoD contractors that handle sensitive unclassified DoD information will be required to achieve a particular CMMC level as a condition of contract award.

The Evolution to CMMC 2.0

In September 2020, the DoD published an interim rule to the DFARS in the Federal Register (DFARS Case 2019-D041), which implemented the DoD's initial vision for the CMMC program ("CMMC 1.0") and outlined the basic features of the framework (tiered model, required assessments, and implementation through contracts). The interim rule became effective on November 30, 2020, establishing a five-year phase-in period.

In March 2021, the Department initiated an internal review of CMMC's implementation, informed by more than 850 public comments in response to the interim DFARS rule. This comprehensive, programmatic assessment engaged cybersecurity and acquisition leaders within DoD to refine policy and program implementation.

In November 2021, the Department announced "CMMC 2.0," an updated program structure and requirements designed to achieve the primary goals of the internal review:

- Safeguard sensitive information to enable and protect the warfighter
- Dynamically enhance DIB cybersecurity to meet evolving threats
- Ensure accountability while minimizing barriers to compliance with DoD requirements
- Contribute towards instilling a collaborative culture of cybersecurity and cyber resilience
- Maintain public trust through high professional and ethical standards

Key Features of CMMC 2.0

With the implementation of CMMC 2.0, the Department is introducing several key changes that build on and refine the original program requirements. These are:

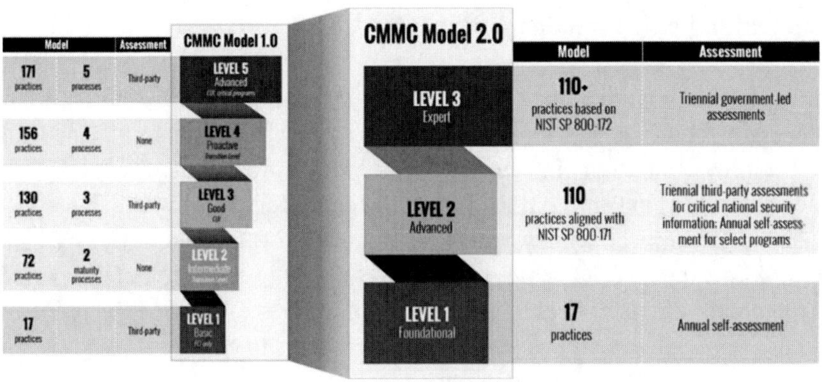

Streamlined Model

- Focused on the most critical requirements: Streamlines the model from 5 to 3 compliance levels
- Aligned with widely accepted standards: Uses National Institute of Standards and Technology (NIST) cybersecurity standards

Reliable Assessments

- Reduced assessment costs: Allows all companies at Level 1 (Foundational), and a subset of companies at Level 2 (Advanced) to demonstrate compliance through self- assessments
- Higher accountability: Increases oversight of professional and ethical standards of third-party assessors

Flexible Implementation

- Spirit of collaboration: Allows companies, under certain limited circumstances, to make Plans of Action & Milestones (POA&Ms) to achieve certification
- Added flexibility and speed: Allows waivers to CMMC requirements under certain limited circumstances

Rulemaking and Timeline for CMMC 2.0

The changes reflected in CMMC 2.0 will be implemented through the rulemaking process. Companies will be required to comply once the forthcoming rules go into effect. The Department intends to pursue rulemaking both in Part 32 of the Code of Federal Regulations (C.F.R.) as well as in the Defense Federal Acquisition Regulation Supplement (DFARS) in Part 48 of the C.F.R. Both rules will have a public comment period. Stakeholder input is critical to meeting the objectives of the CMMC program, and the Department will actively seek opportunities to engage stakeholders as it drives towards full implementation.

While these rulemaking efforts are ongoing, the Department intends to suspend the current CMMC Piloting efforts and will not approve inclusion of a CMMC requirement in any DoD solicitation.

The Department encourages contractors to continue to enhance their cybersecurity posture during the interim period while the rulemaking is underway. The Department has developed *Project Spectrum* to help DIB companies assess their cyber readiness and begin adopting sound cybersecurity practices.

The DoD is exploring opportunities to provide incentives for contractors who voluntarily obtain a CMMC certification in the interim period. Additional information will be provided as it becomes available.

[Summary Statement of Helen Norris]

Cybersecurity presents numerous challenges to the higher education community and our students, faculty, patients and staff. Universities manage complex environments and sensitive data, and need to defend against threats in the form of ransomware, hacking, phishing and social engineering. This presents numerous challenges as outlined below:

- The cost of protecting our universities against cybersecurity threats is very high;
- The threat landscape is complex and ever-changing and the tools needed to manage threats are constantly evolving;
- Ransomware incidents or breaches are disruptive and expensive;
- We have a complex regulatory environment that introduces additional complexity.

Universities protect their students and communities from these threats by:

- Utilizing sophisticated technical tools to protect our systems and networks;
- Educating our communities to be on the alert for cybersecurity risks;
- Working together to share information and best practices;
- Working with Federal agencies to stay up-to-date with new threats; and

- Preparing for the worst by preparing and exercising incident response plans.

In summary, it is important for universities to take a multi-layered approach to managing cybersecurity risks.

The CHAIR. Thank you all for your really excellent testimony this morning. We appreciate it. We will now begin a round of 5 minute questions, and I ask my colleagues to keep track of the clock and try and stay within those 5 minutes.

During the COVID–19 pandemic, we have really seen a significant increase in cyber-attacks, particularly ransomware attacks on critical infrastructure here in the U.S. And those attacks are increasingly professionalized, and oftentimes they are either sponsored or supported by foreign actors like China or Iran or Russia.

A cyber-attack, as we have talked about, on health care or education, can have a devastating impact on safety and well-being of patients and students and communities. So I want to start with this basic question, Mr. Corman. What is driving this increase in cyber-attacks and how can we better prevent and monitor them?

Mr. CORMAN. I will try to be brief, but there is more detail in the written testimony. But for now, there has really been a ransomware revolution. It used to be that Dillinger quote, why do you rob banks? That is where the money is. And most attacker adversary focus on the Fortune 100 or Fortune 500 for funds, for things that could be sold, intellectual property.

The revolution here both fueled by Bitcoin making the payments easy, but more importantly, the unavailability of whatever is important to you can be monetized for the adversary. So everyone and anyone is a target because you are in business or you are a health care institution or a university or an educational foundation, you need to function. So that unavailability became universally monetizable.

The other problem is you—when you get away with something, you keep doing it. And when you are rewarded with financial payment, you keep doing it. So we funded their R&D to come back at us harder and harder to the point where something that may have been manageable and deterrable is now nearly unstoppable.

It is a business model, some ransomware as a service with highly professionalized multi-party coordination. So we have a fairly significant problem where their bold actions went unchecked long enough and things that used to be off limits, like designated critical infrastructure—a cyber-attack on designated critical infrastructure is technically an act of war when perpetrated by a nation state.

The state tolerated and sometimes state directed, have flirted up to and across lines that we need to reestablish. That is more than just the job of Congress here, but we have allowed and tolerated the intolerable. And unless we do significant things both against the adversaries and to shore up minimum hygiene for the defenders, we should expect more of this.

The CHAIR. Anybody else want to add to that at this point. Okay. Well, I think that was pretty clear. And I appreciate that input. Let me go to this, we have seen cyber-attacks target hospitals across the country. From the largest to the smallest health care system, these attacks have really undermined the care for tens of thousands of patients in my state alone but more across the country.

Protecting patients from cyber-attacks requires significant investment in both technology and expert staff by hospitals and other facilities. How can the Federal Government help to strengthen cybersecurity across the health care sector, including actually for our rural or low income communities that have a lot fewer resources? Mr. Corman If you want to start with that, and we will go from there.

Mr. CORMAN. I am sure Denise will add. I call these organizations target rich, but cyber poor. They lack the resources to do minimum hygiene. There are significant Federal, available Federal services, and I added more while I was at CISA.

There is a free cyber hygiene scanning service that can assess your remote attack surface and tell you if you have vulnerabilities. I think one of the big challenges is we don't have sufficient reach to these cyber poor. They don't participate. They don't have CISOs yet. They don't participate in ISACs or information sharing groups. They don't know what CISA is or who is who in the pantheon of the Federal Government and when to work with HHS versus CISA versus someone else.

We have an awareness and adoption gap, but once we do engage them, I have tried to find fit for purpose things that can meet them where they are at their current skill level with empathy and give them a crawl, walk, run.

The CHAIR. Ms. Norris, maybe you can talk to us about what the Federal Government can do with the higher education within them to help support under-resourced institutions to secure their IT systems.

Ms. NORRIS. Thank you. I do agree that expanding the tools that are offered by organizations, by agencies like CISA and the outreach to those more under-resourced universities and colleges would be excellent. In addition, perhaps we could see more tools that are more focused on higher education through agencies like CISA.

For example, the FBI has the campus security program and rolling that out, more awareness of that could be helpful. I also think that for institutions that are, have fewer resources, simplifying the regulatory environment is extremely critical, too, so that they can point their limited resources in the most effective ways.

It would also be helpful if there were some solutions to address the lack of affordability of cyber insurance for under-resourced universities. Actually, for everyone. The cost of cyber insurance and the availability is a problem, is a challenge for all of us, but it hits under-resourced institutions much more—in a much more impactful way.

Finally, it is something that we do and that we could hopefully get more engagement at the Federal level, I have heard some of the other witnesses talk about this, using Federal work study programs. We have had great success in bringing our students into our cybersecurity practice.

More engagement of our students in our universities can benefit all of us. And I know that I myself at Chapman and at other universities have made great use of that work study, for example, to help fund student engagement in this area.

The CHAIR. Thank you very much. Senator Cassidy.

Senator CASSIDY. I am going to defer to my colleague, Senator Tuberville.

[Technical problems.]

Senator TUBERVILLE. There we go. Thank you very much. Thanks for being here today. This is a great topic. I come from education, and we are behind in a lot of things, and this is one that is dear to my heart. I just had a son graduate from college in cyber and I was shocked how many people tried to hire him because we have a huge shortage.

I was a little skeptical four or 5 years ago, really 6 years ago, he was on the 6-year plan of him getting involved in this. But my goodness, we have overlooked this problem. It is going to get worse and worse if we don't address it, especially on the state and in the higher education levels.

But Mr. McLaughlin, what can we do to encourage our younger kids, and how—what kind of programs can we put into our elementary schools to enhance young people to really get involved? They are all into video games and all that. That is totally different. I mean, this is something we have got to get them involved in.

Ms. MCLAUGHLIN. I think that is a wonderful question, Senator. There are all kinds of opportunities to bring students in early. And I think that this becomes part of creating a culture of cybersecurity and cyber safety in schools.

First off, we don't necessarily train students like we do for other safety issues from early on. We all know look both ways before you cross the street, put your seatbelt on when you get in the car. But those kind of integrated messages about cyber safety need to be built into the messaging that students get.

On top of that, we have opportunities to build a pipeline of students who want to grow into these kind of professions later on by involving them and offering them opportunities like cybersecurity camps, cybersecurity courses.

I want to point out, it is really important that computer courses include cybersecurity as a pathway and are focused on actually how the technology works, not how to type, which has become a challenge in some spaces—lack consistency in what is offered.

Then there are some wonderful competitions that actually are offered at the Federal level for students in K–12 education and in higher education on what can they do to prevent hacking and demonstrating their skills.

Involving students and participating in that is really critical for evolving that incoming workforce and having opportunities to work in those spaces once they get to higher education, whether they are at a community college or a university.

It is a really great opportunity when we can fund, as Ms. Norris was mentioning, security operations centers and opportunities for students to develop their skills.

Senator TUBERVILLE. Thank you. In Huntsville, Alabama, we have got a new school that started over the last few years, and it is called the Alabama School of Cyber. And what they do—this is from 9th to 12th grade.

They take the top students from all over the state, rural, urban, and they bring them to Huntsville, and they train them in cyber. And of course, Huntsville is a missile defense agency, NASA, 600 defense contractors, huge. FBI is moving all of their cyber security to Huntsville, and they need more people.

They see upfront front that they are going to need this. Do we need to start doing something like this, Ms. Norris? Can you visit with me on that? All states?

Ms. NORRIS. One thing I would like to just add to what Ms. McLachlin said is that, and I heard Chair Murray refer in her comments to the digital divide. So I think as we want to bring more and more students, both from K–

12 and higher education into cybersecurity, we need to make sure we continue to address that digital divide.

I think in terms of what you just described at Huntsville, we do see centers of security excellence, whether it is at the Federal level or a corporate level across different states. But I think in this new working world where people are working from everywhere, we probably have to think about ways that we can infuse security into a more globally diverse workforce, or nationally diverse workforce, as well as centers where cybersecurity is physically located. And that is one of the challenges that we have.

Senator TUBERVILLE. Yes. It takes a special person to get in this type of field. And, I would like to see in the future our higher educational institutions that accept state and Federal funding get into cyber more. I mean, we are going to need that. I mean, it is National Security.

When we are 400,000 or 500,000 short in people to do these jobs this world is getting more dangerous as we speak in terms of just anything that people can do to us, our water systems, our grids, and all those things over the years, so. Thank you all for being here today.

This will be a great hearing. And again, we are pulling for everybody to start understanding where we are at and why we are at— why we are at this spot, and we need to get better. So thank you very much. Thank you. Thank you, Senator Cassidy.

The CHAIR. Thank you. Senator Baldwin.

Senator BALDWIN. Thank you, Madam Chair. And thank you, Senator Cassidy, for jointly bringing our attention to this. I recently helped to introduce the bipartisan Protecting and Transforming Cyber Health Care, or Patch Act, with my colleague, Senator Cassidy.

This legislation is aimed at helping protect patients from ransomware by implementing critical cybersecurity requirements for device manufacturers. And it would allow manufacturers to develop and maintain processes to update and patch devices throughout the life cycle.

Mr. Corman, you anticipated my first question in your testimony when you were talking and in your answer to a previous question when you were talking about the significant amount of research that shows how ransomware attacks constrain hospitals and ICUs, etcetera, leading to excess deaths.

I want to take my question in a slightly different direction, because while I am really proud to sponsor this legislation, it always helps me to get a more granular view of what devices are at risk of being hacked or being manipulated. You showed us a pacemaker. You talked about insulin pumps.

I am curious to know whether part of our strategy might be to make smart devices into dumb devices. We famously have a colleague on the Democratic side of the aisle who uses his flip phone just because it is safer than are iPhones and Androids.

But what about diagnostic and treatment devices in hospitals? Can they be manipulated? What about—anyways, open that up and give us some more granular examples and whether bringing some of those offline might be actually more helpful to patient, good patient outcomes.

Mr. CORMAN. I appreciate the question. In the Patch Act, I should mention as I prepared my remarks, I called some of the worst victims during the pandemic and said, what are your top three to five things you would want Congress to know? And one of them, one of the biggest victims, said, all five of my top five are, I need the Patch Act.

His point was, they never want what happened to them to ever happen again. And as they have taken a much closer look at their attack surface and their exposures, it is the unsupported software, the hardcoded passwords, the supply chain of devices, whether they be medical or just normal technology.

He can't defend that indefensible kingdom, so he wanted me to express his, I think he said I am dying of thirst and that is the water I need to wear. To your more specific question, pretty much all technologies, even 5 years ago I want to mark Thursday was the 5-year anniversary of WannaCry, the most devastating attack on health care in the world at the time and mostly hit the UK.

I remember it because we were also issuing our report to Congress for our 405c on the same day and it got delayed by 3 weeks. In that, we pointed out that a typical medical technology has over 1,000 known vulnerabilities or CVEs, and it only takes one. During the pandemic, we saw even different types of technologies that could bring down either patient care in an acute sense.

One was a radiation delivery machine that had a heavy dependance on the cloud. So you had this incredible multimillion dollar, expensive piece of gear that does its function but can't calculate how and where to precisely deliver radiation. So for several weeks, you could not deliver time sensitive cancer treatment. So the Internet of Medical Things is going to be everywhere.

It is our electronic medical records. I try to focus people in a practical sense, moving more quickly to some of the things that later in my testimony, these pragmatic security steps, these are the most dangerous practices. Instead of just referring to best practices, I got CISA to publish something called cisa.gov bad practices.

There are currently three, I think there is about to be a fourth, but these are the use of unsupported and end of life software in service of national critical functions and critical infrastructure is dangerous, especially egregious for internet facing. So I try to focus these target rich, cyber poor on their internet attack, surface the things reachable from the outside.

I look for things like unsupported software, hardcoded fixed passwords, and that is really the place to start. This should start to become the definition of negligence.

Senator BALDWIN. Thank you. I fear I am not going to get a full, another question in, but let me just plant a seed. I have some real concern about the third party apps that aren't covered by HIPAA and how we go about striking the right balance between access to data and efforts to protect innovation and security.

Ms. Anderson, I was going to ask you to elaborate on that. I am already out of time, and our Chair has cautioned not to exceed the time. So maybe we will get a second round, or I will submit it for the record afterwards.

The CHAIR. Okay. Thank you very.

Senator CASSIDY. I will let Senator Braun go in my place right now.

Senator BRAUN. Thank you. Thank you, Madam Chair. What I have heard most about not only on cybersecurity, but across the spectrum of workforce and enterprise is, how do we train individuals to actually be ready to take on the new landscape of jobs out there?

Running a company in a very low unemployment area prior to when I got here, I was shocked at how little is being done in the, let's say, middle school through high school time, guidance in directing so many students, and a lot of times with parents okay with it, but into areas that—you are not necessarily going to benefit with a 4-year degree if it hasn't been guided well.

Half the kids that pursue it don't end up with the degree, have got time lost, and debt incurred. We need to do better. And in cybersecurity, since it is something that we talk a lot more about now than we did 10 years ago when I was actually grappling with that, I think the underlying issues are the same.

My question will be for Ms. McLaughlin. Do you think that in middle school and especially high school, are we doing the things that would prepare kids for cybersecurity career? And I would like your opinion on whether a 4-year degree is necessary for the bulk of the jobs that would be in the field, because it would be instructive, because it is the same issue I hear everywhere.

I might add that a third of the kids that get a 4-year degree end up back in the basement because it was poorly guided and there is no market for it. Here at least it looks like there is a strong market for it. Tell me a little bit about whether it is working well, pre, post-secondary education, and what is needed to be successful to fill the job.

Ms. MCLAUGHLIN. All right. Well, Senator, that is a really complicated question so I will do my best. On the middle school and high school level, and now, remember, we have 50 states plus territories. They all have their own school board governance processes, so it is difficult to extrapolate across the board.

But my observation is that curriculum content to cover issues around cybersecurity and training and development of those skills is not up to speed with the threat that we face.

Now, of course, there are exceptions and there are like charter schools or magnet schools, focused schools, and programs that do exceptionally well in this area. But across the board, I would say that we struggle in this area to get consistent training and education for students in middle and high school, and also to make sure that people are aware across the board that this is a really good career opportunity.

Now, your question about the value of a 4-year degree and the educational component for cybersecurity. I think that there are actually a couple paths in the higher education space that I want to point out. There are a number of 2 year associate degree programs at community colleges, as well as 4 year university degree programs that focus on cybersecurity.

They both have their own value ads depending on the program. And I would say that the combination of the degree plus experience working in a program where you are developing actual hands on skills is extremely valuable.

The degree focus is on the theory and the application, and then the actual practice comes from that hands on work experience. Those people often don't actually make it to graduation in a 4-year program because they are getting recruited away faster than people can get through the program.

Having said that, there are a lot of people who find alternative pathways. I would say that developing skills in the U.S. Armed Services, developing skills through training and certification programs, are also very viable paths for developing cybersecurity professionals.

Senator BRAUN. It is a complicated question and a difficult answer, and I certainly wouldn't suggest that we should commandeer it from here. That is the bailiwick, I think, of the states. It might draw your attention.

I watched with interest Sunday morning, this past weekend, and the ex-CEOs of Merck and IBM basically said exactly what I just said. And they are 15 years later and when I was grappling with it in running my own company.

I think that given the time, the cost, it is just good for the spectrum of opportunity to make sure we are not waiting to be trained solely until you get out of, I think, that most instructive period when you are in high school. Thank you.

The CHAIR. Thank you. Senator Hassan.

Senator HASSAN. Well, thank you, Chair Murray. And thank you again to our witnesses for being here. Mr. Corman, I want to start with a question to you. You have pointed out how dangerous cyber- attacks can be to the health and safety of the public.

In your written testimony, you stated that cyber-attacks on hospitals and health care settings can lead to additional patient deaths, and that the impact is not limited to just the health care setting directly affected but also in the surrounding region.

As you know, over the past few years, ransomware has shut down several hospitals and health care settings in and around New Hampshire, including the University of Vermont Medical Center and Coos County Family Health Services. You were working remotely in New Hampshire forces at the time. Can you speak to the impact that you saw of these attacks on the health generally of Granite Staters?

Mr. CORMAN. Sure. The excess deaths were really correlated to ICU strain, irrespective of cause. The top two contributors were not cybersecurity. They were people reluctant to try to seek medical care, introducing self-delay, and then the inability to get seen in a timely manner when they did.

The question we asked is, can cybersecurity make it worse? And we were able to use data science to measure that yes, it can. Just anecdotally, many of those affected systems in our neighboring state of Vermont, a lot of those patients were redirected and absorbed in the institutions in your own state.

I just heard a very sad story yesterday of a cybersecurity professional in New Hampshire whose mother needed an ICU bed. There were none within a 50 mile radius. She had to be treated less attentively in the E.R. and subsequently passed away. Now, this is not this hack, this person who did this. It is that we have finite capacity in our systems, especially during a pandemic.

With the mass exodus of health care workers, any elective strain, preventable, avoidable strain like 4 weeks of downtime for oncology and other things—there is an incredible case study. They were very transparent about the impacts to their oncology program and how those were pushed to surrounding states. There is only so much capacity and when we are cavalier about avoidable, preventable harm, it has consequences.

Senator HASSAN. Thank you. I want to give each of you an opportunity to drill down a little bit on something you started to discuss in response to a question from Senator Murray. The Department of Health and Human Services, the Department of Education, CISA make more—make many affordable and often free cybersecurity resources available to the health care and education sectors.

However, as you discussed, smaller health care settings and school districts that would benefit most arguably from these resources are often just unaware that the resources exist and what the benefits are. So to each of you, in your experience, how effective is the outreach from the Federal Government to smaller entities?

I am really asking about the Federal Government's outreach and how we can improve that outreach so that these smaller entities really know what is out there and can actually connect and get some of this help. And why don't we start with you, and we will go right down the line, Ms. Anderson.

Ms. ANDERSON. I believe education is one of our biggest obstacles as far as the public knowing what services are out there for them to use. The Health ISAC, for example, in health care and many of the ISACs offer a lot of free services.

As I mentioned, the Sector Coordination Council also has free publications as well as we push all the CISA products and the HHS products as well. And so, I am going to use an example from financial services when I was with the financial services ISAC.

Treasury was very supportive of the financial services ISAC, and they actually proposed that as part of the checklist and the audits that were done against financial firms, that they belong to a sector ISAC or that they use products and services from the sector. And they—it was like a tsunami.

We called it a tsunami because people became aware of that and started joining the ISAC. And so there are a lot of ways I believe— I don't believe it is effective right now, but I do believe that if we can educate, that would be a huge great thing to do.

Senator HASSAN. Thank you. And we will go right down the line, and I will ask each of you to be pretty quick.

Mr. CORMAN. Very briefly. It has to be fit for purpose. The kind of information that an expert CISO in the ISAC needs is going to be much more sophisticated than someone who is brand new to this. So a lot of this target rich, cyber poor, pragmatic security suite. We do need to let them know CISA exists, how to work with the various parts of the Federal Government, and then make sure the advice we are giving is applicable.

Senator HASSAN. Right. Thank you.

Ms. MCLAUGHLIN. I think fit for purpose is a really good point. Most of our, 65 percent of our school districts have 2,500 students or less across the country. So having a person—having the person be able, who knows that there is a resource out there for them to use becomes a challenge.

I think one of the challenges, for once you get further—the further West you get is also—having somebody from MS-ISAC who is that point person for a region who can help people connect to the services that they need and understand why they need them.

Senator HASSAN. Thank you, and briefly, Ms. Norris.

Ms. NORRIS. Thank you. I would echo what my colleagues have said and encourage Federal agencies to continue to use the associations of ISACs and in higher ed groups like EDUCAUSE and also internet to get the word out.

Senator HASSAN. Great. And I will follow-up with questions on the record, because I think that we could have some more specific coordinating council just aimed at K through 12 and education sector so that they could have their own special assistance. Thank you.

The CHAIR. Thank you. Senator Cassidy.

Senator CASSIDY. Thank you, Madam Chair. First, Mr. Corman, thank you for your endorsement of the Patch Act, doing with Senator Baldwin.

Just thank you for that. You make an incredibly compelling case. Not to make light of it, but my staff made this kind of funny sort of thing under a hack, and it shows this kind of increasing incidence from Health and Human Services of the amount of hacks that are occurring from 35 percent in 2016 to 22 percent now in terms of information breaches.

I say that because we see it coming. It has been happening. Unfortunately, none of the solutions that we are talking about today are kind of real time. They are like, let's make the investment for the future when we can see the trend, which is occurring now, both in the schools, upper and lower, as well as in the health care system. So I use that to frame the following discussion.

When I read about the poor, cyber poor and I am looking at Ms. McLaughlin and probably you, ma'am, as well, there is probably universities that are cyber poor because their resources are poor.

If there is such a shortage of people to do it, it is difficult to get someone. I think at the elementary school in which I attended. Now, the school system may have it, but not the school. But does therein lie a potential solution?

Mr. Corman, in terms of cyber vulnerabilities, what are the main differences between an on premise facility as opposed to a cloud based system?

Mr. CORMAN. Well, there is many ways to answer that. But one example——

Senator CASSIDY. Try to do it succinctly.

Mr. CORMAN. Yes. The most—the one that immediately comes to mind is Microsoft Exchange is like the most popular email server that you could use on premise and people try to deploy it, harden it, patch it, maintain it. Unfortunately, even though theoretically you could take better care of your own server, we have found that cloud hosted email servers are much better maintained——

Senator CASSIDY. Let me stop you. So if I go to my cyber poor hospital, and maybe I will ask about a cyber poor in university and school, it seems like—it may be difficult for them to get a cyber expert, but if they put it in the cloud, you would get the experience and the whatever of the experts who are doing the cloud based system. Is that a fair intuition?

Mr. CORMAN. There are efficiencies for hardening and security from outsourcing to expertise often in the cloud. It is not inherently riskier or better, but it seems to be less mistakes made——

Senator CASSIDY. Well, it seems like it is going to be inherently safer because you just have the expertise which is concentrated in wherever the person wishes to live, as opposed to kind of walking around to your neighborhood and doing it if you live in a small, rural neighborhood.

Mr. CORMAN. One of the top ways to reduce risk is to reduce complexity. So it is not always defending indefensible things, it is having more defensible, simpler infrastructure.

Senator CASSIDY. What is a relative expense cloud based versus a premise based system?

Mr. CORMAN. It will vary, but one idea I did suggest during my time at CISA is that we subsidize and fund that migration into cloud hosted, more secured, better maintained infrastructure.

Senator CASSIDY. Just like we once gave increased reimbursement on Medicare for people to adopt an EHR, a paradigm could be increased reimbursement for Medicare for people to migrate their system from an on premise to a cloud based?

Mr. CORMAN. Yes. A report 5 years ago had a cash for clunkers suggestion for the most dangerous and egregious technology to be modernized.

Senator CASSIDY. Yes. Now, Ms. McLaughlin, would you—is my intuition correct that we have a lot of school systems that could do better with a cloud based versus a premise based?

Ms. MCLAUGHLIN. We have a lot of school systems that already— yes, Senator. We have a lot of school systems that are already in cloud for a lot of their services. And then that leaves them with a few challenges in the cyber space, which is protecting and defending the large abundance of endpoints and ensuring that their cloud service providers are——

Senator CASSIDY. Now, just stop for 1 second. That is actually cyber hygiene, I think is the terminology as opposed to cybersecurity, correct?

Ms. MCLAUGHLIN. Yes. Well——

Senator CASSIDY. They are connected but still it is hygiene, right?

Ms. MCLAUGHLIN. Yes. And knowing what is happening and being able to respond to incidents, but also those endpoints become a gateway to potentially damage your cloud resources. So there are advantages to being in the cloud——

Senator CASSIDY. But I assuming the cloud has the ability to create cul de sacs in which somebody can't penetrate the whole because they are kind of walled off, correct?

Ms. MCLAUGHLIN. If you properly engineer your cloud services to be split up based on roles and responsibilities and that you don't have an attacker who has figured out how to traverse across the——

Senator CASSIDY. But that is the role of the cloud based service, not of the small elementary school in the rural town?

Ms. MCLAUGHLIN. Correct.

Senator CASSIDY. Yes. That is my point. It seems that—and one more thing, let me ask. It also seems, I have read about—I am out of time.

The CHAIR. You can finish. Go ahead.

Senator CASSIDY. Okay. About federated systems in which there is not a central repository of data, but rather there is a central point which then reaches out into a federation of hospitals or schools.

If you wish to look at something in aggregate, you pull it up and then you put it back. Sounds like a game that you would play in elementary school. But I assume that in a cloud based system that could similarly be allowed because you would have a wall here and a wall there and you would be federating within the system. Is that again a—Mr. Corman?

Mr. CORMAN. The cloud native innovators tend to do a much better job at distributed, immutable, ephemeral segregation, separation like you are describing. It is not guaranteed, but they seem to be doing it better.

Senator CASSIDY. Then to summarize, maybe if we want to do something relatively quickly, it would be to somehow increase funding for entities out there in order to migrate from the premise to the cloud and to put in a strong cyber hygiene program at every level. Ms. McLaughlin?

Ms. MCLAUGHLIN. I do think that would be extremely beneficial.

Senator CASSIDY. Timeline for that completion could be much shorter?

Ms. MCLAUGHLIN. I wouldn't hesitate to guess on the timeline for that completion, given the heavily distributed nature of these systems.

Senator CASSIDY. All involved is Congress to pass a law. That is very easy. So anyway, I yield. Thank you.

[Laughter.]

The CHAIR. Senator Hickenlooper.

Senator HICKENLOOPER. Thank you, Madam Chair. And thank all of you for taking the time today. So illuminating. I had to go to another meeting, but I was watching in my office. I remember when President Obama was finishing his last year, he gave a commencement address at the Air Force Academy.

I went down when I was the Governor, and we ended up having lunch together in the training room. But in that lunch, I asked him after 8 years as being President of the United States, what kept him up at night, what was the single thing that most concerned him, and he said cybersecurity, especially the way it would interface with things like health care that were absolutely essential to our Country.

Which was interesting because I would come back on a trip to Israel and saw how their cybersecurity industry was so connected to their military and so connected to their universities, and that people would come out of the military, and go work in a business, then go to study and then teach.

We set up something called the National Cyber Security Center in Colorado Springs just because we have Northern Command, NORTHCOM, and Space Command, lot of intelligence there, a lot of retired military officials. And I think that building, that citadel toward cyber resiliency and awareness and training and education, just what all of you guys are doing, was one of the most rewarding things I did in the entire time I was in office.

I love, especially love the term, I am cavalry, Iamthecavalry.org, has got to be one of the best names. I wish we could have thought of that. Anyway, this notion of how much there is to do, and I start with Ms. Anderson. How can the Health ISAC work within the National Cyber Security Center or all the other Federal level groups to provide sector specific guidance?

Ms. ANDERSON. We do that every day, actually. We work very closely with CISA and HHS and FDA, as I mentioned in my testimony. We do have weekly meetings where we are looking at issues facing the sector and we are addressing them and trying to figure out what is the best way to handle whatever the situation is.

We are partnering very closely with them. Also, another thing during the whole Ukraine, Russia tensions, we have been part of all of the briefings that have taken place. And then we have foot stumped those messages out to our members and the public writ large about things that they need to really be paying attention to.

Senator HICKENLOOPER. Right. Good. We, like everyone, have experienced devastating attacks and especially ransomware attacks. You had 5 years of records taken from the Parkview Medical Center down in Pueblo. Last year, we—one of our universities refused to pay the ransom of $17 million ransom when they were hit by the Accellion data breach.

When colleges and universities are attacked and hospitals are being attacked with sensitive data like health information and visa status, Social Security numbers, I guess, and Ms. Norris I ask you, why is it so critical that we don't pay these ransoms?

Ms. NORRIS. I think when a ransom is paid, there is no guarantee that you are, a, going to get your data back, although there are some stats show about I think 68 percent of the time it does come back.

In addition, there is no guarantee that your data won't be published. And that is another, I think aspect of ransomware, that while the operational disruption is really critical and really impactful, there is also the threat of releasing that data out into the dark web and for it to be misused.

I think that it highlights the need to be prepared for a ransomware attack to do the things that we need to do, have a good backup, have a plan, test the plan, test the plan before you get a ransomware attack, don't do it the first time when somebody is asking you for a ransom.

I think that is the critical way to go. It is so disruptive because it impacts the operation and the timing is always—they know when to time it, right. So they time it at a university at a time of admission or final exams so that it has the worst impact and that they will be more inclined to pay ransom.

Senator HICKENLOOPER. The only way to deal with it is be prepared. I agree completely. Mr. Corman, real quickly, just because I am almost out of time, we have a large campus of NIST in Boulder, Colorado, and they are currently in the process of updating the framework for improving critical infrastructure cybersecurity.

While this guidance is voluntary in the private sector, it is a critical resource for companies that are looking at how they can protect themselves. Given that health care has been deemed a critical infrastructure sector, how could NIST best tailor the updated guidance to meet the evolving cybersecurity needs of health care systems.

Mr. CORMAN. The NIST framework is nearly a decade now and voluntary. And the recent OIG report showed very little adoption. So it is unnecessary and insufficient.

I think you have seen some excellent work from the 405c in the joint working group in the ISAC and the Sector Coordinating Council, attempting to give that sector fit for purpose advice on how to do it. People do things when they are incentivized to do them and a decade later with voluntary, the adoption is quite low.

Even where it is, it is amongst the haves, not the have nots. I think we need carrots and sticks. If we are going to offer safe harbors, they should be tethered to an attestation about your current state of practice against such a framework tool that isn't being used, did not realize its potential.

Senator HICKENLOOPER. I couldn't agree more. Thank you. I am out of time, but I will have questions for each of you that we will filter through the appropriate channels. I yield back to the Chair.

The CHAIR. Thank you. Senator Casey.

Senator CASEY. Chair Murray, thanks very much for having this hearing. I wanted to pose two questions to Ms. Anderson and one to Mr. Corman. Ms. Anderson, I want to start with the center that you lead.

The question is about data and tracking data. Does the center track data on negative patient outcomes that result from cyber and ransomware attacks? That is one question. No. 2 is, what are the challenges in collecting the data and how can that data be useful?

Ms. ANDERSON. We don't collect data on negative outcomes. We are actually threat—we are operational in nature, so we are looking at threats as they unfold, and we are sharing information.

We do have a saying where one person's defense becomes everyone else's offense, and we are sharing like 65,000 in 2021 actionable indicators. So real time, really true, positive indicators that help defenders put those into their system so that they can defend against attacks. So that is the type of data that we tend to collect. And that is all members shared, by the way.

Senator CASEY. Okay. I wanted to ask you a question as well about rural health care. I represent a state that has 67 counties, but we have 48 counties that are considered rural. And rural, of course, means a lot of small towns.

But communities where there is a great distance between health care institutions and access to care and all of those challenges.

One of the big challenges, of course, is these rural hospitals and rural health centers don't have the resources that some of the big cities do, don't have the research dollars sometimes that the big universities and health systems have, so therefore they lack not only resources, but staffing to ensure that they have the requisite security in place to protect against cyber-attacks.

Just in terms of the what the center is doing, how can you and how do you help those small or medium sized health care networks?

Ms. ANDERSON. We offer many free products. And as I alluded to on the Sector Coordinating Council, their cybersecurity working group, they have put out a number of best practices publications that are freely available on the website. Just basic things that you could do with on a low budget.

There are also things that we are developing actually in the Sector Coordinating Council cybersecurity working group, a series of videos, basic cyber videos for clinicians so that they understand the aspects and impacts of cybersecurity within their practice.

There is a lot of efforts underway. I think, again, it goes back to educating people that these things do exist and that they can use them, and they don't cost anything, really.

Senator CASEY. I wanted to turn to Mr. Corman regarding a question about intelligence. I am a member of the Intelligence Committee, just became a member in 2021.

Given your background with CISA and the work you have done, what role do you envision the intelligence community more broadly playing in developing not just a cyber threat picture for the Joint Cyber Defense Collaborative, but in particular, what role do you think the intelligence community can play in developing a health care specific cyber threat picture?

Mr. CORMAN. Almost—just to be clear, two things. One, I am no longer in CISA. My public service ended in January 2. We kept this in public trust to literally be on the low side or not in the classified side. The role that we benefited from intelligence was having fit for purpose, timely, actionable decision support for the ISACs or for the practitioners that might be targeted.

We issued one of the most full throated alerts in October 2020 in advance of the U.S. Presidential election, with FBI and HHS in a pretty intense collaboration to warn of a plan to disrupt concurrent hospitals across the U.S. to sow panic. And you have now seen that covered in the Wall Street Journal and Wired in possible ties to Putin direction. So that is vital and should continue.

If there were a national agenda to prioritize the weakest or highest consequence sectors, specifically with specific programs that maybe enhance the yield. I think the bigger issue is getting that in a timely way to the cyber poor, the rural organizations.

10 seconds—we keep talking about data. I love my privacy. I would like to be allowed to enjoy it. And most of the current regimes, like HIPAA focuses on the confidentiality of records, not the availability of patient care. So even these best practices pre-date the shift to the unavailability of health care.

Mr. CORMAN. Great. Thanks very much. Thanks, Chair Murray. The CHAIR. Thank you. That will end our hearing today. And I

really want to thank all of my colleagues, as well as our really great witnesses today. Ms. Anderson, Mr. Corman, Ms. McLaughlin, and Ms. Norris, very thoughtful conversation on a really important issue of National Security. For any Senators who wish to ask additional questions, questions for the record will be due in 10 business days, June 2nd, 5 p.m.

The Committee will next meet on Wednesday, May 25th to mark up several nominees, including Kalpana Kotegal to be a member of the Equal Employment Opportunity Commission, LaWanda Toney to be Assistant Secretary for Communications and Outreach at the Department of Education, Nasser Paydar to be Assistant Secretary for Post-Secondary Education at the Department of Education, and Rita Landgraf to be Assistant Secretary for Aging at the Department of Health and Human Services.

Thank you all again.

The Committee will stand adjourned.

Questions and Answers

Response by Denise Anderson, to Questions from Senator Baldwin, and Senator Rosen

SENATOR BALDWIN

I was proud to help craft the 21st Century Cures Act, which worked to address many of the interoperability concerns that we've all heard about from providers and patients. In the process, this legislation made health data much more sharable.

Question 1. Can you share any concerns that you have around the security of the health data that's gathered and used by entities not covered by HIPAA, such as third-party apps? How do we strike the right balance between access to data and efforts to protect innovation and security?

Answer 1. Senator Baldwin, thank you for your question. While there are many third-party applications covered by HIPAA, there are health applications that are provided by non-covered entities to whom individuals provide health information that can potentially be shared with others often without much transparency. I think there are three main points here:

First, while updating HIPAA is not high on the priority list given the other challenges being faced, it is time to update HIPAA. HHS has been doing what they can to provide guidance on applications and cloud, but the reality is that HIPAA is too dependent on defining covered entities and the relationships between them. Instead, HIPAA should focus on the data itself, rather than who holds/transmits it. For example, information about a patient can be shared with a covered entity and the data is protected, but if the exact, same information is shared with a non-covered entity, the data is not protected.

Second, there should be education and transparency around how data is used. There was an article published June 16th, 2022, illustrating how Facebook is receiving sensitive medical data that it can then potentially use to track patients for commercial purposes without patient knowledge: https://themarkup.org/pixel-hunt/2022/06/16/facebook-is-receiving-sensi tive- medical-information-from-hospital-websites.

The Executives for Health Innovation (EHI) published a report in March 2022 that makes the case for why a robust accountability mechanism is needed to govern the use of health data held and used by health tech companies. While EHI is proposing a private-sector solution—a neutral, independently run self-regulatory program that will oversee the data use policies and procedures, the report does point out several value points:

- Defining health information broadly enough to cover all the data that reflects mental or physical well-being or health and applying to all entities that develop consumer technology and may access, hold, or use consumer health data.
- Focusing on how consumer health information is used rather than what information, and putting clear restrictions on the collection, disclosure, and use of consumer data.
- Shifting the burden of privacy risk off consumers and onto the companies collecting and storing consumer data. The detail, length, and density of most company privacy practices make it unrealistic and

untenable for consumers to meaningfully research each technology with which they interact, nor understand the terms of use they are asked—or required— to accept before they can use each tool.

- Enabling consumers selecting health technologies to do so with less confusion and risk.
- Creating a system to receive and review consumer complaints.

https://www.ehidc.org/resources/report-case-health-data-use-accountability-out- side-healthcare-system.

Finally, the security of applications and the cloud need to be continuously reinforced. While that doesn't get to the inherent problems with authorized (or at least marginally legal) sharing of individual health information, it does help address the breach scenarios. Secure software development is a hot topic and one that should be continually talked about and reinforced in every way and venue possible. Holding application developers accountable for good security practices helps to protect all information.

SENATOR ROSEN

Increasing Federal Collaboration and Resource Sharing in the Health Care and Public Health Sector: Healthcare and Public Health Sector entities are increasingly the targets of malicious cyberattacks, resulting not only in data breaches, but also driving up the cost of care and ultimately affecting patient health outcomes. Currently, Federal collaboration and information sharing between HHS and the Cybersecurity and Infrastructure Security Agency (CISA) is fragmented and limited, and many small and rural healthcare sector entities—who arguably need this Federal information sharing the most—are not aware of the many free Federal resources that are available to them. That's why I've introduced bipartisan legislation with Senator Cassidy that would require CISA to coordinate with and make resources available to Healthcare and Public Health Sector entities, including by developing products tailored to the specific needs of small and rural hospitals and health clinics. Our bipartisan bill also would authorize HHS to coordinate with CISA and private sector healthcare experts and provide training to Healthcare and Public Health Sector asset owners and operators on cybersecurity risks and mitigation.

Question 1. Ms. Anderson, I was pleased to work with the H-ISAC in developing this bipartisan bill. As the leader of a major information sharing organization, would additional Federal resources and collaboration be helpful for the H-ISAC to push out to your members?

Answer 1. Senator Rosen, thank you for your question and thank you for working with H-ISAC on this important legislation. I too believe and am a strong proponent of collaboration and while there has been good progress over the years, there is still much more we can do. I think if CISA and HHS could work with Health ISAC and the Health Sector Coordinating Council Cybersecurity Working Group together in partnership to develop and deliver products through joint webinars, workshops, products, and programs, that would be a powerful and productive way to reach those entities that may not be aware of all the resources that currently exist. As I mentioned in my testimony, many entities are not aware these resources exist and are free. The more we can push out education and broad awareness of the resources collaboratively and together as one voice, the better we can help the sector.

Public/Private collaboration during incidents or potential threats is also needed. We do have recent, good examples of collaboration, such as Health ISAC's joint product with HC3 on the geopolitical Russian threat and H-ISAC's foot-stomping of CISA's Shields Up messaging and information from briefings. However, the more CISA and HHS can be encouraged to approach sharing in partnership with the private sector, such as jointly briefing the sector on threats, situational awareness and incident response mitigations and strategies, the more powerful the impact. Again, when we can work together as one voice, the better we can help the sector.

Consideration around encouraging organizations to join the Health Sector ISAC or related ISAOs as a best practice, would be beneficial. Having a strong community of health organization participants strengthens the sector and ecosystem. Many years ago, there was some discussion around providing tax incentives for critical infrastructure organizations to join their respective sector ISACs. ISACs stood up under Presidential Decision Directive 63, are robust, valuable, sharing communities, many of which have been in existence for over two decades. Federal support in the form of incentives or grants to small organizations would go a very long way to helping these entities and the sector at large.

Finally, another area of support would involve improved regulation and control over digital currency to prevent issues like Ransomware and Digital Extortion. Crypto-currency provides for an unregulated, and anonymous money exchange that is widely used by cyber criminals to conduct nefarious activities. Crypto-currency should be highly regulated or eliminated as it is the primary mechanism fueling cyber-criminal activities and money laundering.

Response by Helen Norris, to Questions From Senator Hassan

SENATOR HASSAN

In her testimony, Ms. Anderson highlighted the important role that the Health Sector Coordinating Council has played in improving the cybersecurity of the health care sector. Paraphrasing from her written testimony: The Health Sector Coordinating Council serves as an official advisory council to the Federal Government with critical infrastructure protection functions distinct from the advocacy and member services roles of traditional industry associations. The education sector, however, does not have a dedicated Sector or Government Coordination Council.

Question 1. How might Sector and Government Coordinating Councils help with the critical infrastructure protection function for the education sector?

Answer 1. The coordinating council model fills an important role for sectors designated as ''critical infrastructure'' by the Federal Government, but that carries with it functions and responsibilities that are specific to those sectors ''critical infrastruc- ture'' status. As a result, it may not be the right model for more effective DHS/CISA engagement with areas such as higher education that have national significance while not presenting the same types and levels of systemic risk as sectors like health care, transportation finance, and so forth.

With that distinction in mind, it would be worthwhile to consider how we can build on the CISA Cybersecurity Advisory Committee (CSAC) (https://www.cisa.gov/about-cisa-cybersecurity-advisory-committee) that was established roughly a year ago. CSAC, which includes cybersecurity leaders from a range of private and public sector organizations, serves as an official advisory body that provides the agency with broad-based input on its cybersecurity policies and programs. Given higher education's unique structure, and thus the unique cybersecurity challenges it faces, having a higher education subcommittee of the CSAC could ensure that issues and recommendations particularly relevant to colleges and universities are surfaced, both for the benefit of higher education as well as the overall cybersecurity space that the CSAC is intended to represent. Likewise, establishing such a subcommittee might provide a model for developing CISA's advisory structure so that nationally significant fields with unique structures and characteristics, which would include our colleagues in K–12, have "a seat at the table" as CISA considers how it can best work with us to advance cybersecurity nationwide.

Question 2. The Department of Health and Human Services, Department of Education, and the Cybersecurity and Infrastructure Security Agency make many affordable, and often free, cybersecurity resources available to the health care and education sectors. However, smaller health care settings and school districts that would benefit most from these resources are often not aware of these resources or their benefits.

Question 2(a). In your experience, how effective is the outreach from the Federal Government to smaller entities?

Answer 2(a). Federal agencies employ a variety of tools to reach the education sector, with electronic methods such as email and online groups being among the most effective. However, for many of us in larger institutions, we find our relationships with specific Federal agency offices and/or representatives to be more effective still. They give us an opportunity to have an interactive discussion with an agency, which allows for greater understanding and impact in the results. Unfortunately, such connections are generally not scalable, and as a result, smaller entities often feel out of the loop. In many cases, even if the Federal agencies had the capacity to reach out to every organization, the smaller entities often have limited staff with multiple responsibilities in addition to cybersecurity, adding to the communications challenges that the agencies face. Finally, the volume of information can be overwhelming for smaller entities, especially when one considers that the states are also communicating to colleges and universities.

Question 2(b). How can we improve that outreach to increase support for these entities that have the greatest need?

Answer 2(b). The Federal Government is most effective in outreach to smaller colleges when they partner with states and other organizations. For example, in California we have an organization called AICCU (https://aiccu.edu/) representing independent colleges, many of them smaller entities. They do an excellent job of liaising between their members and the State of California and could be effective in playing the same role with Federal entities. I would also recommend that Federal agencies target communications to non-technical leaders in smaller institutions, ensuring that the communications are clear to a non-technical audience.

In addition, a higher education-specific advisory body, as described above, would be helpful in broadening engagement. Likewise, Federal agencies should establish and maintain consistent channels of engagement and communication with national associations and organizations that support higher education cybersecurity leaders and professionals, such as EDUCAUSE and the Research and Education Networks Information Sharing and Analysis Center (REN-ISAC). The professional and operational connections that these entities sustain are often the most direct and effective ways to reach the higher education IT community at every level, from community colleges through research universities. Finally, Federal agencies could expand their methods of communication, leveraging video and social media to extend their reach given the increased prevalence of those means of engagement following the pandemic.

Response by Amy McLaughlin, to Questions from Senator Hassan

SENATOR HASSAN

In her testimony, Ms. Anderson highlighted the important role that the Health Sector Coordinating Council has played in improving the cybersecurity of the health care sector. Paraphrasing from her written testimony: The Health Sector Coordinating Council serves as an official advisory council to the Federal Government with critical infrastructure protection functions distinct from the advocacy and member services roles of traditional industry associations. The education sector, however, does not have a dedicated Sector or Government Coordination Council.

Question 1. How might Sector and Government Coordinating Councils help with the critical infrastructure protection function for the education sector?

Answer 1. The Health Sector Coordinating Council is coordinated by the Cybersecurity and Infrastructure Security Agency (CISA) and offers the benefit of coordinating Federal cybersecurity resources from multiple agencies through a single working group and providing a central point of access to those resources, giving health sector organizations a single access point and reducing overlap and duplication of services.

From this perspective, a sector coordinating council for K–12 public schools could be extremely beneficial in bringing existing resources together in a single, coordinated location, identifying, and resolving gaps in resources, and reducing the development of duplicative services. Reducing the number of locations and organizations a K–12 district needs to interact with to access available resources would increase efficiency and effectiveness of those resources.

Finally, a sector specific coordinating council offers the benefit of reviewing and curating available resources from a K–12 perspective to determine if they fit the K– 12 environment.

Question 2. In your written testimony, you highlighted the involvement of the Multi-State Information Sharing and Analysis Center (MS-ISAC) in supporting cybersecurity in K–12 public schools.

Question 2(a). How effectively is the MS-ISAC serving the needs of K–12 schools?

Answer 2 & 2(a). The K–12 membership in MS-ISAC has grown steadily and currently represents over 2,000 schools and districts nationally and about one fifth of the organization's membership.[148] MS-ISAC provides a valuable range of services that support the needs of K–12 schools, including:

- Malicious Domain Blocking and Reporting (MDBR)—a free service that blocks students and staff from accessing known bad websites
- Access to MS-ISAC's 4x7x365 Security Operations Center (SOC)
- Training resources including: MS-ISAC Cybersecurity Awareness Month Poster Contest for Students and Kid Safe Online Activity Book[149]

MS-ISAC actively partners with COSN and other K–12 organizations to connect with school districts, offer training and build access to the resources that support K–12 organizations. They continue to improve and expand their effectiveness in supporting K–12 schools.

One area where MS-ISAC's effectiveness has been limited is in their ability to consistently offer Security Operations Center services in a timely manner because of the rapid increase in need for SOC services caused by the increase in cyberattacks against MS-ISAC members. This impacts all MS-ISAC members, including K–12 members and is why we support increasing funding for the MS-ISAC SOC and opportunities to help MS-ISAC in staffing an expanded SOC.

Question 2(b). Do you believe that a dedicated K–12 ISAC would be beneficial?

---

[148] https://www.cisecurity.org/ms—isac/k-12—text—Membership—20is—20open—20to— 20 all—2C—20and—20private—20sector—20partners.

[149] Ibid.

Answer 2(b). MS-ISAC has spent significant time building relationships with K– 12 schools, districts and partner organizations that developing a separate dedicated K–12 ISAC at this point may be more disruptive than helpful. Supporting and funding a K–12 specific segment of MS-ISAC would be extremely beneficial in providing a way for MS-ISAC to customize services and information specifically for the K–12 environment. For example, MS-ISAC regularly releases security advisories that are available free to all members. However, the advisories are targeted to a generic State, Local, Tribal and Territorial Government (SLTT) audience and can be difficult for the K–12 practitioner to translate into actionable activities necessary in the K–12 environment.

Question 3. The Department of Health and Human Services, Department of Education, and the Cybersecurity and Infrastructure Security Agency make many affordable, and often free, cybersecurity resources available to the health care and education sectors. However, smaller health care settings and school districts that would benefit most from these resources are often not aware of these resources or their benefits or they lack the trained personnel required to use them.

Question 3(a). In your experience, how effective is the outreach from the Federal Government to smaller entities?

Answer 3 & 3(a). Outreach from the Federal Government to smaller entities is generally less effective than it could be, for several reasons.

First, Federal Government agencies often expect or assume that there is an individual dedicated to the cybersecurity in place at each organization which is an inaccurate assumption. In smaller entities, time for cybersecurity functions competes with daily technical support and customer service, and in the smallest entities, with teaching and administration of the school. This is especially true in rural and frontier schools and districts, where not only are staff expected to take on myriad responsibilities, they are also hampered by the lack of cybersecurity skills in the local community.

Second, programs to fund additional technologies and support often come with administrative overhead and reporting requirements that are too intensive for small K–12 entities to absorb into their workload, so those programs remain unused by the groups that need them most.

Third, many programs developed by Federal agencies offer one-time grant funding for improvements, for example offering one-time funding for cybersecurity implementation, but don't support the ongoing costs post-implementation and/or require ongoing reporting even beyond the lifetime of the grant. This approach adds financial burden to small K–12 entities that they are unable to absorb the costs into their budgets.

Building the capacity of the Department of Education's Privacy Technical Assistance Center to help schools address their cybersecurity needs could be particularly helpful for the smallest and most resource limited school districts.

Question 3(b). How can we improve that outreach to increase support for these entities that have the greatest need?

Answer 3(b). Outreach to K–12 entities that have the greatest need can be improved by:

- Expanding K–12 access to cybersecurity resources through existing Federal programs, such as E-Rate, that are already widely used by K–12 schools and districts. In 2021, CoSN filed a petition with the FCC urging the agency to make cybersecurity costs eligible for E-rate Category 2 support.[150] The FCC has not yet published a request for comments seeking public input about the ideas featured in the CoSN petition, including modernizing the E-rate's ''firewall'' definition.
- Utilizing the forthcoming results of the CISA study on cybersecurity in K–12 education to develop a coordinated approach to offering cybersecurity resources that scale to fit small entities and are easy to access, and/ or provide centrally funded and offered services that expand the cybersecurity capability of small entities. For example, providing the MS-ISAC Albert Network Monitoring and Management service to small entities free of charge.
- Providing funding to community college and university cybersecurity programs that operate security operations centers that offer low-cost cybersecurity monitoring and incident response services to K–12 schools and districts and serve as a training ground for new cybersecurity professionals.

[Whereupon, at 11:28 a.m., the hearing was adjourned.]

---

150 http://d31hzlhk6di2h5.cloudfront.net/20190903/cc/f3/72/41/228e09116606c764f2d2f2c4/CoSN-Cat-Two-Filing-Final-2019.pdf.

Chapter 2

Examining Ongoing Cybersecurity Threats Within the Department of the Interior and the Nexus to State- Sponsored Cyber Actors*

Committee on Natural Resources

Wednesday, June 7, 2023
U.S. House of Representatives Subcommittee
on Oversight and Investigations
Committee on Natural Resources
Washington, DC

The Subcommittee met, pursuant to notice, at 2:01 p.m. in Room 1324, Longworth House Office Building, Hon. Paul Gosar [Chairman of the Subcommittee] presiding.

Present: Representatives Gosar, Collins, Westerman; Stansbury, Case, and Lee.

Dr. GOSAR. The Subcommittee on Oversight and Investigations will come to order.

Without objection, the Chair is authorized to declare a recess at any time.

The Subcommittee is meeting today to hear testimony on examining ongoing cybersecurity threats within the Department of the Interior and the nexus to state-sponsored cyber actors.

* This is an edited, reformatted and augmented version of Oversight Hearing Before the Subcommittee on Oversight and Investigations of the Committee on Natural Resources, U.S. House of Representatives, One Hundred Eighteenth Congress, First Session, Serial No. 118–36, dated June 7, 2023.

In: Cybersecurity Challenges and Strategies Across Sectors …
Editor: Marybeth Wiskoff
ISBN: 979-8-90134-039-4

Under Committee Rule 4(f), any oral opening statement at the hearings are limited to the Chairman and the Ranking Minority Member. I therefore ask unanimous consent that all other Members' opening statements be made part of the hearing record if they are submitted in accordance with Committee Rule 3(o).

Without objection, so ordered.

The Chairman now recognizes myself for my introductory statement.

Statement of the Hon. Paul Gosar, a Representative in Congress from the State of Arizona

Dr. GOSAR. Good afternoon, everyone. I would like to thank all of our witnesses, both those from the public and the private sector, for being here today, as well as many of the colleagues that will surely be showing up for their participation.

When you think of the House Committee on Natural Resources, a hearing on cybersecurity probably isn't the first thing that comes to mind. However, in today's world of hyperconnectivity, technology touches almost every aspect of our lives. From toothbrushes with apps to children playing games on tablets in restaurants, it seems we cannot escape the growing role of technology in our daily lives. With more connectivity, more information, and more data, there is an ever-increasing need for vigilance, protection, and cybersecurity to guard against these threats. These threats are foreign and domestic, and come from private actors and nation states like China.

As our experts may mention later, cybersecurity refers to the security of our devices: infrastructure, data, and users of computers, computer networks, information, and communication technology, virtual systems, or computer-enabled control of physical components. As individuals, we are increasingly aware of the potential for cyber criminal activities. In both our personal and professional lives, there is more awareness of the need for best practices like changing our password, not clicking on links from Nigerian princes offering us a small fortune if we help them out. But jokes aside, small actions by individuals protect our work from both lone cyber criminals and large-scale hacking groups who hope to make money by exploiting hard-working, earnest Americans. Unfortunately, individual vigilance often gets lost in the large governmental bureaucracies.

Federal agencies are responsible for collecting, processing, storing, and disposing of massive amounts of digital information related to individuals, businesses, and sensitive government matters. As a result, even the slightest cyber vulnerability as government agencies can manifest itself as a large-scale breach and, therefore, our nation's economic prosperity, national security, and our personal privacy.

Sadly, many government agencies, including the Department of the Interior, are increasingly vulnerable to today's world of omni-present technology and information. At the same time, foreign nation states like China are aware of even the slightest cyber security weaknesses, and are increasingly seizing vulnerabilities in America's cybersecurity infrastructure as opportunities to advance their strategic, economic, geopolitical, and military interests.

For example, on May 24, Microsoft, in partnership with the U.S. Intelligence Agency, announced the discovery of stealth and malicious activity aimed at critical infrastructure in the United States. The attack, carried out by a state-sponsored actor based in China called Volt Typhoon, targeted critical infrastructure in Guam and elsewhere in the United States.

In the most recent campaign, communications and government infrastructure sectors were included in the attack. The infrastructure is a key component to maintaining America's interests in the Indo-Pacific region. Unfortunately, this is just one attack of many, and we know of and can speak of those that are unclassified, but we can't even talk about the ones that are classified in an open forum.

China's threat looms large over the national security interests of the United States and the world. Ongoing aggressions in the Indo-Pacific highlight the need to support our territories, including holding the Department of the Interior accountable to ensure their assets are cyber-secure. There are no quick fixes to cybersecurity and the agencies are never done with the project.

Rather, cybersecurity is an ongoing process that requires agency planning, implementing processes, and conducting programing. I am grateful for the men and women in both the private sector and the government services who devote their professional lives to protecting America's information technology assets.

In my own state, we set up the Arizona Cyber Command Center, which is run by the Department of Public Safety's Arizona Counter Terrorism Information Center in Phoenix. I have actually been there. This center works together with the state and Federal officials to protect our assets from cyber criminals.

The critical nature of the mission does not excuse any government agency at the Federal, state, or local level from fulfilling their duties and implementing necessary changes, especially when they are told time and time again that they are falling short.

Today, we will hear from both the Office of the Inspector General and the Government Accountability Office about cybersecurity vulnerabilities at the Department of the Interior. They found absurd levels of password insecurity at the Department and "long-recognized but unaddressed cyber risks to BSEE's offshore energy infrastructure that would be catastrophic to our national and economic security if attacked." I appreciate both the IG and the GAO's work on this important issue, as accountability is a key component to resolving the cybersecurity problem across the government.

In addition to our government witnesses, we have a very accomplished panel from the private sector, all of whom can speak to the very real threat that nation states like China continue to pose not only to the Department of the Interior, but across the Federal Government.

Moreover, these witnesses can speak to the best practices providing recommendations and policies that are available today to make our taxpayer-owned assets more secure and less vulnerable to the Chinese Communist Party. I think that is great news, and something that doesn't even necessarily take a change in the law. Often a change in individual behavior like updating passwords, using two-factor authentication, and increasing interagency collaboration to ensure that those with access to our critical infrastructure keep it safe and secure.

Again, I appreciate the witnesses' time today, and I turn to the Ranking Member, Ms. Stansbury, for her opening statement.

Statement of the Hon. Melanie A. Stansbury, a Representative in Congress from the State of New Mexico

Ms. STANSBURY. Thank you, Chairman. It is actually really wonderful to be here today, and to have had such a productive bipartisan effort to examine these critical issues affecting our nation's national security and our Federal agencies.

While cybersecurity may be a subject that many do not immediately think of when they think about this Committee's jurisdiction, we are well aware of the rising frequency of cyber attacks and the implications for the agencies that this Committee has jurisdiction over. Agency assets are targeted by, as was said, state- sponsored actors, cybercrime groups, and even hobbyist hackers.

Our Federal agencies are particularly attractive targets because of their high profiles, their access to sensitive and privileged information, and, of course, the national security implications. But our Federal agencies are prioritizing cybersecurity, and are prepared to strike back at cyber criminals who threaten us.

And I, too, would also like to thank our cyber professionals who work in the area, especially those who work in my district at our national labs and at our base.

Cyber attacks can affect everyone in our country. In New Mexico, our local institutions have been under cyber attack this past year, including our public school system, our county, and one of our universities. A cyber attack on these systems or operations related to these missions could have devastating and long-lasting effects on any institution.

I look forward to hearing testimony from our government and expert witnesses today to understand the vulnerabilities, what is at stake, and what we can do to address these issues.

A recent GAO and OIG report revealed that there is, of course, significant room for improvement when it comes to modernizing our systems and procedures, identifying and resolving weaknesses, improving coordination between agencies and the private sector, and addressing the risks to our critical infrastructure. These recommendations are particularly important for the Department of the Interior, which manages billions of dollars in assets, including the financial assets of tribal communities and insular areas, as well as operations related to oil and gas leasing, our national parks, and our water supplies across the western United States, as well as our exploration for critical minerals.

One of the OIG reports from February found that offshore oil and gas infrastructure regulated by DOI faces significant risks, and a successful cyber attack could have significant implications to environmental, physical, and economic harm in terms of a potential oil spill or other impacts to our energy systems, not to mention disruptions that could occur to energy supplies and markets, as we saw with the Colonial Pipeline and SolarWinds.

By improving our understanding of our cyber security vulnerabilities as we are going to do in this hearing, as well as bad actors' motivations for launching these attacks, we can prevent them and minimize the damage when they do happen.

Strengthening our cybersecurity infrastructure is more than just patching and having the most state-of-the-art technology. We must also ensure that our agencies have the necessary resources and personnel to properly monitor and address their needs.

I do want to take a moment before we begin to hear testimony to say this to anyone who is involved in cyber attacks or cyber crime: the United States is prepared to respond to, dismantle, and disrupt any cyber criminal enterprise attempting to attack its networks, data, and systems. Earlier this year, the Justice Department completed a disruption campaign against a ransomware group, and the FBI successfully penetrated the network. The stakes with cybersecurity are huge, but so are the consequences. So, if you are coming for the Federal Government, we will be coming for you.

With that, I yield back.

Dr. GOSAR. That was a nice end to that statement.

I now recognize the Chairman of the Full Committee, the gentleman from Arkansas.

Statement of the Hon. Bruce Westerman, a Representative in Congress from the State of Arkansas

Mr. WESTERMAN. Good afternoon, everyone, and thank you to Subcommittee Chairman Gosar and Ranking Member Stansbury for holding this very important bipartisan hearing today, as well as to the witnesses and my colleagues for their time and participation. I think it is safe to say that we all recognize the power of technology in our day-to-day lives. With the devices in our hands we can control the temperature of our homes, monitor weather around the globe, and harness the power of this metadata for all kinds of new uses, even things like monitoring soil moisture to track the growth of trees and crops.

Just like regular folks, government agencies depend on information technology systems for pretty much everything, including national defense, maintaining our critical energy infrastructure, and protecting personally identifiable information for Federal Government employees.

Most of us in this room have probably been targets of a cyber attack. In March of this year, the FBI announced that the personal data of Members and staff were breached in an attack on the D.C. Health Link site. Unfortunately, this is a common occurrence, too common of occurrence, as foreign nation states recognize the growing role that technology plays in America's government operations.

Nation states like China are launching increasingly sophisticated cyber attacks to further their strategic and geopolitical priorities. Because of this growing threat, industry leaders described cyber weapon deployment as "the dawn of a new age of conflict."

Despite the critical and growing importance of cybersecurity, U.S. Government agencies often fall short of best practices and align with the recommended standards. The results can be catastrophic.

For instance, in 2015, affiliates of the Chinese Communist Party hacked systems at OPM and stole personally identifiable information for 4.2 million government employees and security clearance background information on 21.5 million individuals. The Director of the FBI at the time called it a treasure trove of information about everybody who has worked for, or tried to work for, the U.S. Government. His successor said that data theft allows China to identify targets for espionage campaigns, and aids in the nation's development of artificial intelligence systems.

Sadly, this breach was not a surprise to those monitoring cybersecurity vulnerabilities at OPM. The IG issued warnings to the agency for years over alarming cybersecurity security vulnerabilities. Those warnings were ignored, the Chinese Communist Party exploited the vulnerabilities, and our national security suffered. You would think that the lesson was learned, and other government agencies would prioritize cybersecurity, especially when notified time and again that their agencies are vulnerable. However, many agencies still fall short.

The Department of the Interior is no exception. On behalf of the Committee of Natural Resources, I thank both the Inspector General and the GAO for their work highlighting cybersecurity weaknesses at the Department of the Interior.

But let me make it clear that the Department of the Interior is not alone. All government agencies must make a renewed commitment to cybersecurity in order to protect America's information, data, and technology. Indeed, with the ever-increasing role of technology and the rapid rise of artificial intelligence, effective and ongoing cybersecurity is of utmost importance and, quite frankly, it is a matter of life and death.

We have an impressive slate of witnesses today from both the private and public sectors. I look forward to listening to them and learning more about cybersecurity as we work to protect America's information technology infrastructure.

With that, I yield back, and thank you again to the witnesses.

Dr. GOSAR. I thank the Chairman. Now I will introduce our witnesses from the first panel.

First we have the Honorable Mark Greenblatt, Inspector General of the U.S. Department of the Interior; and then we have Ms. Marisol Cruz Cain, Director, Information Technology and Cybersecurity, Government Accountability Office. I work a lot with you, so thank you so much for being here today.

Let us remind the witnesses that under Committee Rules, they must limit their oral statements to 5 minutes, but their entire statement will appear in the hearing record.

To begin your testimony, please press the "on" button on your microphone so we can all hear you.

We use timing lights here. When you begin, you will see a green light. At the end of 5 minutes, that light will turn to red. When you see that red, I will ask you to please complete your statement. I will also allow all the witnesses in the panel to testify before Member questioning.

I now recognize Mr. Greenblatt for 5 minutes.

Statement of the Hon. Mark Greenblatt, Inspector General, U.S. Department of the Interior, Washington, DC

Mr. GREENBLATT. Chairman Gosar, Ranking Member Stansbury, and members of the Subcommittee, thank you for the opportunity to appear before you today.

My office has identified IT security as a top management challenge for the Department of the Interior for more than 20 years. With that in mind, we have prioritized cybersecurity oversight as an important part of our portfolio, and have built a track record, a long track record of effective oversight into these vulnerabilities. Our latest inspection focused on password security at the Department. It goes without saying that passwords are a prime target of attack for malicious actors who are attempting to gain unauthorized access to sensitive data. Our team tested whether DOI's password complexity and enforcement controls were effective to prevent a malicious attack. To do this, our testers spent less than $15,000 to design a system to crack or hack passwords. Our tools compared the Department's 85,000 passwords, on the one hand, with 46 quadrillion potential passwords on the other.

It is important to note two things: first, all of the equipment, tools, and information that our team used is available to malicious actors across the globe; second, the methodology that we used is similar to that used by hackers in the past.

The results of our testing were troubling. In total, we cracked more than 20 percent of the Department's active passwords, which amounts to more than 18,000 passwords. Get this: Our team was able to crack more than 14,000 in the first 90 minutes alone.

Even worse, the cracked passwords included hundreds of accounts belonging to senior government officials, and hundreds more of accounts with elevated privileges such as what a systems administrator would have.

Moreover, our testers found that the most commonly used password at the Department was "password1234." In fact, 5 of the top 10 passwords in the Department included the word "password" and some combination of 1234. Even so, 99.99 percent of the accounts that we hacked met DOI's password complexity requirements. As I said, the results of our tests were disturbing.

But the good news is that there are solutions. The first one is requiring what is called multi-factor authentication, or MFA. MFA refers to the requirement to use at least two factors to access computer systems, and the factors can be broken down into three categories: something you have, such as an ID card; something you know, such as a password; and something you are, such as a fingerprint or a retinal scan. Multi-factor authentication would require at least two of those, such as a password with a fingerprint. MFA is the gold standard for cybersecurity because it is much easier for an attacker to obtain a password than it is to obtain a retinal scan.

MFA is already required on all Federal information systems and has been for decades. But our inspection showed that the Department of the Interior still allowed passwords alone on an unknown number of systems. In fact, our inspection found that nearly 90 percent of Interior's high-value IT assets permitted authentication through passwords alone, or allowed MFA to be bypassed.

Let me say that again, because that might be the most significant aspect of our findings: We found that nearly 90 percent of the Department's high-value assets did not enforce multi-factor authentication requirements. We therefore recommended that the Department prioritize implementing and requiring MFA that cannot be bypassed on all of its systems, starting with the high-value assets. While MFA is the cornerstone for cybersecurity, we recognize that there may be cases in which MFA cannot be fully implemented. So, we recommended that the DOI improve its password policies. In particular, we recommend shifting away from clumsy passwords that have special characters and numbers and are simply impossible to remember.

Specifically, we recommend that the Department shift away from requiring a password, which is hard for a person to remember and easy for a computer to crack, to a passphrase, which is a string of unrelated words which is easy for a person to remember and hard for a computer to crack. Using passphrases is part of the mandatory technical requirements for Federal agencies, and we recommended that the Department adopt policies and controls that are consistent with that guidance.

To its credit, the Department concurred with our recommendations, and has generally provided target dates for their implementation.

Thank you for your time, and I look forward to answering your questions.

[The prepared statement of Mr. Greenblatt follows:]

Prepared Statement of the Honorable Mark Lee Greenblatt, Inspector General, U.S. Department of the Interior

Chairman Gosar, Ranking Member Stansbury, and Members of the Subcommittee, thank you for giving me the opportunity to discuss cybersecurity at the Department of the Interior (DOI) and in particular, our office's January 2023 report, P@s$w0rds at the U.S. Department of the Interior: Easily Cracked Passwords, Lack of Multifactor Authentication, and Other Failures Put Critical DOI Systems at Risk. As you know, inspectors general have a direct reporting relationship to Congress. My office and I take this obligation seriously, and we appreciate the Subcommittee's continued support for our independent and objective oversight. In our recent inspection of the DOI's password security, we found that the DOI's management practices and password complexity requirements were not sufficient to prevent potential unauthorized access to its systems and data. In fact, during our inspection, we cracked 18,174 of 85,944—or 21 percent of active user passwords, including 288 accounts with elevated privileges and 362 accounts of senior U.S. Government employees. As the result of our findings, we made eight recommendations to help the Department strengthen its IT security by improving user account management practices. The DOI concurred with our recommendations.

1. Background

The DOI Office of Inspector General (OIG) has recognized IT security as one of the DOI's top management challenges for many years. The DOI relies on complex, interconnected information systems to carry out its daily operations and spends approximately $1.7 billion annually on its portfolio of IT assets. Our work has found that the DOI continues to face challenges in implementing an enterprise IT security program that balances compliance, cost, and risk while enabling bureaus to meet their diverse missions.

The OIG prioritizes cybersecurity oversight as an important part of our portfolio. For example, our 2023–2024 oversight plan includes planned reviews of the DOI's vulnerability remediation practices and cyber threat hunting efforts. We also currently have an ongoing review of the DOI's public cloud computing security practices.

In April 2023, we issued the fiscal year 2022 annual independent Federal Information Security Modernization Act (FISMA) audit for the DOI.[1] That audit identified needed improvements and made 24 recommendations intended to strengthen the DOI's information security program as well as those of the bureaus and offices. Using FISMA metrics, the Office of Management and Budget (OMB) scored the cybersecurity performance of 23 Federal agencies, including the DOI. The DOI scored a 68 percent and ranked 23rd on the list.

Other recent work published by our office includes the results of our testing of the DOI's cyber threat detection and defense controls. Specifically, in August 2022, we issued a memorandum concluding that this evaluation could be closed without a full-scale report because we were satisfied with the Department's response to our technical tests, conducted between May and November 2021.[2] Our review of the Department's cyber incident tracking system demonstrated that the DOI's IT staff identified our simulated attacks. Moreover, the Department mitigated confirmed technical vulnerabilities identified by our technical tests.

---

[1] Summary: Independent Auditors' Performance Audit Report on the U.S. Department of the Interior Federal Information Security Modernization Act for Fiscal Year 2022 (Report No. 2022-ITA-028).

[2] The U.S. Department of the Interior's Cyber Threat Detection and Defense Controls (Report No. 2020-ITA-067).

In addition, in September 2020, we issued a report of our evaluation of the security of the DOI's wireless networks.[3] Our evaluation revealed that the Department did not deploy and operate a secure wireless network infrastructure. We conducted reconnaissance and penetration testing of wireless networks representing each bureau and office. To do this, we assembled portable test units for less than $200 that were easily concealed in a backpack or purse and operated these units with smartphones from publicly accessible areas and locations open to visitors. Our attacks simulated the techniques of malicious actors attempting to break into departmental wireless networks, such as eavesdropping, so-called "evil twin" attacks,[4] and password cracking. We made 14 recommendations that will help prevent malicious actors from eavesdropping on internal communications and gaining unauthorized access to the DOI's wireless networks. The Department concurred with and has implemented all recommendations.

Given the team's success rate cracking passwords during our September 2020 evaluation, we decided to conduct a formal test of passwords throughout the Department. That prompted this passwords project, in which we inspected the DOI's password complexity requirements after defining rules of engagement[5] with the Department to ensure that it was able to protect its IT systems and that any vulnerabilities could be addressed promptly.

II. The DOI OIG's Inspection of the DOI's Password Complexity Requirements

Identifying and authenticating users is a fundamental security control for granting access to computer systems and information resources. As such, authentication methods such as passwords are a prime target of attack for malicious actors attempting to gain unauthorized access to sensitive data. In this inspection, our objective was to determine whether the Department's

---

[3] Evil Twins, Eavesdropping, and Password Cracking: How the Office of Inspector General Successfully Attacked the U.S. Department of the Interior's Wireless Networks (Report No. 2018- ITA-020).

[4] In such attacks, bad actors seek to capture usernames and passwords and then crack the passwords.

[5] As explained in our report, according to the National Institute of Standards and Technology, ''rules of engagement'' define detailed guidelines and constraints regarding the execution of information security testing. The rules are established before the start of a security test and give the test team authority to conduct defined activities without the need for additional permissions.

password management and enforcement controls were effective enough to prevent a malicious actor from gaining unauthorized access to Department computer systems by capturing and "cracking" user passwords.

A. Methodology

A "clear text password" is what a user types when prompted to log in to a system. To avoid exposing a sensitive password, user passwords are stored in a secure, unintelligible format called "hashes." The hashed version of a password is not usually accepted through typical authentication operations, such as computer login prompts. This restriction prevents a malicious actor from using captured password hashes to gain unauthorized access to a computer system. So, for example, the clear text password "Password-1234" is stored in its hashed form as "A71FB31235347EA75956B6155ED36899."

Hashes are generally considered secure because they cannot be directly reverted to clear text—their original state. However, there are indirect methods attackers can use to attempt to recover hashed passwords. Once attackers have captured hashes, they must attempt to recover their original clear text form through a process referred to as "hash cracking."[6] If successful, this enables the attacker to use the password to gain unauthorized access to an organization's computer systems and data.

To test the Department's passwords, our inspectors spent less than $15,000 on a system designed to crack—or hack—passwords using open-source software and a custom wordlist, consisting of publicly available password lists harvested from past data breaches, dictionaries from multiple languages, U.S. Government terminology, and pop culture references. We created a set of rules and processes for manipulating and combining those words into password candidates; we then attempted to crack the hashes for every DOI user account.[7]

---

[6] "Hash cracking" is the automated process of generating clear text password "candidates" and then computing hashes of those candidates and comparing the results against captured hashes. If the candidate's hash matches the captured hash, it means the password candidate and the clear text version of the captured hash are the same. If the two hashes do not match, the process continues until either a match is found or the attacker gives up and attempts to crack other captured password hashes.

[7] As part of our rules of engagement with the Department, we waited 90 days to begin testing hashes from the Department. At that time, all accounts should have had their passwords changed or been disabled due to inactivity pursuant to departmental policy. As of June 8,

B. Findings

We found that the Department's management practices and password complexity requirements were not sufficient to prevent potential unauthorized access to its systems and data. Over the course of our inspection, we cracked 18,174 of 85,944— or 21 percent of active user passwords, including 288 accounts with elevated privileges and 362 accounts of senior U.S. Government employees.

Specifically, we found that:

1) The Department did not consistently implement multifactor authentication (MFA), including for 89 percent of its High Value Assets, which are assets that could have serious impacts to the Department's ability to conduct business if compromised. This lack of MFA left these systems vulnerable to password compromising attacks.
2) The Department's password complexity requirements were outdated and ineffective, allowing users to select easy-to-crack passwords (e.g., Changeme$12345, Polar-bear65, Nationalparks2014!). We found, for example, that 4.75 percent of all active user account passwords were based on the word "password." In the first 90 minutes of testing, we cracked the passwords for 16 percent of the Department's user accounts.
3) The Department's password complexity requirements implicitly allowed unrelated staff to use the same inherently weak passwords—meaning there was not a rule in place to prevent this practice. For example, the most reused password (Password-1234) was used on 478 unique active accounts. In fact, 5 of the 10 most reused passwords at the Department included a variation of "password" combined with "1234"; at the time of our report, this combination met the Department's requirements, even though it is not difficult to crack.
4) The Department did not timely disable inactive (unused) accounts or enforce password age limits, which left more than 6,000 additional active accounts vulnerable to attack.

2021, we provided the Department with a list of all user accounts with passwords we cracked to ensure that the Department forced those accounts to change passwords.

The Department Did Not Consistently Implement MFA on Its Systems

MFA refers to the requirement to use at least two factors to access computer systems, such as a password plus a PIN from a smartphone app or a PIV card plus a password. When MFA is implemented correctly, it adds a layer of security that protects organizations, even when passwords are compromised.

MFA is already required on all Federal information systems and has been for decades. As our inspection showed, however, the Department still allowed singlefactor authentication (username and password) on an indeterminate number of its systems, including high-value IT assets.

Because the Department relied on authentication methods that were not in line with National Institute of Science and Technology (NIST) recommendations, Governmentwide mandates, and industry best practices, the burden of the Department's security controls rested on obsolete password complexity requirements. Further, the Department did not have a full picture of which systems complied with which standards. Without requiring and enforcing MFA across its systems— including those that contain sensitive information—the Department's data remains at risk of unauthorized exposure.

The Department's Ineffective Password Complexity Requirements Allowed Easy-to- Crack Passwords

Department policy at the time of our inspection required that all passwords have a minimum length of 12 characters and contain at least 3 of 4 character types consisting of uppercase, lowercase, digits, and special characters. We found that these requirements were not sufficient to prevent us from successfully recovering the clear text passwords for 18,174 active user accounts (21 percent) using our hashcracking system. We recovered passwords for 13,924 of those accounts in the first 90 minutes of testing and recovered the passwords for the remaining 4,250 accounts over an additional 8 weeks of testing.

We note that 99.99 percent of the accounts we cracked met the Department's password complexity requirements. These passwords, however, were consistently made up of single dictionary words, patterns, or slightly modified existing passwords—all of which people tend to use to construct memorable passwords. Although the Department's password policy at the time of the inspection appeared to encourage complex passwords, in practice, its policies were not sufficient to prevent users from creating passwords that are easy to crack.[8]

Further, frequent password change requirements, while crucial when weak passwords are permitted, tend to encourage users to continue to use passwords that are easy to crack. NIST states that, when frequent password changes are required, users are most likely to change a single character, or append a character to the end of an existing password (e.g., Password-1234 might become Password-1234!). This ensures that the password remains memorable to the user, but it also remains weak and easy to crack. This creates a feedback loop that frustrates users, perpetuates the weak password cycle, and does not improve security.

The Department's Password Complexity Requirements Implicitly Allowed Hundreds of Unrelated Accounts to Use the Same Passwords

Password reuse is a security risk because it reduces both the time and effort necessary for a successful attack. The risk is greatly increased when the same easy- to-crack passwords are allowed to be used on multiple accounts. We found that the same easy-to-crack passwords (which all met the Department's complexity requirements) were used across multiple active accounts. Even though many of these accounts were unrelated to each other, the passwords were so common that multiple employees from different bureaus and offices independently chose the same passwords. Because the Department did not have an explicit rule in place denying this practice, it implicitly allowed users to create the same passwords across multiple accounts.[9]

We found that 20 percent of all active accounts had passwords that were used across multiple distinct accounts (16,812 out of 85,944). This includes both cracked and uncracked passwords. We were able to identify when the same passwords were used based on the hashes, so even if we did not crack a

---

[8] Most of the passwords we cracked were based on a single dictionary word with the inclusion of enough characters or character substitutions to meet the complexity requirement. For example, ''Password-1234'' was the most used password at the Department. Even though a password of this type meets requirements because it includes uppercase letters, lowercase letters, digits, and a special character, it is, in fact, easy to crack.

[9] In other cases, we found common passwords reused across multiple related accounts, such as new accounts with temporary passwords, shared mailboxes, or service accounts. (Service accounts are often granted elevated privileges over systems or data, and shared mailboxes often contain sensitive data or attachments.) Understanding the purpose and extent of access granted to these accounts was out of the scope of our inspection; therefore, we were unable to identify the extent of the risk posed by these and other nonadministrative accounts.

password, we could identify and determine which accounts shared the same password.

NIST standards require agencies to check potential passwords and disallow them if they are on a list of commonly used, expected, or compromised passwords. We found that none of the Department's bureaus had implemented the ability to check for and prevent weak passwords.

The Department Did Not Timely Disable Inactive Accounts or Enforce Password Age Limits

We found that the Department failed to enforce its own account management policies regarding account disabling and password changes on a significant number of accounts. The Department's policy requires accounts to be disabled after 45 days of inactivity. Enforcing this provision is important because unused accounts pose a higher risk to Department systems and networks, as they offer more opportunities for a malicious actor to gain unauthorized access. Disabling accounts after a period of inactivity reduces this risk. We found that 6,243 of all active accounts had not been used for more than 45 days; the Department failed to disable these accounts as required by its own policy and instead left implementation and enforcement of this policy to the bureaus and offices. We cracked 23 percent (1,405) of these accounts.

We also found that 28 percent of the accounts we cracked did not comply with the Department policy requiring password changes at 60-day intervals, suggesting that these accounts were still using the passwords after we cracked them. Without that password age limit, an attacker is not limited by time. According to Department policy in place at the time of our inspection, an attacker would have only 60 days to intercept or otherwise acquire a hash, crack it, and then use it.

C. Recommendations

Given our findings, we made eight recommendations to the Department to help it strengthen its IT security by improving account management practices. In summary, our recommendations can be grouped into four broad categories:

- First, we recommended that the Department prioritize implementing MFA across all systems and develop a system to track the status of the implementation of MFA.

- Second, we recommended that the Department revise password complexity requirements to bring them in line with current NIST guidance, such as using longer passphrases and less frequent change intervals.
- Third, we recommended that the Department revise policy to prohibit accounts from reusing the same passphrases and passwords.
- Fourth, we recommended that the Department ensure compliance with policies regarding timely disabling of inactive accounts.

In response to the report, the Department concurred with our recommendations and provided target implementation dates. We are engaged in ongoing communication with the Department regarding the status of these recommendations and will report on Oversight.gov when actions sufficient to close the recommendations have occurred.

Conclusion

In the current cyberthreat environment, strong authentication methods and robust account and password management practices are necessary to help protect computer systems from unauthorized access. Overreliance on passwords to restrict system access to authorized personnel can have catastrophic consequences.

The Department's reliance on single-factor authentication only increased the importance of aligning its account management requirements with NIST's recommendations.

To best mitigate the risk of easy-to-crack passwords, the Department should prioritize MFA on all systems and applications. In those instances where MFA has not yet been implemented, password complexity requirements should be updated to comply with NIST guidance.

Thank you for your time. I look forward to answering questions.

Questions Submitted for the Record to the Hon. Mark Greenblatt, Inspector General, U.S. Department of the Interior

Questions Submitted by Representative Gosar

Question 1. Is anything stopping the Department of the Interior from allocating a greater percentage of its existing budget to cybersecurity initiatives?

Answer. The Department of the Interior (DOI) did not address budget issues in its response to our office's report (the DOI's response is included in the report as Appendix 2). The Office of Inspector General (OIG) also has not independently evaluated the DOI's budget. Given that we have not conducted oversight work in this area, we do not have a basis to make findings or draw conclusions about the Department's ability to allocate a greater percentage of its existing budget to cybersecurity initiatives.

Question 2. How can DOI better prioritize cybersecurity initiatives with its existing budget?

Answer. Although we have not conducted specific work regarding the DOI's prioritization of cybersecurity initiatives within its existing budget, we have evaluated various aspects of DOI's IT environment, and 64 IT-related open recommendations have yet to be implemented. We have identified seven of these recommendations as "significant," including four from the passwords inspection report that was discussed at the hearing. Designation of a recommendation as "significant" considers a range of factors but, overall, is an indication that we have concluded that it is a particularly important issue to address. Beyond noting this designation, we do not have a basis to make findings or draw conclusions about how the DOI should make prioritization decisions within its current budget.

Dr. GOSAR. Thank you, Inspector General. I now recognize Ms. Cruz Cain for her 5 minutes.

Statement of Marison Cruz Cain, Director, Information Technology and Cybersecurity, Government Accountability Office, Washington, DC

Ms. CRUZ CAIN. Chairman Gosar, Ranking Member Stansbury, Chairman Westerman, and members of the Subcommittee, thank you for inviting GAO to contribute to this important discussion about cybersecurity risks at the Department of the Interior.

As you know, Federal agencies and our nation's critical infrastructure, such as energy and transportation, depend on technology systems to carry out operations and to process essential information. The security of these systems and data is vital to protecting individual privacy and our nation's security and well-being. GAO has long emphasized the urgent need for the Federal Government to improve its ability to protect against cyber threats. In fact, we have designated cybersecurity as a government-wide, high-risk area since 1997.

Today, I will focus on cyber threat actors and incidents facing Federal systems and critical infrastructure. I will also discuss recent findings related to Interior's cybersecurity program and practices.

Risk to technology systems are increasing. Malicious actors are becoming more willing and capable of carrying out cyber attacks, which can result in serious harm to human safety, the environment, and the economy. Because of this, agencies and critical infrastructure owners and operators need to protect the confidentiality, integrity, and availability of their systems, and effectively respond to cyber attacks.

According to the 2023 annual threat assessment of the U.S. intelligence community, China, Iran, North Korea, and Russia continue to pose the greatest cyber threats. These countries possess the ability to launch cyber attacks that could disrupt the operations of critical infrastructure, including facilities and assets supporting offshore oil and gas production. Recent attacks demonstrate the impact these threat actors can have on critical infrastructure and systems.

The ransomware attack on the Colonial Pipeline Company led to a shutdown of the pipeline, which resulted in widespread gasoline shortages throughout the southeastern United States. Federal agencies have continued to report tens of thousands of information security incidents each year, which further highlights the importance of protecting their systems and those that support our critical infrastructure.

Accordingly, the Department of the Interior has significant responsibilities, both for protecting its own systems and data, and overseeing the safety of the offshore oil and gas infrastructure. However, both we and Interior's OIG have identified needed improvements in the Department's cybersecurity program and practices.

As my colleague mentioned, in January 2023, Interior's OIG reported that the Department had numerous weaknesses in its password management. Also, its computer authentication mechanisms and account management practices had weaknesses similar to those that were allegedly exploited in the Colonial Pipeline attack.

Also, in September 2022, we reported on Interior's efforts to establish a comprehensive privacy program. We found that the Department had addressed several important privacy practices, but had not yet incorporated privacy into its organization-wide risk management strategy. This practice is key to ensuring that the Department has established a strategic approach to identify, assess, and manage privacy risks.

Further, in October 2022, we reported that Interior's Bureau of Safety and Environmental Enforcement had not developed a strategy to identify and assess cyber risks to infrastructure supporting offshore oil and gas. Absent such a strategy, offshore oil and gas infrastructure will continue to remain at significant risk from cyber threat actors.

Much to its credit, Interior generally agreed with the recommendations that we and the OIG have made to address these issues, and has outlined plans to implement them. It will be important for the Department to follow through on their commitments to help ensure that the Department is capable of both preventing and responding to the ongoing cyber threats it faces.

In summary, to protect Federal systems and critical infrastructure from cyber-related threats, Federal agencies such as Interior need to ensure that they are effectively implementing risk-based cybersecurity programs and practices. Doing so provides the best protection from cyber attacks that threaten our nation's economic well-being and national security.

This concludes my remarks, and I look forward to answering any questions you may have. Thank you for your time.

[The prepared statement of Ms. Cruz Cain follows:]

Prepared Statement of Marisol Cruz Cain, Director, Information Technology and Cybersecurity, U.S. Government Accountability Office

Chairman Gosar, Ranking Member Stansbury, and Members of the Subcommittee: I am pleased to be here today to discuss cybersecurity risks at the Department of the Interior, such as threats posed by malicious actors, including nation-state actors. As you know, federal agencies and our nation's critical infrastructures—such as energy, transportation systems, communications, and financial services—depend on technology systems to carry out operations and process, maintain, and report essential information. The security of these systems and data is vital to protecting individual privacy and national security, prosperity, and wellbeing. Moreover, recent incidents highlight the impact that cyberattacks can have on these systems.

We have designated information security as a government-wide high-risk area since 1997. We expanded this high-risk area in 2003 to include protection of critical cyber infrastructure. In 2015, we expanded it again to include protecting the privacy of personally identifiable information.[10]

This statement discusses various types of threat actors and attacks that could compromise federal systems and our nation's critical infrastructure, such as that overseen by Interior. It also discusses cybersecurity risks that we and the Office of the Inspector General have identified at the department.

This statement is based on previously issued GAO reports on cybersecurity at Interior and other federal agencies. We also reviewed Interior Office of Inspector General reports and other public information sources.

We conducted the work on which this testimony is based in accordance with generally accepted government auditing standards. Those standards require that we plan and perform the audit to obtain sufficient, appropriate evidence to provide a reasonable basis for our findings and conclusions based on audit objectives. We believe the evidence obtained provides a reasonable basis for our findings and conclusions based on our audit objectives.

---

[10] See GAO, High-Risk Series: Efforts Made to Achieve Progress Need to Be Maintained and Expanded to Fully Address All Areas, GAO-23-106203 (Washington, DC.: Apr. 20, 2023).

Background

The U.S. Department of the Interior's mission is to protect and manage the nation's natural resources and cultural heritage, provide scientific and other information about those resources, and honor its trust responsibilities and special commitments to American Indians, Alaska Natives, and affiliated Island Communities. The department plays a central role in how the United States stewards its public lands, increases environmental protections, pursues environmental justice, and honors our nation-to-nation relationship with Tribes. The department carries out its mission through 11 technical bureaus:

- Bureau of Indian Affairs
- Bureau of Indian Education
- Bureau of Land Management
- Bureau of Ocean Energy Management
- Bureau of Reclamation
- Bureau of Safety and Environmental Enforcement
- Bureau of Trust Funds Administration
- National Park Service
- Office of Surface Mining Reclamation and Enforcement
- U.S. Fish and Wildlife Service
- U.S. Geological Survey

In addition to the 11 bureaus, a number of offices fall under the Office of the Secretary, Office of the Assistant Secretary for Policy, Management and Budget, the Solicitor's Office, and the Office of Inspector General.

Interior IT Security Responsibilities

Interior is responsible for protecting the confidentiality, integrity, and availability of its information and information systems. Specifically, the Federal Information Security Modernization Act of 2014 (FISMA) was enacted to provide a comprehensive framework for ensuring the effectiveness of information security controls over information resources that support federal operations and assets.[11]

FISMA requires agencies to develop, document, and implement an agency-wide information security program to secure federal information operations and assets of the agency. These information security programs are to provide risk-based protections for the information and information systems that support the agency's operations. FISMA requires agencies to comply with the Office of Management and Budget's (OMB) policies and procedures, the Department of Homeland Security's (DHS) binding operational directives, and the National Institute of Standards and Technology's (NIST) information security standards.

Interior's Office of the Chief Information Officer (OCIO) leads Interior's security management program. The office's mission and primary objective is to establish, manage, and oversee a comprehensive information resources management program. The Interior Chief Information Security Officer (CISO) reports to the Chief Information Officer and oversees the Information Assurance Division. This division is responsible for Interior's IT security and privacy policy, planning, compliance, and operations.

Each of Interior's bureaus and offices have an Associate Chief Information Officer (ACIO) that reports to the department Chief Information Officer and the Deputy Bureau Director. The ACIO serves as the senior leader over all IT resources within the bureau or office. Each also has an Associate Chief Information Security Officer that represents the Bureau and reports to the Bureau ACIO and Interior's CISO.

Interior Offshore Oil and Gas Responsibilities

Interior's Bureau of Safety and Environmental Enforcement (BSEE) is responsible for overseeing offshore oil and gas operations, including cyber risks. The bureau's mission is to promote safety, protect the environment, and conserve resources offshore through regulatory oversight and enforcement. It

[11] The Federal Information Security Modernization Act of 2014 (FISMA 2014), Pub. L. No. 113-283, 128 Stat. 3073 (Dec. 18, 2014) largely superseded the Federal Information Security Management Act of 2002 (FISMA 2002), enacted as Title III, E-Government Act of 2002, Pub.L. No. 107-347, 116 Stat. 2899, 2946 (Dec. 17, 2002). As used in this statement, FISMA refers to the new requirements in FISMA 2014, and to other relevant FISMA 2002 requirements that were unchanged by FISMA 2014 and continue in full force and effect.

is responsible for overseeing offshore operations, which includes the authority to investigate incidents that occur on the outer continental shelf, monitor operator compliance with environmental stipulations, and take enforcement actions against operators that violate safety or environmental standards.

BSEE's regulatory programs advise a wide range of offshore activities and facilities, including drilling, well completion, production, pipeline, and decommissioning operations. The bureau implements advancements in technology and conducts onsite inspections to assure compliance with regulations, lease terms, and approved plans. To date, BSEE's regulations do not explicitly mention cybersecurity, but the bureau has determined that addressing cybersecurity risks to offshore oil and gas infrastructure aligns with its mission to promote safety and protect the environment.

Cyber Threat Actors Pose Serious Risks to Federal Systems and Critical Infrastructure

Risks to technology systems are increasing. In particular, systems and networks supporting federal agencies and U.S. critical infrastructure are becoming more vulnerable to cyberattacks. These systems and networks are composed of, and connected to, enterprise IT systems and operational technology systems.[12] Because of their complexity and interconnections with other systems, these systems are vulnerable to cyberattacks. Such attacks could result in serious harm to human safety, the environment, and the economy.

Overview of Cyber Threat Actors

Key cybersecurity risks to federal agencies and U.S. critical infrastructure also include the growing attack capabilities of threat actors. According to the 2023 Annual Threat Assessment of the U.S. Intelligence Community, China, Iran, North Korea, and Russia pose the greatest cyber threats.[13] Of particular

[12] Enterprise IT systems encompass traditional IT computing and communications hardware and software components that may be connected to the internet. Operational technology systems monitor and control sensitive processes and physical functions, such as offshore oil and gas operations.

[13] Office of the Director of National Intelligence, *Annual Threat Assessment of the U.S. Intelligence Community* (Feb. 6, 2023).

concern, these countries possess the ability to launch cyberattacks that could have disruptive effects on critical infrastructure, including facilities and assets supporting offshore oil and gas production. Further, the assessment stated that transnational organized ransomware actors continue to improve and execute high-impact ransomware attacks, extorting funds, disrupting critical services, and exposing sensitive data. Table 1 describes common types of cyber threat actors.

Examples of Cyberattacks

Cyber adversaries use a variety of tactics and techniques to exploit vulnerabilities and attack systems and networks. According to MITRE's ATT&CK® Framework, attackers tend to follow common methodologies to compromise targets and achieve their goals. For example, threat actors can use multiple techniques, such as compromising the supply chain of hardware and software, to gain initial access to IT and operational technology systems.[14]

Table 1. Common Cyber Threat Actors

Threat actor	Description and potential motivation
Nations	Nations—including nation-states, state-sponsored, and state-sanctioned groups or programs—use cyber tools as part of their efforts to further economic, military, and political goals. Chinese and Russian cyber threat actors have previously targeted the U.S. energy sector, including oil and gas companies. In addition, Iran has previously targeted foreign oil and gas companies using cyberattack techniques.
Transnational criminal groups	Transnational criminal groups, including organized crime organizations, seek to use cyberattacks for monetary gain. Further, cyber criminals are increasing the number, scale, and sophistication of ransomware attacks that threaten to cause greater disruptions of critical services.
Hackers and hacktivists	Hackers break into networks for reasons including the challenge, revenge, stalking, or monetary gain. In contrast, hacktivists are ideologically motivated actors who use cyberattack tools to further political goals. For example, according to U.S. Coast Guard officials, the agency considers environmental groups opposed to petroleum development to be a threat actor that could potentially target offshore oil and gas infrastructure.

[14] The supply chain is a linked set of resources and processes that begins with the design of products and services and extends through development, sourcing, manufacturing, handling, and delivery of products and services to the acquirer.

Insiders	Insiders are individuals (such as employees, contractors, or vendors) with authorized access to an information system or enterprise and who have the potential to cause harm, wittingly or unwittingly. This can occur through the destruction, disclosure, or modification of data, or through denial of service. Bureau of Safety and Environmental Enforcement officials indicated that insiders, such as a disgruntled employee, could cause issues on an offshore oil and gas facility.

Source: GAO analysis / GAO-23-106869.

In fiscal year 2022, federal agencies reported 30,659 information security incidents across nine categories,[15] which represents a 5.7 percent decrease from the over 32,500 incidents reported in fiscal year 2021.[16] Examples of successful cyberattacks demonstrate the impact they can have on federal systems and the nation's critical infrastructure:

- In May 2023, Microsoft reported that it uncovered cyberattacks by Volt Typhoon, a state-sponsored actor based in China. According to Microsoft, Volt Typhoon has been active since 2021 and has targeted critical infrastructure in communications, manufacturing, utility, transportation, government, and IT, among other sectors. Microsoft also reported that Volt Typhoon is aiming to develop capabilities that could disrupt communication infrastructure between the United States and Asia during future crises.
- In May 2021, the Colonial Pipeline Company learned that it was a victim of a cyberattack, and malicious actors reportedly deployed ransomware against the pipeline company's business systems. According to a joint advisory released by DHS and the FBI, the company proactively disconnected certain systems that monitor and control physical pipeline functions to ensure the safety of the pipeline. This resulted in a temporary halt to all pipeline operations, which led to gasoline shortages throughout the southeast U.S.

[15] The nine categories of incidents are (1) attrition, (2) email/phishing, (3) external/removable media, (4) impersonation/spoofing, (5) improper usage, (6) loss or theft of equipment, (7) web, (8) other/unknown, and (9) multiple vectors.

[16] Office of Management and Budget, Federal Information Security Modernization Act of 2014, Annual Report Fiscal Year 2022. The number of incidents are from OMB's fiscal year 2022 annual FISMA report to Congress, which is based on incidents reported to the Cybersecurity and Infrastructure Security Agency by federal agencies. OMB notes that drawing conclusions based on this data point would be premature, particularly as agencies have adjusted to several new sets of reporting guidelines over the last few years.

- In December 2020, the cybersecurity firm FireEye discovered that a SolarWinds product known as Orion was compromised and being leveraged by a threat actor for access to its customer systems. Hackers inserted malicious code into Orion—a product widely used in both the federal government and private sector to monitor network activity and manage devices. The threat actor, the Foreign Intelligence Service of the Russian Federation, used Orion to breach several federal agency networks. The initial breach opened a backdoor to agency systems that enabled the threat actor to deliver additional malicious code. This allowed the actor to move laterally, gathering information and compromising data.
- In 2015, Russian threat actors conducted a cyberattack on the Ukrainian power grid that systematically disconnected substations, resulting in a power outage for about 225,000 customers.
- According to the Cybersecurity and Infrastructure Security Agency and the Federal Bureau of Investigation, from December 2011 to 2013, state- sponsored Chinese actors conducted a spearphishing and intrusion campaign targeting U.S. oil and gas pipeline companies. Of the 23 targeted pipeline operators, 13 were confirmed compromises.

Progress Has Been Made, but Interior's Cybersecurity Practices Have Weaknesses

While Interior has made progress in addressing previously reported cybersecurity weaknesses, both the department's Office of Inspector General (OIG) and GAO have continued to identify multiple weaknesses in the department's cybersecurity program and practices. These include issues affecting both Interior's own security environment and its oversight of offshore oil and gas infrastructure.

Interior's Inspector General Identified Weaknesses in Cybersecurity Practices

In January 2023, Interior's OIG issued a report examining the department's password complexity requirements.[17] The OIG found that the department's

[17] Department of the Interior Office of Inspector General, P@$$words at the U.S. Department of the Interior: Easily Cracked Passwords, Lack of Multifactor Authentication, and Other Failures Put Critical DOI Systems at Risk, 2021-ITA-005 (January 2023).

management practices and password complexity requirements were not sufficient to prevent potential unauthorized access to its systems and data. Specifically, the OIG determined that the department (1) had not consistently implemented multifactor authentication, (2) used password complexity requirements that were outdated and ineffective, (3) used password complexity requirements that implicitly allowed unrelated staff to use the same inherently weak passwords, and (4) did not promptly disable inactive (unused) accounts or enforce password age limits. The OIG noted that if a malicious actor were to compromise an account with elevated privileges, such as a system administrator's account, the magnitude of harm would increase. The OIG made eight recommendations to help the department strengthen its IT security by improving user account management practices. The department concurred with the OIG's recommendations.

In April 2023, the OIG released a summary of an independent audit, carried out by a contractor on behalf of OIG, of the department's information security program.[18] The summary indicated that Interior's program was not effective because it was not consistent with applicable FISMA requirements, OMB policy and guidance, or NIST standards and guidelines.[19] The contractor identified needed improvements in the areas of risk management, supply chain risk management, identity and access management, configuration management, data protection and privacy, information security continuous monitoring, incident response, and contingency planning. To address these weaknesses, the contractor made 24 recommendations intended to strengthen the Interior's information security program as well as those of the bureaus and offices. The department concurred with all recommendations and established a target completion date for each corrective action.

GAO Has Reported on Gaps in Interior's Approach to Managing Cybersecurity and Privacy Risks

Cybersecurity risk management: In July 2019, we reviewed the cybersecurity risk management practices at the 23 civilian Chief Financial Officers (CFO)

---

[18] Department of the Interior Office of Inspector General, Summary: Independent Auditors' Performance Audit Report on the U.S. Department of the Interior Federal Information Security Modernization Act for Fiscal Year 2022, 2022-ITA-028 (April 2023).

[19] According to OMB's fiscal year 2022 Core IG Metrics Implementation Analysis and Guidelines, a security program is considered effective if most of the fiscal year 2022 Core Inspector General Metrics are at least Level 4, "Managed and Measurable." Using OMB's guidance and the CyberScope results, the contractor determined that most of the cybersecurity functions were Level 3, "Consistently Implemented."

Act agencies, which includes Interior.[20] We found that the department had not fully addressed three of five key practices for establishing its cybersecurity risk management program. Specifically, the department had not (1) developed a cybersecurity risk management strategy that addressed key elements, (2) fully documented risk- based policies and procedures, or (3) fully established a process or mechanism for coordination between its cybersecurity risk executive and its enterprise risk management governance structure. We recommended that Interior take steps to address these gaps. Since then the department has implemented all three recommendations. Implementing these foundational practices is a critical step in ensuring Interior can make consistent, informed risk-based decisions to protect agency systems and information against cyber-based threats.

IT workforce planning: In October 2019, we reported on the extent to which the 24 CFO Act agencies had implemented key IT workforce planning activities.[21] We found that Interior had partially, minimally, or not implemented the key practices. This included, for example, assessing gaps in competencies and staffing. Accordingly, we recommended that Interior fully address the workforce planning activities. As of May 2023, Interior had taken some steps, but work remained to fully implement these activities. A key to having a successful cybersecurity program is having a well-trained, highly qualified workforce that is versed in identifying cyber threats and recognizes steps to take once confronted with them.

Information and communications technology supply chain risk management: In December 2020, we issued a public version of a sensitive report reviewing the information and communications technology (ICT) supply chain risk management programs and practices at the 23 civilian CFO Act agencies (which includes Interior).[22] None of the 23 agencies, including Interior, fully implemented all of the foundational practices for supply chain risk management. Fourteen of the 23 agencies had not implemented any of the practices. In the sensitive version of the report, we made a total of 145 recommendations to the 23 agencies to fully implement these practices.

---

[20] GAO, Cybersecurity: Agencies Need to Fully Establish Risk Management Programs and Address Challenges, GAO-19-384 (Washington, DC.: July 25, 2019).

[21] GAO, Information Technology: Agencies Need to Fully Implement Key Workforce Planning Activities, GAO-20-129 (Washington, DC.: Oct. 30, 2019).

[22] GAO, *Information Technology: Federal Agencies Need to Take Urgent Action to Manage Supply Chain Risks*, GAO-21-171 (Washington, DC.: Dec. 15, 2020). This is a public version of a sensitive report that GAO issued in October 2020. Information that agencies deemed sensitive was omitted and, due to sensitivity concerns, GAO substituted numeric identifiers that were randomly assigned for the names of the agencies.

Implementing these practices will help organizations protect against supply chain risks, such as the insertion of counterfeits and malicious software, unauthorized production, and tampering, as well as poor manufacturing and development practices throughout the system development life cycle.

Privacy of personal information: In September 2022, we reported on a review of privacy programs at the 24 CFO Act. Agencies.[23] We found that Interior had addressed most of the key practices for establishing a privacy program. However, the department had not fully incorporated privacy into its department-wide risk management strategy, to include a determination of risk tolerance. We recommended that Interior establish a time frame for incorporating privacy into an organization-wide risk management strategy that includes a determination of risk tolerance, and develop and document this strategy. Interior concurred with this recommendation and plans to implement it by November 2023. Such a strategy will help the agency ensure that it is managing risks to sensitive personal information consistently and within acceptable parameters.

Cybersecurity of offshore oil and gas infrastructure: In October 2022, we reported that BSEE had long recognized the need to address cybersecurity risks to offshore oil and gas infrastructure but had taken few actions to do so.[24] In 2015 and 2020 BSEE initiated efforts to address cybersecurity risks, but neither resulted in substantial action. In 2022, BSEE started another such initiative and hired a cybersecurity specialist to lead it. However, bureau officials said the initiative will be paused until the specialist is adequately versed in the relevant issues.

We recommended that BSEE immediately develop and implement a strategy to address offshore infrastructure risks. Such a strategy should include an assessment and mitigation of risks and identify objectives, roles, responsibilities, resources, and performance measures, among other things. Absent the immediate development and implementation of an appropriate strategy, offshore oil and gas infrastructure will remain at significant risk. In March 2023, the department indicated that BSEE is developing a cybersecurity strategy and anticipates that this strategy will be complete by the end of calendar year 2023.

In summary, cyber threats continue to pose a significant threat to systems supporting the federal government and critical infrastructure. Successful

---

[23] GAO, *Privacy: Dedicated Leadership Can Improve Programs and Address Challenges*, GAO-22-105065 (Washington, DC.: Sept. 22, 2022).

[24] GAO, *Offshore Oil and Gas: Strategy Urgently Needed to Address Cybersecurity Risks to Infrastructure*, GAO-23-105789 (Washington, DC.: Oct. 26, 2022).

cyberattacks, including those carried out by nation-state actors, could have catastrophic consequences for the economy, national security, and human safety and well-being. The Department of the Interior needs to continue to take steps to ensure that its systems and data are protected from cyber-based attacks carried out by malicious actors. Moreover, Interior needs to ensure that it is addressing cyber- security risks to critical infrastructure assets for which it has responsibility.

Chairman Gosar, Ranking Member Stansbury, and Members of the Subcommittee, this completes my prepared statement. I would be pleased to respond to any questions that you may have at this time.

*****

GAO Highlights

Highlights of GAO-23-106869, a testimony before the Subcommittee on Oversight and Investigations, Committee on Natural Resources, House of Representatives

Why GAO Did This Study

More than a quarter of a century has passed since GAO first designated information security as a government-wide high-risk area in 1997. Since then, challenges related to ensuring the cybersecurity of the nation have led GAO to expand this high-risk area to include the protection of cyber critical infrastructure and the privacy of personal information.

The Department of the Interior is responsible for safeguarding its information systems and sensitive data by establishing an effective information security program. The department also has regulatory oversight of critical infrastructure supporting offshore oil and gas production, including identifying and helping to address cyber-based risks.

GAO was asked to testify on threats and cybersecurity risks at the Department of the Interior. This statement summarizes types of threat actors and cyberattacks that could compromise federal systems and critical infrastructures, such as those Interior oversees. It also discusses cybersecurity reports and recommendations from GAO and Interior's Office of Inspector General.

This statement is based on prior GAO work at Interior and other federal agencies. GAO also reviewed Interior OIG reports and other public information sources.

What GAO Recommends

In prior reports, GAO has made several recommendations to Interior to improve its cybersecurity practices. Of the six recommendations discussed in this statement, Interior has fully implemented three.

View GAO-23-106869. For more information, contact Marisol Cruz Cain at (202) 512-5017 or cruzcainm@gao.gov.

June 7, 2023

CYBERSECURITY

Interior Needs to Address Threats to Federal Systems and Critical Infrastructure

What GAO Found

Malicious threat actors continue to present risks to federal systems and the nation's critical infrastructure. Such attacks can result in serious harm to human safety, the environment, and the economy. The table below describes common cyber threat actors.

Common Cyber Threat Actors

Threat actor	Description
Nations	Nations—including nation-states, state-sponsored, and state-sanctioned groups or programs—use cyber tools as part of their efforts to further economic, military, and political goals.
Transnational criminal groups	Transnational criminal groups, including organized crime organizations, seek to use cyberattacks for monetary gain.
Hackers and hacktivists	Hackers break into networks for reasons including the challenge, revenge, stalking, or monetary gain. In contrast, hacktivists are ideologically motivated actors who use cyberattack tools to further political goals.
Insiders	Insiders are individuals (such as employees, contractors, or vendors) with authorized access to an information system or enterprise and who have the potential to cause harm, wittingly or unwittingly.

Source: GAO analysis. | GAO-23-106869

Cyberattacks can disrupt or damage critical infrastructure, including facilities and assets supporting offshore oil and gas production. For example, the May 2021 ransomware attack on the Colonial Pipeline Company resulted in a temporary disruption in the delivery of gasoline and other petroleum products.

In October 2022, GAO reported that Interior's Bureau of Safety and Environmental Enforcement had taken few actions to address cybersecurity risks to offshore oil and gas infrastructure. GAO recommended that the bureau immediately develop and implement a strategy to address such risks.

Interior's Office of the Inspector General (OIG) has identified weaknesses in the department's cybersecurity program and practices. For example:

- In January 2023, Interior's OIG found that the department's management practices and password complexity requirements were insufficient to protect active user passwords, including accounts with elevated privileges. The OIG made eight recommendations to help the department strengthen its IT security.
- In April 2023, the OIG released a summary of a contractor's independent audit of the department's information security program. The summary indicated that the program did not fully comply with applicable federal requirements and guidelines.

Likewise, GAO has reported on gaps in Interior's approach to cybersecurity risk management. For instance:

- In September 2022, GAO reported on the 24 Chief Financial Officer Act agencies' implementation of programs to protect the privacy of personal information. GAO found that Interior had not fully incorporated privacy into its organization-wide risk management strategy. GAO recommended that Interior take steps to do so.

United States Government Accountability Office

Ms. Cruz Cain submitted her prepared statement as a GAO report. The statement as a GAO report can be viewed on the Committee Repository at: https://docs.house.gov/meetings/II/II15/20230607/115966/HHRG-118-II15-Wstate-CruzCainM-20230607.pdf.

Questions Submitted for the Record to Ms. Marisol Cruz Cain, Director, Information Technology and Cybersecurity, U.S. Government Accountability Office

Questions Submitted by Representative Gosar

Question 1. Is anything stopping the Department of the Interior from allocating a greater percentage of its existing budget to cybersecurity initiatives?

Answer. The need to conduct risk assessments and budget constraints due to operating and maintaining legacy systems are stopping the Department of the Interior from allocating a greater percentage of its existing budget to cybersecurity initiatives. Key steps for agencies to ensure adequate funding for cybersecurity initiatives are to identify and assess cyber risks, prioritize initiatives for addressing those risks, and allocate the necessary funds as appropriate. For example, as we reported, the Department of the Interior's Bureau of Safety and Environmental Enforcement (BSEE) had committed minimal resources and demonstrated a lack of urgency in addressing cybersecurity risks to offshore oil and gas production infrastructures.[25] Accordingly, it is critical that BSEE move expeditiously to develop and implement a strategy to guide its most recent cybersecurity initiative. This strategy should include (1) a risk assessment; (2) objectives, activities, and performance measures; (3) roles, responsibilities, and coordination; and (4) identification of needed resources and investments. In March 2023, Interior indicated that BSEE is developing a cybersecurity strategy that includes identifying resource needs, which may be complete by the end of calendar year 2023. By developing such a strategy, Interior will be better positioned to identify and prioritize the funds it needs to support critical cybersecurity initiatives. These priorities can then be reflected in future budget requests. Similarly, we recently recommended that Interior incorporate privacy into its organization-wide risk management strategy.[26] This is a key step for the department to identify, assess, and prioritize risks to the sensitive personal information with which it is entrusted.

---

[25] GAO, Offshore Oil and Gas: Strategy Urgently Needed to Address Cybersecurity Risks to Infrastructure, GAO-23-105789 (Washington, D.C.: Oct. 26, 2022).

[26] GAO, Privacy: Dedicated Leadership Can Improve Programs and Address Challenges, GAO-22-105065 (Washington, D.C.: Sept. 22, 2022).

As we have noted, however, agencies such as Interior are sometimes constrained in making new investments by the large portion of their IT budgets that are allocated to the operations and maintenance of legacy systems. For example, in fiscal year 2023, Interior's budget allocates approximately $297 million to the development, modernization, and enhancement of its IT systems while allocating nearly $1.5 billion to the operation and maintenance of existing systems. As we have previously reported, legacy systems can be costly and difficult to maintain, may have unsupported hardware and software, and may operate with known security vulnerabilities.[27] Such security vulnerabilities may be either technically difficult or prohibitively expensive to address.

Question 2. How can DOI better prioritize cybersecurity initiatives with its existing budget?

Answer. Interior can better prioritize its cybersecurity initiatives within its existing budget by continuing to utilize its cybersecurity risk management strategy and ensuring that it is fully implementing risk-based policies. Federal guidance, such as the National Institute of Standards and Technology Special Publication 800- 39, identifies practices for establishing effective agency-wide cybersecurity risk management programs. Specifically, the practices include aligning agency priorities with resource allocation and prioritization at all levels of the organization, including the enterprise, business, and system levels.

We reported in July 2019 that managing competing priorities between operations and cybersecurity presents a challenge for many agencies.[28] In particular, agencies highlighted the competition for limited resources between cybersecurity risk management activities and operational or mission needs. For example, Interior's Deputy Chief Information Officer noted that the need to balance mission priorities with those related to cybersecurity risk management leads to fiscal and operational challenges when making investment, architectural, and operational decisions. To its credit, as we recommended in our July 2019 report, Interior developed an organization-wide cybersecurity risk management strategy to define how the department intends to identify, assess, and respond to risks. It also updated its policies to require an organization-wide cybersecurity risk assessment and established a process for coordination between its cybersecurity and enterprise

---

[27] GAO, Information Technology: Agencies Need to Continue Addressing Critical Legacy Systems, GAO-23-106821 (Washington, D.C.: May 10, 2023).

[28] GAO, Cybersecurity: Agencies Need to Fully Establish Risk Management Programs and Address Challenges, GAO-19-384 (Washington, D.C.: July 25, 2019).

risk management functions. By establishing and implementing these risk-based policies and procedures, Interior should be better positioned to prioritize cybersecurity initiatives within its existing budget as well as to identify areas for future investment.

Questions Submitted by Representative Grijalva

Question 1. If threat actors were to obtain personally identifiable information during a breach of the Department of the Interior's (DOI) systems, how would federal employees and members of the public be impacted? How would infrastructure under the DOI, such as oil and gas infrastructure, drinking water sources, and power grid maintenance, be impacted?

Answer. A successful attack on Interior's systems involving personally identifiable information (PII) could significantly impact both federal employees and members of the public, leaving them more susceptible to identity theft, fraud, and other crimes. The advent of new technologies and the proliferation of PII has increased the government's reliance on IT to collect, store, and transmit this sensitive information. Consequently, vulnerabilities arising from agencies' increased dependence on IT can result in the compromise of personal information, such as inappropriate use, modification, or disclosure. Recently reported breaches involving PII show that PII such as names, addresses, dates of birth, and Social Security numbers can be compromised when attackers exploit vulnerabilities in IT systems.

With respect to critical infrastructure, we previously reported that cyberattacks against critical infrastructure (e.g., electric grid, water and wastewater systems, etc.) were increasing in frequency, sophistication, and scale.[29] Because of their complexity and interconnections with other systems, these systems are vulnerable to cyberattacks. Such attacks could result in serious harm to human safety, the environment, and the economy.[30] Successful cyberattacks on systems supporting critical infrastructure can compromise sensitive information, such as businesses' proprietary information or individuals' financial or medical information.

---

[29] GAO, Critical Infrastructure Protection: CISA Should Improve Priority Setting, Stakeholder Involvement, and Threat Information Sharing, GAO-22-104279 (Washington, D.C.: Mar. 1, 2022).

[30] GAO, Cybersecurity: Interior Needs to Address Threats to Federal Systems and Critical Infrastructure, GAO-23-106869 (Washington, DC.: June 7, 2023).

Moreover, operational technology (OT) systems, which are used to monitor and control physical equipment, were once largely isolated from internet and business IT systems but are now frequently connected with those systems both within a company and accessible by internet systems globally. As a result, cyberattacks are now more likely to originate in business IT systems and migrate to OT. According to Interior's Bureau of Safety and Environmental Enforcement, results of a successful cyberattack on offshore oil and gas infrastructure could include deaths and injuries, damaged or destroyed equipment, and pollution to the marine environment.

Dr. GOSAR. I thank Ms. Cruz for her testimony. We will now go to Members for their 5 minutes. I first recognize the gentleman from Arkansas, the Chairman of the Full Committee, Mr. Westerman.

Mr. WESTERMAN. Thank you, Chairman Gosar. And, again, thank you to the witnesses.

Inspector General Greenblatt, a lot of interesting stuff in your testimony. The Password Complexity Report discusses how passphrases that you mentioned may be more effective than passwords, and how a "negative feedback loop" has developed for password requirements. Can you explain what passphrases are in a little more detail, what you mean by a negative feedback loop for passwords, how passphrases are a better solution, you alluded to that, but also how AI can be used to crack passwords, and even maybe passphrases?

Mr. GREENBLATT. Passphrases, in short, are just a string of unrelated words. The example that we used in our report is "dinosaur letter trail chants." It takes a computer 550 years to figure that out, as opposed to a password, which might appear to be more complicated. It actually is easier for the computer to crack that. For example, that can take a computer 3 days, as opposed as opposed to 550 years to crack a passphrase.

So, the key is, as hackers have been getting better about hacking into passwords, we have increased the complexity requirements on the passwords, which means as humans, we have to adopt mechanisms to make them easier to remember. Making them easier to remember makes them easier to crack. So, that is this negative feedback loop that, as the complexity requirements have increased, the quality of the passwords has decreased.

That is why the movement throughout government, and this is set by the NIST, the National Institute of Standards and Technology, which is the standard-setting body for the U.S. Government with respect to these issues, has said we should go to passphrases. Again, that is a string of unrelated words which is almost impossible for a computer to crack in a reasonable amount of time.

Mr. WESTERMAN. So, will AI help aid in cracking even those passphrases in a shorter amount of time, my understanding with AI is it can profile you and learn, if you will. Will it somehow be able to know that you picked dinosaur whatever it was?

[Laughter.]

Mr. GREENBLATT. Yes, right. I am sure it is going to get better. The technology is going to get better and better, so we will have to stay in front of it. The key is the length of the passphrase. The longer it is, the more difficult it is for a computer to figure it out.

Mr. WESTERMAN. And then doing the multi-factor authorization on top of a passphrase sounds like the direction we need to head.

Mr. GREENBLATT. That is exactly right. Here is the mnemonic that I use to remember this, because I am a layman, I am not a cybersecurity expert. But the way I remember it is password is bad; passphrase is better; MFA best. That boils down my entire testimony in seven words.

Mr. WESTERMAN. That is pretty easy. Thank you.

Ms. Cain, your testimony declared that DOI had not fully implemented key information technology workforce planning recommendations that were originally made in 2019. What were those recommendations? What are the recommendations DOI has failed to implement, and why have they still failed to implement them 5 years later?

And maybe a follow-up to that is, with this hearing, with your reports, hopefully they have gone in and changed the passwords, the ones that you cracked in 90 minutes, 16 percent of them. Are you seeing any improvements at DOI, or do we know?

Ms. CRUZ CAIN. Much to its credit, we can say today that we have received information from Interior, and we are going to close each one of those workforce recommendations that we had.

Some of the workforce recommendations were looking at their skilled workers and filling up gaps in different types of technical workers that they needed, and they have, to this date, given us documentation to prove that they have closed all of their workforce recommendations.

So, we are very happy about that. Yes, it did take 5 years, but much to Interior's credit, they have been continually working on it, and have gotten to a good place with our recommendations specific to the workforce.

We have not done any password work at Interior, or really haven't looked into Interior's systems. We would be more than happy, if there is a specific

Interior system you would like for us to look at, but we do not have any recent work that has looked into a specific Interior system.

Mr. WESTERMAN. Thank you.

And just real quickly, Inspector General, when did you do the hacks? When did you crack these? How long ago was that?

Mr. GREENBLATT. It was at least a year ago, because we gave the Department a chance to fix much of this. So, it had to be at least a year ago.

Mr. WESTERMAN. OK, thank you. Thank you, Chairman. I yield back.

Dr. GOSAR. I thank the gentleman. The gentleman from Hawaii, Mr. Case, is recognized.

Mr. CASE. Thank you, Mr. Chair.

Mr. Greenblatt, you testified that DOI, I think your words were, generally concurred in your recommendations, or the OIG's recommendations, and established target dates. Are you satisfied with their target dates, are they reasonable?

What kind of time frames are we talking about?

And what are the obstacles to expeditious implementation?

Mr. GREENBLATT. Yes. Generally speaking, they have been very constructive. The relationship we have had has been very productive with them. I have had a number of engagements with the Chief Information Officer there. They, and the Deputy Secretary, frankly, appear to be oriented in the right direction.

In terms of the target dates, they do seem reasonable to us. We would have said so in the report if we did not find them reasonable. We have done that in other contexts. In this context, we found them to be reasonable. In fact, one of the recommendations, they have already submitted the packet of materials to close one of our recommendations, and we are just going through the process of looking at that right now.

I also understand that they have taken some steps already to implement measures with respect to the passwords and shifting over to passphrases. So, that was a very constructive result.

In terms of the problems with respect to timing, this would appear likely on the multi-factor authentication piece, where there are some systems that are so old that they can't handle MFA. So, that is my understanding from the Chief Information Officer.

But this is information you would have to get from them. They know this better than we do, but that is my understanding, is that it is something like that, where they are technologically having difficulty actually handling it on the infrastructure that they have right now.

Mr. CASE. So, is it your understanding, from your perspective, that the target date implementations, are any of them reliant on supplemental funding, or insufficient personnel, or inability or unavailability of technical resources?

I guess what I am asking is, what are the obstacles to getting them done fast, and can we do anything about any of those obstacles?

Mr. GREENBLATT. Well, I think one undercurrent for everything with respect to IT and cybersecurity is finding qualified staff. It is very difficult in the public sector to hire the types of folks with the types of experience that you need in the IT security space, so that is underlying sort of all of this.

With respect to these specific recommendations, I don't know the answer to that, whether there are technological hiccups or supplemental funding. We can get back to you on that. I think that is a fair question that I just don't know, off the top of my head.

Mr. CASE. OK, thank you. I guess I have heard it said or described, or at least my understanding of cybersecurity cyber attacks is they kind of fall into a couple of different categories. One would be state-sponsored for state goals, as we apparently or may well have seen just recently with respect to Guam. Another is issue-oriented to influence a particular issue. Another would be extortion disruption, so money. And then the fourth category would just be to see whether you can get away with it.

Talking about DOI specifically for now, I guess my real question is what is the direct subject of a cyber attack to DOI?

What is the real exposure at DOI?

Ms. Cruz Cain made reference three or four times to offshore oil, so I assume that it is our management of our natural resources themselves, and the implications to our economy and our defense. But where does a cyber attacker tend to engage with DOI?

Mr. GREENBLATT. Again, I think you would have to go to the Department with respect to specific attacks and where they came from. But I think what is fair to say is that DOI houses significant information, be it proprietary information related to oil and gas sales and from the energy leasing, offshore security, offshore oil and gas extraction and security issues as we were saying a second ago.

But you know we have hydroelectric dams that power hydroelectric power plants that feed into the electrical grid. So, I don't know how an attack could compromise, say, an electrical grid or something along those lines. These folks are very, very creative, and very malicious. It is sort of impossible to know at this point. But I think the full scope of the damage is fairly daunting if we were to see an attack unfold.

Mr. CASE. Thank you very much.

Dr. GOSAR. I thank the gentleman. The gentleman from Georgia, Mr. Collins, is recognized for 5 minutes.

Mr. COLLINS. Thank you, Mr. Chairman. I had some other questions, but as you all were speaking, Inspector General, you led me to a whole bunch of other questions.

Being in the private sector, in the trucking industry, I mean, this is something we deal with daily because of the nature of what we are in, and the possibility of getting hacked, mostly from the monetary side of it. So, I have a few I was just going to run by you. If it doesn't apply to you and maybe Ms. Cruz Cain, if you can answer it, then just feel free to jump in there.

You did the study in 2022, and you said you had a reasonable timeline for them to implement this, correct? What was that timeline?

Mr. GREENBLATT. We can get you the dates in particular.

Mr. COLLINS. Was it 6 months, or 2 months, or——

Mr. GREENBLATT. It is probably more than 6 months for us to write the report. We share our findings with the Department, especially in something like this, where we want them to take steps to cure the problems before we were going public. So, it is a good amount of time. It may be a full year.

Mr. COLLINS. OK. So, the problems, though, that you are speaking about are maybe software-related, the reason they can't use multi-factor authentication?

Mr. GREENBLATT. Sometimes, certainly, like——

Mr. COLLINS. Are they just running old systems?

Mr. GREENBLATT. It could be, yes. And that is what I have heard.

That is my understanding, yes.

Mr. COLLINS. OK.

Mr. GREENBLATT. On some of the systems.

Mr. COLLINS. When you do multi-factor authentication that you put in there—we all use phrases now, instead of just passwords, it is easier to remember it, too. Is there a length that you put in there for the password, the passphrase, and then capital letters, numbers, and symbols, as well?

Mr. GREENBLATT. You don't have to do that. That is the beauty of the passphrase, is that it is designed to be easy to remember. So, it can just be words.

What I have seen is between 16 and 64 characters long. That is what I have seen, just generally speaking, out in the world. But the longer you go, the more and more difficult it becomes for a hacker to crack it.

Mr. COLLINS. Yes, I just know that the nature of people, if you say, "Give me three words," it is going to be "at," "the," and "I," you know.

[Laughter.]

Mr. GREENBLATT. Fair enough. But I think what you can do is you can limit the nature of what is a permissible passphrase.

Mr. COLLINS. Yes, that is what I am saying——

Mr. GREENBLATT. You can limit that sort of thing. Again, it is really length, not the quality of the words.

Mr. COLLINS. So, when you recommended that they implement, and you said it was high-quality assets first, is this now agencywide?

Mr. GREENBLATT. The passphrases, yes. My understanding is, again, this is a question that they can give you a better answer. But, yes, my understanding is that they have implemented on the passphrases, getting away from the passwords.

On multi-factor authentication, that is a longer fuse, because they have some of those legacy systems that are very, very old that apparently can't handle multi-factor authentication.

The other thing, by the way, when you were just asking a second ago about the software, they had a number of systems that could handle multi-factor authentication. But they were allowing people to solely use passwords. So, what we are saying is turn that bypass off.

Mr. COLLINS. Yes, are you all doing, for lack of better words, follow-up hacks? I mean, my IT group does it on a monthly basis.

Mr. GREENBLATT. We are doing a number of penetration testing.

We have a number of jobs in the works, and that is what the team does on a day-to-day basis.

But on this issue we now have turned it over to the Department and, hopefully, they will be doing that on their own.

Mr. COLLINS. Is that something, Ms. Cruz Cain, that you would answer?

Ms. CRUZ CAIN. We don't have any work planned at Interior. We really respond as requests from Committees or Members. So, if that is something that you would like us to do, we would be more than happy to take on another password job, or look at multi-factor authentication at Interior.

Mr. COLLINS. I know this may be off subject, but you all don't do phishing expeditions with e-mails to see if people bite, I mean, that is another way that people hack in pretty easy.

Mr. GREENBLATT. The Department should be doing that on their own. Any agency should be doing penetration testing on their own. We could conceivably do that sort of thing, but we take a risk- based analysis on where we can add the most value. But the Department, in theory, should be doing that as part of its regular, day-to-day maintenance, if you will.

Mr. COLLINS. So, you set up the parameters, right, for any agency, you set that up. Do you have password expiration dates, where they have to change the passwords? Do you recommend that?

Mr. GREENBLATT. We did. But if you have passphrases, you don't—

Mr. COLLINS. I know, passphrase.

Mr. GREENBLATT. Yes, you don't need to. For passphrases, they are so robust that you actually don't need to change them. That is part of the problem with the passwords, is that you need to change them every 60 to 90 days, and people need to make them easy to remember. But that makes it easier to hack. With the passphrases, if they are long enough, you don't need to change it.

Mr. COLLINS. My time is expired, but I will tell you that in my world we always say those are famous last words.

Mr. GREENBLATT. There is no question that the hackers and their technology will evolve. There is no question about that. I am not saying that this is the forever answer, but right here, right now, this is the best technology that we can do. And they are going to have to do something pretty robust to figure it out.

Mr. COLLINS. Right.

Sorry, Mr. Chairman.

Dr. GOSAR. Just as long as it is not "Run, Spot, run," right? [Laughter.]

Dr. GOSAR. The gentlewoman from Nevada, Ms. Lee, is recognized.

Ms. LEE. Thank you, Mr. Chairman, and thank you, Ranking Member Stansbury. Before I get into my question for Ms. Cruz Cain I just wanted to ask Mr. Greenblatt.

The software that DOI is using, sometimes when I am using software there are limitations on the length. So, you are saying the software that DOI now uses does not have that limitation, or do we need to invest in new software?

Mr. GREENBLATT. Those are great questions for the agency. They have dozens of different systems at play.

Ms. LEE. Oh, OK.

Mr. GREENBLATT. So, I don't know each and every one of theirs and what their length requirements are, but that is something that I would think they can change, they can modify. But my understanding is that they have moved to passphrases of an appreciable length, like I said, 16 characters or something along those lines. But that is a good question for them to flesh out.

Ms. LEE. Ms. Cruz Cain, in your opinion, does DOI have the sufficient resources to address these threats and make the needed changes?

Ms. CRUZ CAIN. We have made the observation that they are challenged by their IT budget. Most of their IT budget, about 83 percent of it, goes toward just operating and maintaining its IT systems. And that includes a lot of the aging and legacy systems that we have been mentioning, which do not allow newer technologies to be used, such as multi-factor authentication. And it really hinders the ability to deal with the new cyber risks. You are constantly going back to outdated software, outdated hardware, and these legacy systems.

So, that is one challenge that we have noted at GAO, that they are spending about 83 percent of their budget just maintaining. And we really are asking them to shift their focus of their budget to development, modernization of those legacy systems, and making enhancements that would better position Interior to modernize those legacy systems, and then address the associated vulnerabilities with those systems, and be able to engage with the new cybersecurity technologies like multi-factor authentication.

Ms. LEE. Do you have any dollar estimate on what is necessary, or is that something I need to get from DOI?

Ms. CRUZ CAIN. No, that is definitely something you need to get from the DOI.

Ms. LEE. All right. I am also deeply concerned, being from the West, on a potential cyber attack on critical DOI water infrastructure. As you know, 40 million people rely on the Colorado River and its reservoirs, which have long been under DOI care, including Lake Mead, which is the main water source for my hometown and home state of Nevada.

With this in mind, how do you think infrastructure under the DOI, whether it is water resources, power grid maintenance, or oil and gas would be impacted by a hack?

Mr. GREENBLATT. I think it would depend on the hack and what they did. But it could be devastating. Like I said, it just depends on where, and how, and what they do with it. If they are just stealing information versus doing something actively malicious, it is impossible to know.

But also, they could be using the pathway into the Department to then try to get up to higher-level access to other departments that DOI may be connected to. So, that is the kind of thing, they may be a pass-through if they are connected to other networks. It is very difficult to say, but it could be devastating.

Ms. LEE. Can you expand on the measures that DOI is taking right now to ensure that we prevent such a hack?

Are you comfortable that they are taking the measures, or is this a resource issue that we need to give them more funding so they can modernize?

What is the, I guess, the chicken-and-the-egg type of thing? What are the priorities?

Mr. GREENBLATT. So, there are a couple of answers to that.

First of all, with respect to implementing the passphrase requirements, that looks like that has happened, I think that is 100 percent. I remember speaking with the Chief Information Officer, and I believe he said that was 100 percent at this point. So, on the passphrases, that is a good thing.

With MFA, that is going to take a little bit longer. But I believe they are oriented in the right direction with respect to MFA, it is just going to take a little heavier lifting for them.

In terms of their specific timing on all the various systems, you will have to get a breakdown from them in terms of the individual ones.

The thing that was most troubling to me was the MFA, the multi-factor authentication, with respect to the high-value IT assets. The ability to bypass multi-factor authentication on those systems was troubling. So, I believe they have a constructive posture with respect to those systems, I just don't know where they actually sit with respect to all of those that had permitted the bypass or the password alone.

Ms. LEE. Great, thank you. I am over my time.

Dr. GOSAR. I thank the gentlelady from Nevada. I recognize the Ranking Member from New Mexico, Ms. Stansbury, for her 5 minutes.

Ms. STANSBURY. Thank you, Mr. Chairman, and thanks again to our witnesses for being here today. I wonder if we could start with Ms. Cruz Cain.

What exactly did these attacks look like? I think we all think we know what a cyber attack looks like, but what does the experience of a hacker and an attack actually look like?

Ms. CRUZ CAIN. I think it depends on what kind of attack is being executed. My colleague gave the examples of different attacks. If you are looking on attacks to operational technology, and when we did our report on the oil and gas infrastructure, an attack on that operational technology, which is the software and the hardware that are used to control the industrial equipment, that is going to look very different depending on who hacks. So, you can put malicious code into some of the software and hardware, and that might take a little bit longer to detect.

It could be a ransomware attack. Somebody could completely shut down that operational technology, which makes it unable to use the production, which would slow down oil and gas. It could prevent water flow. It could do a lot of harm to the economy, to our well-being.

I think it just all depends on what type of attack you are trying to perpetrate.

Ms. STANSBURY. Yes, and I think, like I said, oftentimes we think we are all talking about the same things, but there are a multitude of different kinds of actors and different kinds of attacks that we are talking about here. So, the implications of whether or not it is the password infrastructure of the individuals who are holding files, who have access to shared systems, who are operating systems that may be related to energy infrastructure or water infrastructure, or it is just the personal identifying information of Federal employees, all of these things are vulnerabilities to these kinds of hacks and these actors.

And as we were preparing for this hearing, I was actually sharing with some of the staff that I am a former Fed myself. I used to work for a Federal agency, and we actually experienced a hack while I was working for a Federal agency by a foreign actor. And I can tell you they were inside our system, we studied them, we shut them down, and we made sure it never happened again. But these hacks can have very significant implications for agencies, so we take them very, very seriously.

And Ms. Cruz Cain, we were interested in particular in the report that you helped to co-author on privacy, dedicated leadership report. And one of the recommendations in that report suggested that our agencies institute privacy leadership in each of the agencies. Could you tell us a little bit more about what that means, what it would look like, and how Congress could help to support an initiative like that?

Ms. CRUZ CAIN. Sure. What we found when we were looking at the 24 CFO Act agencies was that outside of the ones who were mandated by law to have a chief privacy officer that serves at the executive level alongside the CIO, the CFO, and other high-level executives, most of the agencies differed. Some of the chief privacy officers could have been their CIO. They could have been just a person who was in charge of privacy.

So, we also noticed that their responsibilities differed. Some of them solely focused on privacy, which was very few, but others had different responsibilities, some were doing records management, as well; some were doing financial management; some were doing information technology.

And with the increasing nature of these cyber attacks, GAO and all of the agencies that we talked to really think that having someone, some executive-level senior official focused just on privacy as their only responsibility will really elevate privacy to where it needs to be in all of the agencies. Not only do you have the personal information of your employees, you also have proprietary information in many agencies, different types of information that, if leaked, could be very harmful for the Federal agencies.

And in our report, the matter to Congress was to just go into law and say there should be a senior official at that executive level that can have visibility into privacy, and bring that to the table when you are making the high-level decisions.

Ms. STANSBURY. So, really standardizing that leadership within each of the agencies. And I think that brings me to my final question for this panel, which is for Mr. Greenblatt.

We had the opportunity to chat briefly before the hearing, and one of my questions, which you touched on, but I want to just ask you to expand on a little bit more, is about DOI's leadership in addressing not only the password considerations, but also these other cyber risks that have been talked about today in this hearing. Talk to us about what Interior has been doing to address these vulnerabilities, and what we in Congress can do to help support the Department of the Interior and other agencies on their journeys in securing their cyber programs.

Mr. GREENBLATT. Yes, like I said, we have had a very constructive engagement with them. They concurred with all the recommendations with respect to this report, and they have already implemented some of them. We have to close those recommendations. They give us the information for us to close them. They have done that with one of the recommendations that we have to then sort of go through and make sure that it is done. The other ones are pending.

But, so far, the posture has been very constructive. I engaged with the Deputy Secretary and with the CIO on these topics, and I know that they at least have represented to me that they are taking it very seriously, and I have no reason to challenge that.

Ms. STANSBURY. Thank you. And I know we are out of time, but certainly we will be looking to both the OIG, as well as GAO for recommendations for how we can address this at the structural level, whether that is funding, as my colleague brought up, or through statutory and leadership needs within the agency. So, thank you.

Dr. GOSAR. I thank the gentlelady. I am going to start with you, Inspector General.

Are there any problems for the Department of the Interior to access high-end technology?

Mr. GREENBLATT. No, I think they could, subject to FedRAMP authorization and that sort of thing. But no, I don't think there are any barriers that are unique to DOI, as opposed to other Federal agencies.

Dr. GOSAR. So, on these passwords, are there random checks on employees?

Mr. GREENBLATT. I do not know the answer to that question, actually.

Dr. GOSAR. Would that be something of value?

Mr. GREENBLATT. It could be, sure.

Dr. GOSAR. I mean, I get lazy, and all of us get that notice that you have to change your password. So, I mean, from that standpoint it would be nice to know that they are implemented. I think that it sounds like that is one area we can really close.

Mr. GREENBLATT. Certainly, they have certain parameters on what you can do. It has to be a certain length and there may be some prohibited terms, I don't know. But that is the kind of thing that I think in order to set it up, it has to meet those parameters. I don't know if they do checks following the setup.

Dr. GOSAR. OK. Ms. Cruz Cain, the GAO has been sounding the alarm over the cybersecurity vulnerabilities at BSEE since 2015. Finally, in 2022, BSEE hired a cybersecurity specialist to address vulnerabilities to offshore infrastructure. But Bureau officials said the initiative would be paused until the specialist is adequately versed in the relevant issues. Do you have any update on this?

Ms. CRUZ CAIN. The one update that Interior gave us was that they are, in fact, developing their cybersecurity strategy that encompasses all the elements that we recommended, and they anticipate the strategy being done at the end of this calendar year.

Dr. GOSAR. And then you will follow up with that?

Ms. CRUZ CAIN. Absolutely. We do normal follow-up for all recommendations.

Dr. GOSAR. OK. Now, from your vantage point at GAO, is there a prioritization process that you see that should be followed in addressing these cybersecurities?

Ms. CRUZ CAIN. Well, definitely, the strategy is the key. You have to have a strategy. You have to identify your cyber risks. And each sector and each agency is going to have different priorities and different cyber risks.

So, you have Interior's internal systems that will probably have different risks to them. And then, with BSEE, they have the offshore oil and gas infrastructure. So, our report focused on that, and wanted them to just have a strategy. How are you going to identify your risks? How are you going to assess those risks? What are your objectives? What are your activities and performance measures that you are going to measure up to when you are putting your cybersecurity strategy into place? Roles and responsibilities are important, and also coordination with CISA and any other entities that they need to talk to in order to make their strategy successful. But then lastly, as we have mentioned, the needed resources. What resources are they going to need after they have identified all their risks and made the strategy to actually be able to take the actions that the strategy wants them to take?

Dr. GOSAR. I have gone over to see some of these centers, particularly like East Mesa, where we see the active bombardment. It is pretty amazing to see those attacks coming in, and how they are fronting them. Is Interior big enough to have to be doing that type of qualification?

Ms. CRUZ CAIN. I don't have the answer to that question, but I think all Federal agencies have skills that they need. I know that they have recently hired their cybersecurity specialist to take on, specifically, the oil and gas cybersecurity role so they can start there. And in that strategy and any workforce planning that they do for BSEE specific to oil and gas, they should do their skills need. What do they need to make those strategies successful? Where are they going to get them?

As my colleague mentioned and GAO has mentioned, it is an outstanding challenge in the Federal Government to have a qualified IT workforce. So, there are going to be lots of things that go into this strategy and making it successful. But we don't have any indication that Interior cannot handle it.

Dr. GOSAR. OK.

Inspector General, how does the DOI coordinate with CISA?

Mr. GREENBLATT. That is a very good question. Frankly, I don't know the answer to that. I would have to defer to the agency in that regard.

Dr. GOSAR. Sounds good. Do you have any answer to that, Ms. Cruz Cain?

Ms. CRUZ CAIN. I can tell you from the perspective that their regulatory oversight of the oil and gas, they would coordinate with CISA, being that that is a subsector of the energy sector, and CISA being the—they are not the SRMA for the energy sector, but they would have significant coordination with CISA when it comes to attacks or threat information when it comes to oil and gas infrastructure.

Dr. GOSAR. I am going to end by asking each one of you, what was the question you most wanted to have asked that we feel is very important, and what was its answer?

I will start with you, Inspector General.

Mr. GREENBLATT. I guess I am particularly proud of the team, so how they accomplished the password cracking, I think, is pretty fascinating. If you will just bear with me for a moment, and I can explain it, because it was fascinating to this layman.

But, basically, we took the 85,000 passwords from the Department, which are then made into what is called hash, which is 30 characters to prevent. It is a security mechanism designed to protect those passwords. So, we took the hashes of the 85,000 passwords in the Department, and then the team built a dictionary of 1.5 billion words. This is multiple different languages, government terminology, pop culture references, and passwords that had been hacked in prior hacks that were posted online, put that all together and then did permutations of those, 31 million permutations of each one of the 1.5 billion words, which led to 46 quadrillion potential passwords.

Then they compared those two things. They compared the hashes to the hashes of the 46 quadrillion potential passwords, and compared them. That, in the first 90 minutes, led to 16,000 hits. Those are the easy ones. Those are the password1234's of the world. And then it took a little bit longer for them to get through and get those few thousand remaining ones.

So, that is something that I am particularly proud of the team, in how they conceived of this, and how they pulled it off for less than $15,000.

Dr. GOSAR. Wow, that tells me that there is still hope for me as a Pictionary player.

[Laughter.]

Dr. GOSAR. So, Ms. Cruz Cain, your question?

Ms. CRUZ CAIN. Sure. I think pointing out one of the most critical actions that the Federal Government needs to take to better protect our critical infrastructure, I wanted to make a plug for updating our national infrastructure protection plan. The most recent update has been 2003. We have been in discussions with DHS, and they mentioned that it might be until September 2025 that this plan would be fully updated.

So, it is, in GAO's opinion, very important that we have a timely update to this plan. That is going to allow each of the 16 sectors to update their sector plans, and then those subsectors like oil and gas and energy to update their specific subsector plans to address cyber risks.

So, from the top down, the most important action we can take is updating that plan, and also filling the vacant cybersecurity director role. The coordination amongst all Federal agencies can really benefit from getting a permanent cyber director, and being able to have the leadership from that office be how each Federal agency approaches their cybersecurity posture.

Dr. GOSAR. That really helps breaking down the silos, as well.

I want to thank the panel for your testimony today, and there will be some written questions for you from Members.

Thank you very much, and we will seat the second panel.

Mr. GREENBLATT. Thank you.

Ms. CRUZ CAIN. Thank you. [Pause.]

Mr. COLLINS [presiding]. All right, we will get started with the second panel. As you can tell, I am not Mr. Gosar, and I am a freshman. So, I am in the trucking business, this is not what I do for a living. But we are going to go ahead and get started.

I will introduce our second panel of witnesses. And if I mess up your name, I am totally sorry.

We have Mr. Brian Cavanaugh with the Heritage Foundation; Mr. Dean Cheng with the United States Institute of Peace; Ms. Rhea Siers with the Johns Hopkins University; and Dr. Charles Clancy, Sr. with the MITRE Corporation.

Let me remind the witnesses that under Committee Rules, they must limit their oral statements to 5 minutes, but their entire statement will appear in the hearing record.

To begin your testimony, press the "on" button for the microphone.

We use timing lights. When you begin, the light will turn green. At the end of the 5 minutes, your light will turn red, and I will ask you to please complete your statement.

I will also allow all witnesses in this panel to testify before Member questioning.

The Chair now recognizes Mr. Cavanaugh for 5 minutes.

Statement of Brian Cavanaugh, Fellow for Cybersecurity, Intelligence, and Homeland Security, Heritage Foundation, Washington, DC

Mr. CAVANAUGH. Chairman Collins, Ranking Member Stansbury, and members of the Committee, as the government increasingly relies on interconnected systems, cloud computing, and data-driven decision-making, the very fabric of our national security, economic stability, and public trust hangs in the balance.

Cybersecurity is no longer a mere accessory or an afterthought. It is the cornerstone on which the functioning of our government rests. The landscape of cyber threats is ever-evolving, with the cyber threat posed by China to U.S. infrastructure significant and complex.

First, China has demonstrated a high level of sophistication in cyber capabilities, including cyber espionage.

Secondly, China's large-scale and persistent cyber campaigns target every sector of our critical infrastructure, including communications, manufacturing, utility, maritime government, and information technology. Volt Typhoon, a PRC-sponsored hacking group, has been specifically targeting sectors that support Pacific operations for the past 2 years.

Finally, China's ability to leverage vast resources, both in terms of human capital and technology such as AI, quantum computing, and essential chip manufacturing, enhanced their cyber capabilities. The scope and efforts and the nature of their capabilities underscore the potential for significant economic and national security consequences, especially as the United States and China lurch toward an impending conflict.

Meanwhile, Russia, Iran, and North Korea have all focused on improving their ability to target critical infrastructure, including underwater cables, water treatment facilities, and operational control technologies, such as those used by offshore energy platforms. Our adversaries believe that demonstrating the ability to compromise such infrastructure can achieve the goal of influencing foreign policy outcomes.

Meanwhile, the U.S. Government approach to cybersecurity has seen its share of challenges, from a lack of prioritization and chasing trends to its inefficient approach to the private sector and lack of accountability for government employees. To overcome these challenges, it is crucial for the government to recognize and prioritize risk as a fundamental component of its cybersecurity strategy. By prioritizing risk, the government can allocate resources effectively, adopt a proactive approach, and ensure accountability in its cybersecurity efforts.

Technology is rapidly developing and evolving. However, this does not mean that the government can erratically chase after the shiny object. Instead, the U.S. Government should find ways to close the detection gap. A recent IBM report highlights the average time to identify and contain a data breach is 287 days, with malware residing on systems for over 180 days.

More policies and more people are themselves not a solution. The model the government has embraced is flat-footed and clumsy. It is an approach that keeps them in a constant state of response and recovery, awaiting alerts from the private sector and then managing damage control messaging afterward. We must become forward-leaning and take meaningful steps towards addressing the risk and mitigating cyber threats to our critical infrastructure. This includes engaging with small businesses that are driving innovation.

Government procurement practices must evolve and foster innovation, especially in the tech sector. Identifying and authenticating users is a fundamental security control, yet, as we just heard, a recent DOI Inspector General report highlighted lackadaisical policies and procedures that enabled the cracking of 21 percent of active user passwords. The report demonstrated that the front door to the Department had been left open by its employees.

From a repercussion perspective, we all have a role to play in vigilance. And just like how resilience starts with the individual, so too does the responsibility of cybersecurity. The government needs to take a firm stance on accountability at the employee level.

U.S. Government employees are central, important, and have immense power. With that must come responsibility.

We must strike a delicate balance between harnessing the power of innovation and securing our digital infrastructure to counter the evolving threat landscape. To do this, Federal departments and agencies must focus on three things: first, they must prioritize infrastructure by risk; second, focus on closing the detection gap; and third, strengthen personal accountability at the employee level.

Thank you for the invitation to testify today, and I look forward to our discussion.

[The prepared statement of Mr. Cavanaugh follows:]

Prepared Statement of Brian J. Cavanaugh, Visiting Fellow for Cybersecurity, Intelligence, and Homeland Security, The Heritage Foundation

My name is Brian Cavanaugh. I am a Visiting Fellow for Cybersecurity, Intelligence, and Homeland Security at The Heritage Foundation. The views I express in this testimony are my own and should not be construed as representing any official position of The Heritage Foundation.

Chairman Gosar, Ranking Member Stansbury, and distinguished Members of the Subcommittee:

In today's digital era, where technology pervades every aspect of our lives, the critical importance of cybersecurity for federal departments and agencies cannot be overstated. As our government increasingly relies on interconnected systems, cloud computing, and data-driven decision-making, the very fabric of our national security, economic stability, and public trust hangs in the balance. The threats we face in cyberspace are relentless, sophisticated, and pervasive, posing a significant challenge to the integrity and resilience of our nation.

Cybersecurity is no longer a mere accessory or an afterthought; it is the cornerstone on which the functioning of our government rests. Federal departments and agencies store and handle vast amounts of sensitive and classified information, ranging from critical infrastructure blueprints and defense strategies to personal records and financial data. Any breach or compromise in these systems can have catastrophic consequences, undermining our national security, eroding public confidence, and jeopardizing the very foundations of our democracy.

The interconnectedness of our digital infrastructure means that a single vulnerability can ripple across multiple agencies, putting not only individual departments at risk but the entire government apparatus as well. The consequences extend beyond bureaucratic headaches; they can disrupt essential services, compromise emergency response systems, bring a halt to the economy, and undermine the trust citizens have placed in their government to protect their interests. The threats we face transcend borders and adversaries, requiring a unified and robust approach to fortify our cyber defenses.

Threat Landscape

The landscape of cyber threats is ever evolving, with adversaries constantly honing their tactics and exploiting vulnerabilities. Nation-states, organized crime syndicates, and even lone actors seek to breach our defenses, steal sensitive information, manipulate data, and wreak havoc on our systems. The realm of cybersecurity demands constant vigilance, adaptability, and a proactive stance to anticipate, detect, and respond to these threats in real time. We cannot afford to be reactive; we must be several steps ahead, pre-empting attacks and safeguarding our digital assets with an unwavering commitment.

The People's Republic of China (PRC) is an adversary of the United States. After a decades-long engagement strategy toward China, we find ourselves embroiled in a New Cold War with an even more capable adversary than the Soviet Union. The threat posed by China to U.S. infrastructure in terms of cyber is significant and complex. The Office of the Director of National Intelligence assesses China currently represents the broadest, most active, and persistent cyber espionage threat to the U.S. government and private-sector networks.

China has long been recognized as a major player in the realm of cyber espionage, and its capabilities and activities continue to evolve and expand. The Chinese government and affiliated entities have been attributed to a wide range of cyber activities, including intellectual property theft, espionage, and targeting critical infrastructure sectors. China's cyber operations pose a serious concern to U.S. infrastructure due to several factors.

First, China has demonstrated a high level of sophistication in its cyber capabilities, employing advanced techniques and tools to breach networks, infiltrate systems, and exfiltrate sensitive data. Their focus on intelligence gathering, particularly related to economic and technological advancements, underscores the potential for significant economic and national security consequences.

Secondly, China's large-scale and persistent cyber campaigns are a cause for alarm. They have been accused of engaging in long-term, strategic cyber operations, targeting a variety of sectors, including government agencies, defense contractors, technology companies, and energy infrastructure. Most recently, Volt Typhoon, a PRC-sponsored hacking group, has been targeting the communications, manufacturing, utility, transportation, construction, maritime, government, information technology and education sectors in the U.S. The breadth and persistence of these campaigns demonstrate a sustained commitment to cyber operations, posing a persistent and evolving threat.

Moreover, China's ability to leverage its vast resources, both in terms of technology and human capital, enhances its cyber capabilities. The country possesses a highly skilled cyber workforce, often supported by state-sponsored initiatives, and has invested heavily in research and development to develop advanced cyber tools and techniques. This combination of talent, resources, and strategic focus amplifies the potential impact of their cyber operations on U.S. infrastructure, especially as the U.S. and China lurch toward an impending conflict over Taiwan and Chairman Xi's vision for a new world order.

While the Office of the Director for National Intelligence noted Russia's cyber operations during the Ukraine war fell short of the pace and impact they had expected, Russia continues to pose cyber threats to the U.S. Putin is particularly focused on improving Russia's ability to target critical infrastructure, including underwater cables and operational technologies. It appears that Russia's belief in demonstrating the ability to compromise such infrastructure during a crisis achieves the goal of influencing foreign policy outcomes.

Iran has demonstrated a willingness to conduct aggressive cyber operations on critical infrastructure, such as water treatment facilities, and their expertise is improving at an alarming pace. While their approach to cyberattacks remains opportunistic, it does not diminish the susceptibility of U.S. critical infrastructure owners, particularly as Tehran believes it must prove to itself that they can push back against the West.

Cyber operations from North Korea have matured and are capable of causing temporary, limited disruptions of some critical infrastructure networks and disrupting business networks in the U.S. The North Korean cyber program emphasizes cybercrime, focusing on financially motivated cyber operations, such as conducting cryptocurrency heists—with on such heist obtaining $625 million. However, cyber actors linked to North Korea have conducted espionage efforts against a range of organizations and continue to focus on cyber espionage geared toward advancing Pyongyang's military programs.

Another threat that often goes unmentioned is transnational organized criminals whose ransomware attacks continue to execute high-impact ransomware attacks, extorting funds, disrupting critical services, and exposing sensitive data. Critical infrastructure such as health care, schools, emergency services, and manufacturing continue to experience attacks aimed at disrupting services. The cost of ransomware attacks is taking its toll on insurance markets, price increases and a hesitation of new insurance carriers in the market are systemic of an out-of-control problem set.

What Is at Risk

The growing trend of digital transformation within federal departments and agencies brings immense benefits but also amplifies the risks. The adoption of emerging technologies such as artificial intelligence, Internet of Things, and cloud computing introduces new attack surfaces and vulnerabilities that must be addressed with utmost urgency. For its part, the Department of the Interior

(DOI) houses enormous amounts of data on its digital infrastructure. Whether it relates to sustaining the health and productivity of public lands, the development of U.S. Outer Continental Shelf energy and mineral resources, or enhancing the quality of life of American Indians, Indian tribes, and Alaska Natives, the DOI must safeguard the data, resources, and infrastructure it utilizes to deliver its mission.

As noted in a recent Office of Inspector General (OIG) report, lackadaisical policies and procedures enabled the OIG to hack 21 percent of active user passwords at the DOI using basic and inexpensive means. Of the 18,000-plus accounts hacked, 362 accounts were senior U.S. government employees and 288 accounts had elevated privileges. Identifying and authenticating users is a fundamental security control. The OIG was able to demonstrate that the front door to the DOI has been left unlocked by its employees.

With over 1,600 structures on the outer continental shelf (OCS) responsible for a significant portion of U.S. domestic oil and gas production and at least 187 offshore wind farms currently being developed for energy production, the Department of the Interior's Bureau of Safety and Environmental Enforcement (BSEE) must proactively address cybersecurity risks. Modern exploration and production methods are increasingly reliant on remotely connected operational technology, a known vulnerability for cyberattack. A successful cyberattack on offshore energy infrastructure could cause physical, environmental, and economic harm. The effects of a cyberattack could resemble those that occurred in the 2010 Deepwater Horizon disaster or cause market-moving disruptions to energy production or transmission. In the context of cybersecurity, the interconnected dependencies of critical infrastructure mean that a breach or compromise in one sector can have far-reaching consequences across multiple sectors. The ripple effect of such an attack can cause widespread disruption, economic losses, and potentially endanger public safety. The risk of interconnected dependencies lies in the fact that critical infrastructure sectors are often interdependent and share common underlying systems and technologies. This means that a vulnerability or compromise in one sector can be exploited to gain unauthorized access or disrupt operations in another sector. For instance, a successful cyberattack on a Bureau of Land Management system could potentially impact the operations of a U.S. Geological Survey system or even a Department of Commerce system.

Flaw in Current Approach

The U.S. government's approach to cybersecurity has its flaws, from a lack of prioritization and chasing trends and buzzwords, to its approach to the private sector and its soft response to U.S. government employees entrusted with access to systems and data. Addressing these four areas would represent a marked improvement for the government sector of critical infrastructure.

The lack of prioritization of risk within the U.S. government is a significant hindrance to its efforts in cybersecurity. Effective cybersecurity requires a strategic and risk-based approach, where resources and efforts are allocated based on the level of risk posed by various threats and vulnerabilities. However, when risk is not adequately prioritized, several detrimental consequences arise: resource allocation inefficiency, a reactive approach to threats, inadequate risk assessments, misallocation of efforts, and a lack of accountability.

To overcome these challenges, it is crucial for the U.S. government to prioritize risk as a fundamental component of its cybersecurity strategy. This requires a comprehensive understanding of the threat landscape, thorough risk assessments, and the establishment of clear priorities based on potential impacts and likelihood of occurrence. By prioritizing risk, the government can allocate resources effectively, adopt a proactive approach, and ensure accountability in its cybersecurity efforts, ultimately strengthening the resilience of its systems and protecting national interests.

One sign that the government is misallocating efforts is its willingness to chase after cybersecurity buzzwords or new trends. While it is no secret that technology is rapidly developing and evolving, this does not mean that the U.S. government can erratically chase after the shiny object. Instead, the U.S. government should find ways to close the detection gap, something alluded to by the IBM Security Cost of a Data Breach Report 2022. According to the report, the average time to identify and contain a data breach is 287 days, with malware being undetected for an average of 180 days on systems.

The U.S. government's model for addressing cybersecurity is a flat-footed and clumsy approach that keeps them in a constant state of response and recovery— awaiting alerts from the private sector and then managing messaging. Instead of waiting for the private sector to decide to share information, the U.S. government must become forward leaning, and take meaningful steps toward addressing the risk and mitigating cyber threats to our critical infrastructure. This includes engaging with small businesses and start-ups that are driving innovation in cybersecurity. Procurement practices must evolve and foster innovation, especially in the tech sector. Flexibility in requirements, streamlined and agile procurement-process adoption, and incorporation of pilot programs and testbeds would be a great start.

The risk of interconnected dependencies within critical infrastructure highlights the urgent need for robust cybersecurity measures, including personal accountability. From a repercussion perspective, we all have a role to play in vigilance, and just like how resilience starts with the individual, so, too, does the responsibility of cybersecurity. The U.S. government needs to take a firm stance on accountability at the employee level. U.S. government employees are central, important, and have immense power. With that must come responsibility—with the expectation that they become lead adopters in proven security methods. Cyber and information technology policies need to be treated as seriously as those regarding the unauthorized disclosure of sensitive information.

A More Resilient Future

To address the threat posed by China and other cyber adversaries, the U.S. government must take proactive measures to enhance cybersecurity efforts. We must strike a delicate balance between harnessing the power of innovation and securing our digital infrastructure, employing robust encryption, multi-factor authentication, and comprehensive threat intelligence to counter the evolving threat landscape. Moreover, to address the critical importance of cybersecurity for federal departments and agencies, we must prioritize infrastructure by risk, focusing on closing the detection gap and strengthening personal accountability.

Investing in research and development of innovative cybersecurity technologies and techniques is crucial to stay ahead of evolving threats. This includes leveraging technologies such as artificial intelligence, machine learning, and behavioral analytics to detect and respond to cyber threats in real time. While investing in cutting-edge technologies and cultivating a highly skilled cybersecurity workforce, we must promote a culture of cybersecurity awareness and resilience at all levels of government.

Robust cybersecurity practices, threat intelligence sharing, investment in defense technologies, and collaboration with international partners are vital components of a comprehensive strategy to mitigate the risks posed by China's cyber activities to U.S. infrastructure.

The value of cybersecurity for federal departments and agencies cannot be underestimated. It is the shield that safeguards our nation's secrets, ensures the smooth functioning of our government, and preserves the trust and confidence of the American people. We must rise to the challenges that lie ahead, fortifying our defenses, embracing innovation securely, and forging a united front against the ever-present and evolving threats in cyberspace. Our future, our security, and the integrity of our democracy depend on it.

Questions Submitted for the Record to Brian Cavanaugh, Fellow for Cybersecurity, Intelligence, and Homeland Security, The Heritage Foundation

Questions Submitted by Representative Gosar

Question 1. Is anything stopping the Department of the Interior from allocating a greater percentage of its existing budget to cybersecurity initiatives?

Answer. In general, there could be several factors that may influence the allocation of the Department's budget towards cybersecurity initiatives including prioritization and mandates, resource constraints, risk assessment, legislative and regulatory requirements, and awareness and understanding.

The Department of the Interior's public facing priorities include:

- Identifying steps to accelerate responsible development of renewable energy on public lands and waters,
- Strengthening government-to-government relationship with sovereign Tribal Nations,
- Making investments to support the Administration's goal of creating millions of family-supporting and union jobs,
- Working to conserve at least 30% each of our lands and waters by the year 2030, and
- Centering equity and environmental justice.

None of the publicly identified priorities discuss cybersecurity or ensuring the security of stakeholders' data held by the Department. These public facing priorities compete for funding alongside cybersecurity initiatives.

While the Department's overall budget may be limited, given the findings of both the OIG and GAO reports, there should be nothing stopping the Department from re-allocating existing funding and requesting future funding to address appropriate cybersecurity investments. These investments should include cyber risk assessments, investment prioritization, and the adoption of basic cybersecurity protocols.

The department's leadership and decision-makers have demonstrated a lack of adequate awareness of the importance of cybersecurity and its potential implications. If there is a lack of understanding or appreciation for cybersecurity risks, it will adversely impact the allocation of resources to address those risks effectively. The leadership of the Department are focused on centering equity and environmental justice, while leaving the data it has been entrusted with open to our adversaries.

Question 2. How can DOI better prioritize cybersecurity initiatives with its existing budget?

Answer. The Department of Interior could better prioritize cybersecurity initiatives with its existing budget by developing a comprehensive risk assessment which assess the Department's current cybersecurity posture, identifies vulnerabilities and potential threats, and determines the potential impact of cyber incidents on critical operations, systems, and data. This assessment will help in understanding the specific cybersecurity needs and guide resource allocation well into the future.

Additionally, the Department should develop a cybersecurity strategy and policy. Establishing a clear strategy and policy framework that outlines the Department's approach to cybersecurity. This should include goals, objectives, and specific measures to protect sensitive information, secure systems, and mitigate cyber risks. The strategy should serve as a foundation for budget allocation and proper oversight by both the OIG and Congress.

These two steps will help identify a long-term plan to fund and address cybersecurity efforts that are capable of planning for phased implementation as well as be adaptable to unexpected developments in the cybersecurity field. Providing comprehensive training and awareness programs for employees at all levels—especially the leadership level—to enhance the Department's understanding of cybersecurity risks and best practices. Well-trained personnel are essential for implementing effective security measures and responding to potential incidents, just as well trained and educated leaders are to recognize the need for adequate investment in cybersecurity measures.

The Department should also establish a regular review and update of cybersecurity policies. Continuously monitoring and assessing the effectiveness of existing cybersecurity policies, procedures, and controls ensures the Department remains aligned with emerging threats, industry best practices, and regulatory requirements.

Mr. COLLINS. I thank the witness there for his testimony, and the Chair now recognizes Mr. Cheng for 5 minutes.

Statement of Dean Cheng, Senior Advisor, China Program, United States Institute of Peace, Washington, DC

Mr. CHENG. Good afternoon, Chairperson Collins, Ranking Member Stansbury, and other members of the Committee. My name is Dean Cheng. I am a Senior Advisor with the U.S. Institute of Peace, but my comments this afternoon are my own. My comments this afternoon are intended to provide some context for better understanding potential Chinese interest in cyber penetrating and attacking the Department of the Interior.

Broadly speaking, the PRC employs cyber and network penetration operations to gather intelligence, identify vulnerabilities, map out networks, and otherwise prepare to establish information dominance. The Department of the Interior's areas of responsibility span a range of issues that are of particular interest to the People's Republic of China, including mineral and oil leasing, infrastructure management, and relations with key Pacific Island nations.

The Department is, therefore, at great risk to Chinese cyber penetration and attacks.

From the Chinese perspective, what matters is information. Because the CCP sees the world today as living in the information age, information has become the key currency of power, both at the national and international level. Information feeds and supports all aspects of comprehensive national power and, therefore, all elements of information—military, economic, political, technical— contribute to a nation's power and, conversely, are potential elements that should be hacked because they are also elements of vulnerability.

The overall concept underlying Chinese activities is information dominance. It is [Speaking foreign language]: the ability to exploit information at times and places of one's own choosing, the ability to move and analyze information more rapidly and more accurately than competitors, and denying an adversary those same capacities. The PRC and, in particular, the Chinese Communist Party, sees establishing information dominance as central to regime survival. In this regard, Chinese cyber operations are undertaken for a variety of purposes. This includes intelligence gathering.

And let me emphasize here this is not simply military and defense and intelligence community-related information. It also includes business activities in the private sector. And we have seen Chinese Government entities operate against private-sector entities. It includes mapping out networks. It includes political military targeting, but also industrial espionage. For example, we have heard reference to Volt Typhoon, which targeted U.S. infrastructure. We have also seen Chinese entities hack cloud storage systems.

As well as political intelligence gathering, notably here is the case of the OPM hack from several years ago. It is interesting to note, I suggest, that OPM servers were housed bureaucratically within the Department of the Interior. This goes to the broader aspect of Department of the Interior responsibilities, which includes management of public lands, including drilling and mining, fisheries, offshore public lands, offshore drilling operations. All of these are things that, from the CCP's perspective, need to be mapped, monitored, and potentially hacked.

For example, USGS is responsible for creating a critical minerals list. The latest version was undertaken in 2022. What has not yet occurred is a survey of critical minerals on public lands. USGS is undertaking such actions. From the PRC's perspective, not surprisingly, they would love to know the results of a survey of U.S. public lands and what critical minerals—including, for example, rare earths—might reside. And from there, what companies might be contracted to extract that, and what would be the infrastructure that would be built out to move ores to processing facilities.

Finally, it is important to note here that the Department of the Interior, through the Bureau of Insular Affairs, has responsibility for interactions with a number of Central Pacific Island countries, including the Republic of the Marshall Islands, Federated States of Micronesia, and Republic of Palau. Your counterparts on the Armed Services Committee can certainly go into significant detail on the importance of these islands for U.S. operations.

Federated States of Micronesia, for example, surrounds the island of Guam, one of our central geographic locations in the Central Pacific. But the island of Kwajalein in the Republic of the Marshall Islands is a key part of our space and missile defense capabilities. So, with that in mind, I would suggest that it is, above all, important to recognize that, while the Department of the Interior's focus—by its title, of course—is domestic affairs, because of the various bureaucratic responsibilities, it is absolutely a high- priority target for the PRC.

Thank you very much for the opportunity to testify today.

[The prepared statement of Mr. Cheng follows:]

Prepared Statement of Dean Cheng, Senior Advisor, United States Institute of Peace

My name is Dean Cheng. I am a non-resident Senior Fellow at the Potomac Institute for Policy Studies, and a Senior Adviser with the United States Institute of Peace. The views I express in this testimony are my own, and should not be construed as representing any official position of either the Potomac Institute or the United States Institute of Peace.

Chinese View of Information

Over the past half century, the leadership of the People's Republic of China (PRC) has increasingly emphasized the importance of information as it relates to national economic development and national security. Beginning in the 1970s, the proliferation of microelectronics, computers, and telecommunications technology has accelerated the ability to gather, store, manage, and transmit information. From the perspective of the Chinese Communist Party (CCP) leadership, information technology, including computers and telecommunications systems, have permeated all aspects of society and economies and become an integral part of a nation's infrastructure.[31] Chinese analysts have dubbed this process "informationization (xinxihua)," and see the world as shifting from the Industrial Age to the Information Age.

From the Chinese perspective,

> Informationization is a comprehensive system of systems, where the broad use of information technology is the guide, where information resources are the core, where information networks are the foundation,

[31] TAN Wenfang, "The Impact of Information Technology on Modern Psychological Warfare," *National Defense Science and Technology* (#5, 2009), p. 72.

where information industry is the support, where information talent is a key factor, where laws, policies, and standards are the safeguard.[32]

In the face of this broad trend of economic, political, and social informationization, Chinese analysts have concluded that national economic development requires greater integration of information technologies into all aspects of the economy, while defending against threats to PRC national interests and security also must become informationized.

Economic development in the Information Age is built upon accessing, exploiting as well as analyzing and transmitting information. While manufacturing, transportation, and other traditional industries remain an essential part of a nation's strength, even those are increasingly digitized, whether in terms of the designs that they are producing or the electronic controls that govern the manufacturing equipment and power networks that sustain them. Information technology therefore permeates all aspects of the nation's economy, indirectly as well as directly.

The spread of information technology similarly means that potential adversaries have unprecedented access to each others' national economy, as well as the broader population and the top decision-makers. Just as the bomber and ICBM allows an opponent to directly strike a nation without having to first break through ground or naval defenses, information technology similarly outflanks traditional military forces. The proliferation of information technology into society and economics makes a nation broadly vulnerable to a range of new pressures and threats.

These threats extend beyond information networks (e.g., vulnerability to denial- of-service attacks) and component computers (e.g., computer viruses, malware).

Instead, the very information itself can constitute a threat, if, for example, its content erodes the morale of key decision-makers, popular support for a conflict, or the will of the military to fight. Consequently, China's interpretation of its national interests has expanded, in step with the expanding impact of information writ large on China.

More recent advances in information technology, including artificial intelligence and machine learning, the Internet of Things (IoT), big data and cloud computing, have further underscored the growing reach and capability

[32] State Council Information Office, Tenth Five Year Plan for National Economic and Social Development, Informationization Key Point Special Plans (October 18, 2002), http://www.cia.org.cn/information/information_01_xxhgh_3.htm.

of those able to exploit information networks through network warfare and cyber operations. These advances also affect both economic and security calculations.

PRC Employment of Network and Cyber Operations

Because of the growth of interconnectivity, the CCP is able to exploit its network and cyber capabilities for both economic and national security gains.

In the military and security context, PRC network and cyber operations are an integral part of intelligence gathering, just as they are for most other nations, including the United States. Undertaking such efforts is an essential part of the PLA's broader efforts to establish "information dominance," which PLA analysts view as an essential prerequisite to fighting and winning future conflicts. Because of the need to be able to rapidly exploit information more effectively than an adversary in wartime, it is necessary to undertake cyber and electronic reconnaissance of adversaries in peacetime. This includes not only amassing electronic signatures of enemy communications and weapons systems, but also surveying their networks, understanding their organization, and constructing the ability to attack those systems and defend against counter-attacks.

To this end, the Chinese People's Liberation Army (PLA) created a new service, the PLA Strategic Support Force (PLASSF), in the massive restructuring and reorganization announced on December 31, 2015. The PLASSF brings together China's electronic warfare (EW), network and cyber warfare, and space warfare forces into a single entity.[33] As all of these elements are linked to the gathering, exploitation, and transmission of information, the PLASSF is very much China's "information warfare force."

Of special importance here is the Network Systems Department (NSD) of the PLASSF. This component of the PLASSF incorporates element of what had previously been part of the PLA General Staff Department's 3rd Department, which had been responsible for a variety of cyber espionage activities. This includes the infamous Unit 61398, named in a 2013 Mandiant report and the first PLA unit publicly identified as a hacker force.[34]

---

[33] For a more extensive discussion of the PLA SSF, please see John Costello and Joe McReynolds, *China's Strategic Support Force: A Force for a New Era*, INSS China Strategic Perspectives #13 (Washington, DC: National Defense University, October 2018).

[34] Mandiant, *APT1: Exposing One of China's Cyber Espionage Units* (February 2013) https://nsarchive.gwu.edu/document/21484-document-83.

The existence of Unit 61398 as a PLA unit also highlights a fundamental difference between Chinese and Western execution of cyber economic espionage. There are few reports of Western intelligence or military forces being tasked with economic espionage. By contrast, the PLA is part of a vast network of Chinese cyber forces that undertake economic as well as national security espionage. Five members of Unit 61398, for example, were indicted by the US Department of Justice for various cyber economic espionage activities over the period 2006–2014, including attacks on Alcoa, Allegheny Technologies Inc., and Westinghouse.[35]

As the Office of the Director of National Intelligence noted in their 2023 threat assessment, "China probably currently represents the broadest, most active, and persistent cyber espionage threat to U.S. Government and private-sector networks."[36] Similarly, FBI Director Christopher Wray observed in 2020 that Chinese espionage efforts are not just targeting defense sector companies. The Chinese have targeted companies producing everything from proprietary rice and corn seeds to software for wind turbines to high-end medical devices. And they're not just targeting innovation and R&D. They're going after cost and pricing information, internal strategy documents, bulk PII—anything that can give them a competitive advantage.[37]

These efforts in turn incorporate both military and civilian, governmental and non-governmental elements, such that they outnumber the FBI's cyber staff by 50 to 1.[38]

---

[35] Department of Justice Office of Public Affairs, ''U.S. Charges Five Chinese Military Hackers for Cyber Espionage Against U.S. Corporations and a Labor Organization for Commercial Advantage,'' (May 19, 2014) https://www.justice.gov/opa/pr/us-charges-five-chinese-military- hackers-cyber-espionage-against-us-corporations-and-labor.

[36] Office of the Director of National Intelligence, *Annual Threat Assessment of the US Intelligence Community 2023* (Washington, DC: ODNI, February 2023), p. 10, https://www.dni.gov/files/ODNI/documents/assessments/ATA-2023-Unclassified-Report.pdf.

[37] Christopher Wray, ''Responding Effectively to the Chinese Economic Espionage Threat,'' Remarks at the Department of Justice China Initiative Conference, Center for Strategic and International Studies (February 6, 2020) https://www.fbi.gov/news/speeches/responding-effectively-to-the-chinese-economic-espionage-threat.

[38] Lauren Feiner, ''Chinese Hackers Outnumber FBI Cyber Staff by 50 to 1, Bureau Director Says,'' CNBC (April 28, 2023) https://www.cnbc.com/2023/04/28/chinese-hackers-outnumber-fbi- cyber-staff-50-to-1-director-wray-says.html.

Targeting the U.S. Department of the Interior for Network Attacks

Given the roles and responsibilities of the United States Department of the Interior (DOI), at least some of this massive array of cyber and network attackers are likely targeted at the DOI. For example, the DOI has oversight of US public lands, including drilling and mining rights. Within this purview is oversight of development of leasable minerals, such as oil, natural gas, coal, phosphate, potassium, and sodium, as well as locatable (or hardrock) minerals, such as gold, silver, copper, and gemstones.[39] Such resources are clearly of economic importance. As important, the United States government has identified an array of 35 critical minerals vital to national economic security, including cobalt, fluorspar, and niobium.[40] Until recently, there have been no surveys of public lands to determine how much, if any, of these critical minerals might be present. Under President Biden's Executive Order 14017, however, the DOI is encouraged to have the US Geological Survey, along with the Bureau of Land Management and the Department of Agriculture's US Forest Service, begin such surveys. For the PRC, accessing the results would provide useful insight into American reserves and potential production capacity for these critical minerals.

Similarly, the DOI has oversight over leasing of both onshore and offshore sites for oil drilling. Knowing the location of potential new energy reserves, including offshore sites, would be strategically valuable, as it could help the Chinese determine which companies, in turn, to monitor and even penetrate through cyber and other means. As important, sites that are tapped will require the construction of substantial networks of pipelines and other infrastructure to extract and move those resources. As a 2021 Joint Cybersecurity Advisory, coauthored by the Cybersecurity and Infrastructure Security Agency (CISA) and the Federal Bureau of Investigation (FBI), noted, state-sponsored Chinese actors have repeatedly targeted U.S. oil and natural gas (ONG) pipeline companies in the past.[41]

ONG companies may have their operating software attacked. Alternatively, as with the May 2021 Colonial Pipeline incident, the companies

---

[39] Congressional Research Service, *Federal Lands and Related Resources: Overview and Selected Issues for the 118th Congress*, CRS Report R43429 (February 24, 2023) https://crsreports.congress.gov/product/pdf/R/R43429/42.

[40] US Geological Survey Communications and Publishing, ''US Geological Survey Releases 2022 List of Critical Minerals,'' (February 22, 2022) https://www.usgs.gov/news/national-news- release/us-geological-survey-releases-2022-list-critical-minerals.

[41] ''Chinese Gas Pipeline Intrusion Campaign, 2011–2013'' (July 21, 2021) https://www.cisa.gov/news-events/cybersecurity-advisories/aa21-201a.

may be targeted for ransomware attacks, where the data is made inaccessible (but is not destroyed). Although Colonial Pipeline's networks moved oil from refineries to customers, other parts of the overall energy supply chain, including from fields to refineries, could also be targeted.[42]

Finally, as the DOI is part of the overall US government bureaucracy, it offers potential access to a range of systems not necessarily related to its purview. The DOI, for example, housed the data center for the Office of Personnel Management (OPM). This was the center that was accessed when OPM was hacked in 2015, exposing the records of some 4 million current and former federal employees. Notably, hearings into the hack indicated that DOI had some 3000 "critical and high risk vulnerabilities."[43]

Oversight of Pacific Island States

Another reason for concern about Chinese network attacks and cyber intrusions into the Department of the Interior is that the Department is responsible for overseeing US relations with several of the microstates of the central Pacific. One example is the Republic of the Marshall Islands (RMI), an independent nation tied to the United States by a Compact of Free Association. It comprises 5 islands and 29 atolls, with a population of some 58,000 people. While only possessing some 70 square miles of dry land, these islands and atolls are spread across 750,000 square miles of central Pacific territory.[44] As such, they straddle waters that link the American west coast with the east Asian littoral.

This strategic position was made clear during the Second World War, when U.S. forces "island hopped" through the Marshall islands, on their way to the Marianas and eventually to Japan. Indeed, the battles for Kwajalein and Eniwetok provided invaluable experience for later battles on Guam, Iwo Jima, and Okinawa.

In the wake of the Second World War, the United States was granted trusteeship over various central Pacific territories, including the Marshall Islands. The Republic of the Marshall Islands (RMI) gained its independence in 1986. Under the original and subsequently amended Compact of Free

---

[42] ''About Shell Pipeline,'' https://www.shell.us/business-customers/shell-pipeline/about-shell-pipeline.html.

[43] ''Thousands of Cybersecurity Vulnerabilities Uncovered at Interior Department,'' FedScoop (July 15, 2015) https://fedscoop.com/after-opm-hack-interior-cybersecurity-audit-finds-thousands- of-critical-vulnerabilities/.

[44] U.S. Department of State, Bureau of East Asian and Pacific Affairs, ''U.S. Relations with Marshall Islands,'' (July 15, 2018) https://www.state.gov/u-s-relations-with-marshall-islands/.

Association (CFA), RMI citizens can work, live, and study in the United States, as non-immigrants.[45] As of 2019, there were some 27,000 Marshallese in the United States, a substantial portion of the RMI population.[46]

In addition, under the terms of the CFA, the United States provides RMI with economic support and aid. The United States provides RMI with some $70 million annually in various forms. This includes a jointly managed trust fund. US government agencies and offices, such as the Federal Communications Commission and US Postal Service, also provide services to the Marshall Islands. This aid is scheduled to end when the current amended Compact expires in 2023.

In exchange, the United States is granted exclusive and full authority to RMI lands and waterways for security and defense purposes, although RMI is free to conduct its own foreign relations. A key element of both economic and security ties is the leasing of land and lagoon space to the U.S. Army on Kwajalein atoll under the Military Use and Operating Rights Agreement. The missile and space facilities there are the second largest employer in the RMI.[47]

RMI's Role in American Defense Efforts

Throughout the post-war period, the Marshall Islands have played an important role in America's defense, especially in the context of nuclear deterrence.

In the immediate post-war period, the United States conducted an array of nuclear tests in the Marshall Islands. The 67 nuclear tests conducted there between 1946 and 1958 included Castle Bravo, the largest American nuclear test involving a 15 megaton device.[48] It is worth noting that this test was nonetheless dwarfed by four Soviet tests, which ranged from 20–50 megatons.

With the Limited Test Ban Treaty of 1963, which effectively banned above-ground nuclear tests, the islands have no longer been rocked by nuclear explosions. RMI has continued to play an important role, however, in

---

[45] U.S. Department of State, Bureau of East Asian and Pacific Affairs, ''U.S. Relations with Marshall Islands,'' (July 15, 2018) https://www.state.gov/u-s-relations-with-marshall-islands/.

[46] Susanne Rust, ''They Came Here After the U.S. Irradiated Their Islands. Now They Face an Uncertain Future,'' *Los Angeles Times* (December 31, 2019) https://www.latimes.com/world-nation/story/2019-12-31/marshall-islands-uncertain-future-us-marshallese-spokane.

[47] 17 U.S. Department of State, Bureau of East Asian and Pacific Affairs, ''U.S. Relations with Marshall Islands,'' (July 15, 2018) https://www.state.gov/u-s-relations-with-marshall-islands/.

[48] Lawrence Livermore National Laboratories, ''Brief History of Nuclear Testing in the Marshall Islands,'' (July 28, 2021) https://marshallislands.llnl.gov/testhistory.php.

maintaining America's nuclear deterrent posture. Especially important has been the role of Kwajalein and the Ronald Reagan Ballistic Missile Defense Test Site (RTS).

The RTS provides key support to US defense efforts in several ways. The credibility of the American nuclear deterrent is sustained through a program of regular tests of Minuteman III missiles. As recently as August 2021, the US fired a Minuteman III with a Hi Fidelity Joint Test Assembly re-entry vehicle onboard towards Kwajalein.[49] Such tests demonstrate to all observers, including America's adversaries, the continuing functionality and reliability of the American nuclear deterrent. This is becoming an ever more pressing issue due to the aging of the Minuteman III, first introduced in the 1960s.

The fact that these test shots cover some 4200 miles further enhances the credibility of the American deterrent. Russian ICBM tests from the Plesetsk Kosmodrome to the Kura test range in Kamchatka cover some 3800 miles.[50] Longer test flights provide more opportunity for measurements of flight characteristics.

Moreover, given the size of the Kwajalein lagoon (which is one of the largest in the world at over 600 square miles), one can target warheads and dummy payloads into it, and thereby prevent their recovery by other actors. In 2016, Chinese sailors seized an American unmanned underwater vehicle (UUV) from international waters.[51] There should be little doubt that the Chinese, among others, would very much like an opportunity to examine a dummy US nuclear warhead.

The facilities at Kwajalein also support missile defense efforts. The various radars and facilities provide American missile defense planners and engineers with data to help improve missile interception capability. This is of growing concern, as both Russia and China modernize their own nuclear arsenals.

Nor are missile defenses only relevant to the nuclear side of the deterrence equation. The PRC, for example, has deployed anti-ship ballistic missiles,

---

[49] Air Force Global Strike Command Public Affairs, "Minuteman III Test Launch Showcases Readiness of U.S. Nuclear Forces' Safe, Effective Deterrent," (August 11, 2021) https:// www.stratcom.mil/Media/News/News-Article-View/Article/2727368/minuteman-iii-test-launch-showcases-readiness-of-us-nuclear-forces-safe-effecti/.

[50] Joe Saballa, "Russia to Test Launch Advanced intercontinental Ballistic Missile," *Defense Post* (May 5, 2021) https://www.thedefensepost.com/2021/05/05/russia-to-test-launch-ballistic- missile/.

[51] Terri Moon Cronk, "Chinese Seize U.S. Navy Underwater Drone in South China Sea," *DOD News* (December 16, 2016) https://www.defense.gov/News/News-Stories/Article/Article/1032823/chinese-seize-us-navy-underwater-drone-in-south-china-sea/.

such as the DF-21 and DF-26. Both of these are clearly intended to neutralize American aircraft carriers and other maritime strategic platforms. Missile defenses would degrade Chinese confidence that they can sink or damage American carriers, which in turn would help deter China from using force against various neighbors, from Japan to Taiwan to the Philippines.

In November 2020, an American SM-3 Block IIA missile successfully intercepted an ICBM-type missile, launched from Kwajalein.[52] This was the first time that the SM-3, which can be deployed aboard an AEGIS-equipped destroyer or cruiser, had destroyed such a target.[53] This radically improves not only American deterrence, but that of any allied nation that has comparable AEGIS-type systems in their fleet. The SM-3 is already part of the Phased Adaptive Approach for NATO defense against Russian missile threats. It is deployed in the ground-based site in Rumania, and will be deployed to the site currently under construction in Poland. Meanwhile, Japan has chosen to rely on its fleet of AEGIS destroyers to provide missile defense for the Home Islands, against North Korean and Chinese threats. The success of the SM-3 Block IIA test means that this key US ally will be more secure in coming years. The facilities in the Marshall Islands have played a key role in improving American and allied security.

Finally, the facilities in the RMI, including on Kwajalein, play a central role in space surveillance. The United States Space Force currently tracks some 26,000 objects in space. Because of the high speed of objects in orbit, even a bolt or a screw can do enormous damage to the International Space Station or an orbiting satellite. The recently built Space Fence on Kwajalein provides the Space Force with the ability to monitor objects as small as a marble.[54]

This capability is of growing importance as America's competitors and adversaries develop ever more capable space systems, many of which are believed to be antisatellite systems. The Russians, for example, have deployed sub-satellites from larger satellites, much like submunitions from a dispenser.

---

[52] The Department of Defense, "U.S. Successfully Conducts SM-3 Block IIA Intercept Test Against an Intercontinental Ballistic Missile Target," (November 17, 2020) https://www.defense.gov/News/Releases/Release/Article/2417334/us-successfully-conducts-sm-3-block-iia- intercept-test-against-an-intercontinen/.

[53] The War Zone Staff, "The Navy Has Finally Proven It Can Shoot Down an Intercontinental Ballistic Missile," *The Drive* (November 17, 2020) https://www.thedrive.com/the-war-zone/37685/the-navy-has-finally-proven-it-can-shoot-down-an-intercontinental-ballistic-missile.

[54] Sandra Erwin, "Space Fence Surveillance Radar Site Declared Operational," *Space News* (March 28, 2020) https://spacenews.com/space-fence-surveillance-radar-site-declared-operational/.

In 2017, Kosmos-2519 launched Kosmos-2521, a sub-satellite while in orbit. Kosmos-2521 subsequently launched a sub-satellite of its own, Kosmos-2523. Both Kosmos-2519 and Kosmos- 2521 maneuvered in orbit.[55] Meanwhile, China's new reusable space plane apparently released an object while in orbit, and engaged in rendezvous and proximity operations (RPO) with at least one other object over the past year.[56] All of these actions are difficult to track, especially while also maintaining situational awareness over 26,000 pieces of other debris. Russia has since launched other satellites that have behaved in a similar fashion, launching their own sub-satellites.[57] US space surveillance capabilities must maintain watch over all these objects, if America's own satellites are to be preserved.

The ground-based Space Fence radar on Kwajalein is an essential part of the American space surveillance network. It plays a key role in helping the U.S. detect and track potential threats to its satellites, including its missile early warning, strategic communications, and reconnaissance platforms.

In addition to RMI, the United States has comparable special relationships with the Federated States of Micronesia, and the Republic of Palau. Relations with both of these states are also overseen by the DOI. Both of these states are slated for additional US military construction, but have also been courted by Beijing.[58]

For the PRC, which has been seeking inroads into the central Pacific and to build expanded ties to the various states, gaining insider knowledge of American positions, aid packages, and general policy toward those states would be of enormous strategic advantage. Moreover, as both RMI and the Republic of Palau maintain ties with Taiwan, rather than the PRC, Beijing is intensely interested in gaining any leverage it can to shift their diplomatic alignment.

---

[55] Gunter D. Krebs, ''Kosmos-2519/Kosmos-2521/Kosmos-2523,'' Gunter's Space Page Retrieved October 17, 2021, https://space.skyrocket.de/doc_sdat/kosmos-2519.htm.

[56] Andrew Jones, ''China's Mysterious Spaceplane Releases Object into Orbit,'' *Space News* (November 2, 2022) https://spacenews.com/chinas-mystery-spaceplane-releases-object-into-orbit/, and Joseph Trevithick, ''Chinese Spaceplane Docked with Another Object Multiple Times Data Indicates,'' *The Drive* (May 9, 2023) https://www.thedrive.com/the-war-zone/chinese-spaceplane-docked-with-another-object-multiple-times-data-indicates.

[57] Neel V. Patel, ''The U.S. Says Russia Just Tested an 'Anti-Satellite Weapon' in Orbit,'' *Technology Review* (July 23, 2020) https://www.technologyreview.com/2020/07/23/1005568/us-space-command-russia-test-anti-satellite-weapon-orbit-kosmos-2543/.

[58] Kirsty Needham, ''Pacific Islands a Key U.S. Military Buffer to China's Ambitions, Report Says,'' Reuters (September 20, 2022) https://www.reuters.com/world/asia-pacific/pacific-islands- key-us-military-buffer-chinas-ambitions-report-2022-09-20/.

Questions Submitted for the Record to Dean Cheng, Senior Advisor, China Program, United States Institute of Peace

Questions Submitted by Representative Gosar

Question 1. Is there anything stopping the Department of the Interior from allocating a greater percentage of its existing budget to cybersecurity initiatives?

Answer. There may be issues of reallocation of money within a budget, and whether Congressional authorizations allow such reallocations. For example, it may be that money cannot be shifted from, say, Bureau of Land Management to Department of the Interior (DOI) information services without prior authorization. More importantly, however, is even within the DOI's information services budget, how money is programmed. More money spent on cybersecurity will almost certainly mean less money spent on some other aspect of information management and information services within the DOI. It may mean fewer updates of the web-site, or a lagging purchase of new computers. So long as the information technology/ information services budget is (relatively) fixed, additional tasks will be a matter of "robbing Peter to pay Paul."

One consideration, however, may be to determine better metrics of information security, in order to assess the effectiveness of dollars spent on information security. How well is DOI currently doing in terms of securing its information systems?

Question 2. How can DOI better prioritize cybersecurity initiatives within its existing budget?

Answer. Measuring effectiveness and determining efficiency of cyber security is extremely difficult to measure, because it is essentially assessing dogs that do not bark. For example, how does one assess effectiveness of deterrence measures, other than "no war occurred"?

Assessing cybersecurity initiative measure effectiveness might be facilitated by conducting "tiger team" or "red team" attacks. Indeed, this might provide USCYBERCOM with an opportunity to engage in cross-departmental cooperation by staging "attacks" against DOI. Alternatively, asking USCYBERCOM to help assess threats and security capacity of DOI's information security would potentially help both departments improve their level of operation.

Questions Submitted by Representative Grijalva

Question 1. In May 2023, a Chinese Government hacking group successfully launched a malware attack on telecommunications systems in Guam and other parts of the United States. What were the consequences of this breach and what can we learn from it to strengthen our cybersecurity posture, especially in the Indo-Pacific region.

Answer. I believe several lessons have emerged.

- One of the most basic is that the same cybersecurity threat groups are often given different names by different cyber-security firms, making it harder to assess how extensively the threat entity has operated, where it has performed prior penetrations, etc. The group "Volt Typhoon" is also known as "Bronze Silhouette" among other names. Encouraging cyber-security firms to not only share data (they often do), but to either use the same nomenclature would improve overall security by facilitating a common understanding of the threat.
- The threat is constantly shifting. "Volt Typhoon" attacks do not require downloading malware, but exploit existing lines of attack. As important, it apparently involves exploiting cyber security firms as an attack pathway.
- There should be little question that the PRC will engage in disruptive attacks against critical infrastructure in time of conflict, and most likely in time of crisis. This is consistent with known People's Liberation Army (PLA) writings, and suggests that policies and courses of action predicated on the assumption that the PRC and PLA will not conduct such attacks are badly mistaken. It is therefore essential to plan now for both mitigation and response strategies in the likely event of such attacks and ensuing disruptions.

Mr. COLLINS. Thank you, Mr. Cheng. The Chair now recognizes Ms. Siers for 5 minutes.

Statement of Rhea Siers, Senior Advisor (Cyber Risk), Teneo, Washington, DC

Ms. SIERS. Mr. Collins, Ranking Member Stansbury, and Committee members, thank you for the opportunity to discuss cybersecurity challenges. My name is Rhea Siers, and I have worked over 30 years in both the government and private sectors, witnessing the cyber threat to our national security and economic well-being growing exponentially.

I will use a practitioner's approach, as someone who sees the daily realities of defending our networks and responding to cyber incidents.

The cyber playing field has evolved. Initially, cyber was the primary domain of state actors. But to understand the totality of the cyber threat challenge, we must acknowledge the role and activities of non-state actors, as well. Computer technology is now easily available to non-state actors, such as organized criminals and hacktivists. They procure cyber tools from state sponsors or the cybercrime underground: a robust, full-service operation.

Years ago, the hallmark of state cyber actors was their persistence, tenacity, innovation, and exploitation of human error. Now, some of these non-state actors are displaying similar performance and tactics.

Of great concern is the increasing impact of actors that self- identify as non-state actors, but are controlled or resourced by states. These groups often employ cybercrime tactics, but their objectives align with their sponsor's strategy. These groups are supported by our traditional adversaries, such as Russia and China, and our newer cyber adversaries, such as North Korea and Iran.

Two examples: The Russian Sandworm group linked to Russian military intelligence is a very sophisticated cyber presence. In 2017, they caused a shutdown at the global maritime giant, Maersk, leading to significant monetary losses and disruption to the worldwide supply chain. The Lazarus Group is a North Korean- sponsored hacking syndicate. They have pursued numerous attacks on an array of sectors worldwide. Their objective is supplying the North Korean regime with funds with the dual purpose of disruption in world markets and financial transactions. Their cyber mentor in building capabilities, of course, was China.

What are our adversaries after? They want access to confidential data. Thus, their efforts to penetrate government and private sector networks.

This isn't just spy versus spy. The government holds a great deal of sensitive data that can give adversaries a very good idea of our security vulnerabilities, from the financial sector to oil pipelines.

This is not just about data. We see more threats against industrial control systems, the instrumentation that operates the industrial processes, from manufacturing plants to power grids. There is potential for operational disruption and damage. One recent example: the Chinese government-supported hackers who targeted multiple U.S. oil and gas pipelines over the past decade, mapping the industrial controls for potential future operations.

Future cyber challenges are also emerging, from efforts to infiltrate the supply chain of information technology, such as the Russian SolarWinds operation, to the potential to alter algorithms that are increasingly running our operational technology.

So, how do we defend against traditional and newer adversaries with the finite resources we have in the public and private sectors? What we don't want is something I call Chicken Little cybersecurity. Recall the story of Chicken Little. He gets hit in the head by some acorns, and he decides the sky is falling. Every day we are hit with a barrage of bad cyber acorns, threats, malicious software, data breaches. To keep the sky from falling, you must assess the specific risks to your organization, public or private. Your cyber defense ultimately depends on your ability to do so.

The response to state and non-state cyber threats is to focus and strategize; find the key vulnerabilities and risks; realize that no government agency or private company is an island unto itself. We cannot claim that we can repel any cyber attack or neutralize all our cyber adversaries. Instead, we must aim for cyber resilience, collaborative preparation, and agile response that doesn't stop at the public-private boundary.

Thank you, and I look forward to your questions. [The prepared statement of Ms. Siers follows:]

Prepared Statement of Rhea D. Siers, Senior Adviser, Teneo

Subcommittee Chairman Gosar, Ranking Member Stansbury and distinguished Members of the Subcommittee, thank you for the opportunity to appear before to discuss the cyber threats to our national security from State adversaries and their proxies. My name is Rhea Siers and I have spent over thirty years in this area, both in government and in the private sector and have watched the cyber threat to our national and economic well-being grow exponentially. I approach this topic from a practitioner's standpoint, as someone who has seen on a daily basis the challenges of protecting our nation's critical infrastructure and government and business operations from the inside and outside. Those challenges are the direct result of our digital world given the vast amount of personal, proprietary and operational information flowing through all our networks. Frankly, it is a treasure trove of information and potential disruption available to our adversaries worldwide.

Prior to my current position as a Senior Advisory on Cyber Risk to Teneo, I served in a variety of senior operational positions at the National Security Agency including Deputy Assistant Director for policy; since my retirement from the US Government Senior Executive Service, I have worked as an attorney and advisor on Cyber Incident Response, and as a Senior Cyber Defense Strategy Executive at Bank of America. I am also on the faculties of George Washington and Johns Hopkins Universities where I have developed and taught courses on Cyber Threats, Strategy and Policy for the past fifteen years. My approach today is a pragmatic one—not just discussing the changes in cyber threats but the importance of planning for emerging threats as technology continues to develop so rapidly. My advisory focus is not just the response to crisis cyber situations but the very critical need for advance planning to ensure resilience to attacks, disruption or even worse, destruction of data and operational technology in our networks. I'm all about demystifying cybersecurity and helping my students and clients ask the right questions about their cyber defense in the wake of daily hostile cyber activity.

In my testimony today, I will discuss the following issues relating to state and other cyber threats to our national security and economic stability:

1) Cyber Actors: The Playing Field Evolves
2) Potential Implications: Who is Hacking and What Are Their Objectives?
3) Responding to the Cyber Threat Challenge: Avoiding the "Chicken Little Cybersecurity" Syndrome

The Cyber Playing Field Has Changed

I admit, given my background, taking a bit of a long and evolutionary view of cyber threats. When I started in this field, cyber was very much the primary domain of state actors—intelligence services and the military held the keys to cyber operations and were the most successful adversaries. They dominated the activity, the attacks, the use of cyber to penetrate networks to gain a national security advantage, to collect intelligence and to seek economic advantage. They possessed the technological resources to conduct electronic surveillance and warfare both domestically and overseas. While that's certainly still very true today, the cyber playing field has leveled out a bit and the attribution—the "who dunnit" of cyber operations—has become a bit murkier.

If we want to understand the totality of the cyber threat challenge, we must acknowledge the role of non-state actors. Significant technological advances actually make computer network resources more widely available. Thus, nonstate actors, such as organized criminals, and 'hacktivists' are now taking full advantage of available cyber capabilities. Certain tools are readily available—either from state sponsors or the cybercrime underground, which features a full service, one-stop shopping for tools such as ransomware—that hold data hostage until a ransom is paid.

There is a growing and increasingly impactful category of actors that self-identify as nonstate actors but are controlled or resourced by states. They often employ cybercrime tactics and techniques, but their objectives align with the State's strategy against adversaries. One can call them a blended or hybrid threat, but ultimately many are state-sponsored and supported. Of even greater concern, the non- state cyber actors are improving all the time. Years ago, the hallmark of state cyber actors was their persistence, tenacity, great use of technology and exploitation of human error. Now these state proxies are displaying the same persistence and use of more advanced cyber tools and techniques. These proxies allow states to build further capacity and also aid in the state's efforts to hide some of its cyber activity.

Just a few recent examples illustrate the challenge of state sponsored cyber groups:

- The Russian Sandworm group, which is linked to Russian military intelligence, has been quite active. Sandworm is a sophisticated cyber presence and is believed to have conducted the 2015 BlackEnergy cyber attack against Ukraine's power grid as well as the 2017 attack on the global maritime giant, Maersk. Maersk's booking system and loading systems were impacted. Maersk and all its global shipping were shut down resulting in significant monetary losses and great impact on the worldwide supply chain. Sandworm has been active against Ukraine recently as well in an effort to damage the industrial control systems that run high voltage substations there—i.e. shut off power.

- The Lazarus Group is a North Korean sponsored hacking syndicate—they are known to have been involved in the attack on Sony Motion Picture Entertainment here in the US and have pursued attacks on the financial and pharmaceutical sectors worldwide. While their key objective is supplying the North Korean regime with funds, they also often have a dual purpose of disruption in world markets and financial transactions.
- More recently, the Department of Justice indicted a number of Iranians affiliated with the Iranian Islamic Revolutionary Guard Corps (IRGC) for ransomware activities "threatening the physical security and economy of the United States". These activities included the targeting of critical infrastructure with ransomware.

As if the playing field wasn't complicated enough—there are no shortage of targets for malevolent cyber actors. While certainly government agencies at all levels are in the crosshairs of hostile cyber states, the private sector in the US controls about 90% of cyberspace; of even greater concern is the protection of our critical infrastructure. For example, the Cybersecurity and Infrastructure Security Agency (CISA) notes that "more than 80% of the country's energy infrastructure is owned by the private sector, supplying fuels to the transportation industry, electricity to households and businesses and other sources of energy that are integral to growth and production across the nation".

2. Who Is Hacking and Why? Potential Implications

To understand impact on the natural resources sector, it is important to understand three different and multiple cyberattack objectives—i.e., what benefits the cyber attacker is expecting to gain from a successful intrusion or attack.

All of these objectives operate across the three main target areas of commercial, industrial, and government sectors. A single operation can also seek to affect multiple targets and have multiple purposes. The fact that different targets share similar vulnerabilities only strengthens the necessity for collaboration (not just information sharing) across the entire cyber environment, regardless of whether the target is a public or private entity.

Objective 1: Collection of and Access to Confidential Data

You name it, every commercial, industrial, and governing entity is a potential treasure trove of information to the right attacker. This isn't just "spy vs spy." Remember that the government sector holds a great deal of sensitive data beyond plans and strategies including intellectual property, personal and proprietary data. It also includes data related to control systems, such as dams or water treatment facilities—these are potential vulnerabilities that must be protected. In some highly regulated industries, companies are required to report their cyber and physical security strengths and weaknesses to the government. Unauthorized access to those reports by one of our adversaries is obviously a serious concern. This is not only about data being accessed; there is the potential for data being altered with a negative impact on operations and safety.

Of course, these attacks also focus directly on the private sector. Just a few months ago, both the Department of Energy and the US Intelligence Community warned of "custom made" malware targeting the control systems for both electricity and natural gas. The warning indicated that this hacking operation, probably conducted by Russian state supported groups, were mapping the US energy infrastructure. "Mapping" is a key step in intelligence gathering—the precursor to an ability to potential disrupt and even destroy energy industry or other equipment.

Objective 2: Financial Gain

This second cyberattack objective is largely the motive of cybercriminals seeking unauthorized access to funds, personal information that can be used to pose as a victim and obtain funds, or information about pending transactions or deals that can be used to engage in such activities as insider trading.

One recent area of concern: criminal, ransomware and data extortion targeting the industrial sector. We are seeing more and more threats against Industrial Control Systems (known as ICS). ICS are the different types of systems and instrumentation that operate or automate industrial processes, anything from manufacturing plants to power grids. Previously, ransomware used to focus on information technology and data access but has now expanded to this operational technology. An intrepid cybercriminal, including state sponsored groups, can threaten to stop the production line, turn off the power, or in several recent cases, turn off the oil or gas pipeline. They can do this simply by threatening administrative or enabling functions. It doesn't take a lot of imagination to see the potential harm to business and of course, to a utility's customers and operations.

Example:

Colonial Pipeline (2021): Just the threat of a potential release of data by the Cyber Crime group DarkSide caused Colonial Pipeline to shut down its East Coast pipeline delivery system for gasoline, jet fuel, and diesel. And the cybercriminals didn't even target the actual pipeline; they went after its corporate data, encrypting it and demanding a ransom. Unable to bill its customers, Colonial Pipeline turned off the spigot, resulting in a significant shortage of gasoline. This also demonstrated that blended threat that I referred to earlier when cybercriminals conduct activity, sometimes tolerated, and sometimes encouraged, by a nation state that views the attacks a serving their interest, in this case, Russia.

Objective 3: Operational Disruption/Damage

Attacks attempting to disrupt or even destroy operational controls and technology have targeted the entire spectrum of commercial, industrial, and governmental targets and have used the full range of cyber techniques and even cyber weaponry to achieve their goals. The targets include commercial, industrial and government entities that are heavily reliant on their computer network for operations. There has been a steady increase in attacks on industrial control systems that run manufacturing or utilities.

Methods: Disruptive operations often require more advanced tactics including the collection of extensive intelligence and setting up a presence in the target's network for a prolonged period of time without detection. Most recently, ransomware has sometimes been added to the attacks.

Example: Chinese government supported hackers targeted an array of US oil and gas pipelines over the past decade, seeking "strategic access to industrial control networks that run the pipelines for future operations rather than for intellectual property theft."

3. Responding to Cyber Threats

I have briefly outlined state and state-associated cyber threats and the potential dangers to our national and economic security—but it's time for some practitioner pragmatics—the big "so what?"

You may have heard, especially about a decade ago, people referring to cyber threats by states as a potential "Cyber Pearl Harbor," a catastrophic cyberattack on critical infrastructure, like power grids, that would cause physical damage and injuries or death to our citizens. Have we had a Cyber Pearl Harbor? Thankfully not. Is one theoretically possible? Yes, but it is critical to give context to what the threats mean without turning to untethered panic. This debate is also a red herring; it sets a threshold for damage from a cyberattack that is quite high, forgetting that lower-level attacks can cause significant problems in everyday life as well as to our national and economic security, a kind of death by 1000 cuts. And just a cursory look at recent hacks of private-sector companies and government agencies should remind us that smaller-scale intrusions can be disruptive, dangerous and very costly even without catastrophic outcomes.

I tend to think of both the cyber and national security environment as a set of concentric circles. That means simply that this is not just an issue of direct impacts by direct attack on a specific target. Rather this means that cyber state and non-state attackers aim at not just their primary target, such as gas or energy distribution, but the enabling functions often supplied by third party partners. When attackers are frustrated by their primary targets, they turn to those concentric enabling circles—suppliers who have some access into the network or even the physical plant of the target. They gather intelligence, conduct reconnaissance, gather organizational and structural information and they search for the backdoor for unauthorized access. States historically were most proficient at this intelligence work; but that is no longer exclusively true. Once again, state supported non-state actors have proven themselves agile learners at collecting intelligence about their targets and taking the time to penetrate their targets' networks to map them and assess them for further attack.

This is also a problem that I like to call "chicken little cybersecurity." You might recall the story of Chicken Little: he gets hit in the head by a couple of acorns and decides the sky is falling. We are all hit with a daily barrage of bad news about cyberattacks and intrusions—new malicious software, a new advanced persistent threat (APT) group, or new backdoors into our networks. Not every cyber event or newly discovered vulnerability applies to every company, government agency or entity. Throwing money at your cyber problem without incisive analysis and context is not going to keep the sky from falling on you. If you cannot assess or link the specific risk to your organization or to your sector, public or private, you are in serious danger of being overwhelmed. If the risk is not fully assessed and related to actual operations or potential fallout, you are limiting the efficacy of your cyber defense.

The response to state and non-state cyber threats is to focus; find the key vulnerabilities and risks; realize that no government agency or private company is an island onto itself. We cannot claim, nor should we, that we can repel any cyber attack or intrusion; instead, we must aim for cyber resilience—collaborative preparation and well-practiced response.

Thank you.

Questions Submitted for the Record to Rhea Siers, Senior Advisor (Cyber), Teneo

Questions Submitted by Representative Gosar

Question 1. Is anything stopping the Department of the Interior from allocating a greater percentage of its existing budget to cybersecurity initiatives?

Question 2. How can DOI better prioritize cybersecurity initiatives with its existing budget?

Answer. Both of Representative Gosar's questions deal directly with the specific details of the DOI budget. I am unfamiliar with DOI budget details such as mandated vs discretionary spending, the conditions for the reprogramming vs transfer of funds, or whether provisions exist that might limit the movement of funds to new cybersecurity programs or activities. I realize that these represent difficult choices and prioritizations but cannot offer specific guidance.

With that caveat, I want to focus on the reality of funding cybersecurity in federal agencies (and often in private entities). As previously noted, successful cyber resilience necessitates not only sufficient funding but consistent funding. In addition to the monetary costs, there is also the challenge of finding human resources—people with the right cyber and technology skills to institute best practices, stay on top of technological advancement and to move with agility and speed as necessary. Lack of funding and resources result in gaps in our ability to protect today's threats; lack of resources negates our ability to prepare strategically, operationally and coherently for new threats and future risks. It is difficult to make our networks and systems resilient when our resources are so limited that we can, at best, put out fires and try to fend off the latest hack. I'm not arguing for unlimited cyber funding; that would be unrealistic. I am advocating consistent, prioritized funding that is built on a multi-year program without interruptions, annual funding swings or "salami slice" cuts lacking a sound rationale.

Questions Submitted by Representative Gallego

Question 1. Ms. Siers, in your testimony you use the phrase "Cyber Pearl Harbor." Can you elaborate on what this means and the likelihood of such a threat occurring?

Answer. "Cyber Pearl Harbor," a catastrophic cyberattack on critical infrastructure, like power grids, that would cause physical damage and injuries or death to our citizens. It could hypothetically disrupt our daily lives, our welfare and our economy. The use of the term was more prominent a decade ago as we began to understand the potential ramifications of cyber activity and attacks. It certainly attracted much-needed attention to cyber threats at that time. Have we already experienced a Cyber Pearl Harbor? Thankfully not. Is one theoretically possible? Yes, but it is critical to give context to what the threats mean without turning to untethered panic.

This debate is also a red herring; it sets a threshold for damage from a cyberattack that is quite high, ignoring that lower-level attacks can cause significant problems in everyday life as well as to our national and economic security, a kind of death by 1000 cuts. And just a cursory look at recent hacks of private-sector companies and government agencies should remind us that smaller-scale intrusions can be disruptive, dangerous and very costly even without catastrophic outcomes.

Question 2. You've detailed a number of existing threats in your testimony and responses. What are some of the future threats of concern in cyber security?

Answer. Given the pace of technological advancement, there is clearly much potential for future threats in the cyber realm. I'll focus on only two to provide examples of potential cyber risk. First, a supply chain cyber attack—usually when your adversary targets a trusted third-party vendor who supplies software or other services to your agency or company. The Russians hacked by deploying malicious code in management software used by thousands of government agencies and private companies. The hack gave the Russians great access into many public and private networks and is certainly a threat that could be repeated in the future. Even when companies or agencies manage their cybersecurity well, some of this is beyond their control because it resides with software developed outside their own enterprise.

The second is a newer concern—relating to the use of Artificial intelligence and machine learning that relies on data to make predictions and decisions. It's what's used in self-driving cars or translation tools for example. This is called "data poisoning" in which the attackers tamper with the data used to build the models— and "poisons" the data, rendering it unreliable or inaccurate.

Question 3. In September 2022, the U.S. activated the 3rd Multi-Domain Task Force in Hawaii to support the U.S. Indo-Pacific Command and the operations of the first task force activated in the region in 2017. To what extent does cyber play a role in our multidomain operations in the Indo-Pacific region?

Answer. Cyber is a critical part of our military operations—not only via US Cyber Command but in electronic warfare functions, intelligence and integrated into battle plans. The third multi domain task force brings together cyber, electronic warfare and intelligence. This activation supports the national security prominence of the Pacific Theater. Cyber is critical for both readiness and interoperability for all operations.

Question 4. To what extent is a cyber-attack a threat to our military operations and national security posture in the Indo-Pacific region? What are some potential consequences of such an attack?

Answer. In terms of a cyber attack—it would depend largely on the nature of the attack. First, we should note that there is a very good level of cyber preparedness by our military and a good amount of contingency planning to deal with the cyber threat. However, this preparedness does not inoculate forces in the region from disruption; nor can we say with absolute certainty how cyber attacks might lead to a serious escalation even beyond the Indo-Pacific region. There are many potential consequences of such an attack—for example, if the PRC Government makes the ill-advised decision to attack Taiwan, it will have to disrupt our military (and our allies') communications—so that threat is real and present. If an escalation ensues, there will be significant economic consequences with global impact.

Questions Submitted by Representative Grijalva

Question 1. The Offce of the Inspector General Audit found that several DOI components lacked sufficient authorizations, and the DOI did not conduct quality control reviews or submit those systems to FISMA audits. These DOI offices included the National Park Service, which manages Americans' transactions and reservations to national parks through recreation.gov, and the Bureau of Trust Funds Administration, which manages over $5 billion in trust for Native Americans. Please describe how a breach at these two offices might have real consequences for individuals.

Answer. These data breaches can provide unauthorized access to Personal Identifiable Information (PII)—depending on the type of transaction, anything from credit card numbers to birthdays to social security numbers to passport numbers. The real consequences often occur when this type of information is found on what is called "the Dark Web"—kind of the "Star Wars Bar" of cyber criminals where lots of information can be procured. The information can be used for scams, to procure other credit cards, and for any of us who have experienced this form of identity theft—it is quite a hassle and can cause considerable stress. In many cases, the victim has to replace their credit cards or even other forms of identification such as driver's licenses or passports. Victims may have their credit frozen for important transactions like home mortgages or choose to freeze their credit while investigations are being conducted. The other consequence is what the breach does to the reputation of the office/organization that was hacked—there are major reputational issues including a loss of trust by clients/customers.

Question 2. Federal agencies like the Department of the Interior increasingly rely on non-federal entities for services. For example, Booz Allen Hamilton, a major consulting form, runs recreation.gov. What are best practices for protecting federal assets that contractors have access to when the federal government does not control the contractor's cyber infrastructure?

Answer. There are already a number of requirements for contractor cybersecurity especially in the Defense sector, such as those provided by the Defense Federal Acquisition Regulation Supplement (DFARS) and the Cybersecurity Maturity Model Certification (CMMC). These provide good practices and are based on the National Institute of Standards and Technology (NIST) 800-171 (Controlled Unclassified information). General best practices are familiar ones—including such items as Multi-Factor Authentication, certain types of perimeter and endpoint protection and internal penetration and vulnerability scans. I would add that the federal agency itself must take proactive steps to monitor compliance by contractors when possible and establish firm and clear deadlines, accountability and requirements for notification in the case of a contractor breach.

Question 3. There are concerns that the significant budget cuts included in the recent debt ceiling deal would limit funding available for federal cybersecurity, much like how the cuts to agency funding recently proposed by Republicans could negatively impact our ability to fulfill NEPA requirements. What impact does funding insecurity and uncertainty have on an agency's ability to address cybersecurity threats?

Answer. Cybersecurity and cyber resiliency are not inexpensive—and this is not only a matter of dollars. In addition to the monetary costs, there is also the challenge of finding human resources—people with the right cyber and technology skills to institute best practices, stay on top of technological advancement and to move with agility and speed as necessary. Lack of funding and resources result in gaps in our ability to protect today's threats; lack of funding negates our ability to prepare strategically, operationally and coherently for new threats and future risks. It is difficult to make our networks and systems resilient when our resources are so limited that we can, at best, put out fires and try to fend off the latest hack. It is difficult to ensure cyber resilience when we put off replacing legacy systems or do it in a piecemeal fashion. I'm not arguing for unlimited cyber funding; that would be unrealistic. I am advocating consistent, prioritized funding that is built on a multi-year program without interruptions, sudden funding swings or "salami slice" cuts lacking a sound rationale.

Mr. COLLINS. Thank you, Ms. Siers. The Chair now recognizes Dr. Clancy for 5 minutes.

Statement of T. Charles Clancy, Sr., Senior Vice President and General Manager, Mitre Labs, and Chief Futurist, the Mitre Corporation, Mclean, Virginia

Dr. CLANCY. Mr. Collins, Ranking Member Stansbury, Committee members, thank you for inviting me to testify before you today on this topic of critical national importance. My name is Charles Clancy. I am a Senior Vice President at MITRE, where I lead science, technology, and engineering for the company.

MITRE is a non-profit, non-partisan research institution that operates federally funded research and development centers, or FFRDCs, on behalf of the U.S. Government. We provide deep cybersecurity expertise across the executive branch and the Federal judiciary.

Before joining MITRE, I led cybersecurity research and development programs as a professor at Virginia Tech, and as a scientist at the National Security Agency.

Over the past 5 years, the cyber threat environment has continued to change. Organized crime continues to target enterprise network environments with ransomware, including those used by the U.S. Government. China and Russia have elevated their offensive cyber programs into strategic instruments of statecraft.

The Director of National Intelligence's annual threat assessment concludes that China could almost certainly disrupt oil and gas pipelines and rail infrastructure in the United States, and would do so to deter U.S. military action by impeding our decisionmaking, inducing societal panic, and disrupting military mobilization. It also assesses that Russia is focused on attacking U.S. undersea cables and industrial control systems.

But let's, I guess, focus in a bit more on some of the enterprise networks that have been germane to the discussion so far today. I guess I want to differentiate that a bit from the critical infrastructure that Department of the Interior has oversight authority over.

So, starting with the internal enterprise networks that DOI operates, they are all governed by requirements stemming from the Federal Information Security Modernization Act, or FISMA, which was originally passed in 2002 and has gone through a number of legislative updates. This Act emphasizes a risk-based approach to cybersecurity with protections commensurate to the level of data that needs to be protected by those agencies.

Helping agencies implement FISMA is a number of key standards from NIST. So, NIST provides their security control baselines, known as Special Publication 853, and the Risk Management Framework, or RMF. These all cover the things we talked about in the earlier panels, including password complexity and multi-factor authentication, and are best practices across the entire executive branch.

The White House has also taken steps to move beyond these tools and require Federal agencies to implement zero trust architectures, which was part of an executive order 2 years ago. DOI would be well served by developing and executing a plan to implement the NIST Risk Management Framework, or RMF, and the new and emerging Federal Zero Trust cybersecurity principles that go beyond MFA, in terms of securing enterprise networks.

Shifting gears to look at the privately-operated critical infrastructure that the Department of the Interior has some oversight over, this is sort of a different set of authorities, a different set of levers that might be pulled to improve cybersecurity. So, critical infrastructure is most often operated by private organizations, subject to some form of regulations.

Sector risk management agencies, or SRMAs, have been mentioned a couple of times in passing so far during the hearing, are responsible for the cybersecurity of those named critical infrastructure sectors. SRMAs typically promote the use of the NIST cybersecurity framework, another NIST document that is really focused on cybersecurity for privately-operated critical infrastructure systems. While much of this ecosystem today relies on voluntary compliance and information-sharing, the National Cybersecurity Strategy that was published earlier this year by the White House seeks to establish minimum cybersecurity requirements, rather than a voluntary compliance regime for U.S. critical infrastructure.

Recent reports from the GAO highlight cybersecurity concerns with offshore oil and gas industry. While not designated an SRMA, the Bureau of Safety and Environmental Enforcement, or BSEE, does oversee security for this industry. The Bureau could leverage its rulemaking authorities in collaboration with other Federal partners to develop a minimum set of cybersecurity requirements based on the NIST cybersecurity framework, and that is consistent with the National Cybersecurity Strategy.

Major operators of offshore energy and their corresponding onshore transportation infrastructure could implement an integrated strategy for securing both, which the intelligence community assesses as specifically under threat from China.

Recent cyber attacks against Guam attributed to China are also concerning. The tactics used by the CCP are not unique to Guam. Given the strategic importance of Guam's critical infrastructure to the Department of Defense, DOI and DOD could develop a closer partnership on securing the infrastructure upon which both the U.S. military and citizens of Guam depend. This could include leveraging DOD's cyber protection teams and other assets to collaboratively perform a cybersecurity vulnerability assessment of Guam's infrastructure and systems.

Implementing any of these requirements come down to workforce. Certainly, we have talked a bit about the competitive nature of the cybersecurity talent base. I will point out that the Department of the Interior does not have a current permanent chief information security officer, and I would recommend filling that position as soon as possible. Other departments and regulatory commissions have consolidated organizations focused on cybersecurity and resilience within the industries that they regulate.

One option could be to establish a cybersecurity cell within the Office of the Secretary that is focused on coordinating cybersecurity strategy and policy across all segments of DOI's regulatory and oversight apparatus.

Thank you. And with that, I look forward to your questions.

[The prepared statement of Dr. Clancy follows:]

Prepared Statement of Dr. Charles Clancy, Senior Vice President, MITRE

Chairman Gosar, Ranking Member Stansbury, Ranking Member Grijalva, and Committee Members:

Thank you for inviting me to testify before you today on a topic of critical national importance. My name is Charles Clancy and I am a Senior Vice President at MITRE where I lead science, technology, and engineering for the company. MITRE is a non-profit, non-partisan research institution that operates Federally Funded Research and Development Centers (FFRDCs) on behalf of the U.S. Government. Among other technical disciplines, our team of over 1,500 cybersecurity professionals provide deep expertise across the executive branch and federal judiciary, including in support of organizations like the Cybersecurity and Infrastructure Security Agency (CISA), the National Institute of Standards and Technology (NIST), and U.S. Cyber Command. MITRE's ATT&CKTM framework has become the de facto language between government and industry for describing and combatting cyber threats.

Prior to joining MITRE, I spent nine years as a member of the faculty at Virginia Tech where I held the Bradley Distinguished Professorship of Cybersecurity in the Department of Electrical and Computer Engineering, and served as executive director of what is now the National Security Institute. I started my career at the National Security Agency leading research and development programs.

Threat Environment

Over the past five years, the cyber threat environment has changed considerably. Among criminal elements we have seen the dramatic rise of ransomware giving organized crime new business models for exploiting enterprise computer networks and systems. This has fueled secondary industries, such as hacker groups focused exclusively on penetrating organizations and selling that access to the highest bidder. Well-financed criminal hacker groups now develop new cyber tools on par with nation-state hackers. While U.S. action against major ransomware groups has stunted what was astronomical growth in the ransomware economy, it remains a major threat.

Meanwhile China and Russia have elevated their offensive cyber programs into strategic instruments of statecraft.

China's cyber program had been primarily focused on espionage: stealing secrets from governments and intellectual property from companies. However, the Chinese Communist Party (CCP) has expanded their operations to also hack into critical infrastructure systems and preposition access that could be used for strategic effect in the U.S. and beyond.

Russia's espionage and information operations posture has similarly expanded to include critical infrastructure. But unlike China, Russia has the ongoing war in Ukraine as a backdrop for pulling the trigger on their cyber weapons, normalizing destructive cyber attacks against civilian infrastructure as part of military conflict. Beyond shifting international norms, they are also gaining experience they can employ beyond Ukraine, in Europe and North America.

The Director of National Intelligence released their annual threat assessment in February in which they assessed that China could almost certainly disrupt oil and gas pipelines and rail infrastructure in the U.S. and would do so to deter U.S. military action by impeding our decision making, inducing societal panic, and disrupting military mobilization. It also assessed that Russia is focused on attacking U.S. undersea cables and industrial control systems.[59]

Importantly, the goal of inducing societal panic skews the nature of traditional state actor cyber tactics. Beyond targeting specific civilian

---

[59] Office of the Director of National Intelligence, "Annual Threat Assessment of the U.S. Intelligence Community," 6 February 2023. https://www.dni.gov/files/ODNI/documents/assessments/ATA-2023-Unclassified-Report.pdf.

infrastructure that has downstream military impacts, state actors are now acting more like terrorist groups, using cyber attacks—or the threat of cyber attacks—to induce fear.

With this as a backdrop, all federal agencies need to remain vigilant against cyber attacks targeting their enterprise infrastructure and take steps to promote cybersecurity within the industries and jurisdictions they oversee.

Enterprise Security for the Department of the Interior (DOI)

Recent reports by DOI's Inspector General highlighted cybersecurity concerns.[60,61] While I am not able to assess these specific reports, there are a range of recommendations and best practices used by other federal agencies that could be beneficial if adopted by DOI.

Much of the U.S. federal cybersecurity ecosystem is governed by requirements stemming from the Federal Information Security Modernization Act (FISMA) originally enacted in 2002, updated in 2014,[62] and currently undergoing another legislative update in both the House and Senate to account for the modern threat environment and new defensive technologies.[63] The act emphasizes a risk-based approach to cybersecurity, with protections commensurate with the level of data that needs to be protected by agencies. There are a variety of resources that reinforce and provide detailed guidance on implementation of FISMA, including Office of Management and Budget

---

[60] Office of the Inspector General, Department of the Interior, ''Semiannual Report to Congress,'' 31 March 2023. https://www.doioig.gov/sites/default/files/2021-migration/DOIOIGSemiannualReporttoCongressMarch2023.pdf.

[61] Office of the Inspector General, Department of the Interior, ''The U.S. Department of the Interior's Cyber Risk Management Practices Leave Its Systems at Increased Risk of Compromise,'' 2020-ITA-030, February 2023. https://www.doioig.gov/sites/default/files/2021-migration/Final%20Evaluation%20Report_DOI%20Cyber%20Risk%20Management_Public.pdf.

[62] ''Federal Information Security Act of 2014,'' Public Law 113-283, December 2014. https://www.congress.gov/113/plaws/publ283/PLAW-113publ283.pdf.

[63] Dave Powner, ''When it comes to federal cybersecurity policy, the executive branch is far ahead of Congress,'' Nextgov, 17 June 2022. https://www.nextgov.com/ideas/2022/06/closing-gap-cyber-policy-focusing-fisma/368353/.

(OMB) circulars,[64] the NIST Risk Management Framework,[65] and NIST's security control baselines.[66]

In response to continued threats from advanced threat actors, the White House has taken steps to move beyond these tools and require federal agencies to implement zero trust architectures, through executive action[67] and OMB memoranda.[68] These provisions are expected to be part of legislative updates to FISMA. DOI would be well served by developing a plan to implement the NIST Risk Management Framework and Federal Zero Trust Cybersecurity Principles into their enterprise network infrastructure.

Critical Infrastructure Security

A decade ago, a variety of executive[69] and legislative[70] actions created much of the critical infrastructure cybersecurity environment we operate in today. Critical infrastructure is most often operated by private organizations and subjected to some form of regulation. These actions established Sector Risk Management Agencies (SRMAs) responsible for cybersecurity of named critical infrastructure sectors, ultimately led to the Department of Homeland

---

[64] Office of Management and Budget, ''Managing Federal Information as a Strategic Resource,'' Circular A-130, June 28, 2016. https://www.federalregister.gov/documents/2016/07/28/2016-17872/revision-of-omb-circular-no-a-130-managing-information-as-a-strategic-resource.

[65] National Institute of Standards and Technology, ''Risk Management Framework for Information Systems and Organizations,'' NIST Special Publication 800-37, rev2, December 2018. https://nvlpubs.nist.gov/nistpubs/SpecialPublications/NIST.SP.800-37r2.pdf.

[66] National Institute of Standards and Technology, ''Security and Privacy Controls for Information Systems and Organizations,'' NIST Special Publication 800-53, rev5, 23 September 2020. https://nvlpubs.nist.gov/nistpubs/SpecialPublications/NIST.SP.800-53r5.pdf.

[67] The White House, ''Executive Order on Improving the Nation's Cybersecurity,'' EO 14028, May 12, 2021. https://www.whitehouse.gov/briefing-room/presidential-actions/2021/05/12/executive-order-on-improving-the-nations-cybersecurity/.

[68] Office of Management and Budget, ''Moving the U.S. Government Toward Zero Trust Cybersecurity Principles,'' M-22-09, 26 January 2022. https://www.whitehouse.gov/wp-content/ uploads/2022/01/M-22-09.pdf.

[69] The White House, ''Improving Critical Infrastructure Cybersecurity,'' EO 13636, 12 February 2013. https://obamawhitehouse.archives.gov/the-press-office/2013/02/12/execu tive-order- improving-critical-infrastructure-cybersecurity.

[70] ''Cybersecurity Information Sharing Act of 2015,'' Public Law 114-113, 18 December 2015. https://www.congress.gov/114/plaws/publ113/PLAW-114publ113.pdf.

Security establishing CISA, and resulted in NIST creating its Cybersecurity Framework[71] to provide an approach to securing critical infrastructure.

Much of this ecosystem today relies on voluntary compliance and the establishment of communities where sectors can freely share cyber threat information called Information Sharing and Analysis Centers (ISACs). While this approach has dramatically improved cybersecurity, major gaps remain across every industry, and there are periodic calls to shift voluntary compliance regimes to compulsory, with corresponding push back from industry over the associated costs. The National Cybersecurity Strategy published earlier this year seeks to establish required minimum cybersecurity safeguards for U.S. critical infrastructure.[72]

Recent reports from the Government Accountability Office[73] and the National Security Agency[74] highlight cybersecurity concerns connected with infrastructure over which DOI has some oversight. While not a designated SRMA, the Bureau of Safety and Environmental Enforcement (BSEE) does oversee security for the offshore energy industry. BSEE could leverage its rulemaking authorities, in collaboration with other federal partners, to develop a minimum set of cybersecurity requirements based on the NIST Cybersecurity Framework and consistent with the National Cybersecurity Strategy. Major operators of offshore energy infrastructure and their corresponding onshore transportation infrastructure could implement an integrated strategy for securing both, which the Intelligence Community assesses is specifically under threat from China.1

Recent cyber attacks against Guam attributed to China are also concerning,[75] though the tactics used by the CCP are not unique to Guam. Given the strategic importance of Guam's critical infrastructure to the Department of Defense (DOD) strategy, DOI and DOD should develop a closer partnership on securing infrastructure upon which both the U.S. military

---

[71] National Institute of Standards and Technology, ''Cybersecurity Framework''. https://www.nist.gov/cyberframework.

[72] Office of the National Cyber Director, ''National Cybersecurity Strategy,'' March 2023. https://www.whitehouse.gov/wp-content/uploads/2023/03/National-Cybersecurity-Strategy-2023.pdf.

[73] Government Accountability Office, ''Offshore Oil and Gas: Strategy Urgently Needed to Address Cybersecurity Risks to Infrastructure,'' GAO-23-105789, October 2022. https://www.gao.gov/assets/gao-23-105789.pdf.

[74] Joint Cybersecurity Advisory, ''People's Republic of China State-Sponsored Cyber Actor Living off the Land to Evade Detection,'' PP-23-1143, May 2023. https://media.defense.gov/2023/May/24/2003229517/-1/-1/0/CSA_Living_off_the_Land.PDF.

[75] Wired, ''China Hacks US Critical Networks in Guam, Raising Cyberwar Fears,'' 24 May 2023. https://www.wired.com/story/china-volt-typhoon-hack-us-critical-infrastructure/.

and the citizens of Guam depend. This should include leveraging DOD's Cyber Protection Teams and other assets to collaboratively perform cybersecurity vulnerability assessments of Guam's infrastructure and systems.

Workforce and Leadership

A major challenge across the board in cybersecurity is workforce. The cybersecurity workforce gap nationally continues to grow, with 40% of the 1.9 million cybersecurity positions currently being vacant.[76] In this climate, DOI has stiff competition in recruiting and retaining cybersecurity talent. Partnering with an FFRDC could be a good part of the solution, but longer-term, the department needs to build its organic talent base. One option could be to target students graduating from the Cybercorps Scholarship for Service program who have a federal service commitment upon graduation.[77]

The Department needs a permanent Chief Information Security Officer (CISO). Such a position is critical to securing enterprise infrastructure.

Other departments and regulatory commissions have consolidated organizations focused on cybersecurity and resilience for the industries they regulate. While BSEE has that remit, it only focuses on offshore resources and reportedly has only one employee focused on cybersecurity.[78] One option could be to establish a cybersecurity cell within the Office of the Secretary focused on coordinating cybersecurity strategy and policy across all segments of DOI's regulatory and oversight apparatus. The team could participate in interagency efforts like the Cybersecurity Forum for Independent and Executive Branch Regulators.[79]

---

[76] Cyberseek, "Cybersecurity Supply/Demand Heat Map," accessed 5 June 2023. https://www.cyberseek.org/heatmap.html.

[77] Office of Personnel Management, "Cybercorps Scholarship for Service," accessed 5 June 2023. https://sfs.opm.gov/.

[78] Kevin Sligh, "BSEE proactively addressing cybersecurity and offshore energy production," 3 January 2023. https://www.bsee.gov/kevin-sligh-bsee-proactively-addressing-cybersecurity-and-offshore-energy-production.

[79] Cybersecurity Forum for Independent and Executive Branch Regulators, "Charter". https://www.nrc.gov/docs/ML1501/ML15014A296.pdf.

Conclusion and Recommendations

DOI is not alone. It can leverage deep expertise across the interagency to improve its own enterprise cybersecurity, and work with key partners across DHS and DOD to help secure infrastructure over which it has some oversight. With a proactive cybersecurity strategy, it can build momentum by adopting best practices and forging interagency relationships.

Questions Submitted for the Record to T. Charles Clancy, PhD, Senior Vice President and General Manager, MITRE Labs

Questions Submitted by Representative Gosar

Question 1. Is anything stopping the Department of the Interior from allocating a greater percentage of its existing budget to cybersecurity initiatives?

Question 2. How can DOI better prioritize cybersecurity initiatives with its existing budget?

Answer. Thank you for these important and timely questions. As was discussed during the hearing, DOI faces two separate cybersecurity challenges: securing their own enterprise IT infrastructure, and effectively governing the security of certain critical infrastructure under their purview.

In general, some level of improved cybersecurity is possible within current budgets, but robust implementations will require modernization and new funding. The absence of new funding will require evaluating budgetary tradeoffs between existing priorities and critical modernization needs.

Enterprise IT

With respect to enterprise IT security, many of the baseline recommendations from the Inspector General are achievable within their current budget for many of their IT systems. Enabling and requiring passphrases and multi-factor authentication requires little software change, and is primarily changes to system policies. The costs are primarily around user training, which should be absorbable into the broader training requirements for federal employees.

However there are two areas that would likely require additional investment above and beyond their current IT budget: deploying zero trust, and addressing legacy systems.

Executive Order 14028 put into motion requirements for federal agencies to adopt zero trust architectures to deal with increased threats from cyber adversaries. Implementing zero trust requires procuring and deploying additional software systems within the enterprise, and implementing it fully often requires rearchitecting enterprise networks with concepts like micro-segmentation. These changes would best be achieved if done as part of a larger enterprise IT modernization that looked to more fully embrace a FEDRAMP-approved cloud-based solutions. With respect to legacy systems, based on testimony during the hearing, DOI has certain IT systems that are aging and lack the capability to be upgraded with modern cybersecurity defenses. Many federal agencies are facing these same challenges, such as the Internal Revenue Service.[80] While it may be possible to put "band aid" solutions on top of these legacy systems to achieve some level of compliance, they represent serious technology debt whose modernization costs only continue to increase over time. The solution is modernization, the sooner the better. While these represent increased costs in the near term, over time they represent cost savings as smaller IT teams are needed long term when leveraging cloud-based Software as a Service (SaaS) solutions.

Of course, the cybersecurity safeguards being discussed for DOI represent really only the bare minimum for best practices by federal agencies. A more comprehensive solution would be to fully embrace and implement the NIST Risk Management Framework (RMF) within DOI's enterprise systems.

Critical Infrastructure

Addressing cybersecurity for critical infrastructure under DOI's purview, such as offshore oil and gas production, is implemented by an entirely different portion of the DOI enterprise, and is more focused on developing and promulgating cybersecurity policy, and ensuring appropriate compliance auditing across industry. Organizations like BSEE are sufficiently resourced for baseline policy development, but need to prioritize cybersecurity as part of their safety mission. However, BSEE is likely insufficiently resourced to undertake the needed auditing function. Many critical infrastructure sector risk

[80] https://www.gao.gov/products/gao-23-104719.

management agencies lack the needed resourcing to fully provide the needed capacity building and compliance auditing for their industries.

Mr. COLLINS. Thank you, Dr. Clancy.

I want to thank all the witnesses for their testimony. We are going to move into Member questions, and I am going to recognize myself for 5 minutes.

Dr. Clancy, I want to kind of pick up on what you were just talking about. And I may bounce around. I hope we have time for several questions from Members. It looks like there are two of us, so we may.

Government agencies and interacting. You said, if I heard you right, that that may be an answer to find someone to interact with all of these agencies. Is that right?

Dr. CLANCY. Yes, the Department of the Interior has many different pieces of the critical infrastructure apparatus over which they have authority. And having a single point to coordinate across the Department, I think, would be helpful, and also coordinate up with the Office of the National Cyber Director.

Mr. COLLINS. Mr. Cavanaugh, can you add to that? Do they already talk within this agency, or is there any——

Mr. CAVANAUGH. Sir, to answer that question, I think the structure exists for that communication, as they are able to participate in their sector-specific coordinating councils, whether it be government facilities for the vast majority of the Department of the Interior, or if it is the energy sector, or food and Ag, even for the fisheries.

The challenge has been staffing at the Department of the Interior, and identifying the appropriately staffed individual or individuals that can cover those meetings and represent the Department.

Mr. COLLINS. So, pretty much, that is what you would say would be the barrier that is keeping them from sharing——

Mr. CAVANAUGH. Being more proactive in that engagement process. The structure is there, but it has not been a primary focus for the Department.

Mr. COLLINS. And I don't know if any of you all can answer any of this, or how much you delve into the DOI, but when we were asking the first panel some of the questions, we were talking about passwords. And I find it amazing that we have a government agency that is just now identifying maybe changing passwords to passphrases. I am in the private sector. We did that years ago.

Hardware and software, does anybody keep an inventory as to what needs to be upgraded, what hasn't been upgraded?

I mean, are we still using TRS 80 model 2s, or where is the problem at in DOI?

Dr. CLANCY. I guess I will say that, under FISMA there is a set of requirements to specifically identify systems. And based on the Inspector General's testimony, it sounds like there are tens of such systems across the Department of the Interior that have sort of separately received their authority to operate, or ATO, which basically says that they have, among other things, appropriate cybersecurity safeguards.

I believe the way it would work is they would go through each one of those individual accredited systems and look at what the gaps are for implementing some of these more sophisticated cyber-security protections, because each one likely is different, could be run by different agencies or parts of the Department.

Mr. COLLINS. Right. But it just seems like to me that, ultimately, as Mr. Cheng was alluding to, that we would be moving to a cloudbased system, where that is where you would really clamp down on your multi-factor authentication, and that shouldn't be a problem.

Mr. CHENG. Sir, one of the aspects that is, unfortunately, in play here is the software and the hardware that runs it that is embedded in a lot of the infrastructure itself, the supervisory control and data acquisition systems, or SCADA. These are, essentially, very small programs that make sure that the pipelines run, et cetera.

They have operating systems. In many cases, they are still running off of Windows——

Mr. COLLINS. Don't say 98.

Mr. CHENG. Well, a little better, but Windows 7. And the problem is that the chips that are running them, essentially minicomputers, if you will do not have the capacity to be upgraded. It is not like you can go in. You literally would have to rip out the entire machinery, and put a new one in that would be able to run Windows 10, Windows 11. But Microsoft has stopped upgrading and security updating for Windows 7.

So, in addition to the specific computer issues that have already been touched upon, there is that crossover to the literal infrastructure side of what is the level of security that is even possible on systems that were never designed to be updated, and certainly had not expected to be hacked.

Mr. COLLINS. I would agree, I just don't understand how we have agencies in the Federal Government that are that far behind. That doesn't really make sense to me.

Dr. CLANCY. I would say, from my perspective at MITRE, we see the IT infrastructure of much of the entire executive branch, and there are many agencies with 40-year-old systems still running today.

Mr. COLLINS. I know I am out of time, but one last question. I think it was Mr. Cavanaugh, you said hold employees accountable. We don't hold employees accountable for not following safety protocols, as far as even logging in?

Mr. CAVANAUGH. Having almost 13-plus years experience in the Federal Government, there is minimal accountability outside of being remediated by additional training. So, if you had a password issue, you were just assigned to take more security training. There was no actual accountability beyond training for employees.

Mr. COLLINS. I would have thought Colonial Pipeline at least would have been a huge wake-up call.

Ms. SIERS. Sir, let me add to this a little bit. We are successful, and in Federal agencies where there is success and accountability, it is because at the leadership level and the manager level it essentially becomes part of your contract. So, that has the way of changing the culture, focusing people.

I have personally, however, seen people lose their jobs over issues where there is a pattern of poor password usage and other abuses. So, I don't believe there is one answer for the entire Federal Government, but I do also really believe it is a leadership issue.

Mr. COLLINS. All right, thank you. I know my time has expired.

I recognize the Ranking Member, Ms. Stansbury, for 5 minutes.

Ms. STANSBURY. All right. Thank you so much, Mr. Collins. I want to follow up on some of the testimony that all of you have given already.

The first is this set of folks who have been involved in hacking and cyber attacks who are kind of in the interspace between state actors and private actors. And I know Ms. Siers, you talked a little bit about this in your oral testimony here today. But tell us more about what kind of organizations are we talking about. Are these professional criminal organizations? Are they shops that have been set up by state actors that are in a sort of quasi-private space, but doing contract work for them?

And what is their motivation? Why are they attacking the United States, and our systems, and our institutions?

Ms. SIERS. I would say it is a little bit of all of those. Let me just talk more about the purely criminal organizations.

This is an incredibly well-organized effort. You can buy anything you need on the Dark Web, which is kind of the cyber version of the Star Wars criminal bar. And you find all kinds of tools, you find negotiators to negotiate ransom with any victim. So, that is one category.

Then, of course, you have hacktivists, who generally claim to have political purposes and oppose certain operations or certain organizations.

And then you have this other group that we are not entirely sure on occasion where they come from, but we know a couple of things. One is they are either physically present or availing themselves of servers in specific states, and it is the usual suspects, to be honest: Russia, China, Iran, North Korea. And they are at least given tacit approval to do what they do at one end of the continuum. And at the far end of the continuum, they have direct state support. And sometimes that even includes—and we have seen this in Russia— moonlighting intelligence officers, who actually go there after hours and assist these groups.

We have also seen these patriotic hacktivist groups. Russia has used them on a number of occasions. They are using them now, they used them against Estonia. That is to afford them some kind of plausible deniability, so that they are really unable to point to a specific government figure.

So, you have this whole panoply. It makes attribution, which is kind of our whodunit in cyber, sometimes somewhat difficult, and it makes strategies to respond sometimes a little bit difficult, as well.

Ms. STANSBURY. Well, if there is one thing this hearing has been, it is terrifying to really understand the full breadth of the kinds of organizations and activities that are happening out in the world here.

And Mr. Cheng, as you were testifying today, and I know in your written testimony, as well, you mentioned the attack on Guam and its telecommunication systems, and sort of touched a little bit about the implications for a Chinese extension of its sphere of influence in the South Pacific. I wonder if you could talk a little bit more about that, and the implications for the United States and for our strategic and global position in the South Pacific, and our relationship with China.

Mr. CHENG. Absolutely, ma'am. As the People's Liberation Army has expanded its array of missile capabilities, operations within what is sometimes termed the First Island Chain, stretching from Japan through Okinawa, Taiwan, the Philippines, and down to the Straits of Malacca, have become much more problematic. Whether or not U.S. air bases, U.S. aircraft carriers, et cetera will be able to operate in those waters is becoming more difficult.

So, the Department of Defense is intent upon establishing, essentially, a fallback position in the Central Pacific through what is sometimes termed the

Second Island Chain, which would stretch through Guam, the Republic of the Marshall Islands, et cetera.

Notably, the Chinese have been working very hard to invest and to develop infrastructure across this region, but they are also monitoring what is going on there.

The other aspect to keep in mind is, especially on the island of Kwajalein, which is part of the Republic of the Marshall Islands and therefore within the DOI's remit, is an array of key defense facilities, including the Ronald Reagan Ballistic Missile Defense test site, a key site where we test our ICBMs, which is essential to nuclear deterrence, but also the establishment of the space fence, so that we can see what is coming, basically, over the horizon.

These are key targets for Chinese espionage, but as important in time of crisis or conflict would be facilities that would be targeted, ideally, through cyber means simply because of the distance from Chinese military forces. So, all of these are essential to maintaining American dominance through the Central Pacific region, and are primary targets for Chinese kinetic and non-kinetic means of attack.

Ms. STANSBURY. Well, thank you for sharing all that. One of the things that our Committee is doing, and you mentioned this in your testimony, while our Committee is primarily over the domestic functions of the Department of the Interior, this is the Committee that also oversees and does oversight over our relationship with many of the associated states and territories that are in that region. And we have just stood up a bipartisan task force to look at many of these issues, which myself and others are serving on.

I do have one more follow-up, which is really about the last two questions I asked. And Dr. Clancy, I didn't realize when I read your testimony initially that you had worked in the national security space outside of the private sector. So, I was really interested to hear that in your introduction.

You touched on this a little bit in your oral testimony, but since you do have that background, I wonder if you could talk a little bit more about what are some of the things that you see Congress and our agencies can do to beef up that relationship with DOD, and to make sure that we are really protecting these critical, critical assets and pieces of infrastructure on the cyber side so that we are not vulnerable to the kinds of attacks and espionage that we have been talking about.

Dr. CLANCY. Yes. I think, specific to Guam, I think there is a great opportunity for partnership with DOD, given they are a major component of the ecosystem there.

The example I said in my testimony is leveraging DOD cyber protection teams to go out and work collaboratively with the privately-operated Guam utilities to help identify potential vulnerabilities and beef up security.

Other things could be for the Department of Defense to start including language in the contracts that they have with local utilities for power, water, other sorts of things, requirements that they meet additional cybersecurity requirements. And while that would likely increase the cost of those services to DOD, it would also pro vide resources back to those utilities to help beef up the security, given there is such a dependence on that.

I will note that it is not just Guam, though. Hawaii is another big opportunity for DOD collaboration with local utilities, and some of the other territories, as well.

Ms. STANSBURY. Thank you very much. And we will be working on the NDAA in the coming months, and I think this is something we would really love to work with the Majority on, is to figure out how to make sure we are beefing up all of these resources.

So, thank you, Mr. Chairman, and I yield back.

Dr. GOSAR [presiding]. I thank the gentlelady, and she is right on, because we have the Holman Rule, so we can go line item by line item to make those priorities.

And Mr. Cheng, can you elaborate on the fundamental difference between Chinese and Western execution of cyber economic espionage? What is the fundamental difference between the two?

Mr. CHENG. The fundamental difference, sir, is that the West, for most purposes, is dominated by private industry. There aren't too many state-owned enterprises, state-run entities, and there is also a real separation of powers. Posse Comitatus title 10 versus title 50 are just some of the examples of how, in our system, the military is circumscribed in what it can do.

So, the idea that a Western government would put its cyber military elements out there to, say, steal data about X industrial or economic process creates fundamental issues, beginning with can the government order you to do that, to how would you even disseminate that data. If you gave data on new cars to Chrysler, Ford and GM would be unhappy. If you gave it to all three of those companies, you have probably told everyone in the world that you are engaging in cyber economic espionage.

In the case of China, every one of those aspects is different. The Chinese economy has substantial state-owned enterprises, which means that you can share data directly within the government because oil companies, steel companies, shipbuilding, those are part of the government.

And the Chinese have publicly in their own writings noted that the People's Liberation Army, which is a party army, it is not a national military, it is part of the Chinese Communist Party, it is supposed to do what the party needs it to do. And if that means the party needs it to go and steal economic information, intellectual property, map out private company data, establish, you know—that is a legitimate order for the PLA to acquire that data, which can then be shared within the Chinese system because these state-owned enterprises, the main beneficiaries, are part of the government, as well.

So, we are talking about a fundamentally different ecosystem, a fundamentally different view of the role and responsibilities for the armed forces. And let me note here that Chinese description of their cyber forces—again, from their writings—is the military, non-military governmental entities, but also non-governmental entities ranging from universities to private companies. The CCP is able to reach out and employ a whole-of-society approach within which, therefore, Chinese cyber economic espionage occurs. This is a very different model than anything we see in the West.

Dr. GOSAR. Wow. How much has the Chinese cyber capabilities improved over the past 10 years? And have they outpaced the United States in these capabilities?

Mr. CHENG. We are watching the Chinese steadily improve their cyber capabilities. Pre-2015 a lot of their cyber penetrations often left fingerprints. The Mandiant Report on APT1 back in 2013 was able to determine a PLA unit 61398 cyber activities because they were able to identify who some of these players were, who in turn had essentially left digital fingerprints of who they were.

Since 2016, they have become much tighter. It is harder to identify. But I would defer to either other members of this panel or people from our intelligence community who can provide much greater detail.

Dr. GOSAR. We have also heard today about staffing challenges with IT professionals in the Department and government-wide. What would prevent the Department from using its contracting authority to overcome some of these challenges? Could that be a potential short-term alternative?

Dr. Clancy and Mr. Cavanaugh, could you answer that?

Dr. CLANCY. I think, certainly, it is a function of budget. Many agencies and departments leverage outside contractors for IT work all the time. Certainly, MITRE, as an operator of federally funded research and development centers, we are turned to often by many of those agencies for such tasks. It is often just a function of having budget in order to do that.

Dr. GOSAR. OK.

Mr. CAVANAUGH. And from my perspective, the NIST cyber risk framework provides a great opportunity for them to direct a contractor to address some of those outstanding needs that they have.

But I would caution that right now the tendency across government is to chase after shiny objects and things you are hearing in the cyber community: Zero Trust architecture, polymorphic malware. We have spent a long time and a lot of energy and money building walls around our systems, and not a lot of time understanding what is on our systems and how to observe if anything is there, capturing the point of the fingerprints being left behind in other scenarios. It has just not been a priority.

So, we need to prioritize the infrastructure that has the highest likelihood and highest consequence for impact, and in that process also start closing the ability to detect when something is on our system.

Dr. GOSAR. So, is the procurement process part of the problem?

Mr. CAVANAUGH. I would argue, yes. Right now, there is a tendency to lean heavily in contract bundling, which doesn't always net the outcomes that you are hoping for. The current process makes it very hard for small businesses to engage, and a lot of your innovation in the tech sector is being driven by start-ups and small companies that are understanding the edge of technology.

I would risk that the Internet of Things that we have talked about for a few years now is now becoming the leading edge of where cyber vulnerabilities will exist. And the companies that are most apt to understand that and be able to address those needs may not be your larger corporations and Big Tech; it will most likely be small companies that have understood that, and are addressing only that, and not being driven by their corporate priorities.

Dr. GOSAR. I am going to ask this last question for each one of you to answer. What, if anything, is preventing the Department from prioritizing cybersecurity in their annual budget process?

I will start with you, Mr. Cavanaugh.

Mr. CAVANAUGH. I think the point we have seen today is maybe prioritization within staffing and leadership. So, they don't have a CISO, Dr. Clancy?

Dr. CLANCY. Correct.

Mr. CAVANAUGH. Yes, that is a huge challenge. So, not having a CISO and not having someone at the leadership level guide and direct strategies are pointless without leadership buy-in.

In terms of capturing how they get there today and appropriately budget for it, they need to have a strategy that identifies and prioritizes. They need to understand what it is they want to close down on and where they want to look.

We spoke a little bit about offshore oil and gas. I would also surmise that offshore wind, which is going to become a growing thing, is going to be equally vulnerable as oil and gas. Iran has already successfully proven that they are targeting wastewater and water treatment facilities.

Dr. GOSAR. Mr. Cheng?

Mr. CHENG. Sir, if we look at a corporation, and it is anything other than a cybersecurity company, IT security is an overhead problem. It is not a profit center. And I would suggest that, essentially, the same is going to be true not only for the Department of the Interior, but the Department of Commerce, even DOD and elsewhere, which is to say IT security is not seen as the primary mission of the agency. It is part of yes, I have to hire people, yes, I have to keep the lights on, I have to buy new desks for people, et cetera.

As I believe it was the GAO witness testified, 83 percent of the budget, when it comes to IT, is operations and maintenance. It is keeping the computers running. Antivirus software may be part of it, but it is largely, "I have the blue screen of death, how do I get my computer to turn back on?" not "Are the Chinese rummaging through my files?"

So, making it a priority, I guess part of the issue is going to be which part of the other responsibilities that are part of DOI on its web page, are you going to ask us to lower in priority or deprioritize? Is it managing the national parks? Is it overseeing offshore pipelines? Because unless you elevate it to—and that would have to be true across a lot of departments — "This is job two", it is going to be other duties as assigned.

Dr. GOSAR. Ms. Siers?

Ms. SIERS. Well, let me talk about this a little bit from the private sector. It is not a profit center until you are hacked, seriously. And then everything changes. And that is usually a good thing.

But the real problem, having listened to the term "legacy systems" used continuously by the first panel, which, of course, raises many concerns, the real issue is we are fighting fires every day. So, we focus on the tactical, and we don't talk about what Mr. Cheng referred to as the strategic issues down the road.

So, when our funds are limited, we are putting out the fires but we are not trying to consider what might happen, for example, with some of the improvements in AI, and how that is going to impact us. We are generally woefully unprepared for that, because it is human nature to respond to the first thing on your plate.

That involves leadership, again, and a certain form of management in terms of your cyber and your infrastructure. And in order to do that, you have to have a very disciplined budget process, as well, that takes every part of your budget and projects it 3, 4, 5 years ahead to see where the impact is going to be, and see what risk it is really going to help with.

Dr. GOSAR. Mr. Clancy?

Dr. CLANCY. I think that is a great point there. The legacy system issue is, I think, also coupled in with the cybersecurity issue. If you spend a whole bunch of money on cybersecurity Band- Aids to put on top of legacy systems, you may be throwing good money after bad. So, it might be better to think about a broader IT modernization effort that includes improving cybersecurity as part of it to get a more systemic set of solutions.

Also, I want to note that that is specifically with respect to their enterprise IT infrastructure. That is different than having the right experts to help with the regulatory aspects of overseeing the cybersecurity of the private sector-operated infrastructure like the offshore oil and gas.

Many critical infrastructure sectors, specific agencies have workforce shortages there. I think after the Colonial Pipeline hack we realized how ill-staffed TSA was to help respond. Same thing with the Florida wastewater attack a couple of years ago, where EPA, again, was caught flat-footed without a robust team of people who were really paying attention to this.

So, I think there are sort of two different strategies. There is a broader IT modernization strategy, I think, that is needed for the enterprise infrastructure, but also getting the right experts in to help with the regulatory and oversight component.

Dr. GOSAR. So, I am going to ask one thing. What was the question that you wanted asked, and it wasn't asked, and what is the answer? What keeps you up at night?

We are going to go back in reverse order. Mr. Clancy.

Dr. CLANCY. I guess I will just note that I think with China and Taiwan, we are in sort of a couple-year window here to figure out how to combat large-scale cyber attacks against U.S. critical infrastructure. And that window is getting shorter and shorter, and I think we need to take aggressive action to speed this up across all sectors.

I mentioned that, specifically, electric power, rail, oil, and gas are all being specifically targeted by China to incapacitate them so that, if they take action in Taiwan, we are unable to respond effectively. And this is a scenario that is only a few years down the road, potentially.

And the offshore oil and gas production is part of that ecosystem, and is as vulnerable or more vulnerable than many of the other aspects.

Dr. GOSAR. Ms. Siers?

Ms. SIERS. I think the question I would have liked is what are the consequences, truly, of hacking into a Federal agency. I mean, what really happens to you? I am not talking about the person who messes up the passwords.

And I think there are several levels of consequences we have to think about. The first is standard law enforcement indictments. We have seen a lot of them against the usual suspects. They are useful in some ways.

And lately, we have also seen efforts, though, to disrupt vulnerabilities writ large. And what it simply means is we are not just focusing on a vulnerability that affects a Federal agency, something wrong with a Microsoft application, for example. We are seeing vulnerabilities challenged, information being provided, patches being provided by government entities for everyone to use. And the third part of this, which I think is probably the most important, I think the Ranking Member referred to the takedown of Hive recently, a Russian group. In essence, the U.S. Government, the FBI, hacked into it and took it down. It also provided the keys to a whole group of victims of Hive, both, I would believe, government and private sector.

So, I think we have to be clearer about what the consequences are, and I think we have to develop that as we develop this kind of culture in the Federal Government that cybersecurity becomes a priority mission.

Dr. GOSAR. Thank you. Mr. Cheng?

Mr. CHENG. Actually, I guess I had two. My first question that I wish had been asked, and I don't have an answer to at all, is the extent to which, when there is a CISO at the Department of the Interior, how often do they interact in particular with Cyber Command and with the rest of the intelligence community, not simply from a law enforcement perspective, but broader, being informed about the nation state actors, the gray zone actors, et cetera.

And then the other part of this would have been to ask, actually, the two previous witnesses, are your agencies engaging in two- factor authentication? Do you have, personally, passphrases as opposed to passwords?

And what about the rest of the government? Is the Department of the Interior unique, or is the Department of the Interior actually not so bad because they only could penetrate 20 percent of the passwords? Commerce, Treasury, Energy, Education, et cetera. How well do they do?

Dr. GOSAR. Mr. Cavanaugh?

Mr. CAVANAUGH. For myself, I think the question I would have liked to have been asked is the vulnerability aspect. But I can address that in a couple of terms real quick here, which is things that keep me up at night.

Spending 3 years in the National Security Council as a Senior Director for Resilience, the first phone call from the Sit Room was usually to me before they woke other people up. So, I have seen a lot of things that kept me up at night. But I will say the pervasiveness of the nation state actors and the ends to which they will be willing to go, it is a very cost-effective measure, which is very expensive to defend against. So, for them, this is a way to bleed people out. They can instill a million paper cuts while you try and take care of all your paper cuts. It is going to cost a lot of money. And with that in mind, the things we could be doing differently is looking at our vulnerabilities through three lenses. From a software perspective, are we closing the detection gap in our software? Do we see what is on our software that shouldn't be there? And it gets back to the hashes, and it gets back to some of the encryption capabilities. It is not a hard lift, and I am sure there are companies out there that are exploring this, and we just haven't seen it yet. On the hardware side, I think the CHIPS Act is a pretty strong move to get a good understanding of supply chain, and understanding what semiconductors mean to that supply chain. So, I think there were some efforts in the NDAA last year toward semiconductors. The ones that most worry me are essential or legacy semiconductors, because they are the most pervasive semiconductor in our systems, which I think they account for 75 or more percent of semiconductors.

And then lastly, the human factor, which is going back to the accountability piece, which we discussed earlier today, is how do we instill accountability at the employee level with the government employees who we entrust so much with.

Dr. GOSAR. Well, I just have to tell you, we ask that question because that helps us generate more questions, but it gives us a better understanding.

So, I want to thank the panel. It has been an absolute pleasure. I wish more Members would have attended, because it is incredible, what we learned today.

The members of the Committee may also have some additional questions for the witnesses, and we ask that you respond to them in writing. Under Committee Rule 3, members of the Committee must submit those questions to the Subcommittee clerk by 5 p.m. on June 12. The hearing record will be held open for 10 business days for those responses.

If there is no further business, without objection, we are adjourned.

[Whereupon, at 4 p.m., the Subcommittee was adjourned.]

Chapter 3

Evaluating CISA's Federal Civilian Executive Branch Cybersecurity Programs*

Committee on Homeland Security

Tuesday, September 19, 2023

U.S. House of Representatives, Committee on Homeland Security,
Subcommittee on Cybersecurity and Infrastructure Protection,
Washington, DC.

The subcommittee met, pursuant to notice, at 10:05 a.m., at Room 310, Cannon House Office Building, Hon. Andrew R. Garbarino [Chairman of the subcommittee] presiding.

Present: Representatives Garbarino, Gimenez, Ezell, Lee, Carter, and Menendez.

Chairman GARBARINO. The Committee on Homeland Security Subcommittee on Cybersecurity and Infrastructure Protection will come to order. Without objection, the Chair may recess at any point. The purpose of this hearing is to receive testimony from industry experts on CISA's two flagship cybersecurity programs for the Federal Civilian Executive branch. I now recognize myself for an opening statement.

Thank you for our witnesses for being here to talk about a very important topic CISA's Federal cybersecurity programs. One of CISA's core missions is the protection of the Federal Civilian Executive branch, or FCEB. Although

---

* This is an edited, reformatted and augmented version of Hearing Before the Subcommittee on Cybersecurity and Infrastructure Protection of the Committee on Homeland Security, House of Representatives, One Hundred Eighteenth Congress, First Session, Serial No. 118–29, dated September 19, 2023.

In: Cybersecurity Challenges and Strategies Across Sectors …
Editor: Marybeth Wiskoff
ISBN: 979-8-90134-039-4

CISA has been pulled in many different directions in recent years, it is crucial that it continues to focus on its foundational responsibilities, chief among them being the protection of FCEB networks. Today, we will focus on two programs, the Continuous Diagnostic and Mitigation Program, or CDM, and the National Cybersecurity Protection System, or NCPS, which includes EINSTEIN.

In recent years, CISA officials have indicated their intent to revamp and improve these programs. We will discuss with industry partners who participate in and have perspectives on these two programs, some of the successes they have had so far, and the ways they can improve in the future. CDM provides tools to agencies to defend their networks, which feed data into dashboards to allow agencies to monitor their real-time network security. Conceptually, those agency-specific dashboards send data to a Federal Government-wide dashboard that CISA uses to monitor the state of FCEB security. The current model provides 2 years of CISA- sourced funding for CDM tools at agencies, after which point agencies must pick up the bill.

NCPS is a set of capabilities that includes EINSTEIN, CISA's Intrusion Detection and Intrusion Prevention System. EINSTEIN sensors reside on the perimeter of an agency's network and detect and block known malicious traffic. While this perimeter security function is important, it is not sufficient for a cybersecurity program, given the current threat landscape and the ability of bad actors to evade many perimeter security mitigations. What is more, EINSTEIN has faced long-standing downsides, including limitations in detecting and preventing encrypted traffic and focusing only on what we already know is malicious traffic.

NCPS's authorization expires at the end of the fiscal year. In the President's fiscal year 2024 budget request, CISA included a $425 million request for the Cyber Analytics and Data System, or CADS, which is meant to take the place of NCPS. CISA intends to transition certain legacy capabilities of EINSTEIN into the new CAD system, and others will be taken over by new CADS capability. While CISA has not provided many public details about its plans to build CADS, I am looking forward to hearing from our witnesses their thoughts on how CISA should be approaching this new analytic capability.

As the administrator of Federal cybersecurity requirements, CISA has the broad and important role in ensuring the security of Federal networks. While the ultimate responsibility for an individual agency's security is the head of that agency through programs like CDM and EINSTEIN, CISA has the potential to make a real impact on Federal network security. The direction

CISA takes with these programs, and to what extent they are administered as true shared service with the CISA covering continued cost, will dictate CISA's posture toward other Federal agencies moving forward.

Whether CISA acts as a service provider or an advisor toward other agencies is a fundamental question, and Congress and CISA must both be consistent in how they approach it across CISA's many missions and programs. I look forward to our witnesses' testimony and to discussing these questions with them in depth.

[The statement of Chairman Garbarino follows:]

Statement of Chairman Andrew R. Garbarino September 19, 2023

Thank you to our witnesses for being here to talk about a very important topic: CISA's Federal cybersecurity programs. One of CISA's core missions is protection of the Federal Civilian Executive branch, or FCEB. Although CISA has been pulled in many different directions in recent years, it's crucial that it continues to focus on its foundational responsibilities, chief among them being the protection of FCEB networks.

Today we will focus on two programs: the Continuous Diagnostics and Mitigation program, or CDM, and the National Cybersecurity Protection System, or NCPS, which includes EINSTEIN. In recent years, CISA officials have indicated their intent to revamp and improve these programs. We will discuss with industry partners, who participate in and have perspectives on these two programs, some of the successes they have had so far and ways they can improve in the future.

CDM provides tools to agencies to defend their networks, which feed data into dashboards to allow agencies to monitor their real-time network security. Conceptually, those agency-specific dashboards send data to a Federal Government-wide dashboard that CISA uses to monitor the state of FCEB cybersecurity. The current model provides 2 years of CISA-sourced funding for CDM tools at agencies, after which point agencies must pick up the bill.

NCPS is a set of capabilities that includes EINSTEIN, CISA's intrusion detection and intrusion prevention system. EINSTEIN sensors reside on the perimeter of an agency's network and detect and block known malicious traffic. While this perimeter security function is important, it is not sufficient for a cybersecurity program given the current threat landscape and the ability of bad actors to evade many perimeter security mitigations. What's more, EINSTEIN has faced long-standing downsides, including limitations on detecting and preventing encrypted traffic and focusing only on what we already know is malicious traffic. NCPS's authorization expires at the end of this fiscal year.

In the President's fiscal year 2024 budget request, CISA included a $425 million request for the Cyber Analytics and Data System, or CADS, which is meant to take the place of NCPS. CISA intends to transition certain legacy capabilities of EIN- STEIN into the new CADS system, and others will be taken over by new CADS capabilities. While CISA has not provided many public details about its plans to build CADS, I am looking forward to hearing from our witnesses their thoughts on how CISA should be approaching this new analytic capability.

As the administrator of Federal cybersecurity requirements, CISA has a broad and important role in ensuring the security of Federal networks. While the ultimate responsibility for an individual agency's security is the head of that agency, through programs like CDM and EINSTEIN, CISA has the potential to make a real impact on Federal network security. The direction CISA takes these programs, and to what extent they are administered as true shared services with CISA covering continued costs, will dictate CISA's posture toward other Federal agencies moving forward. Whether CISA acts as a service provider or an advisor toward other agencies is a fundamental question, and Congress and CISA must both be consistent in how they approach it, across CISA's many missions and programs.

I look forward to our witnesses' testimony and to discussing these questions with them in more depth.

Chairman GARBARINO. I now recognize the Ranking Member, the gentleman from New Jersey, Mr. Menendez, for his opening statement.

Mr. MENENDEZ. Good morning. I want to thank Chairman Garbarino for holding this important hearing to assess how CISA is modernizing its signature Federal network security programs to keep pace with the rapidly-evolving threat environment and advancements in technology. Two-and-a-half years ago, the solar wind supply chain attack forced the Federal Government to overhaul its approach to securing its networks and supply chains. The Biden- Harris administration made revamping Federal network security a top priority, issuing an ambitious Executive Order that brought to bear the full resources of every Federal agency with a cybersecurity mission.

Together with Congress, the administration made historic investments in improving Federal network security.

Not since the 2015 Office of Personnel Management breach had there been as much momentum for change in how we secure Federal networks. While President Biden and Congress certainly deserve credit for giving needed attention to Federal network security, it is critical that we continue our work to modernize Federal network security to avoid crisis-driven policy making. We must ensure that the programs we rely on to secure our networks can adapt to and integrate with new technologies and modern network architectures. We must endeavor to stay a step ahead of our adversaries, building upon our recent momentum to better detect malicious activity quickly and mitigate the risk posed by cyber intrusions.

CISA plays a central role in securing our Federal networks as the administrator of the National Cybersecurity Protection System, commonly referred to as NCPS, and the Continuous Diagnostics and Mitigation Program, commonly referred to as CDM. These pro grams complement CISA's other important powers, including the authority to issue security guidance and best practices, binding operational directives and emergency directives, which require agencies to take expedited action to secure their networks against a pressing threat or vulnerability.

Over the past 21⁄2 years, CISA has laid out its plans to modernize both NCPS and CDM programs. Earlier this year, CISA announced plans to sunset and replace its EINSTEIN intrusion detection system, which has limited effectiveness against novel threats and newer network architectures and shift remaining NCPS capabilities to a new program called the Cyber Analytics and Data System. Together, the legacy EINSTEIN capabilities and CADS will become the joint collaboration environment, commonly referred to as JCE, which CISA predicts will be, ''best-in-class analytical environment'' that utilizes increased automation to more efficiently analyze classified and unclassified data.

JCE holds tremendous promise, but successful implementation requires a clear vision and buy-in from both Federal and private-sector partners. CISA has worked to rapidly mature its CDM program to ensure that its Federal customers can tailor it to accommodate their unique security requirements. CDM is limited, however, in that it is deployed on IT technologies, not operational technology, or internet of things devices. Moreover, the Government Accountability Office recently found that CISA lacks the authority to test CDM tools on agency networks, which undermines its ability to ensure those tools are working as anticipated. I am interested in learning from witnesses today how we can improve the security value of both programs.

Before I close, I want to remind my colleagues that Government shutdowns are bad for Federal network security. We are nevertheless 2 weeks away from Government funding running out. During the last shutdown, which lasted 35 days, CISA issued its first emergency directive to Federal agencies ever. Having employees and IT contractors across the Government and at CISA furloughed at the time was not helpful. A continuing resolution would also impair CISA's critical work, as it would restrict CISA's ability to start new programs that match the current threat environment.

It is detrimental to our national security to slow investments in our Federal network security programs at such a critical moment in their maturation. Moving forward, the House and Senate need to pass a Homeland Security Appropriations bill that provides needed funding to CISA to carry out its vital missions. Now is not the time to take our foot off the gas. With that, I thank the witnesses for being here today. I look forward to their testimony.

[The statement of Hon. Menendez follows:]

Statement of Hon. Robert Menendez September 19, 2023

Two-and-a-half years ago, the SolarWinds supply chain attack forced the Federal Government to overhaul its approach to securing its networks and supply chains. The Biden-Harris administration made revamping Federal network security a top priority, issuing an ambitious Executive Order that brought to bear the full resources of every Federal agency with a cybersecurity mission. Together with Congress, the administration made historic investments in improving Federal network security.

Not since the 2015 Office of Personnel Management breach had there been as much momentum for change in how we secure Federal networks. While President Biden and Congress certainly deserve credit for giving needed attention to Federal network security, it is critical that we continue our work to modernize Federal network security to avoid crisis-driven policy making.

We must ensure that the programs we rely on to secure our networks can adapt to and integrate with new technologies and modern network architectures.

And we must endeavor to stay a step ahead of our adversaries, building upon our recent momentum to better detect malicious activity quickly and mitigate the risks posed by cyber intrusions.

CISA plays a central role in securing our Federal networks as the administrator of the National Cybersecurity Protection System, commonly referred to as NCPS, and the Continuous Diagnostics and Mitigation program, commonly referred to as CDM. These programs complement CISA's other important powers, including the authority to issue security guidance and best practices, Binding Operational Directives, and Emergency Directives, which require agencies to take expedited action to secure their networks against a pressing threat or vulnerability. Over the past 21⁄2 years, CISA has laid out its plans to modernize both NCPS and CDM programs.

Earlier this year, CISA announced plans to sunset and replace its EINSTEIN intrusion detection system—which has limited effectiveness against novel threats and newer network architectures—and shift remaining NCPS capabilities to a new program called the Cyber Analytics and Data System (CADS). Together, the legacy EINSTEIN capabilities and CADS will become the Joint Collaboration Environment, commonly referred to as JCE, which CISA predicts will be a ''best-in-class analytic environment'' that utilizes increased automation to more efficiently analyze classified and unclassified data. JCE holds tremendous promise, but successful implementation requires a clear vision and buy-in from both Federal and private-sector partners.

CISA has also worked to rapidly mature its CDM program to ensure that its Federal customers can tailor it to accommodate their unique security requirements. CDM is limited, however, in that it is deployed on IT technologies, not operational technology or internet of things devices. Moreover, the Government Accountability Office recently found that CISA lacks the authority to test CDM tools on agency networks, which undermines its ability to ensure those tools are working as anticipated. I am interested in learning from witnesses today how we can improve the security value of both programs.

Before I close, I want to remind my colleagues that Government shutdowns are bad for Federal network security. We are nevertheless 2 weeks away from Government funding running out. During the last shutdown—which lasted 35 days—CISA issued its first Emergency Directive to Federal agencies ever. Having employees and IT contractors across the Government—and at CISA—furloughed at the time was not helpful. A continuing resolution would also impair CISA's critical work, as it would restrict CISA's ability to start new programs that match the current threat environment.

It is detrimental to our national security to slow investments in our Federal network security programs at such a critical moment in their maturation.

Moving forward, the House and Senate need to pass a Homeland Security appropriations bill that provides needed funding to CISA to carry out its vital missions. Now is not the time to take our foot off the gas.

Chairman GARBARINO. I want to thank the Ranking Member for that rousing opening statement. Other Members of the committee are reminded that opening statements may be submitted for the record.

[The statements of Ranking Member Thompson and Honorable Jackson Lee follow:]

Statement of Ranking Member Bennie G. Thompson
September 19, 2023

We all remember learning about the SolarWinds intrusion in December 2020, which highlighted how vulnerable Federal agencies were to foreign espionage campaigns and how outdated our Federal network cyber defenses were. While the creation of the Cybersecurity and Infrastructure Security Agency in 2018 represented a major step forward in developing an organization charged with leading the oper ational defense of Federal networks, Congress did not initially provide the agency with sufficient resources to match the modern threat environment.

Fortunately, upon taking office shortly after the SolarWinds incident, President Biden quickly took critical actions to modernize our cyber defenses. By issuing Executive Order 14028, President Biden began a process of updating the Federal Government's cybersecurity to combat the threats we face from our adversaries. Along with the $650 million Congress provided to CISA in the American Rescue Plan Act and steady increases in CISA's budget, efforts over the last 3 years have brought meaningful gains in improving CISA's visibility and response capabilities throughout the Federal Civilian Executive branch.

Investments in endpoint detection and response technologies across Federal agencies have helped improve the Continuous Diagnostics and Mitigation program and has brought the Federal Government in line with the cybersecurity practices standard in much of the private sector. In recent cyber incidents, we have seen how an improved CDM dashboard and increased visibility have enabled CISA to move quickly to identify vulnerabilities across the Federal Government and mitigate risk. I look forward to hearing from our witnesses about how CISA can continue to improve the CDM program, including how it can gain visibility into operational technology, a priority for me.

In this year's budget request, the administration has now proposed a much-needed restructuring of the National Cybersecurity Protection System. By establishing the Cyber Analytics and Data System, CISA hopes to more efficiently analyze the ever-increasing amount of data it receives from Federal agencies, State and local governments, and critical infrastructure. Hearing from private-sector partners should help ensure CISA develops this new program in a way that reflects the expertise of leading cybersecurity companies, while maintaining and evolving the network detection and prevention capabilities of the EINSTEIN program. Without sustained support for CISA's Federal network security programs going forward, the progress we have made in recent years may stall.

A Government shutdown or a year-long continuing resolution would restrict CISA's ability to move forward with efforts to continue CDM modernization or deploy the new CADS program. Operating under a CR is problematic for any agency; in the world of cybersecurity, where our adversaries are constantly innovating, operating under last year's budget or no budget at all could be devastating for our national security.

I hope my Republican colleagues will stop holding Government funding hostage to their inhumane and ineffective border proposals and instead come to the negotiating table to develop a bipartisan full-year appropriations agreement.

I am proud of the tremendous achievements we have had in recent years to provide CISA the resources and authorities it needs to better secure Federal agencies. Only with bipartisan support for CISA and its mission can we continue to build on our previous work.

Statement of Honorable Sheila Jackson Lee
September 19, 2023

Chairman Garbarino, and Ranking Member Swalwell, thank you for holding today's hearing on ''Evaluating CISA's Federal Civilian Executive Branch Cybersecurity Programs''.

I look forward to the questions that will follow the testimony of:

- Mr. Brian Gumbel, president, Armis;

- Mr. Stephen Zakowicz, vice president—consulting services, CGI Federal;
- Mr. Joe Head, chief technology officer, Intrusion; and
- Mr. Rob Sheldon, senior director of public policy and strategy, Crowdstrike (Democratic Witness).

I welcome the witnesses and thank them for their testimony before the House Homeland Security Committee.

The purpose of this hearing is to assess CISA's efforts to modernize its two signature Federal network security programs, the Continuous Diagnostics and Mitigation program (CDM) and the National Cybersecurity Protection System (NCPS).

The Federal Executive branch is comprised of civilian Federal agencies that provide the full scope of benefits and services to residents of the States and territories as well as support of domestic law enforcement and homeland security needs.

Cybersecurity for non-civilian agencies is primarily managed under the Department of Defense.

The Federal Executive branch cybersecurity coordination was not as robust as national defense networks, but this dramatically changed following the SolarWinds attack.

In December 2020, the Federal Government learned the Russian government had executed a malicious cyber campaign targeting Federal networks and certain critical infrastructure.

Russian hackers used a combination of traditional tactics, techniques, and procedures (e.g.: password guessing) and a supply chain attack to infiltrate targeted networks.

In a supply chain attack, malicious actors infiltrate a target network by exploiting security vulnerabilities in the network of a trusted partner to gain access to the targeted network.

In this case, one of the trusted partners was Solar Winds, a U.S.-based vendor whose Orion Platform provided network monitoring services to entities across the world, including the U.S. Government.

To execute the attack, hackers gained access to SolarWinds and injected malicious code into an Orion software update sent to customers in March 2020.

The malicious code created a backdoor in the affected networks that caused servers to communicate with a U.S. IP address after a dormant period.

In response, hackers sent additional malicious code to some, but not all, affected networks.

Ultimately, the additional malicious code allowed hackers to access elevated credentials and move around a victim's network, monitoring activity and slowly taking data.

To deceive security products on customers' networks, actors disguised their activity as normal network traffic and were able to persist through the creation of additional credentials from other applications.

A total of 18,000 SolarWinds customers downloaded the compromised version of Orion, but far fewer have identified activity beyond the creation of a backdoor.

Nearly 40 Federal agencies downloaded the compromised SolarWinds Orion update.

It is important to note that about 30 percent of both Government and non-Government victims of the Russian cyber campaign had no direct connection with SolarWinds.

According to news reports, hackers also breached networks by ''exploiting known bugs in software products, by guessing on-line passwords and by capitalizing on a variety of issues in the way Microsoft Corp.'s cloud-based software is configured.'' Bugs can also be called Zero-Day Events that if exploited could cost significant disruption in the function of application or services that rely on computers or remote computing services.

The SolarWind Orion exploit was not intended to damage or disrupt computing systems, it was designed to spy on networks and spread to other systems.

The SolarWinds campaign illustrated many of the shortcomings in the Federal Executive Branch civilian cybersecurity, which lacked the ability to effectively monitor and respond to threats on civilian agency networks.

At that time there was also no overarching Federal law requiring private entities to report cybersecurity incidents, there is little public information on the number of victims that installed the infected versions of Solar Winds Orion or experienced second-stage intrusions.

At the time of the attack, there was a critical need to modernize the Federal Government civilian agency cybersecurity and SolarWinds became the catalysis to begin this important work.

Until the SolarWinds attack civilian Federal agencies had been slow to adapt to the demands of new technologies, network architectures, and the evolving threat landscape.

Harnessing that momentum to revamp Federal civilian agency network security, the Biden-Harris administration implemented ambitious policies to transform how the Federal Government and its contractors secure their networks and supply chains, most notably through Executive Order 14028, Improving the Nation's Cybersecurity.

Under the skilled guidance of the Biden-Harris administration CISA has worked quickly to revamp its signature FCEB network security programs, the National Cybersecurity Protection System (NCPS) and the Continuous Diagnostics and Mitigation program (CDM).

These programs complement other authorities provided to CISA under the Federal Information Security Modernization Act, including the power to issue Binding Operational Directives, Emergency Directives, and technical security guidance to FCEB agencies, among other things.

Additionally, the William M. (Mac) Thornberry National Defense Authorization Act for Fiscal Year 2021, authorized CISA to hunt for malicious activity across FCEB's networks, with or without an agency's permission.

CISA's authorities outside NCPS and CDM, though critical to its FCEB network security mission, are outside the scope of this hearing.

Prior to the SolarWinds attack another major civilian agency attack in 2015 involved the Office of Personnel Management.

In 2015, the Office of Personnel Management data breach targeted information provided by security clearance applications submitted under the Standard Form 86 (SF–86).

At the time this attack was one of the largest breaches of Government data in U.S. history, the attack was carried out by an advanced persistent threat based in China.

In the aftermath of the 2015 Office of Personnel Management (OPM) breach, Congress enacted the Federal Cybersecurity Enhancement Act.

That legislation authorized NCPS and directed the department to deploy a Federal intrusion detection and prevention system to better detect breaches of Federal networks.

NCPS is a "system of systems" that, in addition to the EINSTEIN intrusion detection system, includes data analytics, information sharing, and core infrastructure capabilities.

Earlier this year, CISA announced plans to restructure NCPS and, over time, sunset the EINSTEIN intrusion prevention program.

EINSTEIN is designed to observe traffic going in and out of agency networks and relies on detecting known threats and, therefore, has limited effectiveness in modern network architectures or against novel attacks.

The remaining NCPS capabilities include data analytics, information sharing, and core infrastructure capabilities, which will be integrated into CADS.

CADS and the legacy EINSTEIN capabilities will be housed within the new Joint Collaboration Environment (JCE).

CISA boasts that the JCE will be a ''best-in-class analytic environment that centralizes mission-relevant classified and unclassified data to enable more efficient analysis in large part due to increased automation.''

Last year, Congress extended CISA's NCPS authorities until September 30, 2023, and they will expire at the end of the month unless Congress acts.

CISA intends for the new CADS program to support expanded capabilities that will improve the intake, integration, and automated analysis to facilitate the rapid identification, detection, mitigation, and prevention of malicious cyber activity.

According to CISA, CADS marks a significant expansion of NCPS's existing systems engineering, information technology infrastructure, and cyber operations tools and services.

The new JCE—and CADS, in particular—have the potential to dramatically improve how the Federal Government identifies and mitigates threats to Federal networks.

These new capabilities, however, rely on close collaboration with CISA's private- sector partners and vendors.

It is not clear that CISA has clearly articulated a complete vision for how it will implement its plans for JCE or CADS.

CISA also does not have a concrete plan for replacing or retaining EINSTEIN capabilities, even though ''the visibility provided by existing EINSTEIN sensors remains a crucial enabler of CISA's mission to protect FCEB agencies.''

In June, the General Services Administration issued a Request for Information on behalf of CISA seeking industry feedback on how to modernize the ''legacy capabilities'' of the EINSTEIN program.

I am interested in knowing if CISA has responded to the GSA or intends to respond to the question regarding EINSTEIN.

I thank today's witnesses and look forward to asking questions following the testimony of witnesses.

Thank you.

Chairman GARBARINO. I am pleased to have four witnesses before us today to discuss this very important topic. I ask that our witnesses please rise and raise their right hand.

[Witnesses sworn.]

Chairman GARBARINO. Let the record reflect that the witnesses have answered in the affirmative. Thank you. Please be seated.

I would now like to formally introduce our witnesses. Brian Gumbel is the president of Armis, where he leads the company and its efforts to drive innovation in cybersecurity and emerging technology. Mr. Gumbel has spent 25 years in the tech industry, where he has worked for many companies, and is part of several advisory boards.

Steven Zakowicz is the vice president of CGI Federal, where he leads the DHS CISA account for the company. In this capacity, he leads a large team supporting 7 Federal agencies' participation in CISA's CDM program. In part of this role, Mr. Zakowicz oversaw a team providing environmental, health and safety, and regulatory compliance solutions and services to the chemical and energy companies. He also serves as a member of the American Council for Technology and Industry Advisory Council and the Washington Exec Cyber Council.

Joe Head is the chief technology officer and cofounder of Intrusion. He has held many roles with the company since its founding in 1983, and prior to that, he worked at Honeywell Optoelectronics. That was a tough one.

Finally, Robert Sheldon is the director of public policy and strategy at CrowdStrike. He leads corporate engagement on a variety of U.S. Federal, State, and local government policies, programs, and initiatives. He is the company's representative to CISA's Joint Cyber Defense Collaborative and the IT Sector Coordinating Council. In addition to his role at CrowdStrike, Mr. Sheldon serves as an adjunct professor lecturer on international cybersecurity policy at American University School of International Service.

Thank you all for being here today. Mr. Gumbel, I now recognize you for 5 minutes to summarize your opening statement.

Statement of Brian Gumbel, President, Armis, Inc.

Mr. GUMBEL. Chairman Garbarino, Ranking Member Menendez, and Members of the subcommittee, thank you for the opportunity to testify regarding our experience and perspectives on key programs designed to protect our Nation's most critical assets. As the leading asset intelligence security company, we share the mission and passion with all of you to ensure the protection and security of our Nation's critical assets. Many legacy programs tend to focus on what's commonly known as managed IT assets, but the growth beyond traditional managed assets is absolutely staggering. Our submitted testimony has a chart that highlights the explosion in what is referred to as unmanaged assets, or IOT, the internet of things, also operational technology, OT, and IOMT, which is medical technology.

When we discuss critical infrastructure, we must talk about and account for all unmanaged assets. We are encouraged by the focus and resources this committee and key agencies like CISA are putting toward building dynamic, resilient, and effective cybersecurity frameworks. A few of these programs that exist today, namely the CDM and EINSTEIN programs, have been in place for several years but need updating considering the expanding threat surface. In the recent Executive Order on improving our Nation's cybersecurity, there are references made to the Federal Government partnering with private sector. This is a positive development, and Armis looks forward to teaming with those agencies who are most responsible for protecting our Federal Government systems. The Executive Order states, incremental improvements will not give us the security we need; instead, the Federal Government needs to make bold changes and significant investments in order to defend the vital institutions that underpin the American way of life. It mentions that the Federal Government must bring to bear the full scope of its authorities and resources to protect and secure its computer systems, whether they are cloud-based, on-premise, or even hybrid. That the scope and protection of security must include systems that process data, such as information technology or IT, and that those that run the vital machinery that ensure our safety, operational technology, or OT.

The convergence of technologies and the discrepancies between devices offers a more complex and challenging task than the Federal Government has had to face just a few years ago. At Armis, our growing customer base consists of almost 50 percent of the Fortune 100, many large State and municipal governments, airports, ports, defense contractors, and key Federal agencies. These customers partner with us to achieve complete visibility and intelligence for all assets within their converged environments. Without such, we cannot be fully prepared for the growth of today and the uncertainties of tomorrow.

As stated in CISA's Binding Operational Directive, B.O.D. 23–01, continuous and comprehensive asset visibility is a basic pre-condition for any organization station to effectively manage cybersecurity risk. This directive focuses on asset discovery and vulnerability enumeration. To keep pace with technological change and rapidly-evolving threat landscape and deliver upon the letter and spirit of this Executive Order, bold change is needed now. CISA should align the CDM program updates to directives like B.O.D. 23–01 and should ensure that CDM dashboard is reflective and inclusive of existing and innovative technologies.

The Federal Government can no longer rely on legacy models, contracts, or solutions. What has worked in the past simply will not suffice now. Our adversaries are using automation to move at the speed of now, as should we. Armis is committed to working with CISA and other leading agencies to bring a holistic and inclusive approach where more complete and contextual cyber situational awareness and intelligence can lead to a resilient and responsive security posture.

I want to thank you all again for the opportunity to engage with the subcommittee. The resources of our entire organization stand ready to assist in the honorable mission of protecting our most critical national assets. I look forward to any questions that you may have.

[The prepared statement of Mr. Gumbel follows:]

Prepared Statement of Brian Gumbel September 19, 2023

Chairman Garbarino, Ranking Member Swalwell, and Members of the committee, thank you for the opportunity to testify and share our perspective on civilian agency cybersecurity programs. I applaud the committee's efforts in working to provide oversight and help improve impactful programs such as Continuous Diagnostics and Mitigation (CDM) and Einstein. In accordance with a core function of the NIST Cybersecurity Framework that highlights the need to go beyond merely identifying devices but also understand the interdependence each asset has with each other and their relative importance to business objectives, we are honored to bring a contextual asset intelligence platform to our customers, partners, and Federal agencies.

Armis is THE leading asset intelligence cybersecurity company. We have been recognized by industry-leading analysts and publications as a platform provider who brings a level of insight, awareness, and actionable intelligence to our customers. Today it is important to not only know what exists in your network and cloud infrastructure, but the interdependencies and vulnerabilities within each asset. We are honored to be under consideration to become a member of CISAs JCDC, sharing the mission and passion with all of you in ensuring the protection and security of our Nation's critical assets.

We are encouraged by the focus and resources this committee and key agencies like CISA have put toward building dynamic, resilient, and an effective cybersecurity framework in protecting these assets. On May 12, 2021, the Executive Order on Improving our Nation's Cybersecurity states ''Incremental improvements will not give us the security we need; instead, the Federal Government needs to make bold changes and significant investments in order to defend the vital institutions that underpin the American way of life . . . ''. It mentions that ''The Federal Government must bring to bear the full scope of its authorities and resources to protect and secure its computer systems, whether they are cloud-based, on-premises, or hybrid.'' And that ''The scope of protection and security must include systems that process data (information technology (IT)) and those that run the vital machinery that ensures our safety and national sovereignty (operational technology (OT)).''

In the Armis State of Cyberwarfare and Trends report 2022/2023 where 6,021 IT security professionals where surveyed we found that 73 percent of IT professionals in the United States say their company has experienced one or more cybersecurity breaches. Threat activity against the global Armis customer base increased by 15 percent from September to November 2022 with the largest threat activity coming from critical infrastructure organizations followed by health care organizations as compared with other industries.

Our job as the industry leader is to raise awareness and identify areas in need of attention and improvement. Our experience has shown that intrusions outside traditional IT ''managed devices'' have become more prevalent. Programs and frameworks that in the past have been primarily focused on these managed devices will be limited in their ability to address the larger growing attack surface.

At Armis our comprehensive contextual intelligence engine includes over 3 billion assets and growing and includes the entire spectrum of IT/OT/IoT/IoMT assets. We bring a level of contextual asset intelligence to our customers that introduces a holistic and responsive platform to assist in their mission. Our public-sector customers include several States, large city agencies, and cities and counties as well as the following highlighted below:

- An agency within HHS as well as numerous State agencies leverages Armis for Asset visibility and intelligence through integrations.
- A large defense contractor leverages the Armis platform for Asset Discovery, Intelligence, and Vulnerability Management

- A DOD agency leverages our platform for Asset Management and Security Workflow Remediation
- Department of Energy leverages Armis to increase automated identification and organization of the asset infrastructure across an entire lab.

Our enterprise and commercial customers include Drug and Manufacturing companies, Utility, Transportation, Aviation, and Healthcare organizations, and many others.

Our mission is to help organizations understand where and what exists in their environments and help put them in a position to identify and manage vulnerabilities to respond rather than react to a breach. You can't protect what you can't see and without addressing a visibility gap, organizations cannot be fully prepared for the growth of today and uncertainties of tomorrow.

We work with organizations throughout the globe to gain complete visibility into their managed and unmanaged assets. A ''whole-of-nation'' approach cannot be achieved without a complete view and deep level of intelligence of both managed and unmanaged assets.

As you can see in the chart below, the growth and in our opinion the growing attack surface introduce vulnerabilities heretofore unseen and even unknown. The convergence of technologies and the dependencies between devices has introduced a more complex and challenging task for those who are responsible for securing critical assets and operational environments.

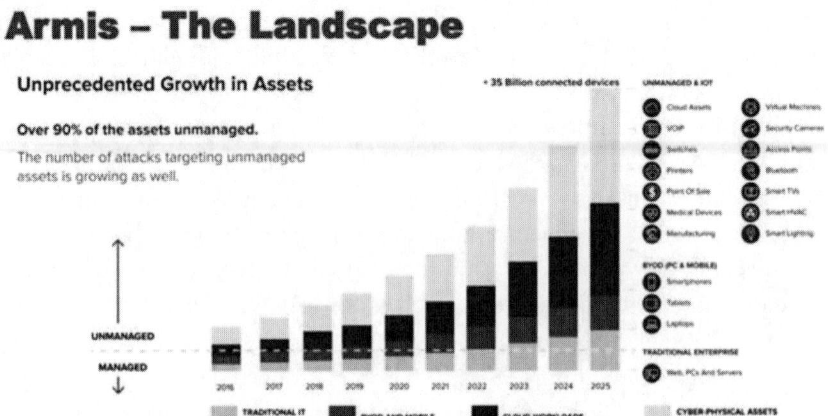

As stated in CISA's Binding Operational Directive (B.O.D.) 23–01, ''Continuous and comprehensive asset visibility is a basic pre-condition for any organization to effectively manage cybersecurity risk.'' This directive focuses on Asset Discovery and Vulnerability enumeration. Many agencies and enterprises are fortunate to have strong endpoint technologies in place (EDR) and solutions that help protect the perimeter, but the attack surface continues to grow and the cybersecurity perimeter which was well-defined just a few years ago is now dynamic and borderless. The introduction of unmanaged devices and operational technologies present challenges that cannot be addressed with legacy models and legacy technology. Present-day challenges and national security threats are now implementing AI and automated capabilities to identify the weakest link in the chain. Automated threats from U.S. adversaries requires automation and scalability delivering prioritization of cyber defense operators.

We applaud the activities toward the next-generation Einstein program, Cyber Analytics and Data System (or CADS). According to CISA's Eric Goldstein the system will integrate data from multiple sources, including ''public and commercial data feeds; CISA's own sensors such as Endpoint Detection and Response, Protective [Domain Name System], and our Vulnerability Scanning service, which has thousands of enrolled organizations across the country; and data shared by both public and private partners,''.

Creating next generation programs are crucial and as our customers would attest, knowing where every asset exists, what the profile of that asset is, and whether it is aged, vulnerable, or compromised in real-time will help to make the investment in next generation and existing solutions more effective.

We are committed to continuing to work with CISA and other leading agencies to bring a holistic and inclusive approach where more complete and contextual asset awareness, contextual intelligence, and attack surface definition can lead to increased resiliency and a responsive cybersecurity posture.

Some important and consistent feedback we hear from existing and former Federal CISOs, and CIOs includes the following:

''The focus should be on building modern security models, not perimeter-based, and should acknowledge and focus on cloud, zero trust, and IT/OT convergence.

''Many of the legacy models and contracts served us well in the past, but a new approach and model is needed.''

These converged technologies deliver more efficiencies in the way we work but they introduce new vulnerabilities and complexities that legacy technologies are not built to identify, profile, or defend.

The ''bold changes'' highlighted in the E.O. call for a collaborative and inclusive programmatic and procurement directive that does not rely on legacy models, contracts, or solutions. What worked in years past will not suffice. Our adversaries are actively trying to exploit our visibility gaps, particularly in critical infrastructure. Our approach should be engaging with new and innovative 21st Century technologies. Lest we forget, bad actors are moving at the speed of now as should we!

Recommendations

- Design and implement a procurement path that allows for more expedient purchase and implementation of newer technologies built to align with the growing attack vectors and surface.
- Improve coordinating between programs like U.S. Digital Services, the Technology Modernization Fund, and CISA to create programs which enable agencies to quickly integrate and maintain newer technologies and services into their framework portfolios.
- Fund the Technology Modernization Fund so that return on investments can reliably cover both the simultaneous deployment of new technology and the retirement of legacy services.
- Align program updates to stated directives. For example, if Directives state cloud-first and all assets, agencies should have the ability to implement those solutions that are not limited to a subset of technologies. Currently the CDM program addresses only IT devices rather than the full spectrum of connected risk: IT/OT/IoT/IoMT. BOD 23–01 focuses on Asset Discovery and Vulnerability Enumeration. Requiring that the full spectrum of converged and connected technologies be inventoried and reported would give these programs more alignment to stated administration and agency objectives. Having only most of your roof covered in a storm won't prevent water from entering!
- The CDM program and dashboard should reflect all existing and upcoming technologies that need integration vs. a limited few to be effective.

- We encourage continued strong support of the CDM program with the appropriate measures taken to be more inclusive of technologies that may not be part of the existing program.

Thank you again for the opportunity to speak with this committee. The resources of our entire organization stand ready to assist in the honorable mission of protecting our Nation's most critical assets.

Chairman GARBARINO. Thank you, Mr. Gumbel. Mr. Zakowicz, I now recognize you for 5 minutes to summarize your opening statement.

Statement of Stephen Zakowicz, Vice President, CGI Federal, Inc.

Mr. ZAKOWICZ. Chairman Garbarino, Ranking Member Menendez, and other distinguished Members of the Subcommittee on Cybersecurity and Infrastructure Protection, thank you for the opportunity to testify today. My name is Steve Zakowicz. I am a vice president at CGI Federal, and for the past 4 years, I have served as a project manager on CGI Federal's contract with the Continuous Diagnostics and Mitigation, or CDM, program. At the subcommittee's invitation, I'm here on behalf of CGI Federal today to provide perspective on the achievements of CDM and its path forward. Since 2016, CGI Federal has played an important role in the CDM program, providing capabilities to participating agencies through tailored solutions and a robust shared services platform.

Our company is currently the system integrator on two CDM Dynamic and Evolving Federal Enterprise Network Defense, or DEFEND, contracts. The first provides tailored CDM solutions to seven large Federal agencies: Departments of Commerce, Justice, Labor, State, FCC, TVA, and USAID. The second provides a state- of-the-art, cloud-based shared services platform currently supporting 65 smaller and independent Federal organizations leveraging those CDM capabilities.

CGI Federal has almost 300 skilled professionals and specialized subcontractors supporting the CDM program today. Given our experience in the CDM program, I would like to use my opening remarks to highlight four points regarding the program's success to date and suggestions to meet evolving objectives.

First, civilian agency partners must be appropriately resourced, funded, and committed for CDM to be successful. CISA cannot do this alone. Congress can help to ensure civilian agencies are approaching cyber preparedness with the appropriate level of attention and investment. Also, funding lapses or limitations stemming from uncertainties surrounding shutdowns and continuing resolutions do impact CDM's continuity and ability to carry forward new initiatives. Second, Executive Order 14028 called Improving the Nation's Cybersecurity enhanced CISA's ability to effectively perform its mission.

For example, authorizing CISA to engage in cyber hunt, detection, and response activities through endpoint detection and response, or EDR, solutions deployed via CDM. Congress could bring stability to CISA's authority to perform these critical activities by codifying appropriate authorities within the Executive Order into law. I understand this is currently under consideration by Congress in pending updates to the Federal Information Security Modernization Act of 2014, also known as FISMA.

Third, emerging opportunities exist to leverage CDM capabilities for State, local, Tribal, territorial, as well as critical infrastructure entities by using this existing shared service platforms and capabilities. The shared services approach can provide these target-rich but resource-poor stakeholders across the Nation the ability to leverage proven capabilities in a cost-efficient way to defend against threats they face, including nation-state actors and ransomware attacks.

Fourth, the evolution of the CDM dashboard ecosystem is an especially promising development. The dashboard has become the first venue of consultation for a wide variety of users within CISA's cybersecurity division, including threat hunt, vulnerability management, and directives and guidance organizations. The level of visibility across the Federal enterprise provided through the dashboard, combined with agency network visibility through EDR, has been a force multiplier and is a terrific case study in the innovation and power of combining data from multiple sources to accelerate progress.

In conclusion, I would like to affirm to the subcommittee CGI Federal's continued and unwavering commitment to our partnership with CISA on its core mission of strengthening America's cybersecurity. Thank you. I look forward to your questions.

[The prepared statement of Mr. Zakowicz follows:]

Prepared Statement of Stephen Zakowicz September 19, 2023

Introduction

Chairman Garbarino, Ranking Member Swalwell, and other distinguished Members of the Subcommittee on Cybersecurity and Infrastructure Protection, my name is Stephen Zakowicz. I am a vice president at CGI Federal Inc. ("CGI Federal"). As a wholly-owned U.S. operating subsidiary of CGI Inc. ("CGI"),[1] CGI Federal and its 7,100 employees partner with Federal agencies to provide solutions for homeland security, defense, civilian, health care, justice, intelligence, and international affairs. During the last 4 years, I have served as the project manager on CGI Federal's contract with the Department of Homeland Security ("DHS") Cybersecurity and Infrastructure Security Agency ("CISA") for the Continuous Diagnostics and Mitigation ("CDM") Program. On behalf of CGI Federal and its employees, I am pleased to submit this written testimony to the subcommittee regarding the CDM Program.

CDM is a mission-critical Federal program that provides participating agencies with solutions and services to identify and combat cybersecurity risk. Since its original contract award in 2016, CGI Federal has provided this support to 100 participating agencies through tailored solutions and a robust shared services platform. CGI Federal is currently the prime contractor on two CDM Dynamic and Evolving Federal Enterprise Network Defense ("DEFEND") Task Orders—DEFEND C and DEFEND F. Under its DEFEND C Task Order, CGI Federal provides tailored CDM solutions to 7 large Federal agencies: Department of Commerce ("DOC"), Department of Justice ("DOJ"), Department of Labor ("DOL"), Department of State ("DOS"), Federal Communications Commission ("FCC"), Tennessee Valley Authority ("TVA"), and United States Agency for International Development ("USAID"). Under its DEFEND F Task Order, CGI Federal developed a state-of-the-art cloud-based Shared Services CDM platform, and currently operates and provides access to that platform to 65 non-Chief

[1] Founded in 1976, CGI is among the largest independent information technology ("IT") and business consulting services firms in the world. With 90,250 consultants and professionals across the globe, CGI delivers an end-to-end portfolio of capabilities from strategic IT and business consulting to systems integration, managed IT and business process services, and intellectual property solutions. CGI works with clients through a local relationship model com plemented by a global delivery network that helps clients digitally transform their organizations and accelerate results.

Financial Officer Act (''CFO Act'') Federal agencies. Roughly 300 CGI Federal employees and subcontractors support the CDM program.

CDM: Current Program Structure

As stated in the DHS fiscal year 2024 Congressional Budget Justification for CISA, ''the CDM program provides the Department, along with other Federal agencies, with capabilities and tools to identify cybersecurity risks to agency networks on an ongoing basis. It prioritizes these risks based on potential impacts and enables cybersecurity personnel to mitigate the most significant problems first . . . Furthermore, CDM enables CISA and agencies to proactively respond to threats through the deployment of multiple different security capabilities, including data protection technologies, Endpoint Detection and Response (EDR), cloud security platforms, and network security controls, and enables CISA to continually evaluate the cybersecurity posture of [Federal Civilian and Executive branch (''FCEB'')] systems and networks.''

As CISA describes on their public website, the CDM program is structured to provide cybersecurity protections and capabilities in four key areas:

- The Asset Management (AM) capability is aimed at providing agencies with a centralized overview of their network devices and the risks associated with such devices. Asset Management enables an agency to maintain and improve its cyber hygiene through 5 capabilities: hardware asset management (HWAM), software asset management (SWAM), configuration settings management (CSM), vulnerability management (VUL), and enterprise mobility management (EMM).
- The Identity and Access Management (IDAM) capability is intended to manage the access and privileges of agency network users. Managing who is on the network requires the management and control of account and access privileges, trust determination for people granted access, credentials and authentication, and security-related behavioral training.
- The Network Settings Management (NSM) capability is designed to provide agencies with greater visibility into what is happening on

their networks, which also gives them a better understanding of how the networks are being protected.

- The Data Protection Management (DPM) capability is intended to provide additional protections to the most critical mission data and systems on Federal civilian networks. While the other CDM capabilities provide broader protections across Federal networks, the DPM capability is focused on protecting sensitive (especially private) data within the agency.

These capabilities are centrally managed and reported through the CDM Dashboard Ecosystem, a cloud-based visualization and data analytics layer that allows agencies and CISA to obtain a top-level view of cybersecurity risk posture and access details regarding how individual systems and endpoints contribute to that risk posture. This allows agency personnel to quickly identify and address the highest risk cybersecurity vulnerabilities first.

The current CDM program consists of 7 individual Task Orders to provide consistent, prioritized CDM capabilities to FCEB agencies. Those Task Orders are:

- CDM DEFEND A: Providing CDM program requirements to DHS
- CDM DEFEND B: Providing CDM program requirements to DOE, DOI, DOT, OPM, USDA, and VA
- CDM DEFEND C: Providing CDM program requirements to DOC, DOJ, DOL, DOS, FCC, TVA, and USAID
- CDM DEFEND D: Providing CDM program requirements to GSA, HHS, NASA, SSA, and Treasury
- CDM DEFEND E: Providing CDM program requirements to DOED, EPA, FDIC, HUD, NRC, NSF, SBA, and SEC
- CDM DEFEND F: Providing CDM program requirements to up to 75 small and medium FCEB agencies through a Shared Services platform
- Dashboard Ecosystem: Developing and hosting a common CDM Dashboard platform on behalf of CISA to receive and consolidate information from participating CDM DEFEND agencies.

CDM Past and Present

Since its inception in 2012, the CDM program has evolved to meet the priorities and relative maturity of the FCEB cybersecurity risk posture. When the CDM program began, it focused on implementing a standard set of commercial solutions to meet CDM-identified technical capabilities for enterprise visibility and protection. At that time, the program implemented cybersecurity risk management across the FCEB enterprise. Over time, however, the program recognized the need for flexibility to accommodate unique requirements and differing maturity levels from one agency to the next. Through CDM DEFEND, CISA addressed that need, and built a model focused on long-term, sustained engagement, delivering custom solutions tailored to each agency's unique environments and cybersecurity needs.

Within the DEFEND model, CISA has further refined its approach to delivering cybersecurity services. For example, CDM DEFEND activities initially focused on delivering a single capability (e.g. Asset Management or Identity and Access Management) to all participating agencies. After deploying these foundational capabilities, CISA evolved to deliver services based on agency readiness model. In advance of agency engagement, CISA works with the agency to identify where program priorities align with an agency's ability to implement and maintain a specific capability. Using this readiness model, CISA validates that both CISA and the agencies are adequately funded and have the resources necessary to successfully deploy, operate, and maintain the cybersecurity solutions.

The evolution of the CDM program is also driven by new regulations and executive guidance. For example, Executive Order 14028 ''Improving the Nation's Cybersecurity'' (the ''EO''), issued on May 12, 2021, provides greater visibility to agency environments as it grants CISA access to object-level cybersecurity data collected through CDM (see Section 7(f)). The EO also authorizes CISA to engage in cyber hunt, detection, and response activities through Endpoint Detection and Response (''EDR'') solutions deployed through CDM. These EO requirements grant CISA unprecedented visibility into agency network environments to proactively identify and remediate threats and apply observations in one agency environment across the FCEB enterprise.

Through the CDM program, CISA has gained critical visibility into the cybersecurity posture across the entire FCEB enterprise and is well-positioned to quickly identify, assess, and remediate potential threats to agency network environments and, by extension, U.S. national security. Specific accomplishments include the broad roll-out of EDR to FCEB agencies and the onboarding of roughly 250 CISA threat hunters to conduct analysis through EDR and CDM Dashboard Ecosystem solutions. That access coupled with the availability of object-level data through the Dashboard Ecosystem has been a ''force multiplier'' in providing CISA the ability to identify, assess, and remediate anomalies across the Federal enterprise network.

Future of CDM

CISA continues to evolve its CDM program to meet the needs of its stakeholders. Further, as CISA prepares for the next generation of CDM, it has actively engaged with industry and identified likely future priorities that include:

- Issuing Task Orders based on CDM capability to be applied across the entire FCEB community to promote consistency in solutions across agencies.
- Delivering CDM capabilities to State, local, Tribal, territorial (SLTT), and critical infrastructure (CI) stakeholders.

Expanding access to Shared Services across CDM capabilities.

- Enhancing alignment and collaboration among CISA, FCEB agencies, and the cybersecurity tool vendor community.

Concluding Observations

As a Federal contractor proudly supporting the CDM program, CGI Federal offers the following observations for consideration:

- Success of CDM's mission depends heavily on FCEB agencies applying the resources and funding to invest in cyber preparedness. Further, funding lapses or delays due to government shutdowns or Continuing Resolutions impact program continuity and ability to operate sustainably.

- Executive Order 14028 ''Improving the Nation's Cybersecurity'' enhanced CISA's ability to effectively perform its mission through, for example, authorizing CISA to engage in cyber hunt, detection, and response activities through EDR solutions deployed via CDM. Congress could ensure stability in CISA's authority to perform these critical activities by codifying these authorities into law.
- CISA could enable SLTT and CI stakeholders to leverage existing CDM shared service platforms and capabilities to defend against cyber threats such as ransomware attacks. These strategies would allow stakeholders to leverage valuable capabilities in a cost-efficient way to defend against threats such as ransomware attacks.
- The use of the Dashboard Ecosystem and EDR as a ''first vcnuc of consultation'' for newly-identified critical vulnerabilities or anomalous network activity by CISA represents a force multiplier and a new era of centralized hunt and response capabilities within the FCEB. These foundational capabilities can be further leveraged in innovative ways to improve our national security risk posture. CGI Federal appreciates the critical nature of the CDM program, as well as CISA's core mission. CGI Federal is proud to support CISA and the CDM program in working to secure the Federal Government's networks for citizens across the United States. CGI Federal also thanks the subcommittee for its continued oversight to ensure the continued success of the CDM program.

Chairman GARBARINO. Thank you, Mr. Zakowicz. Mr. Head, I now recognize you for 5 minutes to summarize your opening statement.

Statement of Joe Head, Chief Technology Officer, Intrusion

Mr. HEAD. Thanks so much. Pleasure to be here with you guys today. We spent a lot of time, as do most I guess, on making the submittal perfect and word crafting, but I think me reading it is boring. So, what I'd like to do is just talk to a few things that aren't on there that I think are important.

You mentioned the CRs. We've got one critical breach we've been waiting on working for 4 years against the U.S. military, and they were first under a CR. Then when they were not under CR, they didn't have a budget.

Then when they had a budget, they were back under a CR again, and we haven't spent dime one on anything yet.

So, when you start looking at major programs like you're discussing today, it is a layup that they will continue somehow. But when you have a reaction to a breach, God help you. There's nobody coming. You can't get budget. You can't get help. So, I would urge you guys, I've talked to Kay Granger about doing some sort of cutout where you say, this percent of your budget can be spent on a breach response. I would encourage you guys to think of a way in law to accommodate that.

If you look at the United States, all of us in the security business would like to say it's good. But I remember there was a comedian that says you go to a college and them bragging about their smarts is like going to an ER and everybody bragging about their health.

The United States is not secure. We suck at security. There's a new breach every 37 seconds. I went to a meeting one time with the STRATCOM chief, and they had all the chiefs of industry lined up at one end, and the rest of us with little companies lined around the outside, and basically said, we spend more on R&D every day than you guys in revenue every year. We got it covered. Well, they don't.

So, what I would urge you guys to think through is, how can you help the threat hunters do better? Then part of the thing that you guys could do with the CISA meetings is ask the simple question like a 4-year-old, if we do this, are we done? Are we finished yet? So, when they finish the program, can you truly say, every threat we have is fixed?

You know, if somebody decides they are going to roll up and sink an aircraft carrier, we're going to unleash holy hell on them. They don't think twice, they won't do it. But in cyber, sure. Take down this, take down that, steal these secrets, bankrupt the only supplier outside of China that can do a thing. They do it with impunity. So, we need to get to the point in cyber where people are scared to hit the enter button, and they are not scared.

So, I would suggest that, you know, I'm not here because I'm part of these programs. I'm here because I see how suck we are at security as a Nation and as a world. The offenders have asymmetry to their huge advantage. One guy in a room doing an all-nighter come up with zero day that ain't nobody going to see. I mean, I named my company Intrusion after intrusion detection systems. My joke was all IDS systems are this helpful system that hands you a Polaroid of the fist that just broke your nose. I don't need that. Can you just give me a system that stops the fist?

So, I think if we ask the questions better. We ought to be asking, if I do this, am I done? Is my COM system undownable? One big thing that I think we need to do in law and policy that you guys could help a lot with is it's—I'm sorry, I'm Texan, so, I don't know about PCness, but, you know, back when the cowboys and the Indians were fighting, the Indians didn't make guns, they didn't make bullets, and the outcome was certain. They were screwed. You can't fight if you don't make the stuff. Right now, there's no computer in any office here that wasn't assembled in China. Everything they wanted on it was on it when they shipped it.

So, when you start talking about being secure, gee, sanitation starts early, you know, and we need to have a cleaner environment to build things on. So, we don't make routers in America, we don't make servers, we don't make computers. We need to re-onshore some stuff.

I think there's room. If you read my testimony, I talked about doing a cyber Manhattan Project and I think we should. There's some of us here at the table, and we could name others that should be on the group. It's not just a contractor loop. There's some genius-level folks around the community that know what to do, but they haven't been tasked to fix it. So, I'd encourage you guys to stir that up a lot. So anyway, for the non-ad hoc stuff, feel free to read what we wrote. Thanks for letting us be here.

[The prepared statement of Mr. Head follows:]

Prepared Statement of Joe Head

Good morning, and thank you Chairman Garbarino, Ranking Member Swalwell, and distinguished Members of the subcommittee. My name is Joe Head. I am the cofounder and chief technology officer of Intrusion—proudly headquartered in Plano, Texas.

It is both a privilege and an honor for me to be here today, sharing my technical expertise and insights, which I have accumulated over four decades of immersion in the cutting-edge realms of the cybersecurity industry. I wholeheartedly commend the dedicated individuals on this subcommittee and their staff for their tireless efforts. They understand the need to enhance the Federal Government's cybersecurity capabilities but are also channeling their energies toward advancing the mission of agencies like CISA, with a strong focus on developing next-generation software and technologies that are critical in the forthcoming cyber conflicts.

I began designing and providing secure networks and other security solutions for the U.S. Government when Ronald Reagan was President. We built equipment for the hotline from the White House to the Kremlin during his second term. I co-founded my company Intrusion in 1983, just 3 years out of college and we've been a public company since the '90's.

I've had more fun designing and securing things than you should get paid for. My goal today is to help the committee spur innovation in security. The United States is not secure. There are some secure networks, but very, very few. Complacency with the state of our security is a serious risk. A relaxed defender is the most naive one. Cyber offense is winning everywhere. A great challenge of our time is to make defenders better able to defend. I have an old friend who liked to say that he'd rather be lucky than smart. A network or system not breached is not a matter of the defender being lucky or smart, it is sadly that an attacker just isn't interested enough to focus on breaching it.

As you read my opening remarks, keep in mind that an outline of the Manhattan Project was not put in the Congressional Record before Los Alamos was built. Our Government needs people with technical depth and a winning mindset. My job is not to inform our enemies what we plan to do to win the cyber war but to methodically ensure we take this domain. We do know what to do. There are core experts both in Government and industry that understand what winning would require and how to get there. This path also includes how not to get there by spending billions unwisely.

Today I too often see security plans and programs looking a lot like children's soccer—a bunch of kids clustered around the ball. In cyber, the kids are always automating the hottest buzzwords without a grand plan to produce an absolute win. The challenge is to wisely architect a plan, put the right people in charge of defining the requirements, manage a design production, and reliably deploy a cyber get-well plan.

We must have a get-well plan in cyber which gets silently built and deployed, representing a master stroke in reversing the reality of our current predicament. Adversaries all over the world are killing it in cyber with massive asymmetry, winning and penetrating millions of systems that we need to be trustworthy. Many are capable hackers working inside adversary cyber operations or just as individuals on their own.

It was in the 1990's while identifying a threat at an automotive manufacturer that I realized we needed a better way to find the needle in the haystack. I built a database to understand what the internet looks like, who owns what, which areas were unsafe to visit. This analytic engine has evolved into a mainstay of defense- in-depth cybersecurity. By the early 2000's we built a tool to inspect and audit internet travels. Today, we know what traffic is coming and going from monitored systems, but more importantly how to stop threats from impacting operations.

Now is a critical time for the U.S. Government, U.S. critical infrastructure, and critical parts of U.S. industry. If the world was awesome at cybersecurity, there wouldn't be a breach every 37 seconds. The more you know, the worse it looks. Is it hopeless? No. Is there reason to believe that the USG will naturally solve the problem? No. But the entirety of the Nation faces continuous and advancing attacks precisely because of U.S. commercial and Governmental successes, so the USG must strategically cultivate protections.

As a student of history, we have seen dramatic examples of innovation in the face of new threats. There were dramatic examples in WW2 when foreign threats and war drove U.S. innovation to new heights. Sadly, few programs in the cyber field are constructed to be game-changers. Mostly they scale up and automate a few elements of a good security approach but are not master strokes of a comprehensive solution. In other words, when the projects are done you won't be truly secure. Well-automated partial solutions don't make you secure, they just delay risk and make companies poorer from the expenses. While we must improve our baseline defensive posture to exponentially increase the cost of attack, profit-motivated hackers, criminals, and adversaries have already doubled-down on their attack investments with extensive resourcing.

We already know that signature-based defenses fall in the face of zero-days and basic offensive threats. Most defenses ignore attacks via trusted sources like supply chains and security tools. The adversary is operating faster than the decision cycle of defenders, hidden in the vast noise of network traffic. Similarly, most budget requests and coding projects are to scale up defenses that cannot see novel compromises that have never been seen before, much less stop these threats completely. We have the capability now to tell if the crown jewels leave on a path headed for the shadows. With the advent of machine learning, network tools have identified and blocked untrustworthy sites, automatically guiding both people and devices to avoid the untamed internet, or offering them a picture of the monster rather than letting them directly reach out and touch it. But the unknowns must also be stopped, which requires knowing what good looks like.

Enemies are already exacting heavy costs on the United States with cyber. Threats have been quietly planted into our infrastructure. Today—our country is still too reliant on foreign factories and vulnerable supply chains. The United States does not make the computers, routers, switches, process controllers, dock cranes, pumps for gasoline, car parts, cameras, medicines, chemicals, and many other electronic things. But in cyber, it is much worse if your adversary made all the computers used in critical infrastructure or weapons systems. If your enemy left a back door or a designed-in a kill switch—they might use it. True security requires covering the supply chain threat as well as all other classes of threats like hackers and the insider threat.

Solutions

Why was I interested in testifying on this topic today? I believe that there is a chance that the United States can re-achieve the needed sense of urgency these threats require. Investments in critical infrastructure, strengthening supply chains, and reshoring critical manufacturing are all necessary investments for our security. We must continue to be proactive in our approach to cybersecurity.

The allocation of over $400 million in funding for the transition from Einstein to CADS is a significant level of funding. It is imperative, however, that the CADS program design and implementation are meticulously executed to deliver not only enterprise-wide system monitoring and control but also the seamless handling of vast volumes of data and information. Intelligent and actionable outputs must be quickly and proficiently delivered to a broad audience. History has shown that well-intentioned technological advancements can be hindered by overly complex and convoluted designs, drowning users in a sea of tools and unnecessary complexity. We must keep in mind that offensive cyber operations can be cheap and flexible. Just like water can find any hole in a ship, building, or computer system and cause massive damage—a cyber attacker needs only to be creative enough to find or create one hole to get in and defeat you with cyber. We must remove those attacks from the shadows of the internet, cut through that barrage of noise, and enable network defenders and analysts to discover the anomalies in the trusted high ground, where the maturing U.S. cyber workforce can collaborate to investigate without having resources overwhelmed. We can start by identifying what good looks like. How should safe software and devices behave? Knowing these profiles drives proficient identification of threats.

Concurrently, we must remain vigilant against the pitfalls of comprehensive coverage leading to comprehensive failure. Adversaries will monitor our progress and respond. In the realms of design, application, and deployment, we must consistently ask ourselves how to intelligently and efficiently innovate new capabilities and approaches into a far more effective solution. This ensures that our legacy solutions, designed to address legacy problems on a massive scale, are agile enough to perform effectively in real-world scenarios.

To achieve success, systems like CADS must work quickly, easily, and reliably. That is difficult. Solutions need to respond immediately to a threat, preventing outbound communications and impact to system operations. The response should be simple and as automated as possible—and not labor-intensive—overwhelming our already-taxed defenders. Plans need to account for integration and sustainment at the outset. And be agile enough to know that new things will need to be included over time. Our systems need to be real-time, 24/7 without a nagging string of alerts. A system that is both powered by quality and comprehensive data.

Beyond the outside threats, the CADS system should support zero-trust principles to mitigate and uncover compromises of accounts and systems. Digitally this means understanding the following about a system and its users:

- Who are the users?
- How do they behave?
- What is their reputation?
- Who have they been associating with?
- What does normal activity look like for mission need?
- What are the indicators of malicious intent?
- What are common traits of targets for a particular attack?
- How can targets reduce their exposure before being targeted?

Moreover, it's essential to examine how a relatively modest investment in pioneering technologies and capabilities could potentially revolutionize our cybersecurity approach. By allocating funding to these ‘‘moonshot'' endeavors, even in the order of a few million dollars, we may uncover the next major breakthrough in cyber defense, at a cost that pales in comparison to the budget required for comprehensive systems like CADS.

We strongly recommend these flagship programs and agencies acknowledge that without specific and targeted funding for strategic research and development, we run the risk of neglecting the cyber defenses necessary for the latter half of the 21st Century. DOD does this with DARPA and other programs. That's one model, but any substantial investment in major cyber defense programs, without accompanying funding for innovative and transformative technologies, could render these programs vulnerable. Much like the Maginot Line, an unforeseen breach in an inadequately defended area could undermine the entire defense system, rendering it futile and ineffective.

As I conclude my opening remarks, I would like to emphasize to the committee that while the introduction of the CADS system seems to represent a significant stride in the right direction, we must not let complacency take root. We should actively seek ways to complement the capabilities of CADS with innovative functions and useable systems that align with our overarching mission of fortifying the U.S. cyber defense posture. By doing so, we can ensure that our Nation remains at the forefront of cybersecurity, prepared to confront the evolving challenges of the digital age.

Just like the Manhattan Project would not have worked without a core team of geniuses backed up with a massive support and implementation program—now is as good a time as any to take charge. Congress can wisely pass laws and fund efforts that guide the course of this cyber conflict. We don't need to wait for our communications, power, logistics, and critical infrastructure to be taken offline in the lead-up to a conflict.

Spending tens of billions on the latest partial buzzwords isn't a winning strategy, let's implement a winning cyber strategy on a tight time line at an achievable budget. This path doesn't stop the kids' soccer teams from doing what kids do with massive pieces of Federal budgets, so let's carve out 5 percent for a cyber Manhattan Project that surprises the world with a defensive cyber solution that came out of nowhere and reversed the asymmetry of this conflict which we are losing. Winning is better.

Thank you again Mr. Chairman and Mr. Ranking Member for inviting me into this subcommittee's discussion today. I would be happy to answer your questions.

Chairman GARBARINO. Thank you, Mr. Head. Mr. Sheldon, I now recognize you for 5 minutes to summarize your opening statement.

Statement of Rob Sheldon, Senior Director, Crowdstrike

Mr. SHELDON. Chairman Garbarino, Congressman Menendez, Members of the subcommittee, thank you for the opportunity to testify today. Government functions are predicated on operable information technology systems. Because these functions underpin national security and other key services, Federal cybersecurity is a topic of paramount importance.

CrowdStrike is a U.S. cybersecurity company with employees in the United States and abroad. We are a provider of endpoint security technologies, cyber threat intelligence, and cybersecurity services to CISA and a host of other Federal agencies. We are proudto be an alliance member of CISA's Joint Cyber Defense Collaborative, JCDC. We also have unique perspectives from being a leading commercial provider serving major technology companies, 15 of the top 20 largest U.S. banks, and thousands of small and medium-sized businesses.

Over the past several decades, the Federal IT landscape has changed drastically. Beyond desktops and servers, we must now defend cloud environments, mobile devices, internet of things devices, and even specialized operation technologies. In parallel, the volume and severity of cyber threats to Federal systems is increasing.

Over the past few years, adversaries like China and Russia have successfully breached the U.S. Government on multiple occasions. In July, Chinese threat actors once again exploited authentication flaws in a major software vendor's email and office productivity platform, this time resulting in threat actors' unauthorized access to the email of two Cabinet Secretaries.

The Federal Government approach to cybersecurity is now evolving. An initial major cybersecurity program launched in 2008, the National Cybersecurity Protection System, NCPS, and its EINSTEIN capability focused on perimeter defense. But this strategy has fallen out of favor as most enterprises no longer even have a perimeter to defend. A complementary program, Continuous Diagnostics and Mitigation, or CDM, was created in 2012. This program offered a flexible portfolio of technologies to defend Federal networks. While CDM had a slow start, it has accelerated meaningfully over the past year, thanks in part to the addition of key end-point detection and response, or DAR, efforts.

This year, CISA officials announced the creation of two associated programs, the Joint Collaborative Environment, JCE, and the Cyber Analytics and Data System, CADS. CADS, in particular, will be central for supporting a variety of new data-intensive operational requirements. Among other things, this includes implementation of the Cybersecurity Incident Reporting for Critical Infrastructure Law, CIRCIA, passed last year.

Beyond programs, Federal cyber policy has changed in recent years to better address threats. Congress provided CISA the authority to threat hunt across Government networks in the fiscal year 2021 National Defense Authorization Act. The White House issued Executive Order 14028 in May 2021. This initiated key efforts for endpoint security, log retention, cloud adoption, and incident response standardization. In 2022, the Office of Management and Budget, pursuant to Executive Order 14028, issued a Federal Zero Trust Strategy that clarifies and aligns Government efforts on implementing zero trust principles. This year, the Office of the National Cyber Director issued a new National Cybersecurity Strategy and an associated implementation plan that provides a roadmap and dates for several important cybersecurity initiatives.

I'd like to offer a few recommendations for Federal cybersecurity going forward. New programs such as CADS must be designed to enable flexibility and be built for scale. The expanded use of cloud workloads, growing log retention needs, and the use of artificial intelligence, or AI, each entail extensive data processing requirements. As noted above, the recent addition of EDR capabilities has strengthened CDM, but when the time comes to modernize that program itself, stakeholders should consider clear terms for long-term cost-sharing and additional shared services approaches. The Federal Information Security Modernization Act of 2014, FISMA, is of a similar vintage as CDM and could benefit from reform. A bill that aligns disparate Federal IT policies accrued over the past 10 years would improve cybersecurity outcomes.

Looking ahead there are a number of emerging technologies that would further strengthen the Federal cybersecurity posture. These include Extended Detection and Response, or XDR, which enables integrated EDR like visibility and control to cybersecurity products beyond the endpoint, identity threat detection and response, which supports zero trust adoption objectives, and expanded use of AI, which can enhance a broader range of cybersecurity solutions, and managed security services, which can enable high-fidelity commercial support to distributed Federal security operations. Each of these is described in more detail in my written statement. Thank you again for the opportunity to testify today, and I look forward to your questions.

[The prepared statement of Mr. Sheldon follows:]

Prepared Statement of Robert Sheldon September 19, 2023

Chairman Garbarino, Congressman Menendez, Members of the subcommittee, thank you for the opportunity to testify today. Materially all Federal Government functions are predicated on operable information technology (IT) systems. Given that these functions include the provision of key services that underpin national security and our way of life, Federal cybersecurity is a topic of paramount importance. CrowdStrike is a U.S. cybersecurity company, with employees across the country and globally. We bring a unique perspective on Federal cybersecurity issues. We are a provider of endpoint security technologies, cyber threat intelligence, and cybersecurity services to the Cybersecurity and Infrastructure Security Agency (CISA) and other Federal agencies. We are proud to be an original plank holder of CISA's Joint Cyber Defense Collaborative (JCDC). We also have unique perspectives from being a leading commercial provider serving major technology companies, 15 of the top 20 largest U.S. banks, and thousands of small and medium-sized businesses.

Over the past two decades, the Federal IT enterprise has swelled in size and scope. No longer basic networks of desktops and servers, Federal IT today includes cloud workloads, mobile devices, internet of things (IoT) devices—and even specialized operational technology (OT).

In parallel, the volume and severity of cyber threats to Federal systems has increased. Nation-state threat actors regularly seek—and too often, succeed—in breaching Federal enterprises. Over the past few years, major incidents have enabled adversaries like China and Russia to collect sensitive intelligence. In July, Chinese threat actors once again exploited authentication flaws in a major Federal vendor's office productivity and email platform—this time resulting in threat actors' unauthorized access to the email of two Cabinet Secretaries.[2] Under slightly different geopolitical conditions or adversarial objectives, these incidents could have enabled scaled destructive attacks.

The evolution in the IT environment and worsening of the threat landscape mean it's important to regularly review and assess the efficacy of Federal cybersecurity measures—which include policies, programs, and strategies.

---

[2] See Nakashima, Ellen. Menn, Joseph. Harris, Shane. *Chinese hackers breach email of Commerce Secretary Raimondo and State Department officials.* The Washington Post, July 14, 2023. *https://www.washingtonpost.com/national-security/2023/07/12/microsoft-hack-china/;* and *Results of Major Technical Investigations for Storm–0558 Key Acquisition,* Microsoft, September 6, 2023. *https://msrc.microsoft.com/blog/2023/09/results-of-major-technical-investigations-for- storm-0558-key-acquisition/.*

A Brief Background on CISA's Primary Federal Cybersecurity Programs[3]

By the early 2000's, Federal IT infrastructure had grown significantly. Cybersecurity protections were still fairly organic, with different agencies adopting different approaches, dedicating disparate resources, and achieving uneven outcomes. A significant uptick in cyber attacks targeting national laboratories, major defense industrial base entities, and the Federal Government agencies themselves highlighted the need for greater investment and more standardization.

National Cybersecurity Protection System (NCPS).[4] Established in 2008, NCPS's goal was to protect Federal networks through a suite of perimeter defense technologies called ''EINSTEIN,'' as well as an associated analytic capability. Leveraging intrusion detection and later intrusion prevention capabilities, EINSTEIN would attempt to defeat threats prior to threat actors accessing sensitive systems, like endpoints, or sensitive data. While the program clearly improved Federal cybersecurity posture from the status quo ante, and the associated analytic capabilities supported broader initiatives, EINSTEIN itself was not ultimately well-suited to meet the full scope of cyber threats to the ''.gov.''

Perimeter defenses are only one small part of cybersecurity. Two concepts help explain why. The first is the assumption of breach. Elite defenders have come to assume that threat actors can—and indeed, already have—breached perimeter defenses. Whether through a supply chain attack, malicious or unwitting insider, compromised identity, or any number of other methods, attacks often sidestep perimeter security measures and other defensive controls. Within this worldview, defenders must operate accordingly.[5] The second concept is defense in depth. This practice essentially layers defensive technologies to provide defenders multiple opportunities to detect and respond to threats. If a threat actor is able to breach the perimeter, defenses at the

---

[3] For brevity, I have not described broader Federal cybersecurity initiatives like Trusted Internet Connection program (2007), the Comprehensive National Cybersecurity Initiative (2009), FedRAMP (2011), the Federal Information Security Modernization Act (2014), or the Federal Information Technology Acquisition Reform Act (2014), but I would like to acknowledge their contributions to the Federal cybersecurity infrastructure that exists today.

[4] See National Cybersecurity Protection System, CISA. https://www.cisa.gov/resources-tools/programs/national-cybersecurity-protection-system.

[5] This assumption leads to the imperative to hunt, described below.

network, endpoint, and identity layers provide additional chances to stop them before they can achieve their objectives.

However useful EINSTEIN was at inception or at its peak efficacy, its value has eroded over time. Mobile devices, remote work, cloud applications, and other changes in the IT landscape have dissolved the perimeter, even as the increased use of encryption has complicated detection of malicious traffic at the perimeter layer. Further, threat actors have become more adept in recent years at targeting endpoints, users, and identities directly. As a result, the security community—including Government agencies and the White House[6] 5—have embraced concepts like Zero Trust, which essentially disavows the defensibility of the perimeter. While it's reasonable to maintain perimeter defenses as part of a layered security architecture for the ''.gov,'' it's also reasonable to consider EINSTEIN a legacy technology and to focus investments elsewhere.

Continuing Diagnostics and Mitigation (CDM). By 2012, DHS had established a complementary, broader program called CDM. Rather than applying a uniform suite of protections across the ''.gov,'' CDM would offer a flexible portfolio of technologies to defend Federal networks. The program would deliver new capabilities in four phases: Asset Management; Identity and Access Management; Network Security Management; and Data Protection Management.[7] A unifying requirement for tools acquired under the program is the ability to offer visibility through an integrated agency-level dashboard, as well as an aggregated Federal-level dashboard.

Despite modest progress in early years, CISA officials report rapidly-accelerating progress over the past few years. According to a recent CISA blog, ''CDM is no longer a static effort to standardize agency capabilities and collect cybersecurity information, but rather the U.S. government's cornerstone for proactive, coordinated, and agile cyber defense of the Federal enterprise.''[8] The post further credits Execu tive Order 14028 with strengthening the program's operational visibility, which highlights the addition of the Endpoint Detection and Response (EDR) program to CDM

---

[6] See Executive Order 14028, Improving the Nation's Cybersecurity, The White House. https://www.whitehouse.gov/briefing-room/presidential-actions/2021/05/12/executive-order- on-improving-the-nations-cybersecurity/.

[7] See CDM Program Overview, CISA. https://www.cisa.gov/sites/default/files/publications/2020%252009%252003 CDM%2520Program%2520Overview Fact%2520Sheet.pdf.

[8] See Evolving CDM to Transform Government Cybersecurity Operations and Enable CISA's Approach to Interactive Cyber Defense, CISA. July 23, 2023. https://www.cisa.gov/news-events/news/evolving-cdm-transform-government-cybersecurity-operations-and-enable-cisas-approach- interactive.

(explained in more detail, below). Further progress is possible with the extension of EDR to cloud workloads and mobile devices.

Recent Policy Developments

While the current major Federal cybersecurity programs administered by CISA are now 10–15 years old, Federal IT policy has accelerated. Stakeholders have made significant progress in the past few years, best illustrated by three key developments.

Threat-Hunting Authorities. A central insight from the influential, bipartisan Cyberspace Solarium Commission Report of March 2020 was recommendation 1.4, which highlighted the need for CISA to perform continuous threat hunting across the ''.gov.''[9] Pub. L. 116–283, the fiscal year 2021 National Defense Authorization Act (NDAA) Section 1705 granted CISA this authority, which positions the agency to act as the operational defender of the Federal Government.[10]

Executive Order (E.O. 14028). The May 2021 Executive Order on Improving the Nation's Cybersecurity advanced a suite of measures to further bolster security of the ''.gov.'' Key among them were requirements to:

- Deploy Endpoint Detection and Response (EDR) capabilities, which among other things serve as the foundational enterprise cybersecurity technology for threat hunting;
- Implement Zero Trust Architectures, as well as generally accelerate cloud and Software-as-a-Service (SaaS) utilization;
- Standardize incident response practices; and
- Maintain more robust and consistent logging, which supports investigations and remediations.[11]

---

[9] See Cyberspace Solarium Commission Report, March 2020. https://www.solarium.gov/report, p. 41.

[10] See NDAA Enacts 25 Recommendations from the Bipartisan Cyberspace Solarium Commission, Sen. Angus King, January 2, 2021. https://www.king.senate.gov/newsroom/press-releases/ndaa-enacts-25-recommendations-from-the-bipartisan-cyberspace-solarium-commission; and The National Defense Authorization Act for Fiscal Year 2021, https://www.Congress.gov/116/bills/hr6395/BILLS-116hr6395enr.pdf, p. 695.

[11] See *Executive Order on Improving the Nation's Cybersecurity,* The White House, May 12, 2021. *https://www.whitehouse.gov/briefing-room/presidential-actions/2021/05/12/executive-order-on-improving-the-nations-cybersecurity/.*

Federal Zero Trust Strategy. In January 2022, fulfilling a requirement from E.O. 14028, the White House Office of Management and Budget (OMB) issued a strategy for implementing Zero Trust across the ‘‘.gov.’’ The memorandum identified specific outcomes and objectives that agencies must achieve over the coming years. This strategy serves a key roadmap that aligns industry and agency efforts over what will be a complex, multi-year process.[12]

Forthcoming Programmatic Developments

Budget request documents released over the past year foreshadow perhaps the most significant shift in the Federal cybersecurity program space since the advent of CDM. Specifically, CISA is in the midst of creating two new, closely-linked programs which will absorb elements of NCPS.[13] First, according to these documents, CISA will create a program called the Joint Collaborative Environment (JCE). At a high-level, JCE would split the NCPS program into two components. The first is EINSTEIN capabilities (i.e., perimeter defense), which would be maintained as legacy technology under JCE.

The second component of JCE is much broader—and is itself a meaningful new program—called Cyber Analytics and Data System (CADS). A summary document for the fiscal year 2024 President’s Budget Request describes CADS as ‘‘a system of systems[] that will provide a robust and scalable analytic environment capable of integrating mission visibility data sets and providing visualization tools and ad vanced analytic capabilities to CISA’s cyber operators.’’[14] CADS would absorb the remaining analytic capabilities from the NCPS program, serve as the hub for Cyber Incident

---

[12] See Memorandum 22–09, Moving the U.S. Government Toward Zero Trust Cybersecurity Principles, Executive Office of the President, January 26, 2022. https://www.whitehouse.gov/wp-content/uploads/2022/01/M-22-09.pdf.

[13] This narrative draws on program descriptions within CISA Budget Overview for Fiscal Year 2024 Congressional Justification. https://www.dhs.gov/sites/default/files/2023-03/CYBERSECURITY%20AND%20INFRASTRUCTURE%20SECURITY%20AGENCY.pdf. See also CISA Strategic Plan fiscal year 2024–2026. https://www.cisa.gov/sites/default/files/2023-08/FY2024-2026□Cybersecurity□Strategic□Plan.pdf. For consistency, I have focused on characterizations from the President’s Budget Request rather than from more recent but yet-to-be-finalized House and Senate Appropriations documents.

[14] See Department of Homeland Security Fiscal Year 2024 Budget in Brief. https://www.dhs.gov/sites/default/files/2023_03/DHS%20FY%202024%20BUDGET%20IN%20- BRIEF%20%28BIB%29_Remediated.pdf, p. 4.

Reporting for the Critical Infrastructure Act of 2022 (CIRCIA) analytics, and support a number of other data-intensive operational activities.

Next Steps in Federal Cybersecurity

A core principle in cybersecurity is that the defender must have visibility into security-relevant events of the systems they defend. Today, this includes the endpoint, cloud, and identity planes in addition to the traditional network. Although stakeholders have made significant progress on Federal cybersecurity over the past few years in enhancing this visibility and control, several points stand out as next steps to further strengthen the security posture of the ''.gov.''

JCE and CADS implementation. Clearly, the JCE and CADS efforts described above will require a significant investment of time and resources. Federal cybersecurity programs historically have a long ''shelf-life,'' and strengths and weaknesses can both compound over time. This underscores two key, future-oriented considerations:

- It's important to design these programs to enable flexibility. Changes in the IT or threat environment over time may precipitate the need to reallocate resources between program areas or initiatives.
- CADS in particular should be built for scale. The processing of data for cybersecurity purposes increased exponentially during the transition from the legacy antivirus age to the current EDR age. This trend could continue for some time, particularly as cloud workloads swell, log retention expectations increase, and adversaries and defenders alike seek to leverage Artificial Intelligence (AI). CISA must build CADS data processing capabilities that can perhaps double (or more) year over year for the foreseeable future.

CDM modernization and sustainment. With the realignment in NCPS described above, CDM will in a sense become the ''mature'' Government cybersecurity program. This raises the question: at what point might CDM itself need to be modernized? From an operational standpoint, the EDR program has clearly breathed new life into CDM, so perhaps this is a question that can be resolved in the future. Nevertheless, when the time comes, stakeholders should consider two questions:

- While some EDR technologies were available through CDM prior to E.O. 14028, it ultimately required a mandate from the White House to deploy this essential technology across the ''.gov.'' Cybersecurity professionals within CISA understood the importance of EDR, and it was clear that EDR would support CISA's hunting mandate. But CDM still works on the model of a catalog. In the future, is there scope for CISA to more proactively enforce the use of CDM technologies to fulfill its mission?
- Although, as noted above, EINSTEIN's operational capabilities have aged poorly, the NCPS program's architecture has aged like a fine wine. Specifically, it worked on a shared services model, meaning agencies got the benefit of EINSTEIN protections without complex budgeting or cost-sharing processes. With respect to the CDM program and associated funding, Federal CISOs still sometimes hesitate to acquire new technologies, given a real or perceived uncertainty about cost-sharing with CISA over time. In the future, is there scope to adapt CDM, or elements thereof (e.g., EDR), to operate more directly as a shared service, where CISA funds the program for users directly?

Emerging cybersecurity capabilities. The cybersecurity industry is evolving at an uncharacteristically rapid rate. So over the next few years, the conversation within the Federal cybersecurity community will shift to new priorities. A few emerging areas to monitor, and further integrate into Federal defenses as appropriate, include:

- Extended Detection and Response (XDR). Mature security programs within the private sector are already augmenting EDR to attain detection and response capabilities at other layers of the enterprise security stack. XDR enables visibility and control over network and identity (described below) data; the aggregation of logs; and the integration of threat intelligence within a unified workflow.
- Identity Threat Detection and Response. As security practitioners increasingly confront risks from IT ecosystem monoculture specifically, and identity-based attacks generally, there's greater interest in defending enterprises at the identity layer. This emphasis comports nicely with broader Federal Zero Trust adoption efforts.

- Artificial Intelligence (AI). While the application of AI to cybersecurity is not new, it is advancing. Although already resident within leading endpoint security tools, multiple other cybersecurity technologies will integrate AI and new AI- based capabilities will emerge over the coming years. This will drive speed, efficiency, and even make some tools more accessible through the integration of a natural language interface.[15] To the extent possible, Federal cybersecurity executives should view this opportunity holistically, consult broadly with industry and academia, and engage in long-term planning.
- Managed Security Services. Enterprises—even very large ones—increasingly leverage commercial managed security solutions. Defenders should be prepared to respond to and remediate cyber threats 24x7x365, and not all entities are able to build programs that can match the agility of dedicated commercial offerings. On the other hand, internal IT and security staff, by virtue of their trust and familiarity with the organization's mission space and constraints, are uniquely positioned to develop processes, address risks, and otherwise strengthen security maturity. So unburdening these internal operators from tactical demands on their time pays enormous dividends. This opportunity clearly applies in aspects of the Federal IT ecosystem.

Thank you again for the opportunity to testify today, and I look forward to your questions.

Chairman GARBARINO. Thank you, Mr. Sheldon. Members will be recognized by order of seniority for their 5 minutes of questioning. An additional round of questioning may be called after all Members have been recognized. I really do appreciate the participation, though, of my colleagues for being here today. This is a dense topic, but it is a very important one. So, I do appreciate you all being here, especially considering CISA right now is under attack from some of our colleagues, ranging from proposed defunding of salaries to up to a 25 percent cut of their budget, something that I think after today's testimony from our witnesses, people will understand

[15] See, for example, Charlotte AI: Accelerate Cybersecurity with Generative AI Workflows CrowdStrike. https://www.crowdstrike.com/products/charlotte-ai/.

how important CISA is and that the focus needs to be on defense, especially when it comes to cybersecurity.

So, I now recognize myself for 5 minutes of opening questions. Mr. Gumbel, for a long time, agencies have been required to maintain asset inventories. The base layer of CDM was meant to help this. You can't defend what you can't see. But even with a requirement in FISMA and tools in CDM meant to help identify and manage assets, agencies consistently struggle to accurately and continuously maintain asset inventories. CISA even put out a binding operational directive at the beginning of this fiscal year, again directing agencies to better manage their assets. What more can the CDM program do to help agencies get this right?

Mr. GUMBEL. Sure. Mr. Chairman, thank you for this question. I think there's a lot that they can do to help get this right. I think some of our recommendations are we need to create a more transparent and collaborative technology assessment process. We also need to, and I think we all can be aware of this, that the procurement process within Federal Government is not the easiest to get through, and it also excludes some of the newer technology, cloud-based technologies, and it's more leaning toward and geared toward legacy technologies. So, I think improvements there within procurement can absolutely help out.

There's also a lot that can be learned from the private sector. The private sector has done incredible advancements around cloud-based technologies, around end-to-end solutions that offer full visibility into unmanaged devices. I submitted in my written testimony a bar chart that showed the explosion of unmanaged devices. Those devices, meaning the ones that you can't see traditionally, IP cameras, HVAC systems, building management systems, and printers, those things need to be looked at when we are looking at securing the American public.

Chairman GARBARINO. Thank you very much. I have heard from many companies that some of our best technologies are being kept out because of the procurement process right now.

So, something we should work on. Mr. Zakowicz, NCPS has traditionally structured as a true shared service with CISA providing and covering the cost of operation. Whereas CISA provides funding and tools for CDM for the first 2 years, with agencies expected to carry on funding after that. Are there changes that would help improve agency adoption of CDM tools? What role does centralized funding play in that?

Mr. ZAKOWICZ. Thank you for the question. As I mentioned in my opening remarks, the funding associated with progress on CDM is not just in the hands of CISA. It's also in the hands of the agencies who have their own mission priorities and focus that they need to balance against the priorities that CISA provides and their own security. I think that one case study under the CDM program that we've seen under the shared services model is that unlike the 2- year funding model that you referenced, that shared services model does provide those services in perpetuity to those smaller agencies and organizations as long as they're using that standardized set of capabilities that are provided to those agencies.

That model is not going to work for the largest, most complex federated agencies out there. They are going to have their unique requirements that won't necessarily allow them to take on a shared services approach. But there are a lot of agencies that currently don't qualify for the shared services program that could take advantage of those and that would allow centralized funding. It would allow reduction in total operating costs due to the purchasing power of that shared services platform, and could ultimately provide some additional benefit.

Chairman GARBARINO. Are there risks introduced by moving toward a true shared services model that increases interdependencies and thus increases the potential for cascading vulnerabilities across agencies?

Mr. ZAKOWICZ. So, I think the risks associated with moving to a shared services model generally, you know, come from an agency perspective around the lack of control in the solution, which can be a risk and a benefit depending on what your IT resources look like. The current shared service model under CDM provides multiple options of any given tool or capability, at least two, so that agencies can pick which one is best suited to their needs. Then it also provides additional watch capabilities so that there's a central organization within CISA keeping an eye on what alerts, what monitoring activities are occurring under those tools, and provides a, you know, checks-and-balances process to then notify those agencies when issues are identified.

Chairman GARBARINO. Thank you. Mr. Head, as the head of your company, both CDM and NCPS—he made me do that, by the way—both CDM and NCPS are critical parts of Federal civilian cyber defense. It seems to me that these two programs, which ultimately are about visibility and continuous monitoring, should work better together. How should CISA be thinking about getting these programs to work better together?

Mr. HEAD. I think if we start with the basics of the roles when we consider the options, you know, what data do I need to see what I need to see? One of the panel members makes a product that says here's your inventory all that stuff on your network. I think we also need to look at role. One of the things I like to look at is, you know, is your printer a bank teller? Is your printer an engineer? If not, why is it accessing customer records? So, when you start looking at things that shouldn't happen the way they are happening, you've got to answer the question, if I have a tool and I choose to make it proactive and to block and, I mean, do we want to spend our whole time analyzing or reporting on how we got eaten? Or do we want to flip the tables and say, no, we stopped this cold and they won't come after us again?

I think a piece of that is you got to do to them what they just did to you. So, you know, we need to have some law changes in terms of punitive damages as well as unleash the military guys to have fun. So, whatever they do to us, we need to do them 10 times until they quit. This is terrible.

Chairman GARBARINO. Thank you very much. I now recognize Ranking Member Menendez for 5 minutes for any questions he may have.

Mr. MENENDEZ. Thank you, Chairman. Government funding is set to expire in just 11 days, creating a dangerous risk of a Government shutdown. Even in a best-case scenario where we keep the Government open, we will have a continuing resolution with no sign of a bipartisan full year appropriations bill in sight. This question is for all of you. What do you see as the main impacts a Government shutdown could have on the ability of CISA to defend networks? We will start with you, Mr. Gumbel.

Mr. GUMBEL. I think the shutdown will obviously cause delays and some cyber projects will come to a halt. The longer we delay, the longer the adversaries will have the chance to get in front of us. So, delays are just terrible for this Nation and it is going to cause some major impact.

Mr. MENENDEZ. Thank you.

Mr. ZAKOWICZ. Thanks. So, having done this for 4 years, I've lived through a couple of, you know, Government shutdowns and the impacts, I think really day-to-day operationally are ones of continuity and ones of resource availability. So, what are we able to do, what are we able to make progress on? Ultimately, what tradeoffs are each one of those agencies making as they're, you know, facing the questions of what, you know, resources are they going to have left, how are they going to keep the doors open? That does have an impact, not just on, you know, that shutdown in the moment, but also continuity, planning, and forward progress in some of these initiatives.

Mr. MENENDEZ. Thank you. Mr. Head.

Mr. HEAD. As I mentioned before, the big programs under a CR continue at the previous funding levels, or 80 percent. The thing that just hits you the hardest is the new initiatives just get stopped completely and we need a lot of innovation in the cybers. So, I think you all need a way to fund during a CR, especially new programs and reactive breach responses. That's sadly lacking across the table and it is sort-of disheartening to the guys that are burn- ing 20-hour days to do the work across all the agencies.

Mr. MENENDEZ. Just to quickly follow up on that, you mentioned the new initiatives. New initiatives are to match the evolving threat environment, correct?

Mr. HEAD. Correct.

Mr. MENENDEZ. So when we are not implementing that, we are not only not keeping up, but we are falling behind in a relatively quick fashion.

Mr. HEAD. Yes.

Mr. MENENDEZ. Thank you. Mr. Sheldon.

Mr. HEAD. You can't start a new effort under a CR, but you can continue an old one. This is all new. It's new every day with a new breach, new zero day, new attack.

Mr. MENENDEZ. I appreciate that. Mr. Sheldon.

Mr. SHELDON. Thank you. You don't get to have good cybersecurity outcomes if you don't have continuity in your cybersecurity programs. The absence of funding could disrupt that.

Mr. MENENDEZ. Thank you. Mr. Gumbel, just to come back to you to sort-of follow up on the point Mr. Head just made. How would a year-long continuing resolution that locks in last year's budget impact the ability of CISA to innovate to match the current threat environment?

Mr. GUMBEL. I'm sorry. Could you repeat that?

Mr. MENENDEZ. Sure. How would a year-long continuing resolution that locks in last year's budget impact the ability of CISA to innovate to match the current threat environment?

Mr. GUMBEL. My view is that we need to obviously match what CISA is doing in order to progress some of the changes in the systems that we're looking to put forth. So, I think it is a big concern.

Mr. MENENDEZ. Thank you. The current CDM program monitors traditional IT assets across Federal agencies. However, the attack surface is growing to include internet of things, devices, and threats to operational technology. As CDM continues to modernize, including all assets will be an important part of the program's maturation. Mr. Gumbel, can you elaborate on why you think including internet of things and operational technology assets in the CDM program is so important?

Mr. GUMBEL. The reason why it's so important is that only 10 percent of networks have managed devices on them. The other 90 percent are unmanaged devices. As you mentioned, Mr. Chairman, you can't protect what you can't see. All of these other devices are out there and they are invisible unless there's modern technology, there's cloud-based technologies, and there's ways in which you can view these assets. Without being able to view these assets, these are vectors for the adversaries to be able to get in and to be able to compromise our environments.

Mr. MENENDEZ. Great.

Mr. GUMBEL. So, it's a real big threat.

Mr. MENENDEZ. A quick follow-up to that you mentioned you can't protect what you can't see. How should CISA go about expanding its visibility into those devices?

Mr. GUMBEL. I think how they go about it is to allow modern companies to be able to bid when there's new contracts that come out. I think they have to evolve from legacy companies that have on premise solutions, allow cloud-based technologies to come in and provide a holistic view. I think the other thing that they can do is start looking at commonality between different leadership groups within organizations. Right now, you have some groups that you have just visibility into OT or IT. You have some that are focused just on IOT. There needs to be a conversion to leadership across all Federal agencies so that there's a holistic view of what's being managed and what's being unmanaged.

Mr. MENENDEZ. I appreciate that. Probably all of us on this subcommittee have had local governments in our district hit by ransomware attacks and other cyber incidents that have denied constituents access to vital Government services. One way to help State and local governments is to provide them expanded access to CDM services. We will ask you to keep this brief because I am over. Mr. Zakowicz and Mr. Sheldon, how should CISA enable expanded CDM shared services to State and local governments?

Mr. ZAKOWICZ. I think they've got a good blueprint to follow in the shared services capability they've already offered to the Federal entities. As you can imagine, the cyber maturity of agencies across our FCEB can, in a lot of ways, mirror the relative maturity of State and local critical infrastructure stakeholders where some are very well-resourced and others are not. So, I think there's a lot of learnings from that rollout of shared services that could be directly applied to State, local, Tribal, territorial, and critical infrastructure.

Mr. SHELDON. Thank you. There are some lessons for sure that State and local entities can take from Federal Government programs like CDM. There are also, frankly, some lessons that the Federal Government can take from State and local entities that kind of more organically operate on shared services models in some instances.

Mr. MENENDEZ. Thank you.

Chairman GARBARINO. I now recognize the gentleman from Florida, Mr. Gimenez, for 5 minutes.

Mr. GIMENEZ. Thank you, Mr. Chairman. Mr. Head, I was listening to your testimony, and it struck me, were you saying basically that the United States' cybersecurity efforts are mainly, if not exclusively, defensive in nature?

Mr. HEAD. I would say that we are reactive defensive in that we are not taking actions to stop it before it happens. You know, and I think, there's, obviously, there's a difference between the offensive side and the defensive side. So, the military guys have offensive capabilities that they hold in reserve and that'll work independent. But my comment was more on the side of don't just wait until something happens and develop a process to know about it and report it sooner. Work on the technologies that stop the attack in the first place.

Mr. GIMENEZ. But I think you also said that our cybersecurity threats, they kind-of operate with impunity. They know that nothing's ever going to happen to them.

Mr. HEAD. Correct.

Mr. GIMENEZ. Which means that they are not afraid of any offensive capability that their target may possess.

Mr. HEAD. That's correct.

Mr. GIMENEZ. Is that because is it illegal for us or a company to conduct offensive——

Mr. HEAD. I think there's——

Mr. GIMENEZ [continuing]. Or retaliatory operations against somebody who just attacked their network, et cetera, or what is that?

Mr. HEAD. I think there's many levels to that. I've been asked several times about, should we take off the gloves and let people that are hit, hit back? I'm not a big fan of that approach because you could end up starting a nuclear war just by, you know, doing something crazy. So, I don't think we want to go vigilante, but I do think we need better clarity.

When I first started looking at this a decade ago, we had a guy that had a bunch of documents stolen, and he put scripts in his documents so that when they got to wherever they were going to, they would call him and let him know where they ended up. They arrested him for operating shell scripts on a computer without permission. That's crazy. So, being able to trace. We need to clarify——

Mr. GIMENEZ. Was that illegal?

Mr. HEAD. Yes.

Mr. GIMENEZ. It was illegal.

Mr. HEAD. He didn't have permission from the guy that attacked him to run scripts on the attacker's computer. So, he included executable files in what was stolen, and he was arrested for that. So, there's a little bit of crack-smoking that goes on in the legal world that we need to fix.

Mr. GIMENEZ. All right. So, somebody attacked him.

Mr. HEAD. Yes.

Mr. GIMENEZ. And he put something in there to make sure that he could find out who it was that attacked him?

Mr. HEAD. Correct. They arrested him.

Mr. GIMENEZ. Then the person that attacked him said, hey, you couldn't do that to me even though I attacked you first, and therefore, the guy that was attacked was the one ultimately jailed?

Mr. HEAD. Yes.

Mr. GIMENEZ. That sounds logical.

Mr. HEAD. You don't have to look far for comedy in the cyber space. But I'm just saying, you know, you guys are really good about—a lot of us that have been in the defensive world forever we try to figure out how to operate within the laws and make it better. The reason I'm here is it suddenly dawned on me, a year or so, just change the law. Let's get rid of the crazy. It helps.

Mr. GIMENEZ. I guess that is what I was trying to get to, that there may be laws that are actually hindering our ability to defend ourselves and maybe, look, I have no problem hitting back every once in a while, OK?

Mr. HEAD. Absolutely.

Mr. GIMENEZ. All right. Because then you should have as an attacker, you need to be fearful of what could happen to you, depending on who you attacked. I mean, can you imagine if we had after Pearl Harbor, we just said, well, I guess we will just wait for the next attack, OK. We are not going to take any offensive capabilities. Or in Europe, well, you know, we are just going to stay here in England, and we were not going to do D-Day because, you know, we are just going to defend ourselves. I don't think you could win too many wars that way. So, I find that very interesting.

I don't know who can answer this, but artificial intelligence. If somebody can put out a crystal, you know, get a crystal ball and say, OK, what will artificial intelligence do in this realm, offensively and defensively? What do you all see?

Mr. SHELDON. I could take a stab at that. Thank you, sir. So, artificial intelligence has made a lot of news recently because there's greater access to some consumer products that make LLMs, especially large language models, available for experimentation. But really, artificial intelligence and cybersecurity is not all that new. My company, for example, has had artificial intelligence and machine learning embedded in it at scale, deployed out across tens of millions of endpoints for the better part of 10 years. That really drives some of our ability to identify and stop even very novel threats, attacks that haven't been seen before. So, there's a lot of ways in which defenders already are using AI and that is poised to continue as AI gets integrated into other product areas. So, it is a very exciting time from the standpoint of what the defenders are able to do.

On the other hand, it's also the case that adversaries and different threat actors are experimenting with large language models and other forms of AI. It's something that us in the defense community need to look out for. It may be the case that there's some more developments in that over the next coming months because there are broader access to some of these tools now than there have been over some time. So, it's something that merits watching.

Mr. GIMENEZ. Thank you. I guess my time is up. I yield back.

Chairman GARBARINO. The gentleman yields back. I now recognize the gentleman from Louisiana, Mr. Carter, for 5 minutes.

Mr. CARTER. Thank you, Mr. Chairman. Thank you all for being here. In 2021, President Biden issued Executive Order 14028, which imposed a host of new mandates on agencies to strengthen the Federal Government's cybersecurity. One positive result of this order was a deployment of endpoint detection and response technologies across Federal agencies as a part of the CDM program. With that Executive Order now already 2 years old, the technological environment continues to evolve with advances that constantly test our defenses. For all of the witnesses, as we seek to constantly evolve the CDM program to stay ahead of our adversaries, what technologies and cyber defense practices do you think are most urgently needed to be deployed at Federal agencies based on today's ever-moving threat?

Mr. GUMBEL. Thank you, Congressman. For Armis, we view the only way for pure protection across all agencies is ubiquity and that view to have 100 percent visibility into all assets. Whether those assets be IT OT, IOT, or IOMT, it is critical that you have visibility into the unmanaged devices within an environment in order to provide that holistic view. Otherwise, you're at risk of adversaries getting one step ahead of the game and being able to infiltrate a network.

Mr. CARTER. Thank you.

Mr. ZAKOWICZ. I agree with the answer. I would say at least with my experience on the CDM program, that yes, historically the focus has been on IT-managed assets. They have done some work associated with operational technology, mobile assets, cloud assets, and I think that needs to be prioritized and accelerated to be able to get that complete view that my colleague's referencing.

Mr. HEAD. I think one aspect that is worth saying is when you look at endpoint protection, there's some really good stuff. We use theirs and love it. But what you want to do is instrument a network in such a way that how do you know when you've been blindsided. So, I think, you know, if you look at IOT devices, there's not going to be endpoint software, you know, on a watch, or on a firmware device, or a lot of IOT things, door alarms, so on. So, you're going to have to have network-based things that look to see if those are acting in ways they shouldn't.

So, you want a layered defense. People talk about that all the time, but when it comes to implementing it, we do sort-of light beer when you're ready for full-bodied. So, we need to really look at a more defense-in-depth with a lot more visibility.

Mr. SHELDON. Thank you. I'd say there's still some progress that can be made within the EDR program itself by way of deploying it out to cloud environments, mobile devices, and the like, just to make sure that you have the same level of visibility control on those types of assets. Then beyond that, really thinking about a concept that the industry calls extended detection and response, which is the same idea of bringing that visibility and control out to other parts of the network security stack. So, making sure that you can get integrated workflows with data not just from the endpoint but also from the network, or from the perimeter, or being able to integrate logs, being able to integrate threat intelligence and similar things then giving people more coherent set of a control plain for being able to do the work that they do from a defensive standpoint.

Mr. CARTER. Mr. Sheldon, in your earlier testimony you discussed the need for CISA's proposed cyber analytics and data systems to be built to scale. I agree on the need to ensure that CADS has the capacity to process significant increases in data we can expect CISA to receive in the upcoming years. How can CISA ensure that it deploys the new program in a way that is flexible enough to handle future demands?

Mr. SHELDON. Thank you, Congressman. This, I think, is probably one of the more interesting questions that CISA has to grapple with today. I think an interesting stress test for whatever plans they've developed for the CADS program is to think about, you know, would this work if we needed to—whatever our sort-of best guess is, or our assumption about how much data we need to be able to process in that environment, would it be able to handle twice that, and then would it be able to handle twice that again? Doing some of those sort-of stress tests would, I think, position them well to understand whether they're developing architectures that can scale to the level that they will need to if they are doing more types of data-intensive programs across the Federal Government.

For our case, we have 2 trillion events per day or more that we stream up to our cloud. So that's the type of big data that——

Mr. CARTER. I got 3 seconds. Let me just cut you off a second. I want to ask Mr. Gumbel, given where we are and the threat as they evolve, and the pace at which technology is moving, if you had a silver bullet that you can use with this committee or with Federal Government, what would that be to make sure that we are staying abreast and ahead of the bad actors?

Mr. GUMBEL. I want to repeat this again, but I do believe the silver bullet is to have end-to-end security for visibility for all of your assets. That's the only way to get full visibility and protection across your enterprise. To take a step further, is once you can identify those assets, understand where those vulnerabilities lie, and then take action upon those vulnerabilities to protect your environment holistically.

Mr. CARTER. How complex is it to do that and how long does it take?

Mr. GUMBEL. It is not that complex at all. We have organizations that, at scale, have rolled out tens of millions of endpoints in weeks. This is something that we can partner with the Federal Government to achieve.

Mr. CARTER. Thank you, Mr. Chairman. I yield back.

Chairman GARBARINO. The gentleman yields back. I now recognize the gentlelady from Florida, Ms. Lee, for 5 minutes.

Ms. LEE. Thank you, Mr. Chairman. Mr. Gumbel, I would like to pick up right where we left off there. You have given us some very useful information today about our general status at this point that we have done a lot of work on endpoint detection, but as the attack surface continues to grow, so do our defenses and our preparation need to evolve. I am interested in what capabilities we need to be integrating into CADS to improve analytics and increase visibility, as you have been testifying about. Specifically, do we need to pay particular attention to the concept of encrypted communication? Are we capturing that now? Is there anything we need to be doing in that space?

Mr. GUMBEL. Sure. So, that was a lot to unpack. But I believe that, Congresswoman, the thing that we still need to do once you have the holistic view of an entire environment, you have to look at other vectors too. You bring up encryption, encryption is definitely of utmost importance and making sure that the encryption standards that the Federal Government holds across all agencies are kept up to date.

You also have to make sure that you're looking at legacy providers and technologies that have been built 10, 20 years ago. Are they really up-to-date? Are they really current today if they are not modern in their approach? Because the adversaries are going to come forth with something new and they are going to bypass and get past those networks that are being defended today by legacy contracts. So, I think all of that needs to be taken into consideration.

Ms. LEE. OK. Mr. Zakowicz, you indicated earlier on the subject of hunt and incident response through CDM that you thought we might need to look at changes in Congressional authority in order to be really utilizing that as part of our approach. Would you tell us a little bit more about that?

Mr. ZAKOWICZ. Sure. Thank you. So, there were two authorities granted within the Executive Order that I think were directly relevant to the CDM program's ability to gain insight and access into agency network environments like they hadn't been able to before. The first was associated with endpoint detection and response, or EDR, hunt and response activities. It's being done through an initiative granting threat hunters access to agency EDR tooling through what's called persistent access or pack capabilities. So, that's given them an opportunity to be able to look in those agency environments real time, directly using tools like CrowdStrike and others to understand what's happening in that space.

Then the second is access to what's called object-level data. So, within the agencies, the detailed information on every endpoint that's being collected and rolled up and aggregated into this CDM dashboard having direct access to that object-level data allows them to within minutes search across the Federal enterprise for the presence of, let's say, zero-day vulnerability or known exploitative vulnerability. Identify the potentially vulnerable assets within an agency environment across the FCEB, and then use EDR in partnership with the agency to go further, interrogate that asset and understand what the risk profile really looks like. I think CISA's seen some success with that combination of capabilities with even recent breaches, being able to identify in minutes what may have taken hours or days or longer through data calls.

Ms. LEE. Mr. Head, I would like to hear from you on what capabilities you think CISA should be including in the CADS program to help improve analytics and visibility.

Mr. HEAD. If you look at the detail that I've seen, you know, publicly, they had things like DNS and signatures in there, but they didn't have flow. I think it is really important to be able to see flow in terms of oversight guidance. There's also the notion of how do you know who somebody is? So, on a network, a lot of the privacy concerns have led manufacturers into anonymizing the Mac addresses so that you don't know what the device is anymore. So certainly on Federal Government agency networks, you need to know what things are and they shouldn't be able to do anonymization and hide their activities.

The other piece I would also mention is you get into the details of things like you ask about encryption. The purpose of encryption is to keep somebody from stealing your stuff. But if you're in the business of stealing stuff, encryption is hiding what you're stealing. So, the answer isn't to give everybody the keys, the answer is encompass in your logging what file moved from his machine to my machine. You shouldn't have your audit system be more prone to invasion and privacy concerns than your original network was. So, we can do things like MD5, all of the files as they flow, and say this file was the unreleased this and you sent it to him, why? So, I think it's possible to build an audit system without breaking the world, but it doesn't do just to start let's opine about things that are impossible. Let's write down methodically things that are easy and very effective.

Ms. LEE. Thank you, Mr. Head. Mr. Chairman, I yield back.

Chairman GARBARINO. Thank you. The gentlelady yields back. I think since everyone is here, I am going to start my second round of questions. I want to start with Mr. Zakowicz. Amidst an increasingly complex threat landscape, technology innovations of the last decade and recommendations for improvements from the GAO and industry stakeholders, the CDM program must evolve to keep pace with the threat and improve Federal cyber defense. Do you envision any gaps in authorities needed to allow CISA to continue to strengthen the Federal Government's information infrastructure?

Mr. ZAKOWICZ. Thank you for the question. I think we've already covered a couple of specific authorities that I think would be beneficial to be codified in order for CISA to continue the mission that they have. I think we've also touched a little bit on I think there was reference in one of the opening statements to CISA's authority to actually conduct testing and verification in agency environments, to run, you know, penetration testing or network testing activities within the individual agency environments. While I'd say personally, I think that, you know, with the responsibility resting with the agencies themselves, that's something that would need careful consideration. I do think continuing to take a look at how actively they are able to engage with agency networks, agency environments, would be worthwhile to understand if that gives them the authorities they need.

Chairman GARBARINO. Thank you very much for that answer. EDR has been rolled out through the CDM program after it was acquired in the May 2021 Cyber EO. A few years ago, CISA was given an authority to proactively hunt for threats on agency networks. Mr. Sheldon, in your testimony you discussed the opportunities for EDR to inform CISA's threat hunting capabilities. How can CISA better leverage EDR data to improve threat hunt efforts?

Mr. SHELDON. Thank you, Mr. Chairman. So, I think CISA is really far ahead of where they were a couple of years ago by virtue of the authorities that I mentioned that were given to them in Section 1705 of the fiscal year 2021 NDAA and then by virtue of having this now-very powerful EDR capability deployed out across many, many Federal agencies. I think the core task now is to ensure that, is it the case that every endpoint that can be protected with that type of capability is. It may be possible for them to think about extending it more over cloud environments and mobile devices, as I mentioned before. Then to think through the next set of problems, which is again, thinking about bringing that same type of control to other parts of the network and then really creating a unified workflow for their analysts to be able to do something productive with that very quickly when there's a threat.

Chairman GARBARINO. Thank you very much. Mr. Head, following up on your response to Ms. Lee before, how can AI be more incorporated into these programs, particularly, as CISA looks to evolve NCPS?

Mr. HEAD. I think in lots of ways. Whenever you're drowning in a sea of big data, like you mentioned, trillions, all of us deal with, you know, tens of trillions of events, you know, on a periodic basis and just slugging through all that with humans just doesn't scale well. So, we all see that as our salvation for doing a thorough job across broad spectrum of assets that need protecting.

I think zooming up a little bit, there's also big data that needs to come to bear outside the—remember the old game where you had to draw lines, three rows of three dots, and you drew your lines? I think a lot of times we are focusing in the box instead of outside. So inside, we are not spending much time to do surveys of what isn't covered and in that you can drive a sinking country through. So, I think we need to kind-of look at what are we missing as a paid research project for somebody.

Chairman GARBARINO. I am not sure how often we think outside the box when it comes to the Government. I only have a little time left. But I said at the beginning of this hearing, we are doing this to talk about the two programs, NCPS and CDM. And we are going to have Government witnesses, one from CISA, someone from somewhere else. This is for all of you and feel free to jump in. What should we be asking them at the next hearing when we have them in front of us specifically about these programs? We can start with Mr. Gumbel, and we can move down the aisle if you want.

Mr. GUMBEL. I think one of the biggest questions, Mr. Chairman, is ask them have they looked at modern technologies or are they only focusing on the contracts that they have with legacy providers that have built technologies 20 years ago? Those technologies that are either on premise, they're not cloud first, there are older ways in their thinking in the way that they protect networks and connect infrastructures. So, I'd say that would be the first thing that I would ask.

Chairman GARBARINO. Mr. Zakowicz.

Mr. ZAKOWICZ. Thank you. So, I would suggest focusing on, you know, across our national security, our economic security, where are the threats? Because I think they certainly exist within the Federal Executive branch, but they also exist outside of the Federal Executive branch. I think as CISA looks at applying their resources, their time, their focus, you know, is it internal to Federal? Is it external to State, local, Tribal, critical infrastructure? Where do we get the most benefit in our improving our security's posture?

Chairman GARBARINO. Thanks. Mr. Head.

Mr. HEAD. I'd ask about how will they map what they're doing to the threat landscape? So, how are you going to stop these things with what you're doing? That gets down to the next level into what are you logging? What are you keeping? What can you see? What can you not see? When do you plan on doing that? You know, I've joked that, you know, there used to be a cartoon with the cat and the mouse, and the mouse would run through the garden hose and there'd be a big lump that was mouse size running through the hose. We don't see our secrets leaving out our ethernet cables like watermelons flowing. So, I think just the simple visibility of have they stolen us blind? Do we have any national secrets left? You know, the cables don't get hot and glow and melt, you know, as they're stealing our stuff. So, I'd look at CISA's programs and say, what are you doing that'll let us see an OPM breach instantly instead of finding it a year later? I found that one myself, you know, looking at data. So, the question is, how is what you're doing going to help that?

Chairman GARBARINO. Mr. Sheldon.

Mr. SHELDON. Thank you. I think it's worth asking CISA if they've seen incidents or other issues on Federal networks that would be protected by technologies that exist within the CDM portfolio and the agency in question hadn't used those technologies than to just try and interrogate where was the disconnect? So, I think some of us have spoken about this today. It may be the case that there's an opportunity to clarify some of the longer-term funding for some of the CDM projects and to make that more consistent and then to really shift that program so it's operating more on that shared service type of basis that you had with NCPS and EINSTEIN. That may resolve some of the issues. There could be others, but it'd be interesting to hear about it.

Chairman GARBARINO. Thank you very much. I now recognize Mr. Menendez for 5 minutes for any questions he may have.

Mr. MENENDEZ. Thank you, Chairman. Thanks to progress made by the Biden administration and support from Congress, CDM has made important strides in recent years and has helped CISA more quickly respond to cyber incidents. Mr. Sheldon and Mr. Gumbel, are there recent examples you are aware of where CDM has helped CISA with incident response or the mitigation of vulnerabilities? What aspects of CDM have been most helpful with strengthening Federal cybersecurity? We will start with you, Mr. Gumbel.

Mr. GUMBEL. I'd actually really like to take this one for the record and get back to you with a thorough answer because I'm currently not aware of anything that's been that beneficial that I could speak to.

Mr. MENENDEZ. I respect that.

Mr. GUMBEL. OK.

[The information follows:]

In response to Ranking Member Menendez's question about examples of where the CDM program has been most beneficial and helped response and mitigation of cyber incidents, we submit the following:

CDM has brought value to small and micro agencies and driven the implementation of new technologies into Federal IT programs. Agencies are better equipped to manage privileged accounts because of the identity efforts leading to more resilient and secure critical citizen services. EDR deployments likewise have been largely successful.

However, our overall assessment of the core CDM efforts is not positive. Many of the original goals of CDM have been achieved and much of the deployment is secondary rather than integrated to agency operations.

The CDM program however relies on a legacy model and approach, and it is our hope that a more open, full-industry approach can help CISA achieve its original CDM mission of: Reducing agency threat surface, increasing visibility into the Federal cybersecurity posture, improving Federal cybersecurity response capabilities, and Streamlining Federal Information Security Modernization Act (FISMA) reporting.

Mr. MENENDEZ. Mr. Sheldon.

Mr. SHELDON. I'll just say briefly that it's sometimes the case that, you know, even we as vendors don't get perfect visibility on how, you know, how particular investigations have unfolded. There may be some good reasons for that from an operational security standpoint, just, you know, people in CISA who are working on different projects, issues, responding to incidents, they'll be in touch from time to time.

The part about this that I do think is helpful and is clarifying is reporting that we will ultimately get from the CSRB, the Cyber Safety Review Board, and they've announced an investigation recently where they were going to look at the July breach of the Microsoft 365 platform that led to the ability of Chinese threat actors to read the email of two Cabinet Secretaries. It'll be interesting to get ultimately a reconciled view from different vendors, from Government agencies that have responded, and from other people out in the security research community about what precisely happened. That's a very useful thing for people to know so that we can learn and integrate lessons as appropriate.

Mr. MENENDEZ. I appreciate it. I just want to give you both a chance on the second part. What aspects of CDM have been most helpful with strengthening Federal cybersecurity? If you'd like to respond.

Mr. SHELDON. I'm sorry, could you say that again?

Mr. MENENDEZ. Sure. What aspects of CDM have been most helpful with strengthening Federal cybersecurity?

Mr. SHELDON. I think we've all mentioned EDR and highlighted that. So, at the risk of beating a dead horse, obviously it's a powerful capability. I think the design of CDM was to make available a portfolio of technologies so that if particular Government agencies had very specific needs, there might be something there that would be able to meet that need. So, it may well differ from agency to agency about what, on top of something like EDR, drives the most value.

Mr. MENENDEZ. I appreciate it. One challenge for Federal agencies is that many rely on outdated technology that is harder to secure. In recent years, Congress has tried to address this challenge by funding the Technology Modernization Fund, which supports efforts to update agency technology. This year, the Appropriations Committee has advanced legislation that would eliminate funding for the program. Mr. Gumbel, why is funding for the Technology Modernization Fund important for strengthening Federal cybersecurity?

Mr. GUMBEL. I think it's very important to be able to fund those projects so it enhances and continues the progress of securing the Nation. Without this continuous funding, there might not be the opportunity to look at modern technologies in ways that could protect the Federal Government. Any type of funding slowdown will halt any progress and the adversaries have the opportunity to just speed up time and be able to come after any of the exposures or links into networks that aren't protected.

Mr. MENENDEZ. You said any slowdown, correct?

Mr. GUMBEL. Any slowdown.

Mr. MENENDEZ. Yes. Following up on that, what kind of investment should be prioritized when looking to upgrade Federal agencies technology? Do you have any specific examples of more investments?

Mr. GUMBEL. Yes, I think the biggest message is don't always look at Government examples to upgrade your technology, look to private sector. Private sector has done in a lot of areas, has done very well in keeping their technologies modern. There's a lot of great use cases that the private sector is using to protect their products, to protect their customers, and to protect their IP. I think the Federal Government can learn a lot from that.

Mr. MENENDEZ. Within private sector, are there any industries that you feel are leading or ahead of the curve that we should potentially pay extra care to?

Mr. GUMBEL. Sure, sure. I think, you know, manufacturing is one, the financial services is another. Some industries that have a lot of operational technology machinery, oil, and gas, I think those are areas to look at as well.

Mr. MENENDEZ. I appreciate that. Thank you, Mr. Chairman. I yield back.

Chairman GARBARINO. The gentleman yields back. I now recognize the gentleman from Mississippi, Mr. Ezell, for 5 minutes of questioning.

Mr. EZELL. Thank you, Mr. Chairman. Guys, about 40-plus years ago, I went to work at the police department in my hometown. What I remember the chief and the administrators at the time talking about was bad communication. Mr. Head, when you were talking there a few minutes ago, it just reminded me of my early life in police service. People don't normally want to call the police unless they got a problem or something's going on. We show up, we respond. When you talked about the aircraft carrier come under attack and what we would do in response to that. I would like to know, and each of you jump in there, what we can do as a Congress to better hold some of these folks accountable for not getting the communication to the proper place so that we can say, why is this happening? Why can we not do something about it? Who can we hold accountable for these things? Anybody?

Mr. GUMBEL. Sure. I'll start off. I believe that there's an opportunity for Congress to look at some of these contracts to bridge some of the gaps of disparity. I will point to something for an example, B.O.D. 23–01 requires agencies to report on all assets con- nected to their networks. But however, CDM, this program explicitly excludes IOT, OT, and other managed technology. So, you have two different programs with two different views. This is just an example of areas or contracts that have this disparity. I think Congress can really help bridge the gap to make sure that everything's on the same playing field.

Mr. EZELL. Thank you. Mr. Head, could you talk just a little bit more about some of your concerns that you were speaking about in your opening statement?

Mr. HEAD. Sure. Reflecting on what you just asked about, one thing I've tried to understand a little bit is when someone reports a breach, FAA for a long time—I'm a pilot just for fun—and for a while there, if you had a near-miss, you report the near-miss and you're excused from losing your license over your participation in that. In the cyber space, it is not usually apparent when you report a thing whether they're going to get you for allowing it to happen or give you a Ferrari for finding it and stopping it. So, we haven't really got the risk/reward down for how do you elicit insightful cooperation and insightful response within and without the organiza tions? I think there's a large jurisdictional—I can't say that—contest between who's supposed to help you.

Mr. EZELL. Yes.

Mr. HEAD. So that would certainly be helpful.

Mr. EZELL. It is kind-of like in police world, if you have a problem and you don't know who to call, what do you do, you're stuck. So, I think that, you know, we as committee Members and you as very concerned folks, we have got to do a better job on our end. We have got to be able to have some very frank conversations because this is not going to stop. There are these bad actors in the world and they want our stuff. Like you were saying, you know, what have we got left that they don't have? So anyway, I want to thank you all for being here today. Mr. Chairman, I yield back.

Chairman GARBARINO. The gentleman yields back. I now recognize the gentlelady from Florida, Ms. Lee, for her second round of questions.

Ms. LEE. Thank you, Mr. Chairman. Mr. Head, I would like to come back to you. You mentioned something in your opening statement and in your written testimony that you refer to as our Cyber Manhattan Project. Would you please share with us a little bit more about your vision there and how you think that would look? Mr. HEAD. Sure. That was the hardest part about writing it because when they started the real Manhattan Project, they didn't put it on public record and put it on C–Span, hey, we're just looking to build a bomb and nuke you. You know, shoot these guys because they are our lead scientists. So, I think what we should do is think about some percentage of our budget. In Texas, I think it was Lady Bird Johnson forever ago that put in the thing for 2 percent of all highway funds will be spent on plants and trees and beautification. We spend a lot of money. I describe it in the testimony that a lot of the cyber efforts remind me of your kids playing 5-year-old soccer. They are all just huddled around the ball chasing the latest buzzwords. At the end of the day, they are not a team and they didn't accomplish anything. That's kind-of prefaced by the we suck at cyber as a country.

Although there's some really good folks in the industry and I think all of us put together in a quiet time would say, let's just fix it. Like the two buzzards' patience, hell, let's kill something. You know, so I think there's room in the oversight process to say to DISA, to DARPA, to somebody, gee, you're in charge of making this suck less every month.

You know, and then there's been some rapid progress made in a lot of fronts, particularly after go back to World War II. But I think, you know, the measure of pissed-offness ought to be higher than it is for us getting attacked every day and doing nothing.

So, I think I would challenge that back to you guys. This is like I told today coming and testifying with you guys, nothing against it, but on my list of top 10 things to do, it's 3,742nd.

But I think now the time is right for doing something and I think that the brains are right for doing something. So, I'd just love to see let's do something that's not ordinary. At the end of the day, we can say, that was bad, we fixed it.

Ms. LEE. On that point, you also just referenced the concept of risk/reward.

Mr. HEAD. Yes.

Ms. LEE. Who is working with us? What are they reporting? When and how are they reporting it? I know I previously worked at an agency that implemented a bug bounty program——

Mr. HEAD. Right.

Ms. LEE [continuing]. To that end, so that in hopes that some of the good guys might help us identify issues that we had prior to the bad guys finding them. What are your thoughts on that type of solution or any other ideas you have to help us properly incentivize risk/reward?

Mr. HEAD. Plenty. I would start, though, with removing the stupid. So, I was looking at one a few years ago that Congress funded and the Pentagon implemented, and it was basically free service for defense contractors. So, you could basically rent this dog that will come in and bite you and your children. So, anything they find, you're on the hook for paying the full cost of remediation, which could bankrupt you.

So, the rightful answer would be don't ask, don't invite, don't participate, because you're renting a dog that could hurt you. Does that make sense?

Ms. LEE. It does.

Mr. HEAD. Because we're going against formidable adversaries and most people don't have the staff to play that game. Like I say, comedy abounds when you look at the rules that we put in place. But I think a reason to pass through all of those to say let's remove the worst first.

Ms. LEE. All right. Mr. Sheldon, and I will ask each of you this preparing to come here today and the things that you think we need to have top of mind and we need to be working on, is there anything you haven't had the chance to tell us about today that you think we should know?

Mr. SHELDON. Thank you for the opportunity. Really, just to drive more focus in the Federal space. So many of the attacks that we see, they don't involve malware, they don't involve classic indicators of compromise that we can block through existing solutions. It is really a compromised credential or something to that effect that might cause the breach.

So, there are some solutions in place and some architectures that try to address that. Zero trust is one of them. That's something that I would encourage all of us as a community to think more about. How do we promote the adoption of that type of solution in the Federal space?

Ms. LEE. Mr. Head.

Mr. HEAD. I think I've talked too much and told you most of my ideas, so.

Ms. LEE. Pass.

Mr. HEAD. Thank you.

Ms. LEE. Mr. Zakowicz.

Mr. ZAKOWICZ. Thank you. I was going to echo my colleague from CrowdStrike, and I'm impressed we went this long before saying zero trust for the hearing. But I think identity is an area we haven't spent much time talking about in this forum but is critically important to understand who is actually on the network.

What are they doing? How do we make sure that people only have access to the things they need to get their job done?

Ms. LEE. Fundamentally zero trust type of thinking?

Mr. ZAKOWICZ. Correct, yes. One of the fundamental pillars of zero trust is identity, and I think that is one that needs the most focus first.

Ms. LEE. Access control.

Mr. ZAKOWICZ. Yes.

Ms. LEE. OK. Mr. Gumbel, what about you?

Mr. GUMBEL. Yes. I'd say last because I've said a lot today, but I think ensure that procurements and programs are aligned to stated administrative, Executive Orders, and agency BODs. I think that's super important.

Ms. LEE. All right. Thank you, Mr. Chairman. I yield back.

Chairman GARBARINO. Thank you very much. I really want to thank the valuable testimony from our witnesses today. Mr. Head, I am glad that the 3,741 other things on your list weren't available to you today. I want to thank the Members for their questions.

The Members of the subcommittee may have some additional questions for all of you, and we would ask the witnesses to respond in writing. Pursuant to committee rule VII(D), the hearing record will be held open for 10 days. Without objection, the subcommittee stands adjourned.

[Whereupon, at 11:25 a.m., the subcommittee was adjourned.]

Chapter 4

Challenges in Establishing a Comprehensive Cybersecurity Strategy and Performing Effective Oversight*

U.S. Government Accountability Office

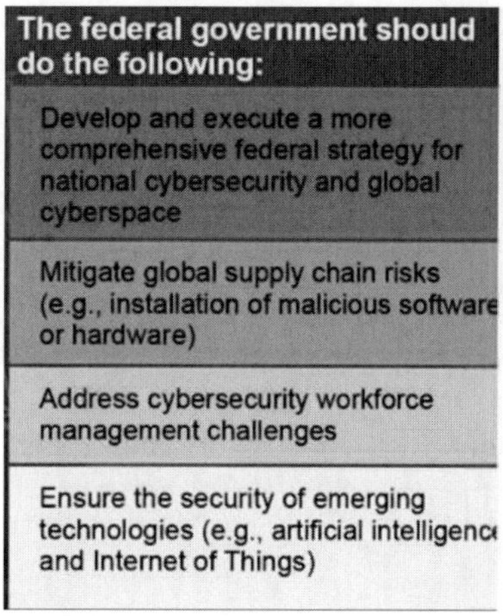

Overview

Federal agencies and our nation's critical infrastructures—such as energy, transportation systems, communications, and financial services—are dependent on technology systems to carry out fundamental operations and to

---

* This is an edited, reformatted and augmented version of the United States Government Accountability Office Report, Publication No. GAO-23-106415.

In: Cybersecurity Challenges and Strategies Across Sectors …
Editor: Marybeth Wiskoff
ISBN: 979-8-90134-039-4

process, maintain, and report vital information. The security of these systems and data is also vital to safeguarding individual privacy and protecting the nation's security, prosperity, and well-being.

However, risks to these essential technology systems are increasing—in particular, malicious actors are becoming more willing and capable of carrying out cyberattacks. Such attacks could result in serious harm to human safety, national security, the environment, and the economy. Agencies and critical infrastructure owners and operators must protect the confidentiality, integrity, and availability of their systems and effectively respond to cyberattacks.

We have designated information security as a government-wide high-risk area since 1997. We expanded this high-risk area in 2003 to include protection of critical cyber infrastructure. In 2015, we expanded it again to include protecting the privacy of personally identifiable information.

This is the first in a series of four reports that lay out the main cybersecurity areas the federal government should urgently address, beginning with the need for a comprehensive strategy and effective oversight.[1] We have made about 335 recommendations in public reports since 2010 with respect to this area. About 190 of these recommendations were not implemented as of December 2022. Until these are fully implemented, federal agencies will be more limited in their ability to protect private and sensitive data entrusted to them.

For more information on this report and others in this series, visit https://www.gao.gov/cybersecurity.

What Actions Can the Federal Government Take to Execute a More Comprehensive Federal Cyber Strategy?

The federal government needs to address missing elements in the *National Cyber Strategy* and *Implementation Plan*.

The White House's September 2018 *National Cyber Strategy* and the National Security Council's (NSC) accompanying June 2019 *Implementation Plan* detail the executive branch's approach to managing the nation's cybersecurity.

[1] In 2018, GAO reported that the federal government needed to address four major cybersecurity challenges related to (1) establishing a comprehensive cybersecurity strategy, (2) securing federal systems and information, (3) protecting cyber critical infrastructure, and (4) protecting privacy and sensitive data.

In September 2020, we reported that the strategy and implementation plan addressed some, but not all, of the desirable characteristics of national strategies. In particular, the *National Cyber Strategy*, when combined with the *Implementation Plan*, addressed three of the six desirable characteristics of national strategies but did not include key elements for three other characteristics (see figure 1). We stressed that moving forward, the incoming administration needed to either update the existing strategy and plan or develop a new comprehensive strategy that addresses those characteristics.

Characteristic	Extent addressed
Purpose, scope, and methodology	●
Organizational roles, responsibilities, and coordination	●
Integration and implementation	●
Problem definition and risk assessment	○
Goals, subordinate objectives, activities, and performance measures	○
Resources, investments, and risk management	○

● Addressed—The *National Cyber Strategy*, when combined with the *Implementation Plan*, fully addressed the desirable characteristics associated with this subcategory.

○ Did not fully address—The *National Cyber Strategy*, when combined with the *Implementation Plan*, did not fully address the desirable characteristics associated with this subcategory.

Source: GAO analysis of 2018 National Cyber Strategy and 2019 Implemenation Plan. | GAO-23-106415.

Figure 1. Extent to Which the National Cyber Strategy and Implementation Plan Addressed the Desirable Characteristics of a National Strategy.

The Congress and Administration took action to establish and fill a critical cybersecurity leadership position. Specifically, in January 2021, the National Defense Authorization Act for Fiscal Year 2021 established the Office of the National Cyber Director within the Executive Office of the President. In June 2021, the Senate confirmed the first National Cyber Director to head the office and serve as the principal advisor to the President on cybersecurity policy and strategy. The Director subsequently issued a strategic statement for the office that summarized its vision, challenge, path, and urgency to improve the nation's cybersecurity. However, until the federal government fully develops and implements a comprehensive national strategy, it will not have a clear roadmap for overcoming the cyber challenges facing our nation.

- We recommended that the National Security Council work with relevant federal entities to update cybersecurity strategy documents to include goals, performance measures, and resource information, among other things. As of August 2022, according to the Office of the National Cyber Director, the development of a national cybersecurity strategy by the administration is underway. The office noted that it is obtaining feedback on the strategy from many other federal entities, including the National Security Council, on this effort.

What Actions Can the Federal Government Take to Mitigate Global Supply Chain Risks?

Federal agencies need to fully implement all of the foundational practices for supply chain risk management.

Federal agencies rely extensively on information and communications technology (ICT) products and services to carry out their operations. However, agencies face numerous ICT supply chain risks, including threats posed by counterfeiters who may exploit vulnerabilities in the supply chain. To assist agencies with effectively managing their ICT supply chain risks, the National Institute of Standards and Technology developed guidance that includes risk-based practices.

In December 2020, our review of 23 civilian agencies found that none had fully implemented all of the seven foundational practices for supply chain risk management and that 14 had not implemented any of the practices (see figure 2).[2] For example, only three out of the 23 agencies had fully developed organizational procedures to detect counterfeit and compromised ICT products prior deployment. In addition, none of the 23 agencies had established a process to conduct agency-wide assessments of ICT supply chain risks. Implementing foundational practices for ICT supply chain risk management is essential to agencies addressing the risks of malicious actors

[2] The 23 civilian agencies are the Departments of Agriculture, Commerce, Education, Energy, Health and Human Services, Homeland Security, Housing and Urban Development, the Interior, Justice, Labor, State, Transportation, the Treasury, and Veterans Affairs, the Environmental Protection Agency, General Services Administration, National Aeronautics and Space Administration, National Science Foundation, Nuclear Regulatory Commission, Office of Personnel Management, Small Business Administration, Social Security Administration, and U.S. Agency for International Development. We did not include the Department of Defense because our scope was the civilian agencies.

disrupting mission operations, stealing intellectual property, or harming individuals.

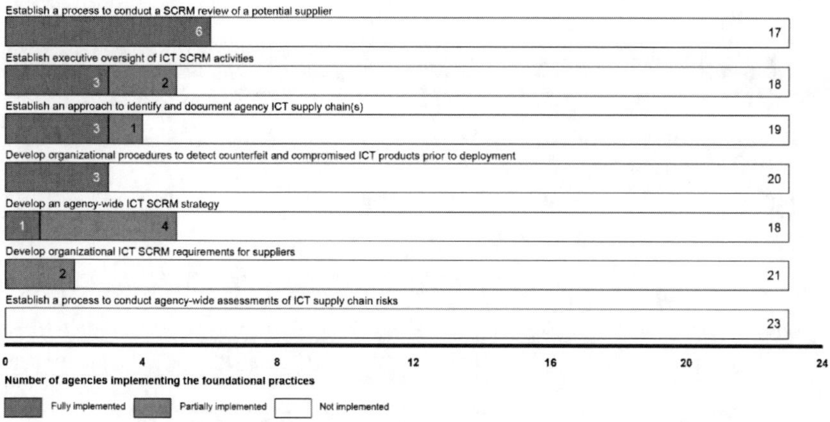

Source: GAO analysis of agency data. | GAO-23-106415.

Figure 2. Extent to Which the 23 Civilian Agencies Implemented Information and Communications Technology (ICT) Supply Chain Risk Management (SCRM) Practices.

- *We recommended* that the 23 agencies fully implement foundational practices in their organization-wide approaches to ICT supply chain risk management.[3] As of December 2022, 130 of our 145 recommendations were not yet implemented; none of the 23 agencies had fully implemented all recommendations addressed to them.

What Actions Can the Federal Government Take to Address Cybersecurity Workforce Challenges?

The Office of Management and Budget (OMB) should develop a government-wide plan to address the cybersecurity workforce shortage.

In April 2020, we examined the extent to which OMB and lead agencies addressed key practices for effectively implementing selected government-wide reforms (see figure 3). These included reforms that prioritized solving the

[3] In the sensitive version of this report issued in October 2020, GAO-21-164SU, we made 145 recommendations to the 23 agencies.

cybersecurity workforce shortage by identifying and closing workforce skills gaps and developing a standardized approach to hiring, training, and retaining qualified cybersecurity professionals.

Key reform practice	Extent addressed	Summary of findings
Establishing goals and outcomes	◐	The Department of Homeland Security (DHS) established goals and outcomes for certain projects and activities, but the Office of Management and Budget (OMB) and DHS have not developed government-wide goals and outcomes.
Involving employees and key stakeholders	◐	DHS conducted outreach to employees and key stakeholders for certain projects and activities but not for the reform as a whole.
Addressing high-risk areas and long-standing management challenges	◐	OMB and DHS have acknowledged cybersecurity challenges, such as our high-risk area of protecting cyber critical infrastructure, but they have not demonstrated how the reform proposal will address these challenges.
Leadership focus and attention	◐	While a May 2019 Executive Order demonstrated high-level leadership attention, OMB and DHS have not yet established a dedicated government-wide implementation team.
Managing and monitoring	◐	While DHS has developed some agency-specific implementation plans and mechanisms to monitor progress, OMB and DHS have not developed an implementation plan with time lines, key milestones, and deliverables for the reform proposal as a whole.
Strategic workforce planning	◐	DHS developed its cybersecurity workforce strategy as required by the Cybersecurity Workforce Assessment Act. OMB and DHS have not developed a government-wide cybersecurity strategic workforce plan.
Employee engagement	○	OMB and DHS have not yet demonstrated how they are monitoring, sustaining, and strengthening employee engagement of affected cybersecurity professionals across the federal government.

◐ Partially addressed—OMB and DHS addressed a practice with significant gaps in their coverage of the actions associated with this subcategory.
○ Not addressed—OMB and DHS did not address this practice or demonstrate coverage of associated actions with this subcategory.

Source: GAO analysis of agencies' plans. | GAO-23-106415.

Figure 3. Extent to Which the Government-Wide Plan to Solve the Cybersecurity Workforce Shortage Addressed Key Reform Practices.

We found that OMB and the Department of Homeland Security (DHS) partially addressed most of the key practices associated with effective reforms through their efforts to implement several projects, such as training employees to fill vacant cybersecurity positions and streamlining hiring processes. However, OMB and DHS had not established a dedicated implementation team or a government-wide implementation plan, among other practices. Without these practices in place, OMB and DHS will likely be unable to make significant progress towards solving the cybersecurity workforce shortage.

- *We recommended* several actions aimed at addressing continuing cybersecurity workforce challenges. These recommendations focused on developing a government-wide workforce plan and related supporting practices such as establishing a leadership team and crafting an implementation plan. Government- wide leadership responsibility for cyber workforce issues transitioned in 2022 from OMB and DHS to the Office of the National Cyber Director. Since the transition, the Director has committed to developing a national strategy that addresses cyber training and education, digital awareness, and the cyber workforce. This commitment is consistent with the current Administration's management agenda, which states that the Administration must identify and address critical skills gaps across the federal IT and cybersecurity workforce. We will continue monitoring efforts to develop the strategy.

What Actions Can the Federal Government Take to Ensure the Security of Emerging Technologies?

Federal agencies need to take action to better secure internet-connected devices.

The nation's critical infrastructure sectors rely on electronic systems, including Internet of Things (IoT) and operational technology (OT) devices and systems (see figure 4).4 In December 2022, we reported that the federal lead agencies of the reviewed critical infrastructure sectors—the Departments of Energy, Health and Human Services, Homeland Security, and Transportation—had cybersecurity initiatives underway intended to help protect three critical infrastructure sectors with extensive use of IoT or OT devices and systems.

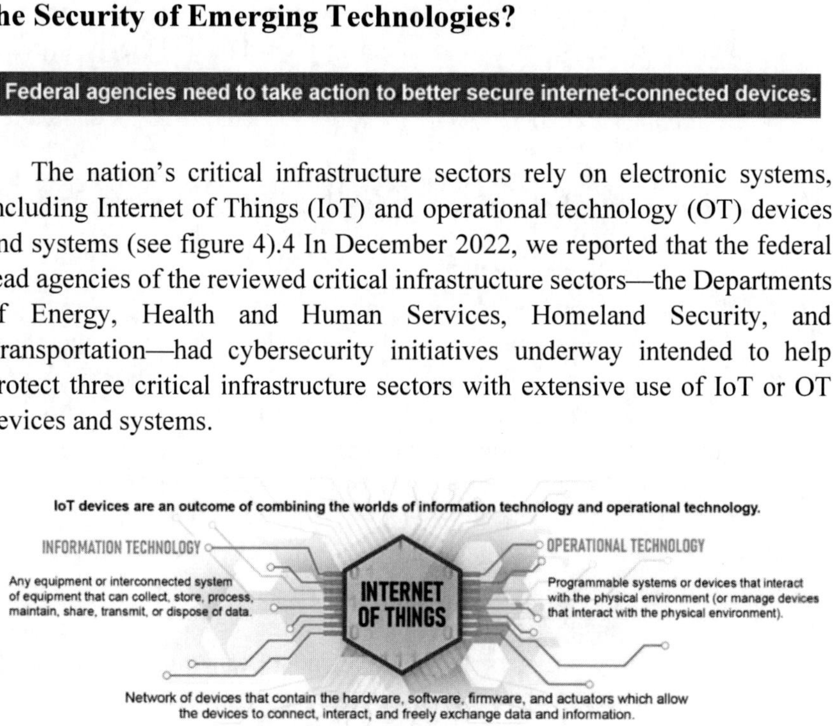

Source: GAO. | GAO-23-106415.

Figure 4. Overview of Connected IT, Internet of Things (IoT), and Operational Technology.

However, none of the lead agencies had developed metrics to assess the effectiveness of their efforts. Further, the agencies had not conducted IoT and OT cybersecurity risk assessments. While agency officials noted difficulty assessing program effectiveness when relying on voluntary information from

[4] IoT generally refers to the technologies and devices that allow for the network connection and interaction of a wide array of "things," throughout such places as buildings, transportation infrastructure, or homes. OT are programmable systems or devices that interact with the physical environment, such as building automation systems that control machines to regulate and monitor temperature.

sector entities, the success of initiatives intended to mitigate risks is unknown without attempts to measure effectiveness and assess risks of IoT and OT.

- We recommended that the Departments of Energy, Health and Human Services, Homeland Security, and Transportation to establish and use metrics to assess the effectiveness of sector IoT and OT cybersecurity efforts and evaluate sector IoT and OT cybersecurity risks. As of December 2022, none of these recommendations had been implemented.

Quantum computing has the potential to create major cybersecurity risks.

We reported in September 2022 that quantum technologies build on the study of the smallest particles of energy and matter to collect, generate, and process information in ways not achievable with existing technologies. Quantum computers could dramatically accelerate computation for some applications, such as machine learning and information decryption. In addition, quantum information technologies could dramatically increase capabilities beyond what is possible with classical technologies, such as having high-value applications in security and cryptography. However, quantum computing has the potential to create major cybersecurity risks. For example, a full-scale quantum computer has the potential to break standard encryption technologies, creating a major information security risk. As a result, the federal government's cybersecurity infrastructure will need to evolve to address this threat.

As artificial intelligence (AI) technologies continue to advance, federal oversight considerations will need to evolve.

In March 2021, we reported that AI might have a number of associated challenges and risks. For example, if the data used by AI are biased or become corrupted by hackers, the results could be biased or cause harm. In March 2021, the National Security Commission on Artificial Intelligence issued a report in which the commission described additional cybersecurity risks associated with AI and recommendations to address them.[5] Specifically, the

[5] Section 1051 of the John S. McCain National Defense Authorization Act for Fiscal Year 2019 established the National Security Commission on Artificial Intelligence as an independent commission to consider the methods and means necessary to advance the development of

commission stated that AI would enable malware to mutate into thousands of different forms, find vulnerabilities, and attack selectively. The commission added that the expanding application of AI cyber capabilities would make cyberattacks more precise and tailored, further accelerate and automate cyber warfare, enable stealthier and more persistent cyber weapons, and make cyber campaigns more effective on a larger scale. The federal government will need to take appropriate action to address these threats.

GAO's Prior Work

We have previously reported on the numerous challenges that the federal government faces and have made recommendations aimed at establishing a comprehensive cybersecurity strategy and performing effective oversight. Key reports focus on the following topics:

Source: Images: (1, 7) VideoFlow/stock.adobe.com, (2) Maksim Kabakou/stock.adobe.com, (3, 4, 5) GAO File Photo, (6) weerapat1003/stock.adobe.com, (8)

AI, machine learning, and associated technologies to comprehensively address the national security and defense needs of the United States. Pub. L. No. 115-232, § 1051, 132 Stat. at 1962. National Security Commission on Artificial Intelligence, *Final Report (*March 2021).

Andrey Popov/ stock.adobe.com, (9) Executive Office of the President, (10) GAO analysis of Ericsson data, (11) GAO analysis of Congressional Research Service data, (12) metamorworks/ stock.adobe.com, (13) GAO analysis of Department of Defense (DOD) information; Thaut Images/stock.adobe.com and U.S. Air Force/Staff Sgt. E. Nuñez (photos).

About GAO

The Government Accountability Office, the audit, evaluation, and investigative arm of Congress, exists to support Congress in meeting its constitutional responsibilities and to help improve the performance and accountability of the federal government for the American people. This document is based on GAO audit products. This work of the United States may include copyrighted material, details at https://www.gao.gov/copyright.

U.S. Government Accountability Office, 441 G Street NW, Washington, DC 20548.

Contact Us

For more information about this Cybersecurity High Risk Series, contact Marisol Cruz Cain, Director, Information Technology and Cybersecurity, (202) 512-5017.

Chuck Young, Managing Director, Public Affairs, (202) 512-4800

A. Nicole Clowers, Managing Director, Congressional Relations, (202) 512-4400

Contributors: Lauri Barnes, Chris Businsky, Corwin Hayward, Elena Epps (Assistant Director), and Keith Kim (Analyst-in-Charge)

Source (cover photo): GAO analysis; Who is Danny/stock.adobe.com.

Chapter 5

Challenges in Securing Federal Systems and Information*

U.S. Government Accountability Office

Overview

Federal agencies and our nation's critical infrastructures—such as energy, transportation systems, communications, and financial services—are dependent on technology systems to carry out fundamental operations and to

---

* This is an edited, reformatted and augmented version of the United States Government Accountability Office Report, Publication No. GAO-23-106428.

In: Cybersecurity Challenges and Strategies Across Sectors …
Editor: Marybeth Wiskoff
ISBN: 979-8-90134-039-4

process, maintain, and report vital information. The security of these systems and data is also vital to safeguarding individual privacy and protecting the nation's security, prosperity, and well-being.

However, risks to these essential technology systems are increasing—in particular, malicious actors are becoming more willing and capable of carrying out cyberattacks. Such attacks could result in serious harm to human safety, national security, the environment, and the economy. Agencies and critical infrastructure owners and operators must protect the confidentiality, integrity, and availability of their systems and effectively respond to cyberattacks.

We have designated information security as a government-wide high-risk area since 1997. We expanded this high-risk area in 2003 to include protection of critical cyber infrastructure. In 2015, we expanded it again to include protecting the privacy of personally identifiable information.

This is the second in a series of four reports that lay out the main cybersecurity areas the federal government should urgently address. It focuses on securing federal systems and information.[1] We have made 712 recommendations in public reports since 2010 in this area. About 150 of these recommendations were not implemented as of December 2022. Until these are fully implemented, federal agencies will be more limited in their ability to protect private and sensitive data entrusted to them.

For more information on this report and others in this series, visit https://www.gao.gov/cybersecurity.

What Actions Should Be Taken to Improve the Implementation of Government-Wide Cybersecurity Initiatives?

The Cybersecurity and Infrastructure Security Agency (CISA) should complete its organizational transformation and fulfill its mission of protecting civilian agency systems and networks.

[1] In 2018, GAO reported that the federal government needed to address four major cybersecurity challenges related to (1) establishing a comprehensive cybersecurity strategy, (2) securing federal systems and information, (3) protecting cyber critical infrastructure, and (4) protecting privacy and sensitive data. For our report on the first challenge area, see GAO, Cybersecurity High-Risk Series: Challenges in Establishing a Comprehensive Cybersecurity Strategy and Performing Effective Oversight. GAO-23-106415 (Washington, D.C.: Jan. 19, 2023).

The CISA Act of 2018 (the act) established CISA within the Department of Homeland Security (DHS) to advance the mission of protecting federal civilian agencies' networks from cyber threats and to enhance the security of the nation's critical infrastructure.[2] The act also assigned five key cybersecurity responsibilities to CISA, including securing federal information and systems, coordinating federal efforts to secure and protect against critical infrastructure risk, and carrying out emergency communication stakeholder outreach (see figure 1).

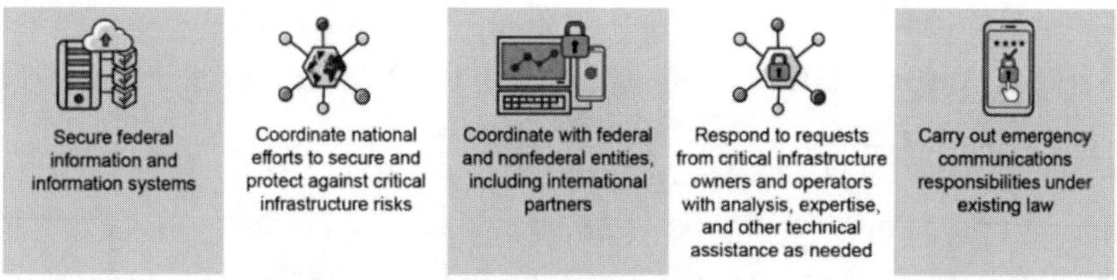

Source: GAO analysis of the Cybersecurity an infrastructure Security Agency Act of 2018; images: Buffaloboy/stock.adobe.com. | GAO-23-106428.

Figure 1. Five Key Responsibilities Assigned to the Cybersecurity and Infrastructure Security Agency.

To implement these responsibilities, CISA undertook a three-phased organizational transformation initiative aimed at unifying the agency, improving mission effectiveness, and enhancing the workplace experience. Also, since its establishment, CISA has been reorganizing offices and functions previously organized under the department's National Protection and Programs Directorate and aligning its new organizational structure with its mission.

In March 2021, we reported that CISA had completed 37 of 94 planned implementation tasks. Critical transformation tasks such as finalizing the mission-essential functions of CISA's divisions and defining incident management roles and responsibilities across the agency had not yet been completed. We also reported that the agency had not established an updated overall deadline for completing its transformation initiative.

Until CISA establishes updated milestones and an overall deadline for its efforts, and expeditiously carries out these plans, the agency will be hindered in meeting the goals of its organizational transformation initiative.

---

[2] CISA Act of 2018, Pub. L. No. 115-278, 132 Stat. 4168, 4169-70, section 2202(a)(1) (codified at 6 U.S.C. section 652c).

Consequently, this could impair the agency's ability to identify and respond to cyber incidents.

- *We recommended* that *CISA establish expected completion dates, plans for developing performance measures, and an overall deadline* for the completion of the transformation initiative, as well as develop a strategy for comprehensive workforce planning. DHS agreed with our recommendations. As of December 2022, it had not yet implemented any of them.

What Actions Can Be Taken to Address Weaknesses in Federal Agency Information Security Programs?

Since 2020, we have reported on government-wide and multiple individual agencies' management of the information security risk to their systems and data. The individual agencies we reviewed were the U.S. Secret Service, the Department of Defense (DOD), the U.S National Institutes of Health (NIH), and the Federal Communications Commission. Key examples include:

The Office of Management and Budget (OMB) should update inspectors general (IG) reporting guidance to increase rating consistency and precision.

To protect federal information and systems, the *Federal Information Security Modernization Act of 2014* (FISMA) requires federal agencies to develop, document, and implement information security programs. Congress included a provision in FISMA for GAO to periodically report on agencies' implementation of the act.

In March 2022, we reported on the information security programs of 23 federal civilian agencies, including annually required program reviews to be conducted by agency IGs. Among other things, we noted that IGs determined that 16 (or 70 percent) of the 23 agencies had ineffective programs for fiscal year 2020.[3] Figure 2 shows the number of the 23 agencies that IGs rated as effective and not effective between fiscal years 2017 and 2020.

[3] The 23 civilian agencies are the departments of Agriculture, Commerce, Education, Energy, Health and Human Services, Homeland Security, Housing and Urban Development, the Interior, Justice, Labor, State, Transportation, the Treasury, and Veterans Affairs; the Environmental Protection Agency; the General Services Administration; the National Aeronautics and Space Administration; the National Science Foundation; the Nuclear Regulatory Commission; the Office of Personnel Management; the Small Business

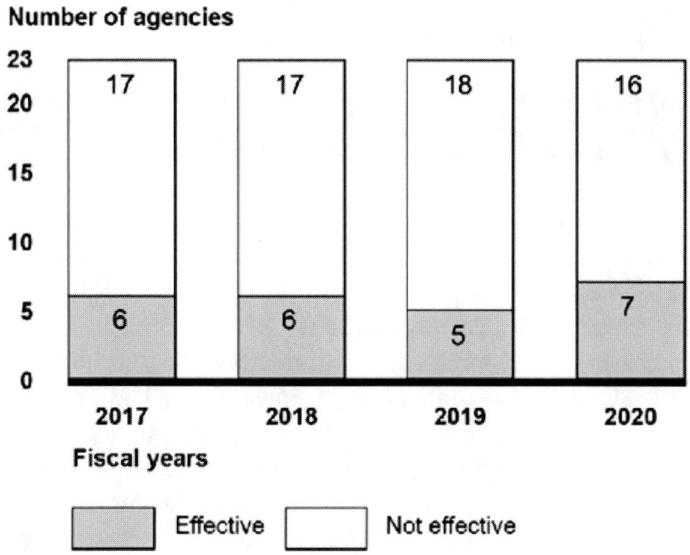

Source: GAO analysis of inspector general report data and office of management and Budget's Federal information Security Modernization Act of 2014 reports to Congress. | GAO-23-106428.

Figure 2. Number of the 23 Civilian Agencies with Effective and Not Effective Agency-Wide Information Security Programs, as Reported by Inspectors General for Fiscal Years 2017-2020.

We found that OMB's guidance to IGs on conducting agency evaluations was not always clear, leading to inconsistent application and reporting by IGs. Further, we reported that the binary effective/not effective scale resulted in imprecise ratings that did not clearly distinguish among the differing levels of agencies' performance. By clarifying its guidance and enhancing its rating scale, OMB could help ensure a more consistent approach and nuanced picture of agencies' cybersecurity programs.

- We recommended that OMB, in consultation with others, clarify its guidance to IGs and create a more precise overall rating scale. OMB did not concur with our recommendations, stating, in part, that they want to provide IGs with the flexibility to adapt their reviews. GAO

Administration; the Social Security Administration; and the U.S. Agency for International Development. We did not include the Department of Defense because our scope was the civilian agencies.

maintains that the recommendations are warranted, but they had not yet been implemented as of December 2022.

The U.S. National Institutes of Health needs to resolve control deficiencies and improve its program.

NIH's duties include researching infectious diseases and administering over $30 billion a year in research grants. NIH uses IT systems containing sensitive data to carry out its mission.

In December 2021, we reported that NIH implemented information security controls— both for its security program and selected systems—intended to safeguard the confidentiality, integrity, and availability of its systems and information. However, we identified numerous control and program deficiencies in core security functions. These issues related to identifying risk, protecting systems from threats and vulnerabilities, detecting and responding to cyber security events, and recovering system operations. Until NIH resolves the associated control and program deficiencies, its information systems and information will remain at increased risk of misuse, improper disclosure or modification, and destruction.

We recommended that NIH address these deficiencies, which resulted in 66 recommendations related to the security program and 153 recommendations related to system controls. As of December 2022, NIH had implemented about 71 percent of the total 219 recommendations. However, it had not yet implemented 15 of the 66 on the information security program and 49 of the 153 on control deficiencies for selected systems.

What Actions Can Be Taken to Enhance the Federal Response to Cyber Incidents Targeting Federal Systems?

Agencies identified multiple lessons learned from SolarWinds and Microsoft Exchange incidents.

Beginning as early as January 2019, a threat actor breached the computing networks at SolarWinds—a Texas-based network management software company. Since the company's software was widely used in the federal government, this incident allowed the threat actor to breach several federal agencies' networks that used the software (see figure 3). In March 2021,

Microsoft reported the exploitation or misuse of vulnerabilities to gain access to versions of the Microsoft Exchange Server that federal agencies hosted and used. Federal agencies formed Cyber Unified Coordination Groups to investigate the incidents.[4]

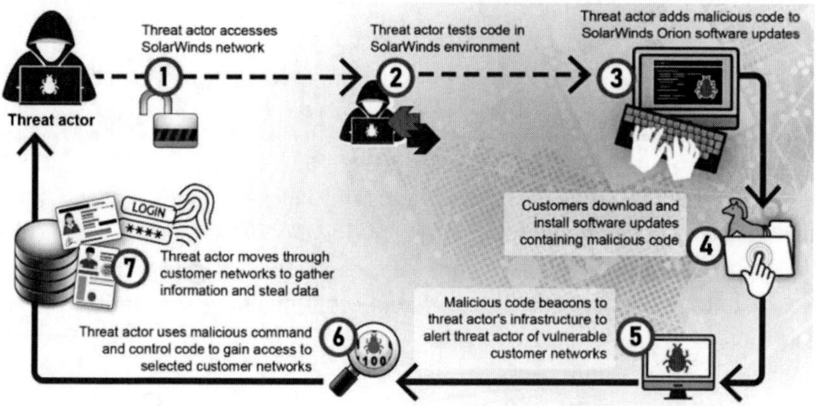

Source: GAO analysis of documentation from publicly released private industry and federal agency reports; images: kras99/stock.adobe.com, anna_leni/stock.adobe.com. | GAO-23-106428.

Figure 3. Analysis of How a Threat Actor Exploited SolarWinds Orion Software.

In January 2022, we reported that the Cyber Unified Coordination Group agencies identified that information sharing and limited evidence collection led to challenges in coordinating and responding to the SolarWinds and Microsoft Exchange incidents. For example, we reported that an official from the Office of the Director of National Intelligence told us that information sharing among law enforcement, private sector, and intelligence groups was difficult and time consuming, as there were different classification levels for information.

In addition, the National Security Council, with input from the Cyber Unified Coordination Group agencies, conducted a review of the SolarWinds incident. The review identified that (1) aligning technology investments with operational priorities, (2) improving public-private engagement, and (3) improving threat intelligence acquisition, sharing, and use among federal

[4] Cyber Unified Coordination Group agencies for the SolarWinds and Microsoft Exchange incidents consisted of the Cybersecurity and Infrastructure Security Agency, the Federal Bureau of Investigation, and the Office of the Director of National Intelligence, with support from the National Security Agency.

agencies may help with preventing and responding to future cybersecurity incidents. If implemented effectively, the areas from the National Security Council review could help address several challenges identified for both the SolarWinds and Microsoft Exchange incidents. We did not make any recommendations in this report, but we maintain that addressing these challenges should remain a priority.

The Department of Defense needs to ensure cyber incidents are appropriately reported and shared.

DOD and our nation's defense industrial base—which includes entities outside the federal government that provide goods or services critical to meeting U.S. military requirements—are dependent on information systems to carry out their operations. These systems continue to be susceptible to cyber incidents as cybersecurity threats have evolved and become more sophisticated (see figure 4).

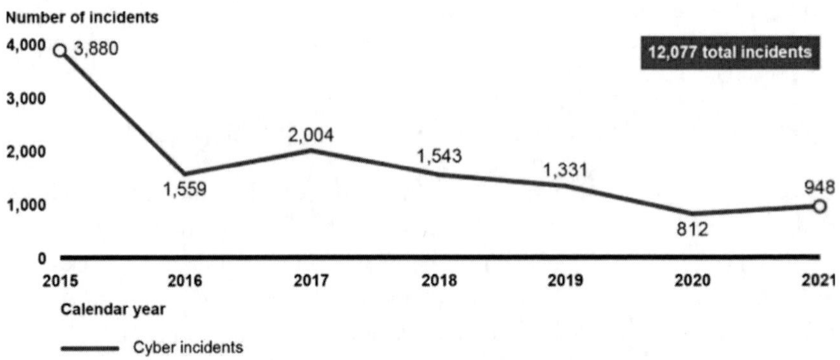

Source: GAO analysis of Department of Defense Joint Incident Management System (JIMS) data. | GAO-23-106428.

Figure 4. Cyber Incidents Reported by Department of Defense's Cybersecurity Service Providers from Calendar Years 2015 through 2021.

In November 2022, we reported that DOD has taken steps to combat these attacks and the number of cyber incidents had declined in recent years. However, we found that the department (1) had not fully implemented its processes for managing cyber incidents,

(2) did not have complete data on cyber incidents that staff report, and (3) did not document whether it notifies individuals whose personal data is compromised in a cyber incident. For example, DOD's system for reporting all

incidents often contained incomplete information, and DOD could not always demonstrate that it had notified appropriate leadership of relevant critical incidents. Without addressing these deficiencies, DOD cannot ensure its leadership has an accurate understanding of the department's cybersecurity posture.

In addition, according to officials, DOD has not yet decided whether the defense industrial base's cyber incidents detected by cybersecurity service providers should be shared with all relevant stakeholders, such as the Department of Defense Chief Information Officer, Under Secretary of Defense for Intelligence and Security, and Defense Counterintelligence and Security Agency. Until DOD examines whether this information should be shared with all relevant parties, opportunities could be lost to identify system threats and improve system weaknesses.

- *We recommended* that the Department of Defense improve the sharing of defense industrial base-related cyber incident information and document when affected individuals are notified of a PII breach of their data. DOD concurred with our recommendations; however, it had not yet implemented these recommendations as of December 2022.

GAO's Prior Work

We have previously reported on the numerous challenges that the federal government faces and have made recommendations aimed at securing federal systems and information. Key reports focus on the following topics:

Improve the Implementation of Government-Wide Cybersecurity Initiatives

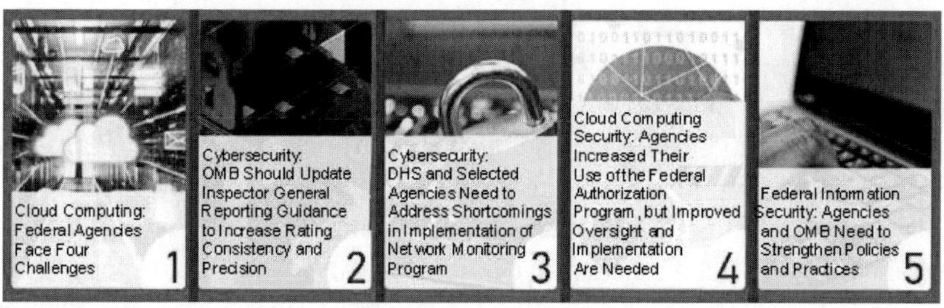

Address Weaknesses in Federal Agency Information Security Programs

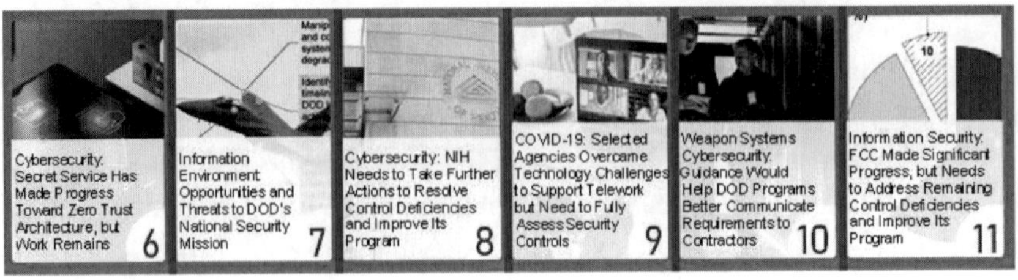

Enhance the Federal Response in Cyber Incidents Targeting Federal Systems

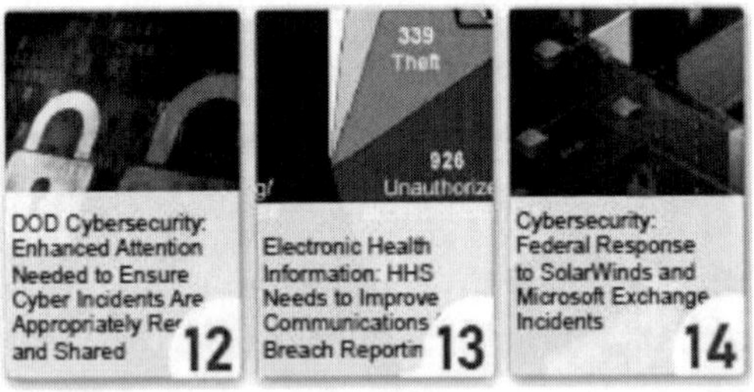

Source: Images: (1, 10) Gorodenkoff/stock.adobe.com, (2, 14) Alex/stock.adobe. com, (3, 5, 8) GAO file photo, (4) GAO, (6) ArtemisDiana/stock.adobe.com, (7) GAO analysis of Department of Defense (DOD) information; Thaut Images/stock.adobe.com and U.S. Air Force/Staff Sgt. E. Nuñez (photos), (9) insta_photos/stock.adobe.com, (11) GAO analysis of Federal Communications Commission data, (12) Maksim Kabakou/ stock.adobe.com, (13) GAO analysis of Department of Health and Human Services' January 2022 data; images: bearsky23/stock.adobe.com, Chor muang/stock. adobe.com. GAO-23-106428.

About GAO

The Government Accountability Office, the audit, evaluation, and investigative arm of Congress, exists to support Congress in meeting its constitutional responsibilities and to help improve the performance and accountability of the federal government for the American people. This document is based on GAO audit products. This work of the United States may include copyrighted material, details at https://www.gao.gov/copyright.

U.S. Government Accountability Office, 441 G Street NW, Washington, DC 20548.

Contact Us

For more information about this Cybersecurity High Risk Series, contact Marisol Cruz Cain, Director, Information Technology and Cybersecurity, (202) 512-5017.

Chuck Young, Managing Director, Public Affairs, (202) 512-4800

A. Nicole Clowers, Managing Director, Congressional Relations, (202) 512-4400.

Contributors: Elena Epps (Assistant Director), Keith Kim (Analyst-in-Charge), Freda Paintsil, Ibrahim Suleman, Lauri Barnes, and Chris Businsky.

Source (cover photo): GAO analysis; images: Gorodenkoff/stock.adobe.com.

Chapter 6

Challenges in Protecting Cyber Critical Infrastructure*

U.S. Government Accountability Office

Overview

Federal agencies and our nation's critical infrastructures—such as energy, transportation systems, communications, and financial services—are dependent on technology systems to carry out fundamental operations and to process, maintain, and report vital information. The security of these systems

* This is an edited, reformatted and augmented version of the United States Government Accountability Office Report, Publication No. GAO-23-106441.

In: Cybersecurity Challenges and Strategies Across Sectors …
Editor: Marybeth Wiskoff
ISBN: 979-8-90134-039-4

and data is also vital to safeguarding individual privacy and protecting the nation's security, prosperity, and well-being.

However, risks to these essential technology systems are increasing—in particular, malicious actors are becoming more willing and capable of carrying out cyberattacks. Such attacks could result in serious harm to human safety, national security, the environment, and the economy. Agencies and critical infrastructure owners and operators must protect the confidentiality, integrity, and availability of their systems and effectively respond to cyberattacks.

We have designated information security as a government-wide high-risk area since 1997. We expanded this high-risk area in 2003 to include protection of critical cyber infrastructure. In 2015, we expanded it again to include protecting the privacy of personally identifiable information.

This is the third in a series of four reports that lay out the main cybersecurity areas the federal government needs to urgently address. It focuses on the need to protect cyber critical infrastructure.[1] We have made 106 recommendations in public reports since 2010 in this area. About 60 of these recommendations have not been implemented as of December 2022. Until these are fully implemented, key critical infrastructures will continue to have increased cybersecurity risks to their systems and data.

For more information on this report and others in this series, visit https://www.gao.gov/cybersecurity.

What Actions Should Be Taken to Strengthen the Federal Role in Protecting the Cybersecurity of Critical Infrastructure?

The Department of Energy (DOE) needs to address cybersecurity risks to distribution systems more fully in its plans to implement the national cybersecurity strategy for the power grid.

[1] In 2018, GAO reported that the federal government needed to address four major cybersecurity challenges related to (1) establishing a comprehensive cybersecurity strategy, (2) securing federal systems and information, (3) protecting cyber critical infrastructure, and (4) protecting privacy and sensitive data. For our reports on the first two challenge areas, see GAO, *Cybersecurity High-Risk Series: Challenges in Establishing a Comprehensive Cybersecurity Strategy and Performing Effective Oversight*. GAO-23-106415 (Washington, D.C.: Jan. 19, 2023) and GAO, *Cybersecurity High-Risk Series: Challenges in Securing Federal Systems and Information*. GAO-23-106428 (Washington, D.C.: Jan. 31, 2023).

The U.S. grid's distribution systems—which carry electricity from transmission systems to consumers and are regulated primarily by states—are increasingly at risk from cyberattacks. Distribution systems are growing more vulnerable, in part because of industrial control systems' increasing connectivity.[2] As a result, threat actors can use multiple techniques to access those systems and potentially disrupt operations (see figure 1).

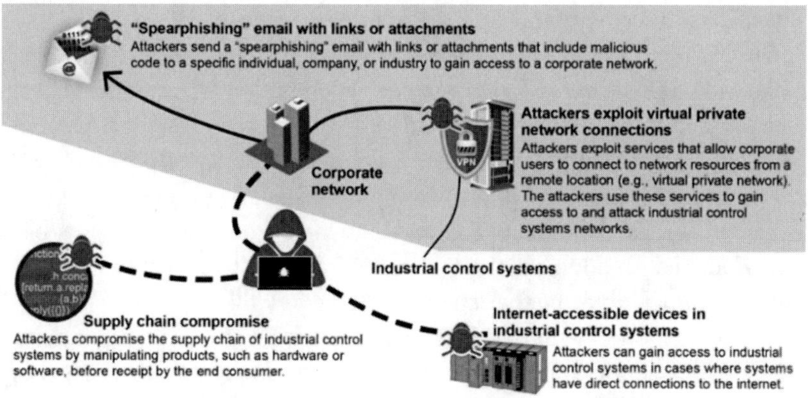

Source: GAO analysis of industry and federal documents. | GAO-23-106441.

Figure 1. Examples of Techniques for Gaining Initial Access to Industrial Control Systems.

We reported in March 2021 that DOE, as the lead federal agency for the energy sector, developed plans to help combat these threats and implement the national cybersecurity strategy for the grid. However, DOE's plans did not address distribution systems' vulnerabilities related to supply chains. As a result, these plans will likely be of limited use in prioritizing federal support to states in addressing grid distribution systems' cybersecurity.

- We recommended that, in developing plans to implement the national cybersecurity strategy for the grid, DOE coordinate with the Department of Homeland Security (DHS), states, and industry to more fully address risks to the grid's distribution systems from cyberattacks. DOE agreed with our recommendation; however, it had not yet been implemented as of December 2022.

---

[2] Industrial control systems monitor and control sensitive processes and physical functions, such as the opening and closing of circuit breakers on the grid.

The Department of Education (Education) needs to increase coordination with its partners to address cybersecurity risks in K-12 schools.

In October 2022, we reported that K-12 schools had experienced significant educational impact due to cybersecurity incidents, such as ransomware attacks. For example, officials from state and local entities reported that the loss of learning following a cyberattack ranged from 3 days to 3 weeks, and recovery time ranged from 2 to 9 months.

The *National Infrastructure Protection Plan* (national plan) established Education as the sector risk management agency that is responsible for the protection of the education critical infrastructure subsector. As such, Education and CISA are to coordinate K-12 cybersecurity efforts with federal and nonfederal partners. For example, Education and CISA offer cybersecurity-related products and services to K-12 schools, such as online safety guidance. In addition, the Federal Bureau of Investigation (FBI) is to provide criminal investigative support. However, the federal agencies had little to no interaction with other agencies and the K-12 community regarding schools' cybersecurity. This was due, in part, to Education not establishing a government coordinating council, as called for in the national plan. Such a council could facilitate ongoing communication and coordination among federal agencies and with the K-12 community and enable federal agencies to better address the cybersecurity needs of K-12 schools.

- *We recommended* that Education establish a collaborative mechanism, such as an applicable government coordinating council, to coordinate cybersecurity efforts, among other things. Education partially agreed with this recommendation; it remained not implemented as of December 2022.

CISA needs to assess the effectiveness of its programs and services to support the communications sector.

The communications sector is an integral component of the U.S. economy and faces serious physical, cyber-related, and human threats that could affect the operations of local, regional, and national level networks, according to CISA and sector stakeholders (see figure 2). In addition to managing federal coordination during incidents impacting the communications sector, CISA shares information with sector stakeholders to enhance their cybersecurity and improve interoperability, situational awareness, and preparedness for responding to and managing incidents.

Type of threat		Description
Physical		• Natural occurrences, such as hurricanes, floods, and ice storms • Human-made occurrences, such as explosive, chemical, biological, or radiological contaminant attacks on communications network infrastructure and personnel
Cyber-related		• Malicious actors, such as adversaries who intentionally disrupt the systems on a communications network • Nonmalicious actors, such as employees that accidentally alter a communication network's configuration, negatively affecting the network's ability to function properly
Human		• Threats to a communications network due to the failure of employees to plan for security incidents and implement protocols to protect networks from the impacts of such incidents

Source: GAO analysis of Department of Homeland Security documents. | GAO-23-106441.

Figure 2. Examples of Potential Security Threats to the Communications Sector.

In November 2021, we reported that CISA had not assessed the effectiveness of its programs and services supporting the security and resilience of the communications sector. By completing such an assessment, CISA would be better positioned to determine which programs and services are most useful or relevant in supporting the sector's security and resilience. We also reported that CISA had not updated its 2015 *Communications Sector-Specific Plan.* CISA officials acknowledged that certain elements of the plan are out of date and agreed the plan should be revised. Developing and issuing a revised plan would help CISA to address emerging threats and risks to the communications sector.

- *We recommended* that CISA assess the effectiveness of its programs and services to support the communications sector and, in coordination with public and private communications sector stakeholders, produce a revised *Communications Sector-Specific Plan.* CISA agreed with our recommendations; however, neither of them had been implemented as of December 2022.

The Department of the Interior's Bureau of Safety and Environmental Enforcement (the bureau) needs to take action to address oil and gas infrastructure cybersecurity risks.

Offshore oil and gas infrastructure faces significant and increasing cybersecurity risks in the form of threat actors, vulnerabilities, and potential impacts. *In October 2022*, we reported that the bureau had long recognized the need to address cybersecurity risks and initiated efforts to do so in 2015, 2020, and 2022. However, the initiatives did not result in substantial action, and the bureau had not yet developed a cybersecurity strategy. To address the lack of progress, the bureau hired a cybersecurity specialist to lead its risk-mitigation initiative in 2022, but bureau officials said the initiative will be paused until the specialist is adequately versed in relevant issues. Absent the immediate development and implementation of an appropriate strategy, the offshore oil and gas infrastructure will remain at significant risk.

- *We recommended* that the bureau develop and implement a strategy for its most recent cybersecurity initiative. Such a strategy should include, among other things, a risk assessment, performance measures, and identification of needed resources. The Department of Interior generally agreed with our recommendation; however, it remained not implemented as of December 2022.

DHS and the Department of Justice need to enhance interagency coordination against ransomware threats.

Ransomware is a form of malicious software that threat actors use in a multistage attack to encrypt files on a device and render data and systems unusable. These threat actors then demand ransom payments in exchange for restoring access to the locked data and systems (see figure 3).

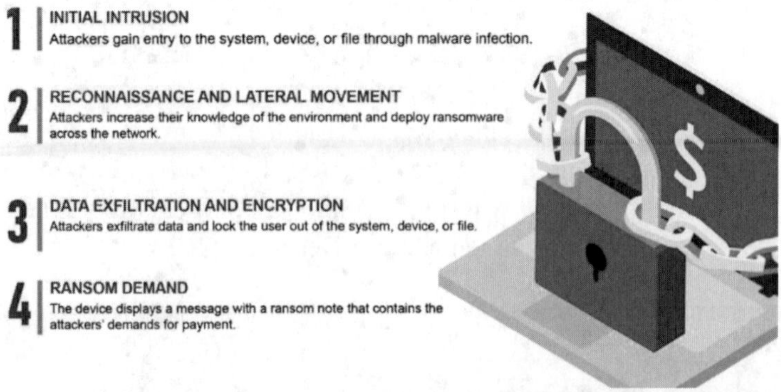

Source: GAO analysis based on information from the Cybersecurity and Infrastructure Security Agency, Center for Internet Security, and Federal Bureau of Investigation; image: tomasknopp/stock.adobe.com. | GAO-23106441.

Figure 3. Four Stages of a Common Ransomware Attack.

In September 2022, we reported that CISA, FBI, and Secret Service provide assistance in preventing and responding to ransomware attacks on tribal, state, local, and territorial government organizations. The agencies coordinated through existing mechanisms—such as interagency detailees and field-level staff—and demonstrated coordination on a joint ransomware website, guidance, and alerts. However, respondents identified challenges related to awareness, outreach, and communication. Further, the three agencies had not addressed aspects of six of seven key practices for interagency collaboration in their ransomware assistance to tribal, state, local, and territorial governments. For instance, existing interagency collaboration on ransomware assistance to tribal, state, local, and territorial governments was informal and lacked detailed procedures.

➢ We recommended that DHS and the Department of Justice address identified challenges and incorporate key collaboration practices in delivering services to tribal, state, local, and territorial governments. Both Departments agreed with their respective recommendations; however, the recommendations had not yet been implemented as of December 2022.

DHS's Cybersecurity and Infrastructure Security Agency (CISA) needs to engage stakeholders and document strategies and goals for the National Critical Functions framework.

In 2019, CISA published the National Critical Functions framework, which is a set of 55 critical functions (such as "supply water") of government and the private sector considered vital to the security, economy, and public health and safety of the nation.

According to CISA officials, this framework is intended to better assess how failures in functions across the 16 critical infrastructure sectors may cascade into key systems (such as public water systems) and assets (including infrastructure such as water treatment plants) as shown in figure 4.

In March 2022, we reported that CISA planned to integrate the National Critical Functions framework into broader prioritization and risk management efforts. However, the federal and nonfederal critical infrastructure stakeholders that we interviewed reported that they did not understand how the framework related to prioritizing infrastructure, how it affected planning and operations, or where their particular organizations fell within it.

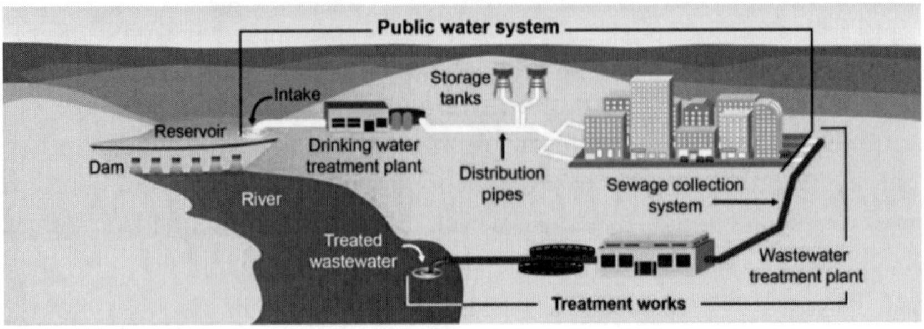

Source: GAO (graphoc) and U.S. Environmental Protection Agency and Department of homeland Security (information). | GAO-23106441.

Figure 4. Examples of Critical Infrastructure Systems and Assets That Support the National Critical Function "Supply Water."

CISA officials acknowledged the need to improve the connection between the National Critical Functions framework and local and operational risk management activities and communications. In addition, CISA lacked documented goals and strategies for its framework. Without such documented goals and strategies, stakeholders' questions regarding the framework will likely persist.

- *We recommended that* CISA ensure that stakeholders are fully engaged in the implementation of the framework and document the framework's goals and strategies. CISA agreed with these and four additional related recommendations on setting priorities, seeking states' input, improving coordination, and sharing threat information. However, none of the recommendations had been implemented as of December 2022.

GAO's Prior Work

We have previously reported on the numerous challenges that the federal government faces and have made recommendations aimed at improving the protection of cyber critical infrastructure. Key reports focus on the following topics:

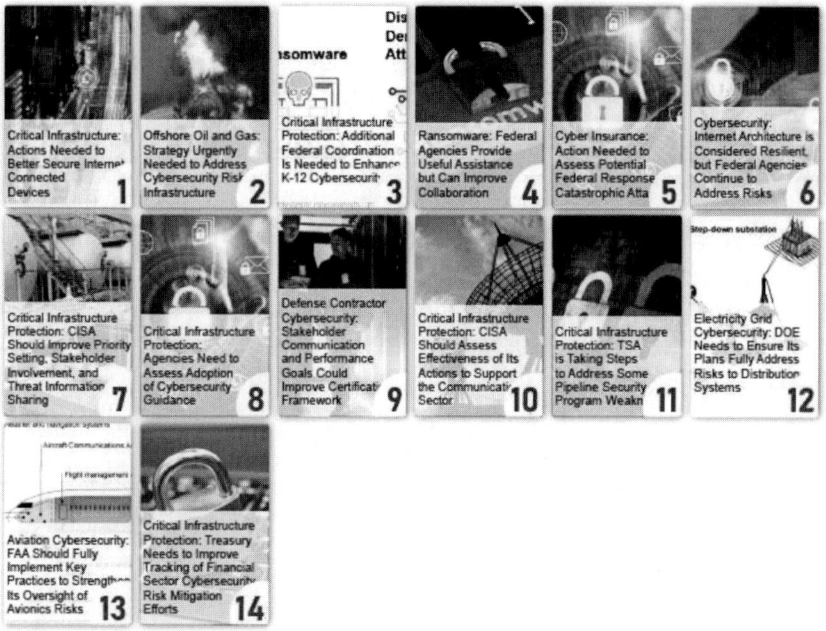

Source: Images: (1) metaworks/stock.adobe.com, (2) United States Coast Guard, (3) GAO analysis of federal and nonfederal documents; images: marinashevchenko/ stock.adobe.com, (4) alexlmx/stock.adobe.com, (5, 8) Murrstock/stock. adobe.com, (6) VideoFlow/stock.adobe.com, (7) Department of Homeland Security, (9) Gorodenkoff/ stock.adobe.com, (10) TebNad/stock.adobe.com, (11) Maksim Kabakou/stock.adobe.com, (12) GAO; Art Explosion (images), (13) GAO analysis of FAA and industry documentation, (14, 15) GAO File Photo. | GAO-23-106441.

About GAO

The Government Accountability Office, the audit, evaluation, and investigative arm of Congress, exists to support Congress in meeting its constitutional responsibilities and to help improve the performance and accountability of the federal government for the American people. This document is based on GAO audit products. This work of the United States may include copyrighted material, details at https://www.gao.gov/copyright.

U.S. Government Accountability Office, 441 G Street NW, Washington, DC 20548.

Contact Us

For more information about this Cybersecurity High Risk Series, contact Marisol Cruz Cain, Director, Information Technology and Cybersecurity, (202) 512-5017.

Chuck Young, Managing Director, Public Affairs, (202) 512-4800.

A. Nicole Clowers, Managing Director, Congressional Relations, (202) 512-4400.

Contributors: Lauri Barnes, Chris Businsky, Corwin Hayward, Ibrahim Suleman, Elena Epps (Assistant Director), and Keith Kim (Analyst-in-Charge).

Source (cover photo): GAO analysis; Who is Danny/stock.adobe.com.

Chapter 7

Challenges in Protecting Privacy and Sensitive Data*

U.S. Government Accountability Office

Overview

Federal agencies and our nation's critical infrastructures—such as energy, transportation systems, communications, and financial services—are dependent on technology systems to carry out fundamental operations and to

* This is an edited, reformatted and augmented version of the United States Government Accountability Office Report, Publication No. GAO-23-106443.

In: Cybersecurity Challenges and Strategies Across Sectors …
Editor: Marybeth Wiskoff
ISBN: 979-8-90134-039-4

process, maintain, and report vital information. The security of these systems and data is also vital to safeguarding individual privacy and protecting the nation's security, prosperity, and well-being.

However, risks to these essential technology systems are increasing—in particular, malicious actors are becoming more willing and capable of carrying out cyberattacks. Such attacks could result in serious harm to human safety, national security, the environment, and the economy. Agencies and critical infrastructure owners and operators must protect the confidentiality, integrity, and availability of their systems and effectively respond to cyberattacks.

We have designated information security as a government-wide high-risk area since 1997. We expanded this high-risk area in 2003 to include protection of critical cyber infrastructure. In 2015, we expanded it again to include protecting the privacy of personally identifiable information.

This is the last in a series of four reports that lay out the main cybersecurity areas the federal government should urgently address. It focuses on protecting privacy and sensitive data.[1] 1 We have made 236 recommendations in public reports since 2010 in this area. About 140 of these recommendations were not implemented as of December 2022. Until these are fully implemented, federal agencies will be more limited in their ability to protect private and sensitive data entrusted to them.

For more information on this report and others in this series, visit https://www.gao.gov/cybersecurity.

What Actions Should the Federal Government Take to Protect Privacy and Sensitive Data?

Federal agencies should fully address key practices for implementing privacy programs.

[1] In 2018, GAO reported that the federal government needed to address four major cybersecurity challenges related to (1) establishing a comprehensive cybersecurity strategy, (2) securing federal systems and information, (3) protecting cyber critical infrastructure, and (4) protecting privacy and sensitive data. For our reports on the first three challenge areas, see GAO, *Cybersecurity High-Risk Series: Challenges in Establishing a Comprehensive Cybersecurity Strategy and Performing Effective Oversight*, GAO-23-106415 (Washington, D.C.: Jan. 19, 2023); *Cybersecurity High-Risk Series: Challenges in Securing Federal Systems and Information,* GAO-23-106428 (Washington, D.C.: Jan. 31, 2023); and *Cybersecurity High-Risk Series: Challenges in Protecting Cyber Critical Infrastructure,* GAO-23-106441 (Washington, D.C.: Feb. 7, 2023).

Federal agencies that collect personally identifiable information (PII)—such as birthplaces and Social Security numbers—are required to establish programs to protect it. In September 2022, our review of 24 agencies found that most had generally established policies and procedures for key privacy program activities. These activities included developing system-of-records notices that identify types of personal data collected, conducting privacy impact assessments, and documenting privacy program plans (see fig. 1).[2]

Agencies varied in establishing policies and procedures for coordinating privacy programs with other agency functions. Further, many agencies did not fully incorporate privacy into their risk management strategies, provide for privacy officials' input into the authorization of systems containing PII, or develop a continuous monitoring strategy for privacy. Without fully establishing these elements of their privacy programs, agencies have less assurance that they are consistently implementing privacy protections.

We also reported that these 24 agencies had each designated a senior agency official for privacy. However, most of these officials did not have privacy as their primary responsibility and had numerous other duties related to managing IT and information security. Legislation establishing a dedicated, senior-level privacy official could enhance the leadership commitment needed to address privacy issues across the government.

- *We recommended* that Congress consider legislation to designate a dedicated, senior-level privacy official at agencies that lacked one. We also made two recommendations to the Office of Management and Budget (OMB) to facilitate information sharing to help agencies address selected challenges and better implement privacy impact assessments. Finally, we made 62 recommendations to 23 of the 24 agencies we reviewed to fully implement all of the key practices for their privacy programs. Twenty out of 23 agencies, including OMB, agreed with the recommendations. However, the recommendation to

[2] Privacy impact assessments are used to analyze how personal information is collected, stored, shared, and managed. The 24 agencies we reviewed were the departments of Agriculture, Commerce, Defense, Education, Energy, Health and Human Services, Homeland Security, Housing and Urban Development, the Interior, Justice, Labor, State, Transportation, the Treasury, and Veterans Affairs; the Environmental Protection Agency; the General Services Administration; the National Aeronautics and Space Administration; the National Science Foundation; the Nuclear Regulatory Commission; the Office of Personnel Management; the Small Business Administration; the Social Security Administration; and the U.S. Agency for International Development.

Congress and 62 out of 64 recommendations to OMB and agencies had not yet been implemented as of February 2023.

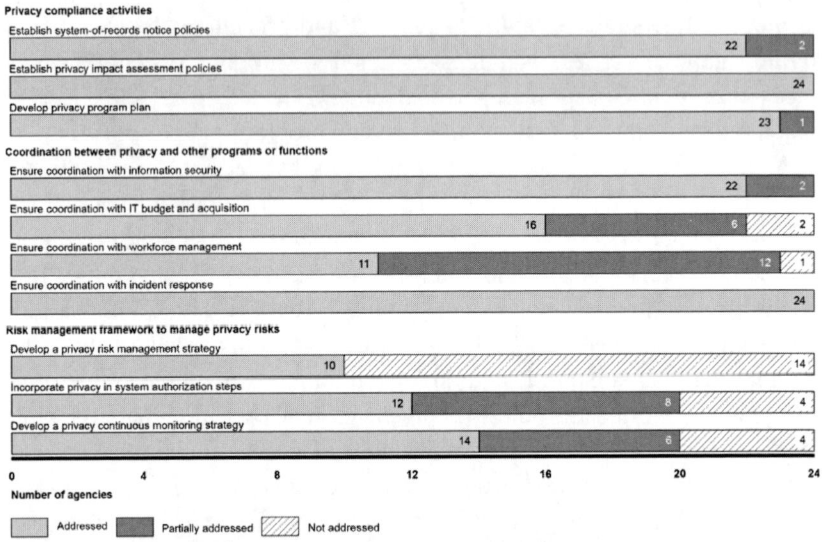

Source: GAO analysis of agency information. | GAO-23106433.

Figure 1. Extent to Which 24 Chief Financial Officers Act of 1990 Agencies Addressed Key Practices for Establishing a Privacy Program.

The Department of Homeland Security (DHS) needs to improve its oversight of contractors handling personal information.

In December 2021, we reported that federal agencies, including DHS, had reported increasing numbers of privacy incidents that have placed sensitive information at risk of potentially serious impacts on federal operations, assets, and people. Figure 2 shows the number of privacy incidents DHS's Privacy Office reported to Congress annually from 2015 through 2019.

DHS is responsible for a wide variety of functions that are critically important to maintaining the security of our nation's citizens. To carry out these functions, the department needs to collect and maintain extensive amounts of detailed and sometimes sensitive PII. In many cases, DHS leverages the capabilities and expertise of contractors to assist in its various missions and grants contractors access to PII to perform the work.

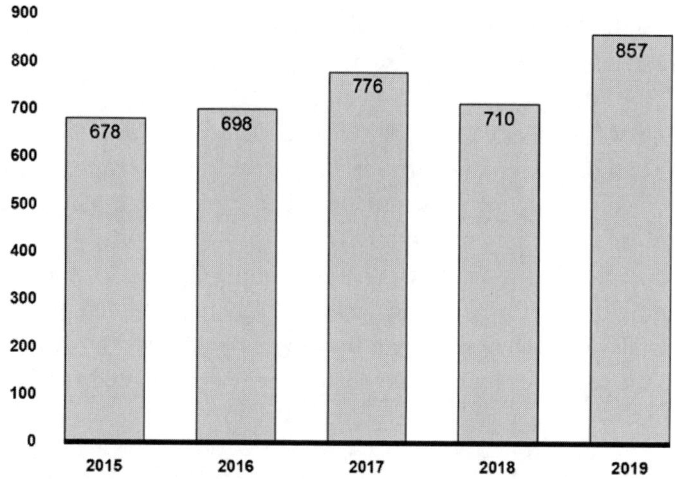

Source: GAO analysis of DHS provided data. | GAO-23-106443.

Figure 2. Privacy Incidents Reported to Congress by the Department of Homeland Security (DHS), 2015 through 2019.

Federal law and implementing policies and guidance from OMB and the National Institute of Standards and Technology require agencies to ensure that agency information, including information collected or maintained by a contractor, is adequately protected.[3] DHS developed policies and procedures to meet these requirements related to the protection of PII that is collected, used, or stored by contractors. We found that the six selected DHS component agencies complied with most of DHS's policies and procedures, but gaps existed.[4] For example, the U.S. Coast Guard did not demonstrate that it identified and addressed gaps in privacy compliance, and DHS's Headquarters did not administer role-based privacy training.

Regarding privacy incidents, one component did not document all necessary remediation activities. Fully documenting remediation activities

---

[3] See Federal Information Modernization Act of 2014 (FISMA), Pub. L. No. 113-283 (Dec. 18, 2014) codified at 44 USC §§ 3551-3559; see also Office of Management and Budget, *Managing Information as a Strategic Resource*, OMB Circular No. A-130 (July 28, 2016); and National Institute of Standards and Technology, *Security and Privacy Controls for Federal Information Systems and Organizations*, Special Publication 800- 53, Revision 5 (Dec. 10, 2020).

[4] The six selected DHS component agencies are the U.S. Coast Guard, U.S. Customs and Border Protection, the U.S. Department of Homeland Security Headquarters, the Federal Emergency Management Agency, U.S. Immigration and Customs Enforcement, and the Transportation Security Administration.

helps ensure that all appropriate steps have been taken to lessen potential harm that the loss, compromise, or misuse of PII could have on affected individuals.

- We recommended that the selected DHS components improve their oversight of contractors' privacy protections and remediation of incidents. The seven actions included providing targeted role-based privacy training to contractors who are responsible for privacy protections and ensuring that recommendations to notify affected individuals of privacy incidents are fully documented in the incident database. DHS agreed with the recommendations; however, none of these seven recommendations had been implemented as of December 2022.

What Actions Should the Federal Government Take to Appropriately Limit the Collection and Use of Personal Information and Ensure It Is Obtained with Appropriate Knowledge or Consent?

Federal law enforcement agencies should better assess privacy and other risks associated with facial recognition technology.

In June 2021, we reported on the results of our survey of 42 federal agencies that employ law enforcement officers about their use of facial recognition technology.[5] Twenty reported owning systems with facial recognition technology or using systems owned by other entities, such as other federal, tribal, state, local, and territorial governments and non-government entities.[6]

---

[5] Facial Recognition Technology is used to help identify an unknown individual in a photo or video surveillance.

[6] The following agencies owned systems with facial recognition technology: the Department of Veterans Affairs, the Federal Bureau of Prisons, the National Aeronautics and Space Administration, and the Office of Protective Services. The following agencies used another entity's system: the Bureau of Alcohol, Tobacco, Firearms, and Explosives; the Food and Drug Administration; the Internal Revenue Service; the U.S. Park Police; the Bureau of Diplomatic Security; the U.S. Fish and Wildlife Service; the U.S. Capitol Police; the U.S. Postal Inspection Service; the Drug Enforcement Administration; U.S. Immigration and Customs Enforcement; the U.S. Marshals Service; and U.S. Probation and Pretrial Services. The following agencies owned systems and used another entity's system with facial recognition technology: U.S. Customs and Border Protection, the Pentagon Force Protection Agency, the Transportation Security Administration, the Federal Bureau of Investigation, and the U.S. Secret Service.

See figure 3 for examples of the types of photos used in federal systems with facial recognition technology.

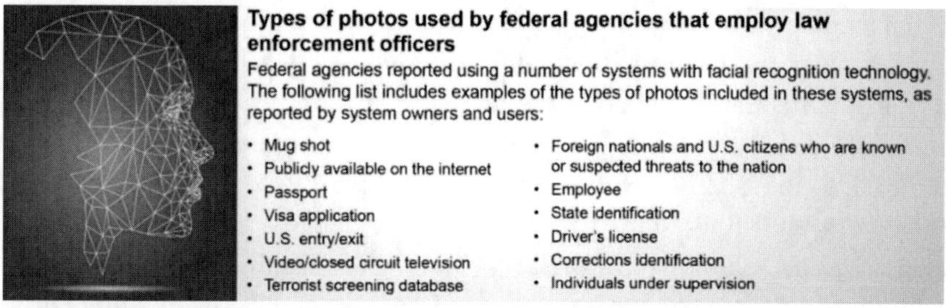

Source: GAO analysis of survey data ; images. Lidiia/stock.aobe.com. | GAO-23-106433.

Figure 3. Types of Photos Used by Federal Agencies That Employ Law Enforcement Officers.

Agencies reported using the technology to support several activities (e.g., criminal investigations) and in response to COVID-19 (e.g., to verify an individual's identity remotely). Six agencies reported using the technology on images of the unrest, riots, or protests following the death of George Floyd in May 2020. Three agencies reported using it on images of the events at the U.S. Capitol on January 6, 2021. All fourteen agencies that reported using the technology to support criminal investigations also reported using systems owned by nonfederal entities. However, only one of those 14 was aware of what nonfederal systems employees used. By having a mechanism to track what nonfederal systems employees use and assessing privacy and accuracy-related risks, agencies can better mitigate risks to themselves and the public.

➢ *We recommended* that 13 federal agencies implement a mechanism to track what nonfederal systems with facial recognition technology employees are using, and assess the risks of using these systems.[7] Twelve of the 13 agencies concurred with both recommendations directed towards them. However, 21 of the 26 recommendations had not yet been implemented as of December 2022.

[7] The 13 federal agencies include the Bureau of Alcohol, Tobacco, Firearms and Explosives; the Drug Enforcement Administration; the Federal Bureau of Investigation; the U.S. Marshals Service; U.S. Customs and Border Protection; the U.S. Secret Service; the U.S. Fish and Wildlife Service; the U.S. Park Police; the Bureau of Diplomatic Security; the Food and Drug Administration; the Internal Revenue Service; the U.S. Postal Inspection Service; and the U.S. Capitol Police.

Federal financial regulators should enhance their protection of personal information.

In January 2022, we reported that the five federal financial regulators we reviewed had built more than 100 information system applications that regularly collect and use extensive amounts of PII to fulfill their regulatory missions.[8] These regulators collect PII directly from individuals and financial institutions and share it with entities such as banks or service providers, contractors and other third parties, and other federal and state regulators. Regulators use the PII to conduct supervisory examinations of financial institutions and to receive and respond to complaints or inquiries from customers (see fig. 4).

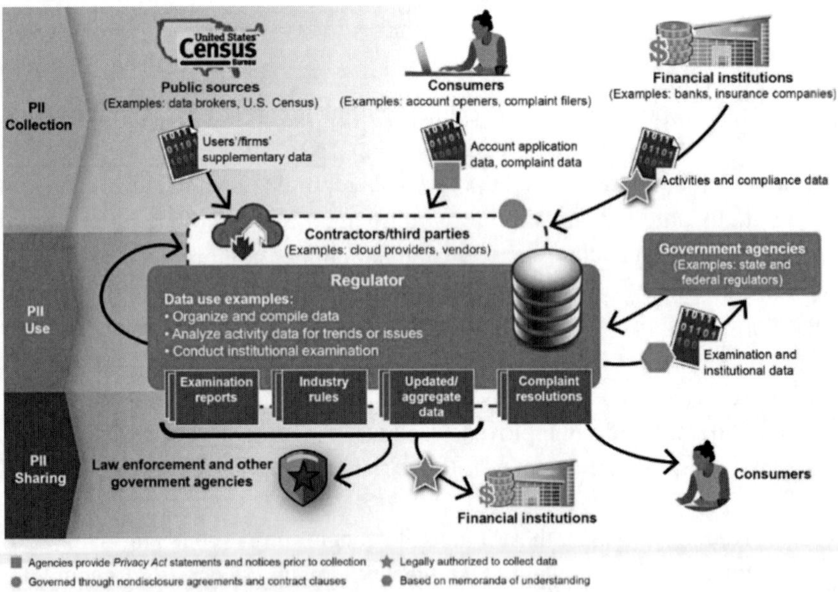

Source: GAO. | GAO-23-106433.

Figure 4. Collection, Use, and Sharing of Personally Identifiable Information (PII) at Selected Federal Financial Regulators.

---

[8] The five selected financial regulators include the Consumer Financial Protection Bureau and the four federal prudential regulators—the Federal Deposit Insurance Corporation, the Board of Governors of the Federal Reserve System, the National Credit Union Administration, and the Office of the Comptroller of the Currency.

We reported that all five financial regulators created privacy programs that generally take steps to protect PII in accordance with key practices in federal guidance. However, four of the regulators did not fully implement key practices in other privacy protection areas. For example, the Board of Governors of the Federal Reserve System (Federal Reserve) and National Credit Union Administration did not document steps taken to minimize the collection and use of PII. We also reported that the Federal Deposit Insurance Corporation (FDIC) and Federal Reserve did not establish agency-wide metrics to monitor privacy controls, and the Federal Reserve and the Office of the Comptroller of the Currency had not fully tracked decisions by program officials on the selection and testing of privacy controls.[9] Until these regulators take steps to mitigate these weaknesses, the PII they collect, use, and share could be at increased risk of compromise.

- We recommended that federal financial regulators better ensure the privacy of the PII that they collect, use, and share.[10] The regulators each described the steps they planned to take to implement the recommendations. However, six of the eight recommendations had not yet been implemented as of December 2022.

Federal guidance could help mitigate cybersecurity risks in 401(k) and other retirement plans.

Defined contribution (DC) retirement plan sponsors and their service providers—record keepers, third party administrators, custodians, and payroll providers—share a variety of PII and plan asset data among them to assist with carrying out their respective functions. The sharing and storing of this information can lead to significant cybersecurity risks for plan sponsors and their service providers as well as plan participants (see fig. 5).

---

[9] Privacy controls are the administrative, technical, and physical safeguards employed within an agency to ensure compliance with applicable privacy requirements and manage privacy risks.

[10] We made recommendations to the FDIC, the Federal Reserve, the National Credit Union Administration, and the Office of the Comptroller of the Currency.

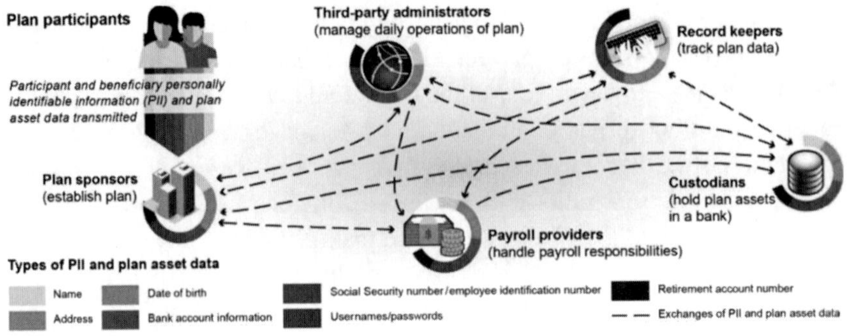

Source: GAO analysis of industry information. | GAO-23-106443.

Figure 5. Data Sharing among Plan Sponsors and Service Providers in Defined Contribution Plans.

In February 2021, we reported that federal requirements and industry guidance could help mitigate cybersecurity risks in DC plans.[11] This includes requirements that pertain to entities directly engaged in financial activities involving DC plans. However, not all entities involved in DC plans were considered to have such direct engagement, and other cybersecurity mitigation guidance was voluntary. Therefore, entities could potentially be left without clear federal requirements or standards to follow to mitigate cybersecurity risks.

In addition, we reported that the Department of Labor (DOL) had not established minimum cybersecurity expectations for protecting PII and plan assets. Without guidance, DOL lacks assurance this sensitive information is being adequately or consistently protected. This potential lack of protection could result in substantial harm to participants and beneficiaries including loss or theft of money, identity theft, or litigation involving plan fiduciaries and their administrators.

➢ We recommended that DOL establish minimum expectations for addressing cybersecurity risks in DC plans. The department agreed

[11] See The White House, *Improving Critical Infrastructure Cybersecurity*, Executive Order 13636, (Washington, D.C., Feb. 12, 2013); and National Institute of Standards and Technology, *Framework for Improving Critical Infrastructure Cybersecurity*, version 1.1 (Gaithersburg, MD: April 2018). Industry guidance includes the Society of Professional Asset Managers and Record Keepers (SPARK) Institute, Inc., *Industry Best Practice Data Security Reporting*, Release 1.0 (Simsbury, CT: Sept. 20, 2017), and the American Institute of Certified Public Accountants' *System and Organizational Control for Cybersecurity Framework* developed in 2017.

with the recommendation and issued new guidance for plan sponsors and service providers on best practices for maintaining cybersecurity in April 2021. However, we maintain that a minimum set of expectations for mitigating cybersecurity risks should be established, and we will follow up with DOL on their efforts to do so.

GAO's Prior Work

We have previously reported on the numerous challenges that the federal government faces and have made recommendations aimed at improving the protection of privacy and sensitive data. Additionally, we made recommendations related to appropriately limiting the collection and use of personal information and ensuring it is obtained with appropriate knowledge or consent. Key reports focus on the following topics:

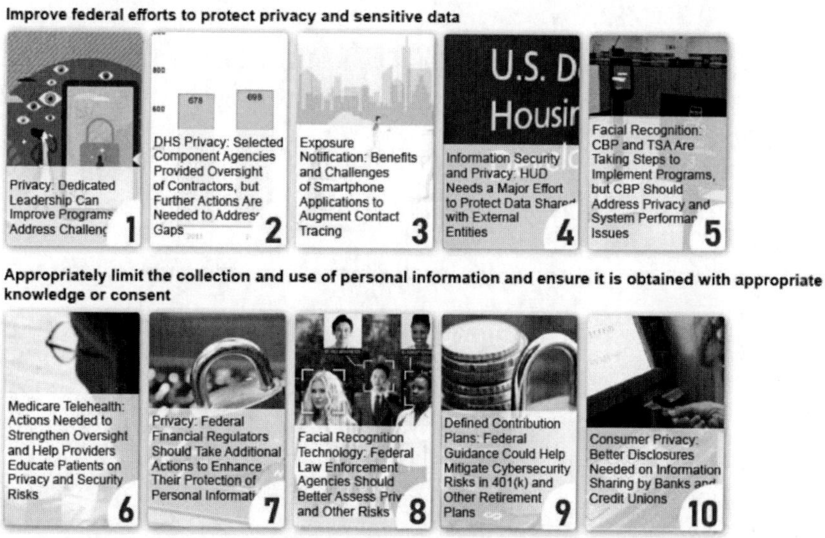

Source: Images: (1) VectorMine/stock.adobe.com, (2) GAO analysis of Department of Homeland Security provided data, (3) GAO, (4, 10, 9) GAO File Photo, (5) GAO, (7) GAO photo illustration; (6) insta_photos/stock.adobe.com, Andrey Popov and polkadot on stock.adobe.com, (9) Jakub Krechowicz/stock. adobe.com. | GAO-23-106443.

About GAO

The Government Accountability Office, the audit, evaluation, and investigative arm of Congress, exists to support Congress in meeting its constitutional responsibilities and to help improve the performance and accountability of the federal government for the American people. This document is based on GAO audit products. This work of the United States may include copyrighted material, details at https://www.gao.gov/copyright.

U.S. Government Accountability Office, 441 G Street NW, Washington, DC 20548.

Contact Us

For more information about this Cybersecurity High Risk Series, contact Marisol Cruz Cain, Director, Information Technology and Cybersecurity, (202) 512-5017.

Chuck Young, Managing Director, Public Affairs, (202) 512-4800

A. Nicole Clowers, Managing Director, Congressional Relations, (202) 512-4400

Contributors: Elena Epps (Assistant Director), Keith Kim (Analyst-in-Charge), Andrea Starosciak, Ibrahim Suleman, Lauri Barnes, and Chris Businsky

Source (cover photo): GAO analysis; images: Monster Ztudio/stock.adobe.com.

Index

F

H

I

M

N

P

Q

R

S

T

U

V

W

Y